Studying popular music

Richard Middleton

Open University Press
Milton Keynes • Philadelphia

Open University Press
Celtic Court
22 Ballmoor
Buckingham MK18 1XW

and
1900 Frost Road, Suite 101
Bristol, PA 19007, USA

First Published 1990
Reprinted 1993, 1995

British Library Cataloguing in Publication Data

Middleton, Richard, *1945-*
    Studying popular music.
    1. Great Britain. Education institutions.
    Curriculum subjects: Popular music. Teaching
    I. Title
    780'.42'07041

    ISBN 0-335-15276-7
    ISBN 0 335 15275 9 (pbk)

Library of Congress Cataloging-in-Publication Data

Middleton, Richard.
    Studying popular music / by Richard Middleton.
        p. cm.
    Bibliography: p.
    ISBN 0-335-15276-7   ISBN 0-335-15275-9 (pbk.)
    1. Popular music—History and criticism.   2. Musicology.
3. Popular culture.   I. Title.
ML3470.M5   1990
781.64'09—dc20   89-34686
                                          CIP   MN

Typeset by Colset (Pte) Limited, Singapore
Printed in Great Britain by
St Edmundsbury Press Limited, Bury St Edmunds, Suffolk

Contents

Preface

'Extraordinary how potent cheap music is.' When Noël Coward's pointed but opaque aphorism (from *Private Lives*) was first uttered on stage in 1930, the 'appalling popularity of music', as Constant Lambert called it (1966: 200), was already a fact and an issue. But neither Coward nor Lambert could have foreseen then just how close to ubiquity this music would come by the 1980s. Nor, probably, were they aware of how the questions they were raising would reverberate for those of us interested in studying popular music. Is mass popularity 'appalling', and if so why? How and why is popular music 'potent'? In what sense – if any – is it 'cheap'? Why is the quip – ironic or outraged, witty or bewildered – a more common response than analysis? Or to put this another way, why is our understanding of popular music still so rudimentary?

Such questions set our initial context. Popular music is everywhere. It is at the centre of several crucial arguments concerning the nature of music, of culture and of modern society. Yet, despite encouraging developments in recent years, the study of popular music has hardly got under way. Traditional musicology still largely banishes popular music from view because of its 'cheapness', while the relatively new field of cultural studies neglects it because of the forbiddingly special character of music. A breakthrough in popular music studies would, in my view, reorientate cultural studies in a fundamental way and would completely restructure the field of musicology. This book, therefore, addresses more than one audience and attempts to carry out several different tasks.

I have tried to write a *cultural study of music*, that is, a study which focuses on music but refuses to isolate it. Since there has been comparatively little work on the cultural theory of music, a good deal of general discussion is necessary in that area. Similarly, because most consideration of the relationship between 'popular' and other kinds of music has been unsatisfactory, nothing can be taken for granted there either. I have tried to survey the most important theories and approaches which have been, or might profitably be, applied to popular music. At the same time, the survey is a critical one. I attempt to argue through the various approaches, formulating a theoretical position of my own, against which readers can assess their own ideas and mount their own criticisms. If this position has any one predominant source, it is the 'turn to Gramsci' so visible in British cultural studies ten years ago but now less prominent (T. Bennett 1986a), in the babble of subsequent intellectual fashions; the justification for such conservatism will, I hope, be found in the book itself.

Since one of my aims is to clarify the question of how popular music may be defined, I shall not engage that question here. Nevertheless, the geographical and historical scope of the discussion needs some explanation. I deal almost, though not quite exclusively, with popular music in the 'developed' societies of the industrialized West, and within that sphere I focus on Britain and the United States. Partly, this is simply because these are the musics and the cultures I know most about. To discuss European popular music before the nineteenth century, or music in the Soviet bloc countries or in Africa, South America or other parts of the Third World would be beyond my competence. But there are less pragmatic reasons, too. It does seem to be the case that, whether it makes sense to talk about 'popular music' in pre-industrial societies or not, many of the resonances presently attaching to the term only appear when these societies undergo the impact of 'modernization' (in all its local variants); at that moment (which may vary from the late eighteenth century in Britain to virtually the present in some isolated enclaves) the entire socio-cultural field undergoes such profound restructuring as to change the terms of the debate. At the same time, it is also the case that, over the last half century particularly, American and to a lesser extent British popular musics have spread more widely than any others; for better or worse, they constitute a dominant sector with which variant or competing musics must come to terms. Moreover, I believe that the theoretical position advocated in this book can, *in principle*, be applied to these other musics – assuming, that is to say, that local modifying factors (such as pre-industrial social relations, state capitalist social formation, or the effects of colonialism and post-colonial dependence) are taken into account. This is not a fully satisfactory position – a comprehensive introduction to popular music studies would take the whole of world music as its subject and would refuse any culturally privileged point of perspective – but I do not think it is unsatisfactory enough to vitiate the book's argument.

To address both students of music and of culture – and possibly historians and sociologists as well – requires a 'linguistic' balancing act. I have tried to make the book as widely accessible as possible. Comparatively little technical musical vocabulary is used; most of the argument can, I think, be grasped without it. Bearing in mind the inadequacies of written music examples, especially for popular music of the last forty years or so, I have used them only when these inadequacies did not detract from the point being made and when the strengths of notation enhanced the point. On the whole, the argument to which the point relates should be comprehensible to readers without musical literacy, especially if the music can be heard.

A book of this kind could not but carry many intellectual debts. I have tried to acknowledge them in the references (including the critical ones). But one must be mentioned specifically. This book has grown out of material originally written for the Open University course, *Popular Culture*. That material in turn reflected changes in my own way of thinking which would not have occurred without the educative process associated with participation in the preparation of the course. I owe an enormous amount to members of the course team, particularly to its chairman, Tony Bennett. To him, and them, my thanks. I am indebted, too, to all those connected with the journal *Popular Music*, for constant stimulation; to Simon Frith and Paul Oliver, for helpful comments on an earlier draft of the book; to the National Sound Archive, especially Andy Linehan, for facilities and information; to Ray Cunningham, a tactful editor; and to members of the Open University's secretarial staff, Val Moggridge and Hildegard Wright in particular, who transformed scribble into legible prose. The result is my responsibility, of course; but whatever errors, omissions and misunderstandings it may still contain, ten years' suckling of however voracious an infant is enough, and it is surely time for it to be weaned and sent out to fend for itself.

Part one
Charting the popular:
Towards a historical framework

1

'Roll over Beethoven'? Sites and soundings on the music-historical map

What is popular music?

So riddled with complexities has this question proved to be that one is tempted to follow the example of the legendary definition of folk song – 'all songs are folk songs; I never heard horses sing 'em' – and suggest that all music is popular music: popular with *someone*. Unfortunately, this would be to empty the term of most of the meanings which it carries in actual discourse. However, it does have the merit of beginning to touch upon the multiple sources of these meanings: what *I* think 'popular' *you* may not. And it follows from this that all such meanings are socially and historically grounded: they come bearing the marks of particular usages and contexts, and are never disinterested.

The briefest 'archaeology' of the more general term 'popular' reveals both the plurality of its inflections and some of their historical movements (see Williams 1976: 198–9). It has to do with 'the people' (but who are they?), though often this has the sense of the *vulgus*, the *common* people, and to describe something as 'popular' may then have the (depreciatory) implication that it is inferior or designed to suit low tastes. Under the influence of democratic ideologies, on the other hand, this usage may be turned round and then 'popular' can become a *legitimating* term; this was the case in post-revolutionary America. A different sense – 'well favoured' (but with whom?) – became predominant, at least in Britain, by the late eighteenth century, and in the nineteenth this could shift to 'well liked' (that is, judged *good* – but by whom?). The origins of a positive, class-orientated usage – something 'popular' as the type specifically produced by the lower classes – lie in this period also; and this has become one of the common twentieth-century senses.

In music, the quantitative usage ('well favoured') seems to have come to the fore in the eighteenth century – alongside the development of a (bourgeois) commercial market in musical products; and when, in the first half of the nineteenth century, songs for the bourgeois market (including what we would now call 'drawing-room ballads') were described as 'popular songs', the intended implication seems to have been that they were good (that is, well liked by those whose opinion counted). Older senses survived, too; and, under the impact of Romanticism, 'popular songs' could in the nineteenth century also be thought of as synonymous with 'peasant', 'national' and 'traditional' songs.[1] Later in the century, 'folk' took over these usages from 'popular', which was transferred to the products of the music hall and then to those of the mass market song publishers of Tin Pan Alley and its British equivalent.

In the twentieth century, many of these meanings coexist and intertwine, in a variety of usages. Frans Birrer has provided a useful summary of the main categories (Birrer 1985: 104), which exist in combination as well as in pure form).[2]

1 *Normative definitions*. Popular music is an inferior type.
2 *Negative definitions*. Popular music is music that is not something else (usually 'folk' or 'art' music).
3 *Sociological definitions*. Popular music is associated with (produced for or by) a particular social group.
4 *Technologico-economic definitions*. Popular music is disseminated by mass media and/or in a mass market.

All these categories are interest-bound; none is satisfactory. The first relies on arbitrary criteria. The second gets into trouble on the boundaries – where neat divisions between 'folk' and 'popular', and 'popular' and 'art', are impossible to find – and also tends to use arbitrary criteria to define the complement of 'popular'. 'Art' music, for example, is generally regarded as by nature complex, difficult, demanding; 'popular' music then has to be defined as 'simple', 'accessible', 'facile'. But many pieces commonly thought of as 'art' (Handel's 'Hallelujah Chorus', many Schubert songs, many Verdi arias) have qualities of simplicity; conversely, it is by no means obvious that the Sex Pistols' records were 'accessible', Frank Zappa's work 'simple' or Billie Holiday's 'facile'.

The third category of definition fails because musical types and practices, even those of the most minority sort, can never be wholly contained by particular social contexts. Social mobility and class fluidity make this obvious today, as does the increasingly undifferentiated character of media diffusion and cultural markets. But even in the nineteenth century, the drawing-room ballads and theatre tunes 'of the bourgeoisie' were heard and reproduced by many workers, just as 'art' music was regaled to them by brass bands and in promenade concerts; while ownership of 'folk' songs would be a matter of dispute between 'peasants', industrial workers, petty bourgeois writers and artisans, and patrician collectors. Putting this point on a more theoretical level, the *musical field* and the *class structure* at any given moment, though clearly not unconnected, comprise different 'maps' of social/cultural space, and they cannot be reduced one to the other (see Williams 1981).

The fourth category is unsatisfactory, too, this time for two reasons. The development of methods of mass diffusion (first printed, then electromechanical and electronic) has affected *all* forms of music, and any of them can be treated as a commodity; if a widely distributed recording of a Tchaikovsky symphony turns the piece into 'popular music', then the definition is, to say the least, unhelpful. At the same time, *all* forms of what would usually be considered popular music can in principle be disseminated by face-to-face methods (for instance, in concerts) rather than the mass media, and can be made available free, or even structured as collective participation, rather than sold as a commodity; it is hard to believe that a few friends, jamming on 'Born in the USA' at a party, are not producing 'popular music'.

There are two definitional syntheses that have a particular currency, both in everyday discourse and among scholarly approaches. The first is *positivist*. It centres on the quantitative sense of 'popular', proposing 'to deal with the pieces which are demonstrably the *most* popular items of "popular music", with the most widely disseminated items of music disseminated in the mass media' (Hamm 1982: 5; see also Hamm 1979: xvii–xxii; 1982, *passim*). It draws, therefore, mostly on category 4 but also to some extent on categories 2 and 3. The second synthesis can be described in terms of *sociological essentialism*. Here the 'essence' of the popular is constant, though whether this is seen as proffered from above or engendered from below, whether 'the people' is regarded as an active, progressive historical subject or a manipulated dupe, varies. This approach draws mostly on category 3 but also to some extent on categories 1 and 4.

The positivist approach claims to be objective but it is no more ideology-free than any other. It takes its primary level of analysis to be that characterized by the question of *size* and by the phenomenal form of the *series*. It is methodologically bound, therefore, to the requirements of *measurement* and to the mechanisms of the *market*, and excludes anything that does not fit these. What this tends to lead to is indicated in Keil's sharp review of Hamm's history of American popular song (Keil 1980: 577; Hamm 1979):

> a steady reporting of names, dates, song titles, musical examples, from the procession of songs in commodity form that began . . . in 1789. [But] the author excludes too many dialectical tensions from the book at the start: no church music will be considered; no worrying about those Americans who couldn't afford sheet music and a piano in the parlor is allowed either; and no room for primarily instrumental music like marches, ragtime, jazz, or polka music up to 1950. Leaving out white and black American Christians is leaving out a lot. Leaving out poor and working people doesn't seem right. And my grandfather, who used to weep over the 'Second Connecticut March', why can't he be included? And all those dancing immigrants?

Even within its own terms of reference, the positivist approach has problems. The reliability of sales figures, record charts and airplay statistics is notoriously suspect. The bases of statistics are often unclear or unsatisfactory, and comparability is often impossible. Figures are open to manipulation and corruption (hyping, payola, and so on). What they represent is also influenced by institutional constraints, and choices of output by record companies and radio stations (see Frith 1987d: 137–8; Street 1986: 116–25; Wallis and Malm 1984: 242–52; Harker 1980: 94–100). But the terms of reference themselves pose problems, too. The most obvious are:

(i)   the tendency to treat heterogeneous markets as parts of an aggregate; thus, an example of relatively high dissemination in one sector may be lost among the larger figures of the whole;

(ii) the tendency to privilege the category of 'youth', because, for some time now, young people have spent a disproportionately large part of their disposable income on leisure commodities such as records; this leads to

neglect of older age-groups who may use different musics and use them
differently;

(iii)   the focus on the 'moment of exchange' rather than the 'moment of
        use' – for example, dissemination through radio-listening, background
        music, live performance and home-taping;
(iv)   similarly, non-commodity-form musical practices are ignored;
(v)   there is a tendency to standardize different time-scales – but in fact
        different musical types, and sometimes different pieces within a type, may
        sell at different rates over different time-spans; thus the Beatles' 'Can't Buy
        Me Love' sold a million copies in a week while Ken Dodd's 'Tears' took
        five months to do the same (Harker 1980: 98–9).

At best, positivist approaches measure not 'popularity' but sales. The result is to
reify popular music, treating songs solely as objects, neglecting their role in
cultural practice or 'way of life'. The circularity of the method – 'popularity' is
conceived in terms of 'how many', the numbers are totted up, and are then used
to define popularity – means that what it can tell us about is limited, first, to the
data themselves, as categorized, and, second, to its own assumptions. It cannot
tell us about the meaning of the term 'popular music', since that meaning,
ideologically replete, has been pushed outside the frame of reference.

In the methods I described as essentialist, the underlying assumptions are
qualitative rather than quantitative. Indeed, here it is precisely a particular
conception of 'qualitative shifts in cultural relations' which supports the
ideological basis of the approach (Hall 1978: 11). As a rule, the essentialist
perspective is brought to bear either from 'above' or from 'below'. In the first
case, the organizing principle goes under such terms as 'manipulation' and
'standardization', and 'popular' is more or less equated with 'mass' or
'commercial'. In the second case, the important concepts are 'authenticity',
'spontaneity', 'grass-roots'; and 'popular' means, in a particular sense, 'of the
people'. In both cases popular music is located, implicitly, within a larger field,
for in both cases the nature of popular music is established through comparison
with something else, an absent Other. And both, implicitly or explicitly, organize
this field historically, for the non-popular is, depending on the perspective, either
what the popular has tried to replace or what has tried to replace the popular. In
both cases the problem is that concrete cultural processes, in particular historical
locations, are reduced to abstract schemata. *Contradictions* within the productive
process are ignored. Consumers are regarded either as blank receptors, by the
mass culture theorists, or as an inherently oppositional class, by ultra-leftists
searching for pure proletarianism. But in practice, neither popular music,
however understood, nor its Others – 'folk song', 'traditional music', 'art
music', 'bourgeois music', or whatever else – walk on to the historical stage in
this uncontaminated form.[3]

All the approaches mentioned so far are engaged in dividing up the musical
field in a particular way – between this and that, better and worse, elite and
mass, higher and lower, aristocratic and plebeian, and so on. Of course, in
internally differentiated societies, distinctions *are* necessary, otherwise important
tensions and conflicts will pass unremarked. The danger is of over-rigid
definition, usually built on a failure to recognize the framework of assumptions
underlying every distinction. It is noticeable that in other languages, in other

societies, different terms are used and different distinctions are made.[4]

Whichever terms are used, their contents should not be regarded as absolute. Moreover, this conclusion points to two additional guidelines. 'Popular music' (or whatever) can only be properly viewed within the context of the *whole musical field*, within which it is an active tendency; and this field, together with its internal relationships, is never still – it is always *in movement*.

A theoretical framework

We need, then, to locate musical categories *topographically*. 'Popular culture is neither, in a "pure" sense, the popular traditions of resistance . . . nor is it the forms which are superimposed on and over them. It is the ground on which the transformations are worked' (Hall 1981: 228). If one must assert, against the positivists, that it is impossible simply to wipe out the ideological accretions to a term like 'popular music', it is also necessary to insist, against the essentialists, that these accretions, and the musical practices to which they refer, cannot be simply disentangled, either from each other or from cultural relations as a whole. They always contain contradictions. This is because, in class society, the *society* is internally contradictory. What the term 'popular music' tries to do is to put a finger on that space, that terrain, of contradiction – between 'imposed' and 'authentic', 'elite' and 'common', predominant and subordinate, then and now, theirs and ours, and so on – and to organize it in particular ways.

The relationships crossing this terrain take specific forms in specific societies, and must be analysed in that context. And, since they are also active, the field never quiescent, the possible meanings of 'popular music' must be historically located, too. Indeed, the very appearance of 'popular culture' within discourse arises at specific moments in specific societies; in Britain this is the mid-eighteenth century, with the rise of mature bourgeois society. Significantly, the terms 'society' and 'culture' themselves, in their modern usage, appear at the same time. In this sense, and at a rather high level of abstraction, the very *possibility* within discourse of a historically located cultural field, marked by internally contradictory relations and hence by particularly difficult questions of causation and explanation, is part of the problematic of bourgeois society; that is, it is internal to, and historically related to, a particular historical-social stage (see Burke 1981).

Much recent historical work, notably Michel Foucault's, has stressed the importance of investigating the discursive formations through which knowledge is organized. If we do not try to grasp the relations between popular music discourses and the material musical practices to which they refer, and at the same time the necessary distinctness of level between these, we are unlikely to break through the structures of power which, as Foucault makes clear, discursive authority erects. And we are likely to abandon the sphere of the concrete to the positivists and that of theory to the essentialists, rather than to theorize the relationship of the two at a higher level.

Though the structure of the musical field is *related* to structures of power, it is not *determined* by them. We need to talk of the *relative autonomy* of cultural practices, and it is helpful to introduce Gramsci's insight that the relationship between actual culture, consciousness, ideas, experience, on the one hand, and economically determined factors such as class position, on the other, is always problematical, incomplete and the object of ideological work and struggle. This is linked to Gramsci's general conception of the relationship between economic forces and 'superstructural' elements.[5] While retaining a determinative role for the former, he insists on the relative autonomy of the latter: these have their own modes of existence, their own inertia, their own time-scales, such that we have to speak of a 'necessary reciprocity' between economic/social and cultural/ideological levels. Cultural relationships and cultural change are thus not predetermined; rather, they are the product of negotiation, imposition, resistance, transformation, and so on.

In class societies this process will obviously be mediated primarily – though not exclusively – through class relationships and class conflict. Thus particular cultural forms and practices cannot be attached mechanically or even paradigmatically to particular classes; nor, even, can particular interpretations, valuations and uses of a single form or practice. In Stuart Hall's words (1981: 238) 'there are no wholly separate "cultures" . . . [no "bourgeois" hit-song, no "proletarian" industrial folk song, no "petit bourgeois" musical comedy, or "working-class" rock and roll] . . . attached, in a relation of historical fixity, to specific "whole" classes – although there are clearly distinct and variable class-cultural formations'. 'Class does not coincide with the sign community' (Volosinov 1973: 23); therefore the best approach is one that

> treats the domain of cultural forms and activities as a constantly changing field . . . looks at the relations which constantly structure this field into dominant and subordinate formations . . . [and] at the *process* by which these relations of dominance and subordination are articulated' (Hall 1981: 235).[6]

The meaning, the *accentuation*, and the form, of, for instance, early British music hall, early syncopated dance music, early rock 'n' roll, were subject to precisely this kind of struggle.

What is the nature of this process? How are musical forms and practices appropriated for use by particular classes? Hall used the word 'articulate', and other writers, too, drawing on Gramsci, have talked of a 'principle of articulation' (see, for example, Mouffe 1979). The argument is that while elements of culture are not directly, eternally or exclusively tied to specific economically determined factors such as class position, they *are* determined in the final instance by such factors, through the operation of articulating principles which *are* tied to class position. These operate by combining existing elements into new patterns or by attaching new connotations to them. Examples of the latter – attaching new connotations – would be the way musical elements of the bourgeois march were made to connote something different in nineteenth-century labour anthems; or the way the supposedly liberated individualist eclecticism of countercultural 1960s rock – 'liberated' in the Marcusian sense – was, in a process of recuperation, rearticulated to the long tradition of *bourgeois* individual bohemianism. Examples of the former – recombining existing elements – would be the way this eclecticism in 1960s rock came into being in the first place, formed as it was from disparate sources, including many elements from bourgeois 'art music'; or the way rhythmic techniques derived from working-class black American music were combined with other elements in 1920s dance music to signify a kind of safe but exotic, hedonist escapism for a broad grouping of classes in Britain.

Particularly strong articulative relationships are established when what we can call 'cross-connotation' takes place: that is, when two or more different elements are made to connote, symbolize or evoke each other. This is what seems to have happened in the late Victorian music hall, when a style evoking a particular class subject – the 'remade' working class described by the historian Gareth Stedman-Jones (1974) – is crossed with political elements – the ideology of imperialism – resulting in a relatively unified mode of 'popular imperialism' within this song category. Similarly, early Elvis Presley managed to link together elements connoting youth rebellion, working-class 'earthiness' and ethnic 'roots', each of which can evoke the others, all of which were articulated together, however briefly, by a moment of popular self-assertion. In the 1960s, the connection to a political theme – the supposed new energies released by a Labour-led 'swinging Britain' – of the notions of boy-next-door, man-in-the-street 'classlessness' constructed around the early Beatles, was one way in which the music's meaning was secured for the dominant social interests.

When the articulative process works well, the pattern of elements that it organizes comes to seem 'natural'; in this form it usually spreads widely through society. An example would be the mid-Victorian 'song synthesis' which spread across a wide spectrum of musical types, from operetta and parlour ballad to music hall and pub singing, displaying variants within a broad congruence of musical code. Another would be the Hollywood/Broadway/Tin Pan Alley synthesis of the 1930s. A third, perhaps, would be the generalized notion of pop/rock represented in chart hit/Eurovision Song Contest/mainstream rock in the 1970s and 1980s. These patterns represent moments when cultural hegemony is relatively unquestioned. It is in this context that we must understand the reception of syncopated dance music in the early 1900s, of rock 'n' roll in the 1950s, and of punk in the late 1970s, as not only new but *unnatural*. These are moments involving elements of social crisis, or at least social unrest, when the strength of accepted articulated patterns declines.

The theory of articulation recognizes the complexity of cultural fields. It preserves a relative autonomy for cultural and ideological elements (musical structures and song lyrics, for example) but also insists that those combinatory patterns that are actually constructed do mediate deep, objective patterns in the socio-economic formation, and that the mediation takes place *in struggle*: the classes fight to articulate together constituents of the cultural repertoire in particular ways so that they are organized in terms of principles or sets of values determined by the position and interests of the class in the prevailing mode of production. This theory seems to me the most sophisticated method at present available of conceiving the relationship between musical forms and practices, on the one hand, and class interests and social structure, on the other; more sophisticated, say, than the theories of homology put forward by some ethnomusicologists and subcultural theorists, which suggest the existence of structural 'resonances', or homologies, between the different elements making up a socio-cultural whole.[7] Such theories always end up in some kind of reductionism – 'upwards', into an idealist cultural spirit, 'downwards', into economism, sociologism or technologism, or by 'circumnavigation', in a functionalist holism.

However, I would like to hang on to the notion of homology in a qualified sense. For it seems likely that some signifying structures are more *easily* articulated to the interests of one group than are some others; similarly, that they are more easily articulated to the interests of one group than to those of another. This is because, owing to the existence of what Paul Willis calls the 'objective possibilities' (and limitations) of material and ideological structures, it is easier to find links and analogies between them in some cases than in others (Willis 1978: 198–201). Consider, for example, János Maróthy's (1974) distinction between what he calls 'collective-variative' methods, which he connects primarily to proletarian musical practice, and the symmetrical solo song forms typical of bourgeois music culture, from the Middle Ages onwards. It would be a mistake to regard these two categories as simple products of class needs. But it is clear that, for objective structural reasons, it was, during a certain long historical period, *easier* for the bourgeoisie to make meaningful use of the second, and the working classes the first, than vice versa. Similarly, working-class musical practice found it hard to deal with the elements of bourgeois solo song except by acquiescing in the norms of the dominant musical culture, or by treating them parodistically or through other methods of distortion.

Moreover, however arbitrary musical meanings and conventions are – rather than being 'natural', or determined by some human essence or by the needs of class expression – once particular musical elements are put together in particular ways, and acquire particular connotations, these can be hard to shift. It would be difficult, for instance, to move the 'Marseillaise' out of the set of meanings sedimented around it – hence around other tunes of the same type, too – which derive from the history of the revolutionary French bourgeoisie. Similarly, it is not easy to disturb the connotations of those types of 'folk song' constituted by bourgeois romanticism as signifying (sentimentalized) 'community', an organic social harmony. The romantic-lyrical ballad style of twentieth-century Tin Pan Alley clings stubbornly to its role in the representation of gender relations within the norms set by the stereotype of the bourgeois couple, despite attempts made from time to time to move it into new patterns with new meanings. Thus a theory of articulation does not mean that the musical field is a pluralistic free-for-all. It is not *un*determined but *over*determined, and the ruling interests in the social formation take the lead in setting the predispositions which are always trying to constitute a received shape. As Gramsci points out (1971: 260), 'the bourgeois class poses itself as an organism in continuous movement, capable of absorbing the whole society, assimilating it to its own cultural and economic level', and this would-be universalizing push provides one of the most important elements in music history of the last two hundred years. Thus, underlying the other side of Gramsci's picture – the continuous construction of class alliances, with its articulative dimension in the cultural domain – there is a basic dichotomy, organized around the relationship of 'hegemonic' and subordinate blocs, 'power bloc versus popular classes' (Hall 1981: 238–9), the content of each and the terrain it controls being precisely the object of cultural as well as economic struggle.

It should be added that cultural formations are not only conditioned by class position, central though that is; age, gender, ethnicity and nationality are also important. Each of these can mediate any or all of the others. Thus, it can be argued that the impact of the young Elvis Presley was due to the way in which, taking a range of pre-existing musical, lyric and performance elements, he rearticulated them into a new pattern set by the intersection and intermediation of certain images of class (proletarian), ethnicity (black/poor white), age ('youth'), gender (male) and nationality (American South). The articulating principle governing the social meaning of this music for its audience must be defined in terms of a conjunction of new representations of leisure, the body, gender relations and capitalist consumption, tied in turn to the objectively new social-economic position of this audience in post-war capitalist society. This is how the romantic-lyric elements in Elvis's style, for example, could take on new meanings, mediated as they were by country and western's and black music's previous appropriations of them, by the 'underview' of the working class of the South on the American Dream, and by an awareness of a new freedom in adolescent leisure behaviour.

Of course, the effect of such a 'constellation' is nuanced by the social situation of *listeners*. The 'nationality' factor in early Elvis signified rather differently for British adolescents in the mid-1950s; it was mediated through the image presented by the 'American South' within their national tradition, and, more widely, through the rather different gender, generational and class structures obtaining in Britain. (This is no more than to say that, within the operation of articulation processes, production and consumption are inextricably tied together.) Similarly, the effects of early Elvis (and of early rock 'n' roll in general) change over time, as the articulating factors change. Sometimes this affects the production of the music; in any case, it always affects the ways in which it is received. Thus the class orientation of early Elvis was shifted as his music was articulated to the interests of the dominant elements in the music business; at the same time, his generational sharpness was muffled. Subsequently, revivals reinvest in meanings closer to the originals but inevitably transformed by the effects of the intervening struggles over the ownership of rock 'n' roll and of its meanings. Elvis – that particular musical agglomeration – never *belonged* to anyone in particular, then; he – it – was there to be fought for.

A historical framework

It will be clear by now why, in order to study historically located forms of popular music, it is necessary to place them within the context of the whole music-historical field. 'The assumption . . . that you might know before you looked at cultural relations in general what, at any particular time, was a part of élite culture or a part of popular culture is untenable' (Hall 1978: 6–7). Thus, to grasp properly the significance of popular dancing in the mid-nineteenth century – the waltz, for example – it is necessary to look not only at the waltz culture of the popular classes but also at such factors as: the peasant sources of the waltz; the use made of those sources in bourgeois culture; the changing social relations involved in the growth of industrial capitalism, to which the romanticizing of popular culture found in bourgeois waltzing, together with its cultivation of an explicit sensuality, was probably a reaction; the tendency of the social developments to result in the atomization of established collective social patterns and modes of corporeal expression, leading, among avant-garde composers, to a music more overtly of thought and feeling, as against a music of social gesture; the way these same composers, by way of reaction to that situation, incorporated spiritualized versions of dance elements in their music. The internally contradictory form, waltzing, as a genre, cuts across classes, and, as a practice, is inscribed in the overall relations of cultures and classes in the period.

Similarly, one could not satisfactorily analyse modalism in rock music without also dealing with the decline of modal folk song, in its traditional social contexts; the urban folk revival; the use of modal techniques by elite composers, and the 'discovery' of modal medieval and renaissance music; the commodification of major-minor tonality by Tin Pan Alley and Hollywood, against which modalism could be seen as 'exotic' or 'primitive'; the internationalization of capital bringing, through American cultural imperialism, the influence of modal Afro-American musics which, at the same time, could be seen as offering a potential for critique *vis-à-vis* the dominant, major-minor musical language; and so on.

These are examples of synchronic analysis: slicing through the relationships obtaining at any one time in the social-cultural formation. But the field is continuously in movement. Articulated syntheses have vectorial qualities – not only a weight within the field but also a direction. Raymond Williams's terminology of 'dominant', 'residual' and 'emergent' forms provides a useful way of mapping such qualities (1981: 203–5). In Britain around 1900, for example, it is clear that the forms of 'high' music hall were dominant, those of street ballad and indigenous rural song were residual, and those of syncopated dance music (ragtime, foxtrot, and the like) were emergent.

But within the whole network of movement, some moments are more critical than others, and there is a definite rhythm of change. Gramsci makes a distinction between two levels of structure, the 'situation' and the 'conjuncture'. 'Situation' refers to the deepest, the organic structures of a social formation; movement there is fundamental and relatively permanent, the result of crisis. 'Conjuncture' refers to more immediate, ephemeral characteristics, linked to the organic structures, but changing at once more rapidly and less significantly, as the forces in conflict within a situation struggle to work out their contradictions. For Gramsci, these two levels are dialectically interlinked. But at the same time it is clear that some periods display radical situational change, while others, in between these, are periods of relative situational stability, when day-to-day conjunctural movement assumes a more prominent position in the historical picture (see Gramsci 1971: 175–85). In this way of analysis, the importance of changes in economic and social relations is retained – particularly at the level of the situation, where homologies, in the sense defined earlier, may be thought to operate – while relative autonomy for cultural and ideological elements is especially noticeable at the conjunctural level, for these elements may change at differing speeds, in differing ways.

In sketching out a music history for the last two hundred years, one can identify, I believe, three 'moments' of radical situational change. These seem to be found in all the developed Western societies, though the dating differs.

First is the moment of the 'bourgeois revolution', marked by complex and overt class struggle within cultural fields, by the spread of the market system through almost all musical activities, and by the development and eventual predominance of new musical types associated with the new ruling class. Conventional music history's delineation of the period through rigid Classical/Romantic periodization or 'great man' physiognomies hides a complex web of interactions, as old and new elements were articulated into a variety of patterns and meanings. In Britain, this moment has several phases during a long and turbulent period from the late-eighteenth century to the 1840s.

By the end of this period, most musical production is in the hands of or is mediated by commercial music publishers, concert organizers and promoters, theatre and public house managers. For the first time, most music is bought, not made for oneself. Over the preceding half century, new kinds of bourgeois song, for theatre and home, emerge; new kinds of social dance develop; there is an explosion in urban street song, often using new kinds of tune; the commercialization of traditional (especially Scots and Irish) song begins; new kinds of song from industrialized working-class areas are produced; new kinds of public house entertainments evolve; organized mass choral singing and wind-band movements begin. Along with conflicts between different musical techniques, there are immense struggles over what form music should take and what role it should play: this is as evident in pub, school and street as, on another level, in orchestral concert music, opera, the fashion for virtuoso piano music and the work of the avant-garde composers of the Romantic movement.

By about 1850, the musical map has been drastically redrawn, in the context of the new norms represented by the values of the various fractions of the bourgeoisie. The period of greater stability – the 'mid-Victorian equipoise' – which followed has been somewhat more adequately mapped by research than the upheavals that went before (see, for example, Bailey 1978; 1986a; Bratton 1986; D. Russell 1987; Scott 1989). The striking feature is the extent of congruence across a range of different musical practices, resulting in a not exactly homogeneous musical field but one clearly dominated by a bourgeois synthesis. With variants, this relative congruence of musical technique, repertoire and practice stretched across light opera, bourgeois domestic song, the brass band and mass choral movements, and the now more rationally organized music hall; it even penetrated the broadside and orally transmitted song genres of the industrial areas. Street music was gradually banished, political song pushed into tight proletarian enclaves, and the musical avant-garde characteristic of earlier in the century was either marginalized or assimilated, as brass bands played Wagner and parlour singers juxtaposed Schubert and Schumann with more commercial products.

By the 1890s, the start of a second major situational fracture can be seen. This is the moment of 'mass culture', characterized by the development of monopoly-capitalist structures. National lineages remain important, but as one pole of a tension counterbalanced by a growing internationalization of culture, associated particularly with an emerging American hegemony. This shows itself both in musical content – the impact of ragtime, jazz, Tin Pan Alley songs, new dance forms, and so on – and in new methods of mass production, publicity and distribution: in short, a drive towards 'one-way communication' in homogeneous markets. Characteristic symptoms of monopolization can be seen in the reorganization of music hall as early as the 1880s; corporate ownership, national and regional syndicates and chains, and restrictive licensing policies combined to freeze out the small entrepreneur (see Bailey 1986a, *passim*). By the First World War, musical production and dissemination are coming to be concentrated in a new alliance consisting of a centralized publishing system (in New York's Tin Pan Alley and London's Denmark Street), the quickly developing gramophone companies (by 1910 dominated, world-wide, by Victor of the USA and the Gramophone Co. of Britain) and, a little later, the new medium of radio; by the late 1920s, we can add the movie industry as well. The language of formula and the mass market, already appearing in the world of 1880s British music hall song (see A. Bennett 1986: 9–10), is heard particularly clearly in the United States against the backdrop of the new industrial methods of 'Fordism'. According to the song-writer Charles K. Harris (quoted in Hamm 1979: 288), 'A new song must be sung, played, hummed, and drummed into the ears of the public, not in one city alone, but in every city, town and village, before it ever becomes popular'.

There are thus both economic and ideological reasons why the new musical energies of this period should come from American sources. As for the avantgarde, we can see the development of modernism as precisely an outraged and deliberately esoteric response to the new drive towards total commodification. Henceforth 'industry' and 'art' would always be in symbiotic struggle, within popular as well as elite genres. While there were many conflicts over all the new music (and dance) forms (see, for example, Hustwitt 1983), by the mid-1920s we can see the outlines of a new, laboriously constructed consensus, 'hotter' and radical elements squeezed out, new techniques smoothed and assimilated within a musical framework with links back to bourgeois traditions, socially centred on 'respectable' dancing and home-listening, and on traditional kinds of concert- and opera-going (see Frith 1983b; 1988b).[8] The consensus popular music repertoire of the late 1920s, 1930s and 1940s[9] covers a relatively narrow stylistic spread, bounded by theatre song on the one side, novelty items deriving from music hall and vaudeville traditions on the other, with Tin Pan Alley song, Hollywood hits and crooners in between. Contesting articulations of musical practices could as a rule now arise only at the level of consumption. Even within elite culture, where producers (composers) were nominally autonomous, the modernist challenge tended to subside into a conservative 'neo-classical' hegemony.

The third moment of situational change begins sometime after the Second World War – most strikingly with the advent of rock 'n' roll – and can be termed the moment of 'pop culture'. In this period, against the background of a developing world market, within a 'global economy' dominated by multinational corporations, the existing monopolistic cultural formation both confirms itself and, at another level, becomes noticeably fissured, through the development of an assortment of transient subcultures. There are changes in technology: electronic systems take over from the electromechanical mode typical of 'mass culture' (just as that had taken over from the purely mechanical production and distribution methods of the earlier bourgeois period, epitomized by music printing). These create the potential for new production methods – magnetic tape replaces music scores, the 'three-chord' electric guitar puts in question the existing professionalized instrumental skills. There are changes in relations of production, too, most importantly, the first significant encroachment on music-production resources by the working-class young, and accompanying this is the opening up of a new youth market, which is structurally less tied to established class roles than older generations. This group, with its 'margin for rebellion', looks to new musical sources, notably in black American rhythm and blues, many aspects of which are predisposed to connotations clustered around feelings of 'oppression', on the one hand, and relatively non-alienated use of the body (potentially subversive of capitalist work disciplines) on the other.

Parallel upheavals occur at roughly the same time in jazz, where modern styles, and, in a different way, the revivalist movement, challenge the hegemony of crooners and commercial dance-bands; and in elite music culture, where the earlier modernist outburst, headed by Schoenberg and Stravinsky, is matched by the iconoclasm of the post-war avant-garde led by Boulez, Stockhausen and Cage.

The efflorescence of rock 'n' roll, and of the 1960s rock movements, took place against the background of a new social-historical phase, that of the 'long boom', 'welfare capitalism' and an ideology of liberal tolerance. Official permissiveness was seen to be justified as, at both moments, 'rebellion' was to a large extent articulated to predominantly safer musical patterns with less subversive meanings. Demands for greater 'freedom' and 'authenticity' can often be channelled into established stereotypes of rebellion and expression, and thus articulated to the framework of the dominant musical ideology, mediated by a discourse which is organized round notions of 'youth', 'modernity' and 'pleasure'; the result can be used across the age-range and across classes, securing the interests of cultural reproduction and of liberal tolerance.

By the late 1960s, the new social patterns, technologies and musical styles had been substantially assimilated into a reorganized music-industrial system: a transnational oligopoly of vast entertainment corporations, supplied to some extent by 'independent' producers; serviced by mass audience radio and TV channels (with some 'minority' shows and channels), by a symbiotically pliant music press and by related leisure-products businesses; and directing itself at a series of separate audiences whose distinctness is less subcultural than a creature of market researchers' consumer profiles. Whether the startling but short-lived explosion of punk rock represented the first sign of a new situational fracture (new production methods; 'outrageous' music; independent operations), or the last twitch of the moment of 'pop culture' (a rerun of rock 'n' roll do-it-yourself amateurism), or a less organic, *conjunctural* tremor (like hip hop, 'charity rock', Bruce Springsteen, Billy Bragg and many more) is difficult to say. From the perspective of the late 1980s, the latter two interpretations seem more plausible than the first; the terms of the conjunctural negotiations, while by no means monolithic, seem to be set by chart pop, 'stadium rock', disco, and middle-of-the-road styles.

It is interesting, however, that Ernest Mandel's model of the stages of industrial capitalism (1975: 108–46), whose sequence of 'long waves' seems to correspond to the sequence of 'situations' described here, would locate our society now in the second half of the current 'wave'; and such periods are characterized, for him, by incipient crisis. But one should not expect such economic movements to determine the details of changing musical practice in any mechanical way.[10] The link between socio-economic structure and the specificities of cultural and ideological practice is provided by processes of articulation, as we saw earlier; and it is therefore these processes which now require further investigation.

Articulation in practice

The apparent coherence of most musical styles, and of the relationship they have with the societies in which they exist, is not 'natural' but contrived; it is the product of cultural work. Particularly in complex, internally differentiated societies, musical styles are assemblages of elements from a variety of sources, each with a variety of histories and connotations, and these assemblages can, in appropriate circumstances, be prised open and the elements rearticulated in different contexts. Sometimes this is obvious, as when parody (in the widest sense of the term) is used. At other times it is relatively hidden, smoothed over by extensive cultivation, familiarity and the techniques of what Bourdieu calls 'legitimation', only to be revealed when constituent elements are wrenched away and placed in a new setting. This happens, for instance, when the *volkstümlich* tunes so popular in early nineteenth-century bourgeois domestic song (where they signify according to romantic conceptions of nation and community) are used by working-class singers for disaster ballads; when sentimental Tin Pan Alley ballad melody is 'gospelized' by Ray Charles or Otis Redding; or when the heavy four-four of the quick march (goose step?) is appropriated by the early punk bands as a mode of critique.

The strength with which particular potentially contradictory relationships are held together depends not only on the amount of objective 'fit' between the components but also on the strength of the articulating principle involved, which is in turn connected with objective social factors. John Lennon's 'Imagine', so powerful when one is listening to it, may afterwards be quite easily broken down into fairly disparate elements: radical text; rock-ballad melody, harmony and orchestration; singer-songwriter ('confessional') piano; soul/gospel-tinged singing. What is tying these together is an ideal, or to put it more concretely, a certain position associated with some alienated intellectuals in late capitalist society. This hard-fought-for (and affecting) 'coherence' lacks sufficient material support (in terms of defined social interests) and ideological legitimacy (or threat) to sustain itself as more than a personal, transitory, hence ultimately sentimental reorientation of the musical traditions concerned. The dominant sectors of society found no difficulty in tolerating or even nodding approval of its message, a development which reached its apogee when the 1988 Conference of the British Conservative Party bellowed out the song with no hint of embarrassment.

Compare this case with a more collective process of rearticulation. The American revivalist hymn 'Amazing Grace' (*c.* 1800) is an excellent example of the symmetries Maróthy ascribes to bourgeois song (Maróthy 1974). The words are organized around symmetrical pairs (grace/wretch; lost/found; blind/see) and the tune, at least in its best known version, not only divides into an open/closed parallelism, through its cadence structure, but within this, the subsidiary phrases form complementary pairs; moreover, the overall pitch contour follows the arch shape typical of this song type (see Ex. 1.1). There are many 'folk' variants of this tune which adapt it to rather different musical traditions. But the more recent adoption of the tune by British football crowds probably follows the Judy Collins 1971 hit, which retains all the features of the 'bourgeois' version. Now, however, the words become repetitive (just the name of the team). And a simple change to the tune has radical results. It is shortened to just the second and third phrases, both of which are cadentially 'open', and so what had been a self-sufficient arch shape is turned into continuous, open-ended variative repetition (see Ex. 1.2). 'Spiritual lyricism' is transformed into an unending, circling chant of collective support for the team. It is easy to see how the two versions 'fit' typical articulating principles traditionally associated with the bourgeoisie ('individual-ism') and the working class ('collectivism'). The football chant articulates its

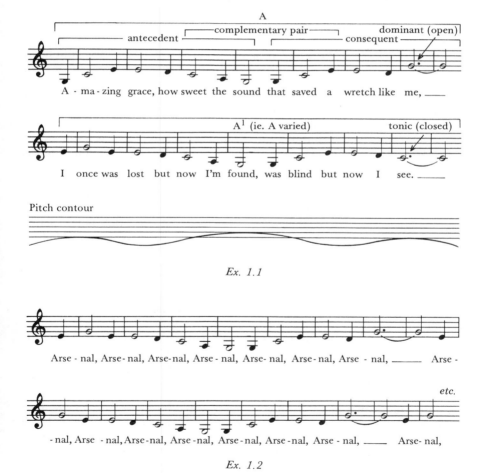

Ex. 1.1

Ex. 1.2

tradition to the specific interests of team supporters and soccer gangs. When, within the wider discursive context, it can be related to 'typical (mindless) working-class collectivism', it is tolerated; transmuted into the beery conviviality of a pop group like Slade, the culture represented by such chants can be patronized. But the latent threat deriving from the social power behind such chanting can often be felt, and of course erupts in the panic over 'football hooliganism'.

It is instructive to apply this analytical perspective to early rock 'n' roll – to Elvis Presley, let us say. At first rock 'n' roll was generally seen in terms of *rebellion*: this was viewed positively, by fans and fellow-travellers, or negatively, by outraged defenders of established cultural interests; in any case, it was a new music, set against existing popular types. Subsequently a more sophisticated interpretation historicized this account, describing what happened to popular music in the late 1950s and early 1960s in terms of the *incorporation* or *co-option* of rock 'n' roll into the repertoire of the hegemonic bloc. But still, the vital point is missing – that rock 'n' roll was internally contradictory from the start: not just boogie rhythms, rough sound, blues shouts and physical involvement but also sentimental ballad melodies and forms, 'angelic' backing vocal effects and 'novelty' gimmicks.

In the case of Elvis, this problem is particularly striking because within the rock discourse he has been widely seen as both the music's first hero and its most prominent backslider. Most rock critics take this line, seeing Elvis's career as a progressive sell-out to the music industry, a transition from 'folk' authenticity (the Sun singles of 1954–5) to a sophisticated professionalism (epitomized by the ballads and movies of the 1960s) in which the dollars multiplied but musical values went by the board. But in post-war America a pure 'folk' role, untouched by commercial influences, had become impossible. The dissemination of music by radio and gramophone record permeated the whole country and every social stratum. The performers whom the young Elvis heard and learned from – gospel singers, bluesmen like Arthur Crudup, Bill Broonzy, Junior Parker and Howlin' Wolf, country and western stars such as Bob Wills, Hank Williams and Roy Acuff – were *commercial* artists; they, like Elvis himself, did not separate themselves from the whole wash of music that was available. When Sam Phillips, founder of Sun Records and 'creator' of Elvis Presley, said, 'If I could find a white man who had the Negro sound and the Negro feel, I could make a billion dollars' (quoted in Hopkins 1971: 66), the twin motivations, artistic and commercial, were not separated or separable. If we look at the music Elvis produced throughout his career, we find confirmation that the 'decline-and-fall' view will not stand up.

Elvis's two most notable contributions to the language of rock 'n' roll are first, the assimilation of 'romantic lyricism' and second, what I call 'boogification'. Both techniques can be found in classic form in his first national hit, 'Heartbreak Hotel' (1956). This was by origin a country and western song but its vocal has the shape of a typical blues shout. Nevertheless the rough tone, irregular rhythms and 'dirty' intonation that most blues singers would have used are for the most part conspicuously absent in Elvis's performance; his tone is full, rich and well produced, his intonation is precise, stable and 'correct', the notes are sustained and held right through, and the phrasing is legato. At the same time this lyrical continuity is subverted by 'boogification'. As in boogie-woogie, the basic vocal

rhythms are triplets (♪♪♪ , ♩ ♪) and, again as in boogie-woogie, the *off-*
beat quaver is often given an unexpected accent (e.g. ♩ ♪), producing
syncopation and cross-rhythm. The effect is physical, demanding movement, jerking the body into activity. Elvis, however, extends the technique. He adds extra off-beat notes not demanded by words or vocal line, often splitting up syllables or even consonants, slurring words together, disguising the verbal sense (see Ex. 1.3). Occasionally, a 'sustained' note has something like a rhythm vibrato (in triplet rhythm): listen for instance to 'Although' at the start of the second and last choruses, 'Now' at the start of the third, and 'Well' at the start of the fourth.

The overall effect of the boogification technique is, of course, sexy, but it is also a bit jittery and absurd; the sensuality seems almost out of control. The combination of boogification with romantic lyricism in 'Heartbreak Hotel' – one element deriving from established Tin Pan Alley technique, the other from the black American subculture – produces a style already, at this early stage in Elvis's career, teetering on the edge of that melodrama into which he was so often to fall. The articulation of the two together, in terms and in a context set by the values of the new youth culture, epitomizes the overall problematic proposed by this music-historical moment; broadly speaking, we can think of romantic fantasy 'made young', 'given flesh', made to 'move' physically, while conversely an increased corporeal freedom is presented, in line with the experience of adolescent sexuality in Protestant bourgeois society, in a guarded, personalized, even ironic manner.

The same fusion of techniques can be found even earlier, while Elvis was still recording for Sun. 'Milkcow Blues Boogie' (1955) is perhaps the best example since the techniques are so well integrated, though Elvis's treatment of the song is at such a quick tempo that the operation of the techniques themselves is less clear than in 'Heartbreak Hotel'. The lyrical approach – the rich tone, the singing

(a) lo - one - ly   stree - ee - eet

(b) be - e so lo - one-ly ba - a - by , heart - break ho - tel - l - l I'll - ll be

(c) they'll ne' - er 'ey 'e - 'er look ba - ack 'll make you so

Ex. 1.3

(a) Well — ah wo-oke up — this_ a morn-ing a-and ah-ah loo-ooked ou-ou-out the door. _

(b) you're gon-na nee-eed your a-lo - o-vin'-a - da - a-ddy here_ some   day.

(c) Well-ll — ah   tried ev'-ry   thi-ing — to   git a-long with-a you-ou. _

Ex. 1.4

through the note, the sustained legato, the controlled phrase-endings – is most apparent for the last line of each chorus. Boogification pervades the entire vocal, though the quick tempo means there is less scope for accenting off-beat notes, and often the effect is so fast as to be a rhythm vibrato. The tempo also makes accurate notation harder. However, Ex. 1.4 gives some typical manifestations.

Both romantic lyricism and boogification not only date back to the beginnings of Elvis's career but also continue to be used throughout its development. There is no watershed, or 'fall from grace'. What we do see, however, is a kind of stylistic specialization. Songs which integrate the techniques like 'Milkcow Blues Boogie' (or 'Mystery Train') in the Sun period or 'Heartbreak Hotel' in the early Victor period, become less common. The techniques tend to diverge, romantic lyricism being channelled into ballads, boogification into a particular kind of rock 'n' roll song which I shall call 'mannerist'.

Elvis's huge ballad repertoire needs little commentary here, save to stress that it began not with the move to RCA but at Sun, 'Love Me Tender' (1956) and 'That's When Your Heartaches Begin' (1957) being preceded by equally sentimental ballads cut for Sam Phillips; indeed, it began earlier – when, as a boy, Elvis was entered for a talent contest at the Mississippi-Alabama Fair, it was the sentimental country and western number 'Old Shep' that he sang.

'Mannerist rock' is associated most clearly with songs, many written for Elvis by Otis Blackwell, like 'Don't Be Cruel' (1956), 'All Shook Up' (1957) and 'Please Don't Drag That String Around' (1963). The techniques of boogification are exaggerated, overplayed, even parodied. By pushing them into mannerism, Elvis distances himself from their demands, physical and psychological. In 'All Shook Up', for example, the old techniques are still there (Ex. 1.5), but the triviality of the lyrics and Elvis's light, amused vocal tone tell us that this is not serious. Mannerism is usually seen as an RCA development; but once again we find that it was already developing during the Sun period, notably in 'Baby Let's Play House' (1955). Clearly, it is the certain amount of 'slack' within the articulative relationships, the fact that the combination of techniques does not fix a - well - a - bless - a - my   soul - a - what's-a - wrong with me ⎯

Ex. 1.5

any constituent 100 per cent to the others, that explains the possibility of differential development of elements in the mixture – rather than 'changes in style'.

Elvis's importance, then, lies not so much in the mix of elements (blues/country/Tin Pan Alley) which he helped to bring into being in rock 'n' roll, but in what he did with it. He transformed them – articulated them – into particular patterns. The only workable categorization of Elvis's music, as we have seen, is not by historical period but by song-type – or more precisely, by apparently self-contradictory assemblages of musical elements as they are mediated by the differential demands of varied songs at various moments. What *does* happen historically is that integrated songs become gradually less common through the course of Elvis's career, while the song-types tend to diverge, as the relatively small, well-defined audience of the Sun days gives way to a large, heterogeneous market demanding different types for different sub-sections. Elvis is all things to his audience *throughout* his career, but the nature of the audience changes, and with it the nature and range of the articulations of the musical materials. The unifying factor is Elvis himself – or rather, Elvis constructed in particular categories, acting as embodiments of particular articulating principles, tied to particular sets of social needs and interests.

Without this kind of analytical framework, respecting the complex levels of mediation involved and their relative autonomy, Elvis becomes simply the plaything of naked political forces (rebellious/manipulative); and the fact that the young rock 'n' roller sang ballads from the start, that the older Hollywood star could still sing rock 'n' roll songs and was still respected by rock 'n' roll fans, that his 'blues' were 'romantic' (a kind of fantasy), his ballads often 'realistic' (given flesh), or that he could make boogification ironic – all this is inexplicable.

The complexity and energy of the early rock 'n' roll moment are probably symptomatic of its position as a manifestation of quite deep situational change. There is a richness of musical resources – many previously unavailable to a mass audience – and an excitement about new technological possibilities, new social relations and new kinds of musical behaviour which account for the fact that cultural struggle could take place here within musical production itself. It is instructive to turn, by contrast, to a location which is more settled, less varied in available musical resources, and characterized, apparently, by heavily weighted relations between the class-cultural formations.

Ned Corvan was a song-writer, fiddler and performer in the working-class concert halls and pubs of Tyneside in North-East England during the 1850s and early 1860s; in his final years he also worked in the first of the new kind of music halls, owned by commercially ambitious entrepreneurs and orientated more towards a nationally organized market and production system. Corvan's career was sufficiently close to the industrial conflict and Chartist agitation of the turbulent 1840s to draw inspiration from them; but, by the 1850s, the musical culture of most British workers was taking on a less class-specific quality, characterized by the consumption of commercially supplied music hall song, the replacement of old tune-types by newer types originating in bourgeois theatre and drawing-room, and a shift from protest, street music and spontaneous sing-song to formalized performance in choirs and brass bands.

Despite strong regional cultural traditions, Tyneside was affected by these developments. But Ned Corvan, it seems, continued to work for a solidly working-class audience and address working-class concerns. How did he do it? He had relatively restricted resources: tunes drawn from rural and urban proletarian traditions and from new bourgeois sources; text-methods, turns-of-phrase and verse forms derived from drawing-room, popular theatre, broadside and working-class entertainment. Many of the originally proletarian elements had been appropriated and reorientated by petit-bourgeois writers and publishers during the previous half-century. To rearticulate them back to working-class interests required considerable ideological *work*. Yet Corvan 'established himself as spokesman-in-song for his own class'; his first published song collection was dedicated to his 'Friends and Patrons', the 'Skippers, Colliers and Working Men in general, of Tyneside and Neighbourhood' (Harker 1981: 48).

The first important point to the argument here concerns Corvan's choice of tunes. There are no newly invented tunes; like almost all proletarian performers at this time, rural and urban, he draws on existing melodies. But at a time when tunes from bourgeois sources were increasingly popular and when traditional, so-called 'folk' tunes were in decline, certainly in the music hall, Corvan used comparatively few of the former and actively retained many of the latter. In a study of his four published *Song Books*, I found that of the forty-two tunes I could identify (four I could not), some 60 per cent are 'traditional', mostly of rural origin (the bulk Scottish), while only about 12 per cent come from comic music hall songs and about 25 per cent from bourgeois sources (parlour ballad, light opera). Furthermore, three of the parlour ballad tunes and one of the comic song tunes contain pseudo-'folk' elements; and two of the 'bourgeois' tunes derive from American minstrelsy and have a melodic style similar to that of some Anglo-American 'folk' traditions.

It may be argued, of course, that in themselves these facts demonstrate comparatively little. 'Folk' tunes, especially of Scottish origin, had long had a strong presence in the North-East regional culture; and, as in other areas of the country, they had also been taken up by middle-class circles. But the weight of received connotations is important here. Given a continuity of working-class usage of such tunes, a sub-stratum of associations in the culture facilitated their articulation towards working-class needs. Their long-lived presence made it possible for them to act as a kind of semi-permanent critique of newer cultural trends.[11] Whether that process would take place clearly depended very much on the texts to which the tunes were put, and the way the songs were performed. Contemporary reports suggest strongly that Corvan's performance style was dramatic, intimate, high in spontaneity and very dependent on audience rapport – as against the more fixed, formalized renderings of the tunes which would be typical of performances in the bourgeois drawing-room or the ballad concert.

As far as texts are concerned, consider 'The Toon Improvement Bill'

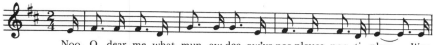

Noo, O dear me, what mun aw dee, aw've nee pleyce noo ti play,— Wor

can-ny Forth an' Spit-al te, eh man, they've tune a - way, ___ Nee

pleyce ti bool wor peyste eggs noo, to lowp the frog and run, ___ They're

al - ways beel-din sum-muck new they'll spoil New-cas - sel seune. __

Ex. 1.6

(Ex. 1.6).[12] This is an attack on speculative urban development, which has resulted in the disappearance of the open spaces where working-class children used to play. Corvan seems to draw on the 'traditional' associations – the feelings of continuity – clustered around the Scottish tune, 'Na Good Luck about the House', to support his nostalgically cast complaint. Similarly, for 'Astrilly', a song about the plight of the suffering pitmen, which led many to resort to emigration (often to Australia: 'Astrilly'), Corvan makes use of the traditional tune, 'All Around My Hat', with its history of texts to do with farewell and absence, here transposed from the sphere of love to that of work.

Corvan also uses 'traditional' tunes for celebrations of working-class life and characters: again cultural continuity within social change is affirmed, and other claims on these tunes, other reworkings of these traditions, are resisted. The virtues of the 'Lads o' Tyneside' are described to the modal Scottish tune, 'Laird o' Cockpen' (working-class 'lairds', these!) (Ex. 1.7), and 'The Factory Lass' gets a similar tune, 'Sunny Banks of Scotland'.

All the tunes mentioned so far were, so to speak, rescued from the hands of 'folk' song collectors and those of 'refined' parlour performers; Corvan's texts articulate them to the needs of *his* class, at a particular moment in its history. But he also made use of tunes from bourgeois sources – and transformed their meanings in the process. The tune to 'Bow, Wow, Wow' originated in the late eighteenth-century bourgeois repertory of London ballad opera, pleasure garden and harmonic society. In 'Jimmy Munro's Troubles' (Ex. 1.8) Corvan uses the banality of its phrasing, repetitions, sequences and harmonic structure to help construct a mock-simpleton persona, which enables him to cloak the bite of his

I've had ma-ny sweet-hearts, in maw woo-ing life An'
The first time I saw him 'twas on the fair night, He

had ma-ny of-fers to be a guid wife; But maw
baith cut and shuf-fled the keel row sae light; Sae ___

heart beats for yen, aye an' faith it beats true; He's a
smart and sae hand-some, not one spark o' pride. Oh! my

bon-ny keel lad-die wi' bon-net sae blue. *For it's*
heart beats a-lone for the Lads o' Tyne-side.

doon the burn Jin-ny maw can-ny hin-ny and doon the burn

Jin-ny aw'll wan-der wi' thee and___ then they'll ca-ress ye, an' so

co-sey they'll press ye o' the bon-ny Tyne lad-dies for e-ver for me.

Ex. 1.7

social criticism in humour; he plays at 'acting the fool', in tortuous verbal
constructions and juxtapositions of the serious and the trivial – just as the 'Bow,
Wow, Wow' song originally did – but the real problems of railway accidents,
rent and ragged clothes turn the joke around. Similarly, in 'The Rise in Coals'
Corvan takes the tune of 'The Mistletoe Bough', an early nineteenth-century
'gothic' ballad mixing melodrama and sentimentality, and puts it to words
describing a situation of *real* emotion for working people: a rise in the price of
household coal during the coldest weather of the winter (Ex. 1.9).

1. Ex - cuse me friends if trou-ble-some, may aw trou-ble ye a while, Sirs for troub - lin' you, for troub-lin' me, to trou-ble you to smile, sirs, Ye'll ma- bies say its dou-ble trou- ble 'void it nae man can, Sirs We've been born in trou- ble, bred in trou-ble since the world be - gan Sirs Bow wow wow The trou-bles of the times are ve - ry bad just now.

2 Nae, Cursmis time comes once a year, wi' roast beef lots to feed at,
An' Cursmis bills they trouble then, but some folks niver heed that;
The landlords trouble you for rent, and smile so when one pays it,
Other poor souls sigh and say they're troubled hoo to raise it.
Chorus.

3 Some married folks that hez nae bairns seem troubled hoo to get them;
Others in the street to cadge noo varry often set them;
Railway accidents trouble us, directors say they cannot mend them,
So they varry often trouble us, an' sometimes wor troubles end then.
Chorus.

5 Aw've maw troubles like the rest o' folks, as on through life aw jog, Sirs;
To tell the truth, aw's troubled sair hoo to reinsuit my togs, Sirs.
Tailors' bills don't trouble me, but the bobbys they take note, Sirs,
An' take me on suspicion 'cause there's nae change in my coat, Sirs.
Chorus.

Ex. 1.8

As an alternative to such subtle rearticulations, Corvan can provide a straightforward send-up. In 'The Sunday Morning Fuddle' the insufferably sentimental parlour ballad 'Before the Bells Did Ring' is given new words which turn it into a comic epic about Sunday morning boozing, in which the hero ends up so 'fuddled' he is arrested (Ex. 1.10).

Corvan's achievement, then – with a narrow stock of materials and against a background of retrenchment, in which the bourgeoisie's musical values, like its

1. The snaw fell doon fast, an' poor folks seem'd shy, Clos'd

up i' thor hyems as the storm pel-ted by; An they wished roond their nooks such times

soon wad pass, For pro - vi-sions had ri - sen an' they'd saved lit -tle brass, And as

mon-ey an' fir - in' was melt - in' a - way Thor seemed nowt but caud dops for us

poor sons of clay, The wo-men folks flew ti' fill thor coal holes, To the

de - poe but hang them they've raised wor small coals. *O what a price for sma'*

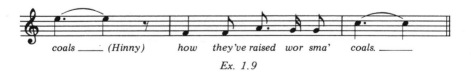

coals ____ *(Hinny)*   *how   they've raised   wor   sma'   coals.* ____

Ex. 1.9

money, were increasingly setting the framework of socio-musical relationships – was to articulate those materials to the needs of his own particular
audience. In a clearly stratified society, the interests of this audience were
predominantly defined by class. Horizons were inevitably restricted, the weight
of traditions heavy, the invention of new techniques and modes of expression
limited. Corvan's basic method was that of parody: transforming the meaning of
a tune through new words (and by performance methods). Even this kind of
intervention in the productive process could not long survive him: the means

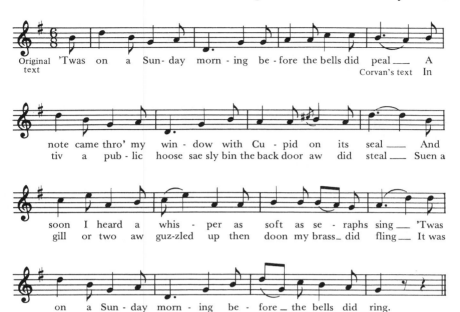

Ex. 1.10

of musical production were taken more and more into the hands of large commercial interests, while parody as a method retreated into informal niches in the fabric of working-class life.

The cases of Corvan, and to a lesser extent that of early Elvis Presley, are relatively straightforward to analyse. In the first, the shape into which the social formation is predisposed to settle, though contested, is obvious and is a powerful influence on the culture; the second – despite an underlying complexity in the cultural relationships – possesses brilliant if temporary clarity arising from its historical position at the beginning of a period of great situational adjustment. How, though, would the method used here perform if applied to a subject right in the middle of complex situational change, where the social formation and the musical culture are characterized precisely by heterogeneity and seemingly transient affiliations? A look at some examples of the so-called progressive rock of the mid- and late 1960s may clarify this question.

Within the rock discourse of the time, progressive rock was widely regarded as associated with, indeed as the music of, the 'counterculture'. How, theoretically, this connection could be said to work was rarely explained. There is an argument that the development of rock in the 1960s was determined mainly by intramusical factors – from a desire to explore the technological and musical possibilities of the new conditions of production set up in the rock 'n' roll moment. How, in that case, could late 1960s progressive rock be specific to the counterculture? And how would such an affixation cope with the evident fact that the techniques, modes of expression and performers claimed by the counterculture as their own were apparently so easily appropriated by the established music industry interests, and the music spread into every social corner and function? Another problem is the sheer eclecticism of progressive rock, both in terms of the variety of sources on which it drew and the range of styles contained within the genre. By the mid-1960s rock as a whole was hardly monolithic; but progressive rock was a particularly heterogeneous genre (compared to, say, rock 'n' roll, which is fairly tightly defined). Is progressive rock, then, a single phenomenon at all? If so, what makes it such? Is the variety itself significant? Is it connected with the variety of radical movements actually making up the counterculture? And how can the use made of elements and attitudes characteristic of 'legitimate' musics be squared with the counterculture's 'oppositionalism'? A brief 'reading' of four diverse but typical recordings will reveal examples of these characteristics – eclecticism, 'art' influences, technical exploration – together, also, with clear countercultural references, and thus will make the inner contradiction more concrete.

A comparison of the Beatles' 1967 single 'Strawberry Fields'[13] with rock 'n' roll, or early Beatles for that matter, immediately reveals a much greater variety of instruments – woodwind, brass and strings are added to drums, keyboard and guitars – and they have obviously been 'scored' for: written arrangements creating varied textures have replaced a simple, consistent rock-band texture, produced largely 'by ear', 'in performance'. Much of the sound has been produced through electronic 'treatment'. These two changes – instrumentation and electronic treatment – suggest two points immediately: that this is music created in a recording studio using quite complex equipment and recording techniques (the Beatles had in fact just given up live performance); and that it is music for listening rather than dancing. This is suggested too by the coda, which transforms the structure of the song and makes use of collage. The structure is also disrupted by the way the regular phrase-lengths and pulse usual in popular songs are subverted. In the first phrase, for example, the normal eight bars are stretched to nine. Throughout the song the rhythm of the vocal follows not the regular periods of dance music but the irregular accents of the words. The harmonic language has become more complex, less predictable, too.

What does the song 'mean'? The electronic treatment suggests 'abnormal experience' (presumably, so the lyrics suggest, psychedelic): this is achieved through implied contrast with the 'normal' timbres previously used in pop songs, which are about 'real life' (love, dancing, and so on). The use of collage, together with the irregular rhythms and lurching harmonies, may signify 'in the unconscious' (which often manifests itself in irrational jumbles of material). Finally, the heterogeneous texture, the ever-changing relationships of instruments, may on one level simply suggest 'influence of art music'. On another, the varied perspectives and changing landmarks may signify 'a complex landscape' (which, given the other signifiers mentioned, is mental not physical). Tagg has argued that conventional melody/accompaniment textures signify the relationship of individuals (foreground) to their environment (background) (Tagg 1979: 123–4; 142–3). It may be suggested, then, that the shifting perspectives, as instruments zoom into the foreground, then out again, together with the relative lack of foregrounding of the voice, signify the dislocation of the individual's dominant position and of the single point of view. The (mental) environment displaces the ego from centre-stage – an important countercultural theme, of course – though it is articulated using, among others, musical techniques familiar in the official culture.

A rather different, and in some ways opposite, trend in progressive rock may be represented by Cream's 'Spoonful'.[14] Pieces in this category used a restricted range of basic harmonic and melodic materials, favoured improvisation as a means of building structures, and achieved their most characteristic results in live performance. Usually they drew heavily on blues traditions. 'Spoonful' is a version of a song associated with one of the most celebrated Chicago blues singers, Howlin' Wolf. Like many Chicago blues songs of the 1940s and 1950s, it draws heavily on the traditions of rural Mississippi blues – evident, for instance, in the vocal (falling shapes, largely pentatonic, lots of repetition of phrases and short motifs, not much 'tune', instead close to speech, shouted as much as sung), and second, the use, throughout, of only one chord – a kind of drone. Other features derived from blues are the use of a riff (the two-note idea which starts the song off and forms the basis of the refrain), the use of call-and-response (between vocal and guitar), and the instrumental styles, especially that of the guitar.

The simple harmonic structure has the effect of freeing melody and form; melodic lines are not constrained by having to fit changing chords and the form is not constrained by a particular harmonic sequence. This encourages improvisation, and enables the improviser to play at length and elaborately, as in the guitar solo by Eric Clapton. The building of extended forms over drones or very simple harmonic progressions (often two alternating chords) or riffs was, of course, to become a staple of hard rock and 'heavy metal' music, and encouraged the development of virtuosic soloists, especially guitarists. Thus while most of the blues-derived techniques I have mentioned appear to set the music in opposition to mainstream musical language (including that of many contemporary pop songs), they are developed in such a way as to lay stress on individualistic virtuosity and personal expression, achieved through 'professional' mastery of instrumental technique; and this could be seen as at least compatible with the traditions of bourgeois art.

Of course, blues-derived rock was not specific to the counterculture. It is interesting to compare the style of a recording like Cream's 'Spoonful' with that of earlier British rhythm and blues (the Rolling Stones or the Who, for example). A record like 'My Generation' or 'Satisfaction' *states a position*: its meanings are collective; Cream extract from this musical language the possibility of individualistic elaboration. Does the appeal of Cream to the counterculture reside here, in the possibility of spontaneity, personal expression and 'freedom'? It can be argued that techniques of drone and repetition are particularly sympathetic to connotations having to do with 'collectivism': they play down 'difference', privilege the 'typical'. By superimposing on these techniques an ideology and a practice of self-expression, Cream's music seems to establish a dialectical relationship between the two, articulating each via the other into a new position – a position, perhaps, of 'fraternal individualism'.

For a third distinct trend in progressive rock we can turn to Pink Floyd, known for avant-garde experiments, often making use of collage, electronics and 'free-form' techniques. In a recording like 'Astronomy Dominé',[15] there are no obvious divisions into the conventional chorus structure of popular song; instead the impression is of a piece *composed* as a whole. There is no really memorable melody, and the complex structure and varied rhythms and harmonies suggest this is music 'for the mind' rather than a simple pop song for dancing. However, there *is* a basic four-chord harmonic sequence, used as a structural underpinning for much of the piece; in a conventional rock song this might well have been deployed as a riff or worked into predictable phrase-structure patterns. But here it is 'covered over' with collages made up of vocal, instrumental and electronic materials, ranging from pre-recorded effects to improvised solo lines. This short chord progression, which in Cream or the Rolling Stones might have been foregrounded, is pushed into the background, the joins between its statements are disguised, and links, an introduction and a coda, are added, so that the music seems to flow on continuously. The effect is that the structural level on which our attention fixes is the whole piece. Similarly, elements of rhythm and blues phraseology remain (drum techniques, guitar phrases and techniques) but they are subsumed within a heterogeneous mixture of styles.

The elements in this mixture barely seem to hang together; or rather, radical disjunctions are part of the effect. Similar experiments (free form, electronics, wild improvisation, collage) were taking place among the jazz and 'straight' avant-gardes during this period, and Pink Floyd were undoubtedly influenced by them. And if the diverse references of the materials used in such music do have a coherence, it mainly rests on a kind of formalist and/or surrealist playing with sound-combinations and their mental associations and images, characteristic – in its implied position of social isolation – of almost all avant-garde music in the twentieth century. This changes the terms on which the music could conceivably be appropriated by the music industry. At the same time, the references to the rock tradition, especially rhythms, are really all that serve to affix the music to the location of a 'popular' audience.

If Pink Floyd's music displays a congruence with avant-garde developments outside rock, then Procul Harum's 'A Whiter Shade of Pale' (a big hit in the summer of 1967)[16] can stand as an example of a complementary trend: the influence of *older* art music sources. The basic materials derive from a harmonic sequence (with melodic elaboration) taken from a cantata by J.S. Bach. On the one hand, this typifies the interest in rock/classical fusions shared by many progressive rock musicians at this time. On the other hand, it asks questions about the *rock* roots of the music: how can such a fusion take place? What happens to rock techniques? What does the fusion mean?

The influence is of a particular kind, from a particular source. Late Baroque music tends to be relatively formulaic. Like rock music, it generally uses conventional harmonic progressions, melodic patterns and structural frameworks, and operates through imaginative combinations, elaborations and variations of these, rather than developing extended, through-composed forms. It also tends to have a regular, strongly marked beat; indeed, its continuo section could be regarded as analogous to the rhythm section of jazz and rock. The harmonic sequence I mentioned is used as a riff. It appears as the instrumental introduction (and two instrumental interludes), it comes four times in each of the two choruses, and it is still going when the song fades out. In all, there are eleven complete statements (plus the fade). Structurally, there is nothing else. The phrase itself is, by rock standards, quite complex harmonically (though to Baroque musicians it was something of a cliché). The use of a repeated harmonic progression is typical of rock. However, it also occurs quite often in Baroque music. There is no conflict here.

We can say, then, that between the two codes involved – Baroque and rock – there are differences but also a relatively high syntactic correlation. Many other examples of rock/classical fusions fall apart because this element is lacking. This tells us something about the limits to fusion as an articulative method (as against other methods, such as parody or deliberate disjunction) and about the limits to the expropriation of meaning: some syntactic structures are simply incompatible. It tells us something also about the weight with which received connotations attach to long-established traditions: it was probably the pre-modern (or at least pre-industrial), and at the same time the quasi-ritualistic motoric-gestural associations clinging strongly to the high Baroque style which attracted the rock group and their countercultural followers.

Nevertheless, these associations *are* articulated into a new pattern, and it is the vocal which plays an essential part in that process, in making the song a *rock* song. Procul Harum superimpose on the Bach harmonies a vocal whose style derives from soul music. This influence manifests itself in melodic shapes (largely pentatonic falling patterns, but, unlike, say, Chicago blues, also lyrical, sustained, long-breathed); vocal timbre (rich, open-throated, sensuous); and the use of melisma. To carry the argument further, it might be suggested that 'A Whiter Shade of Pale' adapts the genre of 'soul ballad' created by Sam Cooke, Ray Charles, Otis Redding and others; it is rather similar, in fact, to Percy Sledge's 'When a Man Loves a Woman'. Once again there is a congruence of codes – from Baroque music and from soul music – but once again, also, the non-congruent elements in each source act to reorientate the effects of the other. 'A Whiter Shade of Pale', we might speculate, marks a trend within the counterculture which sees itself as, so to speak, 'sensuously spiritual' (Bach mediated by soul singing) and is 'immanently oppositional' *vis-à-vis* bourgeois culture (rock made baroque).

As this discussion of four songs shows, there *are* links between the music and elements of countercultural ideology; at the same time, though, there are many references to mainstream cultural traditions. There *are* unifying factors – an ethos of 'personal' expression, for example – but equally there is a radical eclecticism of style and method; indeed, it is no easier to determine the limits defining the musical genre than the exact social composition and boundaries of the counterculture. The subcultural specificity of the songs is hard to establish; all contain techniques which continually threaten to widen the field of cultural reference. Subcultural ownership of music is very hard to protect. Within the counterculture, moreover, the response to each of the songs would have been different among different subgroups.

The relationship of progressive rock and the counterculture is thus uneasy and internally contradictory. Failure to recognize this leads to circular arguments. For example, psychedelic elements in the musical style – blurred or tinkly timbres, for instance – are typically interpreted as such by reference to a subculture of drug usage; in other words they are defined in this way primarily because hippies said they should be. A whole group of connotations, arising from our knowledge of the drug culture, then settles on the music. But this culture has already been defined in this way partially because of the existence in it of this particular kind of music. The meaning of drug usage is affected by the meaning of the associated music. The method is perfectly structured internally but has no

necessary connection to anything outside itself; there is no analytical *purchase* on it
from without. In contrast, blurred or tinkly timbres should be understood in the
context of general timbre-codes in popular music (and, more generally, in
Western music as a whole). These codes set limits to meaning – 'objective
possibilities' – while at the same time they leave open a space within which the
operation of other elements in the music, its context and reception, can pull them
into a more specific place in the network of social meaning, in line with the work
of the articulating principles involved. This explains, for instance, how elements
of bourgeois 'art' music can be rearticulated in progressive rock. They do not
lose the overall parameters of meaning which they bring with them, but the
precise meanings these take on are orientated through the effect of the new
context in which they find themselves. Thus, in 'Spoonful' the 'corporeal'
meanings of rock 'n' roll rhythms, without being destroyed, are shifted by the
complex rhythmic overlays, the instrumental technique, the lyrics and so on,
while in 'Strawberry Fields' and 'Astronomy Dominé', the principle of extended
forms is reworked, still having an implication of 'thinking', but now thinking of a
different kind from that suggested by, say, Beethoven.

But this also explains why the music of the counterculture could be so easily
co-opted and its radical implications defused. For the articulating principle of
hippie ideology is, in the final analysis, and despite its potential for opposition,
embedded within the ideology of the dominant culture itself (see Clarke *et al.*
1976: 57–71). Bourgeois individualism has a long history of subversive bohemian
variants; and the struggle for control of the elements of countercultural musical
style was a struggle between different aspects of the same principle. Cream's
'fraternal individualism', for instance, is easily metamorphosed into 'elitist
exhibitionism' (musically, this is the development from Cream to what has often
been described as the 'empty virtuosity' of many later 'guitar heroes'); similarly,
the 'thinking' of unpredictable extended forms, given the predictable lulling
rhythms and bland timbres of Mike Oldfield, is turned into LP-length 'easy
listening'; the 'psychedelic sound' becomes exactly that: a fetishized label,
isolated from the radical harmonic/rhythmic context it has in 'Strawberry
Fields', and pinned on to simple Top Ten dance tunes, as a tribute to the middle-
class ideology of riskless hedonism. The class-historical location of progressive
rock thus had cultural effects which explain its specific meaning and evolution.

What is to be done?

The approach outlined here leaves much still to be investigated. The discussion
has several times strayed into semiological terminology and it has taken the
nature of ideology largely for granted; both signification and ideology in popular
music demand detailed study. The relationships between social formation,
cultural patterns and musical practice have been touched on, but require more
extended analysis. We need to look more closely at processes of change (and
structures of stasis), particularly the roles of the forces and the relations of
production.

From the music's political economy to the pleasures it offers (another area for
examination), the question of the 'popularity' of popular music will continue to

reverberate. Punk raised this question in a particularly clear form, asking whether, in capitalist society, a really popular music is in fact possible. The research areas listed above are important not just for themselves but even more for the contribution the results might make to thinking about present and future musical practice. A historical theory must validate itself against a future whose demand, ultimately, is the redemption of the democratic claim buried within the long struggles for and by 'the people'.

Notes

1. Chappell (1859) exemplifies this usage.
2. I have reworded Birrer's summary slightly. A good example of a combinational definition (drawing on categories 2, 3 and 4) can be found in Tagg (1979: 20–8). Other useful critiques of common approaches to popular music definition are Cutler (1985a); Fiori (1985); and Shepherd (1985).
3. For a critique of 'essentialism', see T. Bennett (1986b).
4. *Populäre Musik, musique populaire, musica popolare, Unterhaltungsmusik, chanson, Schlager, canzone, variété*, and so on – all make their own distinctions and carry their own connotations. The same is true of the cultivated/vernacular dichotomy favoured by some American musicologists (see, for example, Hitchcock 1974) and of the trichotomy art/folk/mesomusic invented by the ethnomusicologist Carlos Vega (see Vega 1966; Aharonián 1985).
5. While Gramsci retains the term 'superstructure', I prefer to think of the sphere of ideology, consciousness, culture, as an *instance* or *level of practice* rather than as located 'above' (and therefore, by implication, derived from) an economic base.
6. For a similar approach, see also T. Bennett (1986b).
7. These are discussed in Chapter 5.
8. On the links between the consensus repertories of the Victorian period and the 1930s and 1940s, see Hamm (1979: 358–75).
9. Musical styles (as against lyric content) changed little during the war; see, for example, the LP *Britain Can Take It* (World Records SH 213).
10. As occurs in yet another apparently analogous model, that of the Soviet musicologist B.V. Asaf'ev (1977), whose history revolves around 'intonational crises'.
11. Mike Pickering (1982: 7–8) discusses similar tactics in late nineteenth-century Oxfordshire.
12. All the Corvan songs referred to here except 'The Sunday Morning Fuddle' are reproduced in full, together with many others, in Gregson (1983). I am grateful to Keith Gregson for permission to reproduce my examples.
13. Parlophone R 5570.
14. *Fresh Cream*, Polydor CP 594–001.
15. On *The Piper at the Gates of Dawn*, Columbia SX 6157.
16. Deram DM 126.

2

'It's all over now'. Popular music and mass culture – Adorno's theory

Music for entertainment . . . seems to complement the reduction of people to silence, the dying out of speech as expression, the inability to communicate at all. It inhabits the pockets of silence that develop between people moulded by anxiety, work and undemanding docility . . . It is perceived purely as background. If nobody can any longer speak, then certainly nobody can any longer listen . . . Today . . . [the] power of the banal extends over the whole society (Adorno 1978a: 271–4).

Why Adorno?

T.W. Adorno's polemic against 'popular music' is scathing. It possesses, nevertheless, a striking richness and complexity, demanding to be examined from a variety of viewpoints, notably that of musical production (in relation to general production in capitalist societies), that of musical form (discussed by Adorno in terms of 'standardization') and that of musical reception and function (which he sees as almost totally instrumentalized, in the service of the ruling social interests). At the same time, Adorno argues – rightly – that these aspects are actually indivisible, and that it is essential, therefore, to retain a sense of the wholeness of the musical process. First, though, there is a need to say something more general about Adorno's position, in the context of the approach outlined in the previous chapter – particularly in light of the fact that Adorno evidently had little time for popular music! Why devote a chapter to him in a book which explicitly encourages its readers to pay attention to this music?

Adorno has many strengths. He insists – correctly – that the division of the cultural field into 'popular' and 'serious' segments is relatively superficial; it should be grasped as a whole. In a memorable remark to Walter Benjamin, he stated that 'Both are torn halves of an integral freedom, to which however they do not add up' (Bloch et al. 1977: 123). His own view of the way this field is structured posits two contradictory tendencies – on the one hand, music which affirms or accepts the social status quo; on the other, music (of the avant-garde) which refuses such affirmation. While this approach is problematical, his emphasis on the totality remains important. It is still far from being accepted.

For the music industry, critics, listeners, musicians, musicologists and students of culture, the primacy of a 'light'/'classical' dichotomy is generally still taken for granted.

The previous chapter argued for a conception of music which maintains both the relative autonomy of its techniques and its ultimately social meaning, and which sees these as constructed within a historical dialectic. In outline, Adorno's general position on music is not seriously at odds with this approach. Again, the way he applies it to the specific case of popular music poses problems: the utopian promise which, for Adorno, is the mark of great art's autonomy is in his view relevant to popular music solely by its absence, for here, he thinks, social control of music's meaning and function has become absolute, musical form a reified reflection of manipulative social structures; and this moment in the historical process actually represents, in effect, the end of history – the possibility of movement by way of contradiction and critique has disappeared. Still, by developing a historical materialist theory of musical development which in principle rebuts reductionism, both economistic and formalistic, Adorno's general position opened up new ground, in ways which often remain of value. At the same time, his specific treatment of the social situation of popular music, by proceeding, in his usual way, 'through the extremes', does have the negative virtue of exaggerating real trends; the tendential strategy of the music industry in the period of 'mass culture' has nowhere been more incisively presented. As Simon Frith puts it (1978: 195), 'Adorno's is the most systematic and the most searing analysis of mass culture and the most challenging for anyone claiming even a scrap of value for the products that come churning out of the music industry'. The flaws, if such they are, are in the physiognomy of a giant. Anyone wanting to argue the importance of studying popular music has to absorb Adorno in order to go beyond him.

In doing this, it is useful to bear in mind the historical location of Adorno's writings on popular music. His approach, in its essentials, was formed by the early 1930s, and he extends it during the 1940s only in the direction of even greater pessimism: cultural 'totalitarianism' becomes absolute. Later writings, despite important musical developments such as rock 'n' roll and the 1960s counterculture, show no significant changes. Thus Adorno's major contribution dates from a period described in the previous chapter as one of relative situational stability and consensus, when, more than at any other time, the machinery of 'mass culture' worked to considerable effect. His musical examples are always drawn from the repertoire of this period. In a wider cultural perspective, this was the period too of Fascism and Stalinism, of the apparent collapse of socialist revolutionary possibilities in the advanced capitalist countries, and of the emergence within 'Western Marxism' of varied attempts (by Lukács, by Gramsci and by the Frankfurt School, to which Adorno belonged) to adapt Marxist theory in ways which took account of these developments. Adorno should be read against this background.

Production

Adorno did not write a history of music, nor did he describe his picture of the music-historical field in any great detail. But his theory of popular music is predicated on a distinct historical model, itself bound up in a Marxian analysis of the development of bourgeois society, and the main outlines of this model are clear enough.

The decreasing significance of patronage in the nineteenth century and the permeation of musical life by market relations has two dialectically related effects: commodification of musical works and rationalization of the production system are accompanied by a new level of musical autonomy associated with market freedom and a decline of social function. Music is caught between these two tendencies, and good music embodies both in a satisfying unity, at once affirming the objective movement of bourgeois society and also negating this through subjective critique. In a sense, the struggle is between developing compositional technique (for Adorno, the most important force of production) and prevailing relations of musical production, which represent contemporary technological, musical and social norms. Beethoven is the historical fulcrum; in his work the two aspects are perfectly balanced, and the uniqueness of the individual musical idea is organically integrated into a socially comprehensible but freely worked-out totality. After Beethoven, the two split apart. Compositional autonomy is closed off in the sphere of avant-garde negation, while commodity musical production takes on an increasingly standardized character, coupling formula and fetishized effect in both 'serious' and 'popular' markets.

Because people like to think that culture is different from other commercially produced goods ('art' embodies individual expression), standardized methods and forms are masked to some extent by a show of artisan craftsmanship and by 'pseudo-individualized' effects. But in reality the 'culture industries' create, control and exploit musical desires, forming 'a circle of manipulation and retroactive need in which the unity of the system grows ever stronger' (Adorno and Horkheimer 1972: 121). Any sense of expressive immediacy is an illusion: use-value is replaced totally by value in exchange; autonomy disappears as music turns into nothing more than 'social cement' (Adorno 1941: 39); production is reduced, in effect, to reproduction.

From the time of the early modernists (Schoenberg and others), only the radical avant-garde has resisted this situation, and that at the price of social isolation and deliberate incomprehensibility: the only way left to refuse the market. As this suggests, Adorno's theory of avant-garde music has no room for any form of popular music. For him, the vital aesthetic principle of individuation can now be found only in the esoteric discontinuities of modern art, and is alone capable of subverting the status quo. On all counts this view will have to be questioned. But before this, Adorno's whole theory of popular music production, and its historical development, must be subjected to a wider-ranging critique.

Whatever its problems, the *force* of this theory is undeniable. In an age when a symphony orchestra can appear in uniforms designed to advertise tobacco-industry sponsors, conflating music and cigarettes into a single narcotic (*Guardian*, 26 March 1984: 13); when in Japan the record companies and the large industrial corporations co-operate to produce 'image-songs' which both advertise the corporations and play an important role in the hit parade;[1] when a small selection of endlessly permutated pop songs provides the background for almost every social activity; when rhythm tracks on disco records can be behaviouristically planned and electronically produced, for maximum precision and control: one cannot, at this time, avoid the feeling that if Orwell's '1984' ever arrives, it might well consist of a continuous Eurovision Song Contest; that the ideal of the music industry would be to turn *everything* into muzak (Philip Tagg's entertaining account of the way muzak is used to 'programme' a Swedish office-worker's day gives an idea of what this would be like (Tagg 1984)). Similarly, even a brief acquaintance with the dance-band and Tin Pan Alley hit repertories of the 1930s – when Adorno's views were formulated – reveals a level of same-ness that is stultifying. This is backed up by the accounts we have of many aspects of the economic structure of the music business then: the drive for profit, the trend towards monopoly and conglomeration, the conservative appeal to the predictable and universally understood (see for example, Peterson and Berger 1975: 160–4; Laing 1969: 43–5; Sanjek 1988). As far as the 'artisan'-pro-ducer is concerned, Carole King's picture of institutionalized song-writing in New York in the early 1960s – 'squeezed into our respective cubby-holes . . . you'd sit there and write and you could hear someone in the next cubby-hole com-posing a song exactly like yours' (Frith 1983a: 131–2) – fits into exactly the same frame of reference as Abner Silver and Robert Bruce's classic 1939 text, *How to Write and Sell a Hit Song*, which describes the 'standard' forms and techniques, and from which Adorno quotes with withering relish (1941: 17–18). Adorno, then, is certainly talking about *real* things. The problems come when empirical evidence is turned into totalizing theory, tendential strategy into achieved fact.

First of all, there is little doubt that the general political economy of the Frankfurt School, on which the notion of the 'culture industry' is based, generalizes too much, on the basis of an analysis of only one historical moment: 1930s Germany. Moreover, it overstates the homogeneity of the components making up the ruling structure (the state; the economic units; administrative and ideological apparatuses). Persistent conflicts of interest, resulting in periodic political and economic crises, bear this out. Similarly, the importance of class-related tensions, both within the ruling alliance and between it and the masses, is underplayed. What is missed is that alongside an increase in centralized control has been persistent dissent; domination – social, economic and ideological – has been maintained only through *struggle*.

This is as true of culture industries as of other sectors. Most accounts make clear not only the trend towards monopoly and control but also the elements of lack of 'fit' – between institutions (record companies, broadcasters, publishers, and so on), and between functionally differentiated individuals and groups within each institution. Without an awareness of this it becomes very difficult to explain such phenomena as, for instance, the rise of 'independent' record companies in the 1940s and 1950s, and again in the 1970s; the 'war' between the American Society of Composers, Authors and Publishers (ASCAP) and Broad-cast Music Incorporated (BMI) in the 1940s; the jaundiced reception by Tin Pan Alley of syncopated dance music and, later, of rock 'n' roll; music–political struggles within the BBC; the often stylistically heterogeneous content of the hit parades; numerous policy arguments between musicians and their record companies; and so on. Particularly striking examples, as Simon Frith points out (1983a: 146–7, 154), are that some of the 'most creative uses of the recording studio have also been the most "manipulative" in commercial terms' – he mentions Phil Spector, Giorgio Moroder's disco hits and Jamaican reggae – while 'in the USA . . . the most open and imaginative audiences, deejays and radio programmes work in disco, the most obviously commercialized musical genre'. In a study of the French record industry, Antoine Hennion describes how the coexistence of, and tension between, the large multinational concerns, on the one hand, and small producers and independent companies, on the other, are structurally essential to the system's viability (Hennion 1981; 1983). Similarly, the now standard account of the Anglo-American industry traces a cyclical pattern of continual conflict between conservative major companies and innovative 'grassroots' independents and entrepreneurs: break-through–assimilation–breakthrough–assimilation. This would be impossible within the assumptions of Adorno's model (see Peterson and Berger 1971; 1975). Equally impossible would be an adequate explanation of taste-changes: is it reasonable to account for the advent of jazz, rock 'n' roll, beat and punk in terms of 'pseudo-individualization' within an underlying process of simple reproduction? If not, where did these new tastes come from? What was responsible for their emergence? Why *those* changes, and why *then*? Above all, perhaps, there is the point, established beyond doubt, that the creation of hits is not simply a matter of continually plugging into a self-sustaining circle linking producer and customer. Companies certainly try to control demand, to channel it in known directions, but they are never *sure* of their market; the best they can do is to offer a 'cultural repertoire', to cover a spread of the likely possibilities in order to minimize the risk – and it is this which accounts for the colossal overproduction of records and the large number that make a loss (see Laing 1985: 9–10, 20; Frith 1983a: 92–102; Denisoff 1975: 92–4).

Admittedly, the situation in the 1930s and 1940s was *more* settled, the institutions *more* congruent – though even within Tin Pan Alley the Hoagy Carmichaels and George Gershwins were introducing, in however mediated a form, new musical techniques, derived from black traditions. But one can ask why Adorno did not investigate the *origins* of swing before so quickly assimilating it to the prevailing Tin Pan Alley dance-band style. This would have taken him into working-class black dance-halls, bars, churches: more generally, by extension, into the whole network of subterranean currents beneath the bland surface of the metropolitan American musical mainstream. In the same way, he might have looked at the *conflicts* between institutions, genres and styles during the 1890–1930 period (for instance, between old-fashioned vaudeville and new syncopated styles; or between the requirements of public dance and private listening), rather than just the more homogeneous synthesis established by the time it ended.

Clearly, to answer Adorno completely would require nothing less than a complete 'production history' of popular music from 1890 to the present. As yet, this exists only in scattered fragments. What we can say, though, is that the picture which emerges from these is not of a monolithic bloc but of a constantly mutating organism made up of elements which are symbiotic and mutually contradictory *at the same time* (see, for example, Sanjek 1988; Hirsch 1969; Peterson and Berger 1971; Hardy n.d.; Frith 1978; 1983a; 1988a). Over and above the nature of the general economic and social developments, the main reason for this is what can be termed the specificity of *cultural* goods: that is, the fact that 'music can never be *just* a product (an exchange value), even in its rawest commodity form; the artistic value of records has an unavoidable complicating effect on their production' (Frith 1983a: 10). This leads record companies to treat musicians not as wage-labourers but as contracted 'artists', who are paid not a fixed sum for their labour-time but in royalties, in proportion to their success (ibid: 130). Adorno, we have seen, acknowledges this specificity – indeed, for him it explains the (unfulfilled) potential of jazz and the hangovers of 'real' creativity in some Tin Pan Alley songs; but he subsumes it into a theory of 'false individualization', designed, in his view, to disguise mass cultural production as 'art'. But an *empirical* recognition that in some circumstances a particular productive force (say, a composer or a performer) may not be wholly homogenized means that such a possibility must be allowed on the level of *theory*.

Hennion argues that the monopolies *need* the independent small producer for economic reasons – to maintain a flow of new products and to ensure communication with an active market (Hennion 1981; 1983). Jon Stratton has suggested that he is needed for ideological reasons too (1983): in Stratton's view, the 'romantic' image of the creative artist is no false veneer nor confined to 'mass culture', but part of a larger tradition, within which the dialectic of 'romanticism' and commodification is basic to capitalist culture as such; thus it implicates the 'individualism' of, say, Beethoven as well as that of pop stars and composers. If these arguments are valid, they create *spaces* which the system cannot close off or remove, however much it wants to, and which ensure the *possibility* of conflicts within the productive forces as a whole.

At times, such spaces are invaded by new kinds of musician from previously untapped social sources. Bix Beiderbecke and Eubie Blake, Billy Mayerl and Nat Gonella cannot easily be assimilated, or at least reduced, merely to a preformed role in the machinery of a dominant system of musical craftsmanship; nor can Bob Dylan and John Lennon, Chuck Berry, Bob Marley and Merle Haggard, let alone Joe Strummer or John Lydon; though, equally obviously, they all, in another sense, come to be umbilically attached to that system. Peter Wicke has argued that the 'street' origins of beat music on Merseyside reveal a new sort of *collective* practice, in which modes of production and levels of musical technique and technology are geared to, and support, an interactive group spontaneity, emphasizing joint composition, arrangement and decision-making (Wicke 1982).[2] Whether this is too optimistic or not, the phenomenon he describes – and he could have added other examples, from Afro-American 'street-corner' vocal groups or Jamaican reggae, for instance – is clearly not amenable to an Adornian analysis, based on a dichotomy between a radically fragmenting division of labour, on the one hand, and an integrating individual consciousness, on the other. On a different level – 'professional' rather than 'amateur' – Antoine Hennion's account of studio recording methods emphasizes that a variety of differentiated roles are brought together into a 'creative collective': each member has a specific job, but they interact critically and continuously (Hennion 1983). The aim, 'to introduce the public into the studio', is achieved through the 'working relationships, constituted by mutual criticism . . . subjective listening . . . and collective anticipation' of public response. In particular, it is the producer's task to have 'the ear of the public', thereby representing in the music the feelings and values of 'a kind of imaginary democracy' (ibid: 160–1, 188–92). In place of Adorno's search for an authentic *individual* productive subject in popular music, we may see glimpses here of new kinds of mass or collective subject.

Adorno disputes the possibility of such 'committed' practices, and the nub of the problem here lies in his conception of musical autonomy: for this conception is essentially inscribed within the problematic of bourgeois individualism. The fact that Adorno's thinking on the question is locked into a model which pits individual subject against reified social totality leads his picture of the social meaning of music to take on a monolithic appearance. Determined, rightly, to avoid the crude class reductionism of many earlier Marxist approaches to the sociology of cultural forms, he stressed the importance of *mediation*, but then went further and insisted that music

> reflects the class relationship *in toto* . . . Instead of searching for the musical
> expression of class standpoints one will do better so to conceive the relation
> of music to classes that any music will present the picture of antagonistic
> society *as a whole* (Adorno 1976: 68, 69, emphasis added).

The more completely and clearly music represents *the totality*, in all its contradictions, the better – the more autonomous – it is. This approach has two effects. It privileges the music which Adorno chooses as best representing the contradictory whole – thus alongside Beethoven and the tradition following him, other kinds of music (Berlioz, Rossini, Verdi, Elgar, Stravinsky, Eisler, let alone Lehár, Louis Armstrong, Walter Donaldson or Elvis Presley) are inevitably presented as *partial*, that is to say more socially specific, less *autonomous*; it also reduces the possibility of *struggle* over the specific uses and meanings of musical materials and forms: competing 'viewpoints' are dismissed as 'regressive' or 'false'.

This is also partly the reason why in Adorno's theory music in a sense takes on *too much* autonomy, so much as to create a danger of a relapse into idealism. Since music's function is to represent a contradictory totality, social critique is taken into the workings of the musical structure itself. Self-negation requires an internally complex dialogue within the musical language, so that the working of 'musical problems' (in terms of the state of technique) can 'stand for' the play of social contradictions. The picture is of a freely developing microcosm whose internal dynamics nevertheless parallel those of the social macrocosm. The theory depends on agreement over the nature of technical 'progress' at any given time. But since such progress is conceived as immanent to musical history itself, independent of variants of musical practice, social usage and reception, the theory moves dangerously close to a hypostasis of technique; at the very least it confines the relationship between musical and social structures to the level of the *longue durée*, since at that level society is 'encapsulated' in music, while in between, music's 'autonomous unfoldment . . . follows the social dynamics without a glance or any direct communication' (ibid: 206–7), still less putting itself at the service of particular social subjects. But if it is the case, simply and conclusively, that music 'must intervene actively in consciousness through its own forms and not take instructions from . . . the consciousness of the user' (quoted in Held 1980: 83), the baby has gone as well as the bathwater and utopian critique begins to look suspiciously like spiritual determinism, autonomy like repression.

As we saw, the historical model on which this concept of autonomy is based has

Beethoven as its fulcrum. This model, too, raises several questions. Many tendencies in 'commercial' nineteenth-century music which Adorno singles out for criticism – 'mechanical', formulaic composition, for instance, or 'effects' writing such as that of the piano virtuosi, or the interest in sheer sound – can be traced back, as he himself is aware, to the eighteenth century – to dance music, operatic virtuosity, the early symphonies, and so on. The argument is that with the Beethovenian 'advance' the meaning of such techniques is changed; they are no longer valid because they do not meet the needs of the new historical situation. But why can they not be reused, redefined, in new contexts – 'effects', for instance, as 'shocks'? There seems no a priori reason why the intellectual collapse of the radical bourgeoisie in the early nineteenth century should necessitate a *single* line of avant-garde response – rather than a multiplicity of struggles, which, instead of leading irrevocably to extreme Schoenbergian individualism, might, for example, 'preserve' (that is reuse) older elements, to be rearticulated to the interests of new group subjects if and when they emerged. That change of historical focus would allow composers who did not so much 'negate', as *work through* the social conflicts of the time (such as Verdi, Elgar, Liszt) to be readmitted to the 'progressive' ranks.

Adorno argues that with Beethoven the *potential* of music is so raised that older assumptions are shattered. But this could be seen as simply a more than usually coherent version of a familiar Austro-German interpretation of nineteenth-century music history, which sets an over-privileged Viennese tradition at its normative centre. Adorno's preference for 'immanent method' – analysing and evaluating works in terms of the implications, the immanent tendencies, of their own mode of existence rather than approaching them comparatively – means that, having set his criteria for 'autonomous bourgeois music' from his interpretation of Beethoven, he exports those criteria to all music of the period and finds the rest of it wanting. At the same time, Beethoven himself is a less comprehensive representation of the totality of the social struggles of his age than Adorno pretends; in a way he is just as 'partial' as his far more popular contemporary, Rossini. Indeed, at times Adorno's Beethoven comes close to being a fetish: the image objectifies those musical tendencies Adorno wants to privilege. The 'integral' structures which he idealizes are far less in evidence in late Beethoven – the late string quartets and piano sonatas, the Ninth Symphony: here the formal principle is as much that of 'shock' as of 'totality'. Even in earlier Beethoven, works were often performed (with Beethoven's agreement) in unintegral ways: movements were separated, popular sections repeated on request, improvised changes made. (Adorno's ingenious but unpersuasive attempt to rescue Beethoven from these contradictory circumstances of reproduction relies on a *post facto* construction of the 'real' Beethoven: 'unity has become clear only today and largely through the efforts of later production in music' (Adorno 1978b: 149).)

Thus the *idea* of this privileged type of music is a product of the very culture of which the music is part. Indeed, this 'autonomous music' is affixed in its own way to bourgeois culture just as its 'functional', 'commercial' contemporaries are, in theirs. The very concept of autonomous music, defined this way, is a construct of the culture. When first developed in the late eighteenth and early nineteenth centuries, it was designed – so it could be argued – to neutralize music's potential political power, bracket off its critical threat in a 'utopian' enclave and confine negation to individual statement. But this mode of autonomy is dependent on this kind of society, for which music takes on specific private, 'spiritual', leisure functions. In what sense, then, is it 'free' – rather than a different kind of functional music?

Another way of putting this is that Adorno analyses – with great insight – the conditions of a specific mode of musical autonomy but then makes the mistake of reading what is a qualitative change, a historical variant, as an epistemological category; the truth-content of music is seen as directly related to its degree of autonomy of this kind. But on the level of epistemology *all* music is relatively autonomous; no sound-structures can be reduced to social, economic or ideological determinants. Functionality has nothing to do with that; all that different kinds of functionality do is affect the forms which relative autonomy takes. Adorno, in the grip of German idealism which, from Kant, had reckoned the essence of art to be its *disinterested* quality, absolutizes a specific musical ideal as the condition of productive musical work as such – at least, under capitalism.

We can now see clearly why Adorno's conceptualization of the twentieth-century avant-garde is so narrow: it must meet the criteria established by his theory of autonomy. In fact, even *within* these criteria, it has been argued that Adorno wrongly omits some forms of 'light' music (Paddison 1982). In addition to the two avant-garde poles represented for him by Schoenberg and Stravinsky, he has a minor category consisting of music that makes use of materials 'which fell by the wayside . . . waste products and blind spots . . . all that which did not fit properly into the laws of historical movement'; the 'anachronistic quality' of this material 'is not wholly obsolete since it has outwitted the historical dynamic'. The material is used in a 'montage-style, which . . . juxtaposes and cements ruins and fragments up against one another'; as examples he cites Mahler and 1920s Weill. The result is that 'the used parts win a second life' (quoted in ibid: 213–14). While Adorno confines this category to 'serious' music, Paddison points out that there seems no reason why it could not include a good deal of avant-garde jazz and such rock groups as Frank Zappa's Mothers of Invention, the Velvet Underground, and – he might have added – some post-punk bands. Even if the musical language *is* seen as totally shop-soiled, then, it is still possible to rearticulate the fragments.

In a broader perspective, something of an avant-garde role has often been assigned to whole styles or genres in twentieth-century popular music, or to aspects of them. Behind this, as a rule, stand familiar bohemian images, usually mediated by stereotypes from urban Afro-American culture: the 'existential' ghetto hustler-figure, as model for alienated urban man under capitalism, is a familiar one. It was in this context that the Beats reverenced modern jazz – and the influence of their ideas (not necessarily tied to that specific music) spread widely through marginal counter- and subcultures (see Brake 1980). Earlier jazz was also often seen in terms of a 'defence of individualism' (spontaneity, self-expression, and so on). Škvorecký's *The Bass Saxophone* describes the particularly intense form this has taken under totalitarian regimes – both Fascist and Stalinist – when 'the ideological guns and sometimes even the police guns of all dictatorships are aimed at the men with the horns'. Jazz here is 'about fidelity, about the sole real art there is, about what one must be true to, come hell or high water; what must be done to the point of collapse (Škvorecký 1980: 8, 20); and in Škvorecký's own Czechoslovakia, the persecution in the mid- 1980s of the 'Jazz Section' – which has supported rock and punk as well as jazz – confirms the subversive potency and 'alternative' status, still, of this music. The history of jazz and rock is no less littered with tragic deaths, breakdowns and martyrdoms – from Bix Beiderbecke and Charlie Parker to John Lennon, Janis Joplin and Sid Vicious – than that of the mainstream modernist arts.

Blues too is commonly regarded as centrally to do with the expression of alienated subjectivity caught within oppressive social structures; in a previous book (Middleton 1972) I argued that the effects of this are apparent in the musical form itself – in disjunctive structures, an immanently contradictory musical language and a commitment to 'authentic' self-expression – and I drew parallels with modernist art. Blues, of course, has been widely influential, indeed formative, on the development of rock. In rock too, the 'refusal of sentimentality' – as Dave Laing calls it – has been seen as a radical subversion of the culture represented by Tin Pan Alley song, and many of the formal innovations of 1960s and 1970s rock have been viewed in quasi-modernist terms (see Laing 1969: 60, 154–60, 176–9). It would not be difficult to construct a lineage of 'shock' within the history of jazz and rock, from the esoteric lyrics and quotations of some Harlem jazz in the 1920s and 1930s, through 'scat' and 'jive', and the 'noise' of rock 'n' roll, to the calculated unpredictabilities of punk. An important aspect might be embodied by Baudelaire's characterization of modernism in terms of '*mouvement brusque*' (see Berman 1983: 156ff.).

Interestingly enough, sociologists have noted the emergence of an Adornian distinction between 'commercial manipulation' and avant-garde 'authenticity' within the discourse of the jazz and rock communities themselves (see Becker 1972; Frith 1983a: 52–88; 1988b). Frith also comments on the importance of an ideology of bohemianism within the appeal of rock in general (1983a: 75–84). While such simple dichotomies are misleading – *all* categories of music live in the world of capitalist cultural production, while none can be entirely reduced to it, and a more accurate picture is of a spectrum of possibilities marked by internal conflict – their existence not only confirms the influence of the critique of mass culture in musical practice and popular consciousness, it also indicates that, within the premises of such a critique, Adorno draws the net too tightly. But further, if species of jazz and rock *are* accepted as potentially 'authentic', this knocks a *theoretical* hole in the approach, for in the recordings of, say, Frank Zappa, Carla Bley or The Art of Noise (the last inspired by Luigi Russolo's 1913 futurist manifesto *L'arte dei rumori*) we have examples of avant-garde *commodities* – a combination which, according to Adorno, is impossible.

Adorno has another small category, that of 'folklorist modernism', into which he fits such composers as Bartók and Janáček. He is a bit embarrassed by this category because, despite its 'archaic' elements, he finds himself unable to deny its authentic power. His explanation is partly geographical (these composers, and the 'folk remnants' they use, came from relatively 'backward' Eastern European countries, where such archaic traditions still had valid life) and partly on the grounds that the old materials are reinterpreted through incorporation in the composers' radically alienated perspective and progressive language (Adorno 1973: 35–6). It is hard to see why these arguments cannot be applied (in differing proportions) to blues and jazz; to white American country music; to their derivatives (rock 'n' roll, and so on); and to Third World popular musics with links to 'folk' traditions (in Latin America, the Caribbean and Africa).

This missing dimension in Adorno's analysis results from the weakening effect of an ethnocentric and culture-centric perspective – and this emerges in other ways, too. For example, he was clearly insensitive to many specific characteristics of American culture. He transferred his observations of the commercialization of German 'light' music to the United States and found the trends confirmed and amplified in the mainstream music-industry production of the 1930s and 1940s; indeed, he seems to have seen American popular music simply as a historical continuation of these trends, the line running from European operetta, revue and beerhall schmaltz to Tin Pan Alley, Broadway and Hollywood. He did not look beyond, let alone 'below', that. Similarly, he could find no American avant-garde, on the model of Central and Western European modernism. But the American experience had been different in many ways. The development of industrial capitalism came later and more quickly; there were continuing influxes of working-class immigrants from 'backward' parts of Europe; in the South, isolated rural-proletarian and quasi-feudal cultures persisted; the vitality of a 'popular-bourgeois' culture, embracing workers and higher social strata, continued into the twentieth century, when European equivalents were long dead or distorted into passivity. The whole net of relationships between community and subculture, class and centralizing monopoly capitalism thus took on a different shape. For one thing, there was much greater continuity of pre- and early capitalist musical forms. These were still available to twentieth-century American popular music, as analogous genres were to Bartók and Janáček; but further, they could then become available also to *European* workers whose own cultural traditions had been much more nearly shattered and who could, by plugging into still vital transatlantic networks, renew or restart aspects appropriate to potential class-cultural formations. At the same time, late nineteenth-century American *petit-bourgeois* music culture still retained 'progress-ive' elements, unlike its European equivalent, which by then was mostly intent on hedonistic quiescence; and the active, energetic components of this anti-elitist, common-man tradition (in vaudeville for example) fed through into early Tin Pan Alley song where they formed an uneasy synthesis with the tendency to conservative mass-production stereotypes. Indeed, if one side of the initial impact of American twentieth-century popular song was its 'Taylorist' production-line quality, the other was its thematizing of shockingly ebullient, vernacular, everyday *noise*.

Adorno's refusal to read such *class* references into twentieth-century popular music is, of course, the result of his obsession with the category of the individual producer-subject; as we have seen, for him the shocking, the new, the unassimi-lated can be mediated only by alienated individuality. But the discussion here has shown that this is far too limited a conception of the productive process, and a more persuasive picture is of a *variety* of modes, cross-cutting individuals, classes, other groups and mass market requirements. Indeed, one schema for interpreting the music would be in terms of a continuous struggle to constitute *collective* subjects (defined by mixes of class, gender, age, nationality and ethnicity criteria), against both the culture industry's tendential 'mass subject', and, equally, the 'individual subject' of the avant-garde (or in another sense, of bourgeois memory). Needless to say, this is an oversimplification; the struggle is partial as well as, always, enmeshed in both the opposing trends to varying extents. Adorno's recognition of the radical *potential* of what he called jazz (see, for example, Adorno 1976: 33–4) could have given him the theoretical space for such an approach (it certainly means he has no *logical* grounds for the theoretical closure he operates, only a self-fulfilling pessimism); but he fails to follow his quest into places where he could have found what he sought, and, more damagingly, he excludes the possibility of any other mode of critique than that associated with alienated individualism. At the same time, the concept of the *unitary* individual subject, on which he relies, should come under fire – as it has done in recent years, under the influence of post-structuralist thought. The idea of the 'split subject' provides a way of grasping, precisely, the position occupied by the various human productive forces. Composers, performers and other productive agents are not either wholly 'manipulated' or wholly 'critical' and 'free'; their subjectivity – or the positions being continually constructed for that subjectivity – is traversed by a multitude of different, often conflicting lines of social influence, bringing them into multiple, often overlapping identities and collectivities. Neither for them nor for their music are the simple categories of 'mass' or 'individual' appropriate.

Form

One of Adorno's strengths is his insistence that changes in the circumstances of musical production affect musical *form*. His stress on music's 'social content' meant that he could never accept the tendency of positivist music sociology to treat genres, styles and forms as so much freely-existing data. At the same time, this strength brings with it a weakness. Since, as we have seen, Adorno overestimates the homogeneity of culture under advanced capitalism, he is led to a similar interpretation of popular musical form. His key concepts here are *standardization* and – in order to explain the apparent elements of variety – *pseudo-individualization*.

Basically his argument is that all aspects of musical form – Adorno instances overall structure (the thirty-two-bar chorus), melodic range, song-types and harmonic progressions – depend on pre-existing formulae and norms, which have the status virtually of rules, are familiar to listeners and hence are entirely predictable. There is no necessary relationship between these schemata and the actual details of a song; the details could be substituted without affecting the essential meaning, while conversely the overall structure does not depend on the details. Thus the music is 'pre-digested': 'the composition hears for the listener' (Adorno 1941: 22). In 'serious music', by contrast – examples of which Adorno draws, predictably, from Beethoven – the significance of the details and of the totality mutually create each other, with the result that every piece is unique.

An example of the kind of popular song Adorno had in mind – though no doubt he thought of his argument as applying to all kinds – is 'Down Mexico

Way', a 1939 hit by the British song-writing team of Michael Carr and Jimmy Kennedy. This is a typical Tin Pan Alley-style ballad, and like most it uses the thirty-two-bar form. In this form, the musical structure of each chorus is made up of four eight-bar sections, in an AABA pattern. (Actually the A sections here are doubled in length, to sixteen bars – but this affects the overall scheme only marginally. See Ex. 2.1.)

Thousands of Tin Pan Alley tunes share this scheme and Adorno is quite justified in arguing that to listeners of the time it would be totally predictable. Moreover, *within* the chorus, the identical music is heard three times: it is, to use Adorno's phrase, 'the same familiar experience' that is emphasized (1941: 18).

As for predictable harmonies – 'the harmonic cornerstones . . . emphasize the most primitive harmonic facts' (ibid: 18) – each of the four sections begins and ends on the tonic chord, and in between, complications are minimal: the primary triads (Eb, Bb, Ab – tonic, dominant, subdominant) are overwhelmingly in charge. The harmony, then, is no more than a comfortable background; it represents what, as Adorno points out, had come to seem the 'natural' musical language.

Ex. 2.1

Sections are marked by square brackets, phrases by an oblique dash.

Ex. 2.1 cont'd

Similar techniques are at work in the structure of the tune. Within the A sections, every phrase is based on variants of a single rhythm (♪ ♩ ♪ | o ,

♩ ♩ ♩ | o , ♪ ♪ ♪ ♩ | ♩ | etc.). The opening gesture of the first

phrase ('South of the Border'), itself a familiar tonic chord arpeggio, is repeated sequentially at the start of the second ('That's where I fell in love'). The third phrase uses the same device: the second half ('my thoughts ever stray') repeats the first ('And now as I wander') at a higher pitch. The fourth phrase is a variant of the first. Throughout, there are no awkward melodic leaps; everything proceeds smoothly, by arpeggio or by step. Similarly in the B section (the 'middle eight' or 'bridge'), the first three phrases all use basically the same rhythm, while the melodic shape of the first is repeated almost exactly in the third, sequentially in the second.

Altogether, then, we can say the tune is predictable, not in the sense that without knowing it we are sure exactly what is coming next but in the sense that when we hear the next phrase, our reaction is, 'yes, I thought something like that was coming'. We could make the same kind of comment about the lyrics: the predictable rhymes; the clichéd phrases ('South of the Border', 'stars above', 'my thoughts stray', 'she was a picture', and so on).

The thirty-two-bar form was pervasive between the wars, but it has remained important since – even in rock. It is, for example, one of Lennon and McCartney's favourite schemes (though quite often they vary the section lengths). However, with rock came also a different formal scheme, the 'twelve-bar blues'. This, together with many variants and extensions to its basic pattern, is now at least as ingrained in the popular musical consciousness as the thirty-two-bar ballad form was between 1920 and 1950. In a way it is even more predictable, for it not only has a standardized melodic/lyric structure (first phrase: four bars; second phrase: four bars, more or less repeating the first; third phrase: four bars, contrasting or complementary) but also a schematic sequence of (highly 'primitive') chords:

Bars	1	2	3	4	5	6	7	8	9	10	11	12
Chord	I				IV		I		V	(IV)	I	

Moreover, quite often the third phrase repeats the melodic shape of the first two; and frequently there are riffs – often of traditional or clichéd types – in the instrumental accompaniment. All these aspects can be heard in Joe Turner's rock 'n' roll classic, 'Shake, Rattle and Roll' (Ex. 2.2), where again, predictability is high, both within the specific song and as between the song and the general characteristics of the genre.

This has not remained altogether true of rock, which to some extent has developed more individual formal patterns, especially in progressive rock. As we saw in Chapter 1, unexpected chord sequences, irregular phrase-lengths, unschematic structural relationships have all been introduced. But still, most rock songs are strophic (that is, the same music, a *chorus*, is repeated to changing words), and this has its effect even when within the chorus the musical structure

Ex. 2.2

is less standardized. Still, too, there are generally lots of repetitive and conventionalized elements (riffs, and so on); and still there is a tendency to favour 'the most primitive harmonic facts' and standard phrase-lengths. Moreover, many 'new' structural ideas soon evolve into *types*, with their own conventionalized schemes. One could distinguish, for instance, the *riff song* (Led Zeppelin's 'Whole Lotta Love'); the *call-and-response* or *antiphonal song* (the Who's 'My Generation'); the *tension/release song*, built on an alternation of narrative or repetition and lyrical release (from Elvis Presley's 'Jailhouse Rock' to the Rolling Stones's 'Satisfaction', 'Sympathy for the Devil', 'Jumpin' Jack Flash', and many others); and a revival of its close relative, the *verse-and-refrain* song form (probably derived from 'folk' traditions: many of Bob Dylan's songs are classic examples). Altogether, then, at this macro-structural level it is certainly true that almost all popular music works within the sphere of the known.

Such differentiation of detail as Adorno recognizes he explains as 'pseudo-individualization'. A song must be not only 'familiar' but also 'new' – that is, must stimulate attention – and this contradiction is surmounted by introducing 'pseudo-individualized' effects (which at the same time, of course, reinforce the ideology of 'creativity' and 'uniqueness' necessary for cultural goods). There are two aspects to these effects, in Adorno's view. They are a façade: they are confined to the most superficial aspects, and scope for *real* variety is so limited that they in fact quickly become clichéd, standardized, themselves. At the same time, they are always heard in relation to the basic framework or expected effect which lies behind them and which they are varying: they are *substitutes* for the 'correct' formulae; they can thus excite but not disturb. Adorno discusses five categories of pseudo-individualized effects: (1) complicating harmonies, functioning as embellishments of the expected primary chords (in 'Down Mexico Way' the diminished seventh in bar 6 and the tune's chromatic passing notes in bars 8 and 10 would be examples; both are themselves clichés); (2) complicating rhythmic effects, such as syncopations, again heard as 'distortions' of the 'straight' rhythm (for example, the pattern which begins each phrase in the A sections: ♪♩ ♪ ♩ , instead of ♩ ♫♩ ♩); (3) colouristic and especially 'dirty' timbres; (4) 'blue' notes; and (5) improvisations and 'breaks'. The latter three aspects are interpreted as decorative distortions of 'legitimate' timbres, 'pure' intonation, and the 'straight' (that is, the written) tune, respectively (note the valorizing adjectives, used by popular musicians themselves, as well as cultural critics).

Certainly, recordings of Tin Pan Alley tunes from the 1920s, 1930s and 1940s contain plenty of persuasive evidence for Adorno's thesis. Often simple tunes are 'showcased' harmonically and texturally, with elaborate introductions, interludes and codas, and clever instrumental interplay; often, too, syncopation is applied rather mechanically and 'dirty' effects take a clichéd form (for instance, brass 'growls' and glissandos); most dance-band 'improvised' solos are, as Adorno points out, improvised in only a very limited sense: they use stock patterns and depart very little from the written tune, and then by way of 'spicy' effects rather than inventive melodic construction. An important part of the arranger's function was to create a band *style* (hence its 'image') and a song *atmosphere*. Thus many performances of 'Down Mexico Way' used approximations of 'Latin' rhythms in the accompaniment, just as the basic structure is extended at the end by a 'sub-flamenco' coda.

Since the 1950s, many of these functions have been taken over by the record producer. Because of popular music's ubiquitousness and vast scale of production, it has been possible to establish in the collective mind a set of conventional musical 'colours' – 'Spanish', 'pastoral', 'cowboy', 'blue', 'hippie', 'punk', and so on – and arrangers and producers can simply lift the technical devices needed for these ready-made veneers off the shelf when needed. Similarly, the 'mechanized spontaneity' typical of some late 1930s dance-bands can easily be matched by the artificial excitement and synthetic ecstasy of some rock performances – just as rehearsed 'improvised' solos are still common. In a sense, anything – even 'modernist' dissonance or punk 'anti-vocal' singing – can become clichéd and pseudo-individual, as many TV commercials testify. But does what is an undoubted tendency justify Adorno's extrapolation of a monolithic law, today or in respect of the 1930s?

Let us look at another 1930s Tin Pan Alley tune, Jack Strachey's 'These Foolish Things' (Ex. 2.3). Its thirty-two-bar form is pretty rigid (though the bridge is only four bars), the A sections, and much of the B section, are based on *the* Tin Pan Alley harmonic cliché, the circle of fifths, and the tune is full of rhythmic repetition, and melodic repetition and sequence. That said, there seems to me something unaccounted for; the tune *rises above* the conventions. Partly this is the result of the shapely overall curve of the A melody; partly, perhaps, it has to do with the way a certain simple ('innocent'?) *pentatonic* inflection (the melody of section A is based entirely on D E F# A B, apart from a solitary G in bar 6 and the cadence in bar 15) rubs against the 'romantic' harmonies, diatonic with rich chromatic alterations. Similarly, can the foreign harmonies of the bridge be dismissed as a pseudo-individual distortion of an expected D major? They seem, rather, to function as a disturbance – admittedly small-scale – of the A section's tonal stability; this is a technique derived directly from the nineteenth-century *Lied* and piano character piece.

As this suggests, the appeal of such a tune could be seen as a 'leftover', an 'echo' of a bygone era of craftsmanship; and Adorno recognizes the possibility of this – indeed, he acknowledges that it is precisely in popular music that the category of the 'idea' (a relatively independent, memorable element within a totality, a phenomenon more or less abandoned by 'serious' music) lives on, and with it a sense of creative spontaneity (Adorno 1976: 34–7). The music industry term for this is a 'hook'. But having allowed these possibilities, Adorno does not accept the implications of his own gesture. The 'individualism' at issue here is, of course, enmeshed in bourgeois categories; but, in its own way, it seems no more 'crippled' for that than the different but equally 'bourgeois' individualism of a Schoenberg.

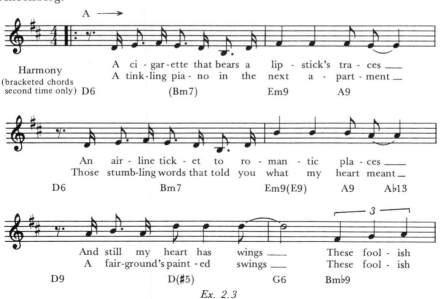

Ex. 2.3

The winds of March that make my heart a dan-cer

A te-le-phone that rings but who's to ans-wer?_ Oh, how the ghost of you

clings! These fool - ish things ___ re-mind me of you.

Ex. 2.3 cont'd

One could carry the critique further and ask why Adorno never examined specifically the Tin Pan Alley songs which *break* with aspects of the standard conventions – in particular, songs by the 'Broadway masters'. Admittedly this repertory is not in *exactly* the same category as the hit song material; nevertheless it is stylistically and functionally continuous with it. Here we find songs which use the thirty-two-bar form but fill it with angular melody and tonally shifting harmony ('All the Things You Are'; 'Body and Soul') or with polyrhythms ('Fascinatin' Rhythm'); we find, too, a song like George Gershwin's 'A Foggy Day', which does *not* use a standard form, boasts a tune consisting almost entirely of leaps, rather than innocuous conjunct motion, and is structured with such motivic tightness as to be almost serial in method (see Ex. 6.3, p. 184 below). A theory of standardization must be able to account for such songs; and Adorno's approach surely begins to crack at this point. A pity he could not have read Alec Wilder's *American Popular Song* (1972) which, using basically the same musical criteria as Adorno – derived from European bourgeois art music – could have been designed as a riposte to his view of this repertory.

As well as the compositional contribution, there is, of course, that of the performer to consider. Adorno's view of performance is restrictive: basically, he sees its proper contemporary role as no more than faithful reproduction of the composer's intentions. The 'spontaneity', 'improvisation' and 'personalized' interpretations of popular singers he explains in terms of a combination of pseudo-individualism, fake immediacy (part of the false veneer of 'art') and the psychological appeal of the 'star'. For him, such performers cannot be forces of production in their own right. But if the moment of performance is considered as potentially an act of composition, a different perspective can emerge.

In Billie Holiday's 1936 recording of 'These Foolish Things'[3] it is not too much to say that the melody is recomposed. The bridge is lengthened to eight bars, the melody 'stretched out', altered and given new harmonies. In the A sections, the tune is more subtly transformed: the basic melodic shapes are still there, for listeners familiar with the original, but they are 'glossed', 'paraphrased', by changing a few notes here, a few notes there; the repetitions of the original all but disappear. In addition, one is struck by the importance of such factors as: *vocal quality* – this is Billie Holiday and could not be anyone else; *phrasing* – that is, the way she places accents, alters the rhythm, often by stretching out notes so that they sound behind the beat instead of on it, and joins notes together, for example smoothly or with attacked consonants; and *pitch inflection* – the way she sometimes slides up to or away from notes, hits them slightly 'off-pitch', and so on. These techniques are geared to the interpretation of the lyric. Thus, they are all particularly clearly in play at moments like 'heart has wings' (bar 5), where a rhythmic stretching-out makes the voice try to fly, while at the same time it is poignantly connected to earth by a descending glissando on the last note; and the 'how the ghost of you clings' phrase, which is given a strikingly tremulous 'clings'.

Most jazz listeners would regard a recording like this as a unique creation, formed precisely in the *tension* between received schema (the written song) and the 'authentication' provided by concrete realization in a specific moment. Of course, Billie Holiday is not 'typical' of all popular singing. But jazz vocalism – and with it this kind of tension – has been a strong influence on popular singing, from Bing Crosby and Frank Sinatra down to many recent performers. And many instrumental solos in popular music owe their form to the same conceptualization. Even before jazz and rock – in music hall song, for instance – numerous accounts stress the importance of the transforming power of performance, often of admittedly banal material. Did the decline of performance in European 'art' music to the status of 'mechanical reproduction' produce a blind spot in Adorno's thought here, such that its contribution in popular music was interpreted as mystifying illusion?

This, among other factors, points to the conclusion that Adorno's theory of standardization, which wants to be a *total* theory, is in fact strictly limited in its applicability. It certainly identifies a central tendency in a particular repertory; but it goes on not only to consume that repertory in every aspect but also to gobble up *all* kinds of popular music. On a macroscopic level, the problem is that there is no allowance for diversity of musical practice or song-type. There is no awareness that differentiated practices, related to national, ethnic or class traditions, have survived, nor that historical breaks – for instance, that represented by rock 'n' roll – could be anything other than pseudo-individual. It is notable that when Adorno mentions examples of songs or musicians (not often), they are always drawn from one narrow band of the spectrum: the hit songs and most popular dance bands (such as Guy Lombardo's) of the 1930s. When he writes that 'the jazz audience is split . . . The full-fledged technical experts vilify the screeching retinue of Elvis Presley. It would take a musical analysis to find out whether the offerings to which these two extremes respond are really worlds apart' (Adorno 1976: 13), we know that the question implied in the final sentence has already been answered in his own mind, just as surely as we know that he has not *done* the musical analysis but simply conflated Elvis and . . . whom? Glen Miller?

On the microscopic level, this problem manifests itself in abstractionism. The lack of analysis of specific songs in Adorno's writings means that it is impossible to know whether he is talking about real pieces or, more likely, ideal types. In fact, there seems to be a kind of *Ur*-pop song in Adorno's mind – to which *no* actual song, however standardized, could totally conform.

But there are problems, too, *within* the theory of standardization. Adorno sees the prevalence of conventions and repetitive norms in twentieth-century popular music against the background of a musical tradition – European bourgeois art music of the late eighteenth and the nineteenth centuries – which evolved in a strongly *non*-schematic direction. A history which limits 'progress' to the sphere of a certain conceptualization of individuality can only see the collective associations of conventions and repetitions as regressive; they represent the manipulative mould of mass society, together with a pseudo-archaism which that society uses to establish its historical credentials. Standardization is seen in terms of a 'pseudo-eternity', a regression to a world of 'simple reproduction', 'a kind of higher-potency feudalism' (Adorno 1967: 123–6). It cannot undertake 'the expression of free solidarity', since, today, 'only individuals [and individualistic treatment of musical material] are capable of consciously representing the aims of collectivity' (Adorno 1978a: 298–9).

We have already seen how questionable this historical picture is. Even within the world of mass-produced culture, it is possible to approach the question of standardization differently. Hennion's account of popular song form accepts, in both words and music, a similar dialectic of the known – clichéd frameworks and transparent effects – and the striking or illuminating detail (Hennion 1983: 171–82). But he treats the former, unpejoratively, as an aspect of grammatical neutrality and obviousness designed to permit communication to a mass audience, and to represent the everyday context; and the latter not as 'false' but as 'interruptions' of the grammar, relatively autonomous 'metaphors', intuitively selected but acting 'like tiny reservoirs briefly holding the social significations of the moment'. Here the mass subject is not treated as abstract but takes concrete and variable forms.

In a broader perspective – that of 'world music' as a whole – standardization, with its pejorative implications, might be more usefully renamed 'formula'. Formulaic schemes are common in very many kinds of music (most nineteenth-century European 'art' music is a striking exception). Many tunes from European 'folk' traditions follow predictable, well-known melodic and rhythmic patterns. A good deal of Middle Eastern and Asian music (for example, music based on the *raga* or *maqam* principle) and of African music consists of pre-existing ideas, schemes, rhythmic and melodic formulae, which are 'filled' out in performance. Obviously this method is highly appropriate for traditions of *oral* transmission; collectively known schemes provide a basis for the act of performance-cum-composition. But European Renaissance and Baroque music, usually written down, often works out sets of variations on existing tunes or harmonic schemes, or uses formal and stylistic clichés for structural, expressive or dramatic purposes (in opera recitative and arias, for instance). And standard structures associated with dance and song, together with characteristic melodic types and rhythmic patterns, survive into the eighteenth and even the nineteenth centuries (symphonic minuets, Viennese waltzes, domestic strophic songs, Italian opera arias). Adorno himself notes this – but his historico-sociological picture ensures that 'since Beethoven', in 'good music' such survivals must, for him, be individualistically transformed. But if, as argued above, 'popular-bourgeois', proletarian and even pre-capitalist musical traditions have *not* been totally broken or irreparably damaged, the possibility of links between them and twentieth-century popular music is a real one. Formula might then work not only as a symptom of 'mass mind' and homogenized thought; the 'people', condemned by Adorno to inertia while the processes of rationalization work themselves through to their totalitarian conclusion, might find that, drawing on old, collectively used methods, they can *act*, if only in compromised, ambiguous forms. Formula can, on the one hand, itself take on a positive significance, and on the other, it can provide a traditionally understood basis for the performance of individual variants (which is what we found in the Billie Holiday recording). In 'Shake, Rattle and Roll', even if it is interpreted as *totally* devoid of the non-formulaic (far-fetched, once one listens carefully to performance nuances), the collectivizing repetitions can take on a positive cultural significance, in the context of use by young working-class dancers.

Adorno's mistake here is of course grounded in his Euro- and class-centric theory of musical evolution. (It is notable that he equates the simple, the sensuous, the repeated, with the childish.) Because he draws his criteria from a particular musical tradition – a 'music of thought', characterized by the working out of themes over extended, integrated forms and requiring concentrated, 'intellectual' listening – he regards other forms of music as either primitive in comparison or as corruptions of this tradition. Adorno overprivileges elements of musical language which are characteristic of the Austro-German symphonic tradition: integrated forms, sophisticated harmony, tonal tension, and so on. Conversely, he underprivileges aspects which are not characteristic, but which may conceivably be important in other musics: among them 'sound', motoric stimulus, nuances of pitch inflection. At the same time, where the same aspect appears both in his tradition and in others, he interprets it through the ears of the former. Dissonance, for example, he treats within the criteria set up by bourgeois art music. In that tradition, it works in relation with consonance to establish tension/resolution structures, with narrative, expressive or dramatic functions. Alternatively, in the extension of the tradition by the Schoenbergian avant-garde, dissonance is felt to reflect an agonized response to the reified stability associated with (absent) consonance. In popular music, such functions are either lacking or much weaker. But Alan Durant (1984: 58–85), in pointing out the historically variative significance of dissonance, has discussed the interpretatively partial nature of these criteria. In popular singing and instrumental soloing, for example, dissonance often works *vis-à-vis* the underlying harmonies in a very different way, as an aspect of the variant/schema tension. Clearly, different criteria are needed to understand this practice. In fact, it may not always be correct to regard such effects as 'dissonances' at all. Adorno's criteria force him to see, for example, blue notes as 'distortions', pseudo-individual embellishments of 'correct' pitches; but blue notes may conceivably be part of a different pitch system with its own correctness.

Another effect of Adorno's historical 'absolutism' is his undervaluing of *performance*. The importance of on-the-spot variation and creation in almost all kinds of popular music (as in most non-European musics) is striking. And just as the growing dependence of European art music on written scores in the eighteenth and nineteenth centuries led to a differential development of certain elements of musical language, so the replacement of popular song scores by recordings has increased the importance of performance, and with it *different* elements. But to Adorno, seeing performance variation and realization as a false façade, the decreasing role of the traditional composer-figure and the relative thinness of many popular song scores can appear only as defects. The extent of Adorno's misunderstanding here is often amusing. He describes guitar tablature in hit song sheet music as 'intended for players who cannot read the notes': 'musical traffic signals'; and he assumes that the numerous mistakes in the piano scores, for which such sheet music has always been notorious, are consciously planned by publishers, to satisfy the listeners' 'infantile amateurism' (Adorno 1978a: 290–1). In fact, of course, such mistakes result from hasty and inexpert transcription from the real music – recordings and band parts – and are symptomatic precisely of the *lack of importance* of the score; just as the tablature reflects a need to direct the player towards *performance*, as against the way the abstract symbolism of staff notation is focused on the needs of contemplative written *composition*.

Such composition, which reached a peak in the large-scale abstract instrumental music of nineteenth-century Europe, coexisted even then with simpler songs and dances. But functional differentiation of genres seems to disappear in Adorno's picture; all art apparently must aspire to the condition of the most 'autonomous'. Yet songs *qua* songs cannot be the same as symphonies; dances must satisfy certain basic functional requirements. It is hard to see why these considerations should have changed under mass culture. Adorno's preferred picture for music listeners seems to be of inert, private critical spirits, without bodies, without vocal sensuality. Will mankind, even under advanced capitalism, let alone any future more liberated society, ever cease to sing and dance?

Reception

To Adorno, listeners to popular music are far from being private critical spirits, of course; they are a passive mass which is prepared to accept standardized musical forms precisely because it is the product of the same processes as the musical forms themselves. 'The composition listens for the listener . . . [both] are kneaded by the same mode of production . . . [creating] a pre-established harmony . . . between production and consumption . . . The people clamour for what they are going to get anyhow' (Adorno 1976: 29; 1941: 38). The music at one and the same time offers *escape* from the banalities of social life and is *continuous* with them; its twin functions are thus *distraction* (music as narcotic) and *affirmation*: 'accepting what there is . . . identifying . . . with the inescapable product' (Adorno 1976: 41; 1978a: 288). From both points of view, the demands of real listening – to autonomous works – are replaced by functions of psycho-social conditioning; Adorno's most complex typologies of listening behaviour are elaborations of this basic position (Adorno 1941: 32–48; 1976: 1–20). 'Plugging', in all its aspects, represents an authoritarian distribution system which produces psychologically weak individuals eager to identify with authority; for such immature personalities, listening can be described in terms of neuroses. Any musical 'needs' apparently satisfied by the music are false, for, as use-value is destroyed, all consumers really consume is the 'success' they themselves have helped to produce.

As usual, the *force* of Adorno's argument has to be admitted. In an age of 'background music', listening *is* often distracted, and popular music is often used as a drug or as a 'switch' to trigger preplanned narcissistically comfortable sensations or as an instrument of group conformity. But, again, the argument is taken too far. In the first place, its validity depends in part on the acceptability of Adorno's theory of musical form – for the (standardized) 'composition listens for the listener' (who becomes equally standardized). But if this theory fails its claim to universality – as I have suggested – then so, too, does the theory of listening; relative autonomy, variants, contradictions in the musical work allow the possibility of individual response, while repetitive structures, if defined as 'formulaic' rather than 'standardized', raise the possibility of still-valid collective meanings (rather than passive mass consumption). But, even if the musical system *were* as constrictive as Adorno supposes, could listeners be *so* unfree? In other words, can the web binding production and consumption be conceived as drawn so tight as to collapse the two together?

Part of the problem is Adorno's class-centrism and the cultural prejudice it brings. Thus his social psychology assumes the traditional bourgeois family structure as a norm. When he diagnoses a crisis in this structure – a tendency to replace paternal authority with external role-models and peer-group norms – this is inevitably interpreted as a crisis in the process of socialization itself. Whether such a tendency must result in narcissism and authoritarianism, as Adorno believes, is dubious, however; similarly, the traditionally greater dependence on such external sources in working-class communities as compared with bourgeois culture suggests that the effects of modern social pressures here may not necessarily be uniform across classes. There are hints (no more) in writings by Adorno's colleague Max Horkheimer that 'out of the suffering . . . there can arise a new community . . . to replace the individualistic motive as the dominant bond in relationships' (Horkheimer 1972: 124), and that, as the family fulfils fewer of the tasks of socialization, this new community would arise outside the family (see Held 1980: 134). It would be premature to describe the youth groups and subcultures associated with many popular music styles in these terms; but the importance they have assumed in adolescents' development is suggestive – just as the older class-based behavioural models and moral norms of proletarian communities, though weakened and modified, have not been entirely smashed. Class-linked youth subcultures, such as those of mods, teds and rockers, could be explained as a crossing of both tendencies.

Similarly, Adorno assumes without question the superiority of certain kinds of listening, notably what he calls 'structural' or 'integrative' listening. Just as he privileges a particular mode of production (focused on the bourgeois composer), a particular kind of musical form (integrated, self-generating) and particular parameters of musical language (those foregrounded by notation), so he privileges the concomitant mode of listening. But this perspective is dependent on the evolutionist music-historical model criticized above; for Adorno, 'after Beethoven' any type of listening other than contemplative cognitive effort is necessarily regressive. Other listening modes – for instance, those where music is associated with activities of various kinds, the sounds perhaps impinging on muscles, skin, nerves as much as conscious thought processes – have a long and continuous history, however; and, still, as anthropologists have shown, a living ethnography. If, in popular music, these take on to some extent an 'automatic' quality, this should not blind us to the *contradictory* potentials of such historical continuities.

In the same way, Adorno despatches all 'amateurism' and 'participation' in music culture without mercy. Whether it be participation through music-making or through response to performance (dance, other body-movement, shouts of enthusiasm, the social paraphernalia of shared fanship, and so on), the increased specialization of musical labour together with mass media distribution, which together deliver 'high-quality' professional products into our homes, render all such 'participation' anachronistic; it becomes an exercise in self-deception since it is manipulated from above by the consumer industries, the fetishistic relation hidden beneath a mask of self-directed activity and 'spontaneity'. While do-it-yourself rock, fan-club organizations and dancing-in-the-aisles are certainly not independent of industry interests, such a breathtaking theoretical closure reduces the musical role of the vast majority of humankind to a subservient attempt to match up, as listeners, to the demands of 'advanced' producers; Marx's vision of a future with everyman an artist certainly seems to be definitively buried, but on a less exalted level, there is once again no attempt to look for the possibility of *contradictory* meanings in the actual practice of real listeners.

If 'the active experience of music' (Adorno 1976: 133) is held to take place now solely in the imagination, more 'functional' kinds of musical practice can hardly be condoned, still less allowed the possibility that they embody social critique. This is as narrow a view of critique as it is of musical response (which in fact traverses the entire body, the activity of the ears being just as 'physical' as that of the dancing limbs or the sensating nerves). But Adorno assumes that 'the process of internalization, to which great music as a self-deliverance from the external world of objects owes its very origin, is not revocable in the concept of musical practice' (ibid: 133), and so he is bound to consider the 'functionalism' of popular music as regressive, explaining it by reference to social-psychological defects. Against this – or alongside the importance of conscious thought – we must affirm the possibility of *practice as critique*; the legitimacy (however compromised) of subsuming 'music', narrowly defined, within other social activities; and the necessity to consider its effects in relation to the structure of the 'external [social] world'.

Even in the sphere of bourgeois 'art' music Adorno allots the listener a strictly limited role. It is the dialectically functioning relationship between musicians and listeners which accounts for the state and the viability of the musical language at a given time, and for changes in the language over time. But in respect of specific works, the listener's role is to measure up to the demands imposed by the work itself, to comprehend what is already present. Certainly social reception of the work – and in that sense its 'meaning' – may, in subsequent periods, diverge from that (socially defined) content; but the content still exists, inviolable. There is no conception in Adorno of listeners coproducing musical meaning *directly*, at the moment of creation; clearly this has to do with his undervaluing of performance and overvaluing of the written score, as well as with the centrality in his thinking of a relatively narrow, homogeneous musical culture, in which variations in musical interpretation were not significant. For Adorno, then, the meaning of musical works is *immanent*; our role is to decipher it.

When Adorno comes to popular music, as we have seen, the listener's role is subsumed still more within the mechanisms of the work itself – only now active deciphering is replaced by passive compliance. And it is here that we come to the nub, theoretically, of the problem with Adorno's whole approach to listening. Dick Bradley (n.d.) points out that within a Marxist framework production and consumption *cannot* properly be given the near-identity which Adorno attributes to them. While Marx presents them as constituents of a unified, continuous process, each nevertheless has its specificity. Thus consumption represents the *individual* appropriation of the *social* product; 'it has its irreducible moment, that of satisfying a "need" '. But Adorno thinks that the listener, buying the music-commodity and

> 'making' the success but failing to 'recognize himself in it', is *alienated* in the same *primary* sense as the labourer in relation to the product. In arguing this he not only collapses the *specificity of consumption* but also misrepresents the relationship between the 'individual' and the 'social' in Marx's argument, for it is not for the *individual* consumer to recognize *himself* in another individual's product anyway, but to recognize the socially-imprinted character and meaning of the product . . . and so to find in it the satisfaction of 'need' (ibid: 30).

Moreover, Bradley continues, the specific nature of *cultural* goods, which Adorno recognizes, cannot be adequately covered by his argument that the apparent use-value of popular music (its 'immediacy', its status as 'art' and as a repository of 'human' feeling, and so on) is an illusion which actually functions in the service of exchange-value (it is an aspect of what people buy). For this argument wrongly denies the existence of *any real relationship at all* between the listener and the musical object itself, turning that relationship into an abstract reflection of the laws of the capitalist system, and 'ignoring . . . what is irreducibly extra-economic in consumption' (ibid: 48); and this denial depends in turn on an implicitly idealist definition of 'needs', against which the satisfactions gained from actual listening can be unthinkingly described as 'false'. To put this more concretely, there can be legitimate arguments about the nature, quality and function of a listener's response to the actual sound and structure of, say, an Elvis Presley or Bing Crosby song; what is not legitimate is to move this 'thrill', however defined, bodily across the theoretical topography so that it sits wholly under the sign of commodity-fetishism. On the contrary, Bradley goes on, a properly 'worked-out view of the specificity of cultural goods . . . [would recognize] the co-production of meanings which goes with them' (ibid: 47). For Adorno, though, the audience – indeed, the entire production-consumption process – has become an abstraction, resting on 'an idealist inversion of the abstract and the concrete' (ibid: 49), in which real historical moments and differentiations of practice have no place.

Once this abstractionist tendency is grasped, the disparities between Adorno's theory and what we see around us are explained. We can accept the possibility that reception of cultural products is not always as passive as Adorno suggests, that it is often class-differentiated, that consuming subjects are not necessarily unitary conformists so much as sites traversed by conflicting interpretative schemas. Similarly, it becomes obvious that such reception does not always represent a direct appropriation of the consumer into a pre-given framework but is *mediated* by other, varied interpretative assumptions associated with other social institutions and values (which may be mutually contradictory). The growth of user-subcultures takes on enormous importance, and not only those associated with deviant youth groups: the British audience for American Country music, the Adult-Orientated Rock audience, successive rock 'n' roll revivals, swing band enthusiasts, and many others, would repay attention, for often they use mass-media products, perhaps radically shifting the original meanings. In fact, some recent work stresses the *active* role of such groups – and of individuals in selecting the group they want to join – either in *choosing* from among the diverse products available (see Van Elderen 1984), or in asserting exclusivity *vis-à-vis* particular mass-produced music forms through a process of 'excorporation' from the hegemony of industry-defined meanings (as against incorporation into those meanings) (see Grossberg 1984). It becomes clear, too – especially when studying youth subcultures since rock 'n' roll – that the spheres of work and leisure are not always so closely intertwined as Adorno suggests, the latter simply duplicating the reified forms of consciousness which may be characteristic of the former. Indeed, very often cultural *styles* – those of the mods and the punks, for example – have been used precisely as forms of rebellion or critique, in relation to the everyday world of work and consumption (see Hebdige 1979). As with modes of production and musical form, then, there are altogether many more alternatives and contradictions here than Adorno's totalizing account can allow.

Historicizing Adorno

The strengths of Adorno's basic approach – the stress on mediation, on music's social content, on the importance of the systemic nature of the production process, on critique rather than description – are real; and as he works it through, there are many specific insights. It is at its strongest when applied to production; indeed, one can think of the Adornian picture of a totally administered, homogeneous, determining process as the ideal type to which the industry constantly aspires (though, for reasons discussed above, this state is never actually reached). For the dissemination and reception of popular music, the approach is weaker, as we have seen. The imbalance derives from the fact that, generally within his social theory of music, Adorno insists on the priority of production in defining the musical language, determining meaning and moving music history forward. This may make some sense for the bourgeois 'art' tradition (though probably not as much as he thinks) but when the elements of the entire musical production–consumption process become both more unified and interdependent, and more 'socialized', it becomes less appropriate. In the mid-twentieth century, the circulation of musical messages comes to look more like a continuous coproduction process, with inputs at many points. And – contrary to Adorno – the more apparently homogeneous the product, the more important and potentially productive the role of reception, and of the mediations interposed between the two (DJs, peer-group opinion, subcultural appropriation, use-situation, and so on).

Adorno's mistake here seems to rest on two aspects of his position, which in fact turn out to provide the two central explanations for the flaws in his argument. The first is his use of the 'immanent method'; the second is his own historical location, or more precisely what we can call his ontologization of history. These need to be grasped if we are to *understand* him – and so to make use of him, rather than simply dismissing him as an embittered elitist pessimist.[4]

The immanent method assumes that the 'truth' of a work is to be found within the work itself: or rather, it can be discovered by critical confrontation of the work's ideal or concept – what it 'wants to be' – with its reality. The problem here, of course, is how to decide what the work's ideal or concept is, and by what criteria. Adorno's criteria, formed within a close knowledge of a particular musical tradition, tended to be exported wholesale to other traditions. At the same time, his chief object of popular musical study, the Tin Pan Alley hit, *was* governed to some extent by those criteria, thus confirming him in his approach, and discouraging any consideration of possible *new* criteria. A greater use of *comparison*, in addition to immanent critique, might have led to a lessening of prejudice, elitism and class- and Euro-centrism.

The importance of the historical location of the formation of Adorno's ideas was mentioned earlier. Paul Piccone has argued that the relative success of monopoly capital in the 1930s and 1940s in incorporating much of social and cultural life within its own orbit led Adorno to

> the ontologisation of the socio-historical predicaments of American society in transition from entrepreneurial to advanced capitalism . . . with the result that the historicity of this transitional phase was altogether ignored . . . the dialectic becomes de-historicized to cover the whole of western

civilization . . . Consequently, critical theory . . . becomes purely defensive . . . [It] brilliantly captures the Cold War period, the plastic 50s and in general the post-New Deal American society which was rapidly hegemonising most of the world. It was unable, however, to foresee or come to grips with what Habermas in *Legitimation Crisis* calls the rationality or planning crisis (Arato and Gebhardt 1978: xviii–xx)

– that is, with the fact that, from the 1950s on, the dominant interests needed, in order to ensure their continued hegemony, to permit a certain amount of 'free space' within the rationalized structures for relatively unplanned 'opposition'. This space, intended both to obtain the invention of new products, leading to enhanced consumption and profit, and to maintain ideological support, in response to apparent liberalism, allows at least the possibility that permitted pluralism can grow into radical dissent.

Adorno's view made *some* sense in 1930 or 1940, then; but subsequently, when semi-stasis gives way to more obvious conflicts, its flaws show through. In the previous chapter, this periodization was described in terms of the 'moment' of 'mass culture' giving way to that of 'pop culture'. For musical production, this transition has the effect of revealing with increasing clarity that any would-be homogeneity of industry, form and audience cannot permanently disguise the fact that in reality the form is 'squeezed out between two conflicting pressures' (Ian Birchall, quoted in Laing 1969: 189) – and this marks its mode of existence as immanently contradictory. On the level of social meaning, the transition could be seen as associated with the move from a period dominated by the modernist critique of mass culture to the period of 'post-modernism'. Adorno speaks from the vantage-point of modernism (though, as we have seen, he arguably gives this too monolithic an interpretation): his ideal is an individual critique, which is negative in relation to society but also constitutes a positive synthesis – an alternative. The interrelationship of modernism and post-modernism is a matter of some controversy (see, for example, Jameson 1984). We can say, though, that with the at least partial collapse of the modernist perspective, there appears to be a certain potency in the post-modernist position, which takes the dominant system as given and proposes as method of critique the *fragment*: subversion takes the form of 'guerilla activity' which exploits fissures and forgotten spaces *within* the hegemonic structure. An 'either/or' (to the extent it existed) is replaced by an 'and/and', a confrontation between unitary subjectivity and its destruction by an acceptance of multiples and contradictions.

The fragments can have many sources, the *past* as well as the present. And, if we can understand and thus make use of Adorno only by historicizing him, we can go *beyond* him by historicizing his historicism, which reacted to the shocks of Fascism, the demoralization of the Left and the rapid consolidation of administrative capitalism by assuming that past popular cultural traditions had been not merely damaged but shattered, and which asserted a single progressive cultural trajectory, developing from radical bourgeois art (Beethoven's, for example) through to modernism. There are more helpful world-historical pictures than that one. For example, Adorno's Frankfurt School colleague, Walter Benjamin, put forward a more optimistic view of the potentials of the productive forces within advanced capitalism; this will be discussed in the next chapter. Secondly, there is the attempt by another contemporary, Ernst Bloch, to, as it were, reinvent the category of utopia for Marxism by introducing into the field, for possible reuse, the *Erbe* – the heritage of the world's pre-capitalist cultural past. Just as, beyond a certain point, the terms of capitalist political economy ('development', 'progress', 'production') can be rearticulated to the needs of a radically different society only through their transformation in the light perhaps of older ecologies, so, arguably, the assumptions of the bourgeois music tradition can, beyond an equivalent point, be most easily articulated to the interests of a future, more liberated order if critically combined with techniques drawn from older, popular traditions (see Jameson's comments in Bloch *et al.* 1977: 209–11). And if this process can be conceived as relevant not only to a possible future but to processes of critique and struggle *now*, then to point to the emergence of black American, non-Western and European 'folk' elements within mass produced popular music commodities – with however ambivalent results – may be the historically most significant way in which we can put Adorno's critical pessimism in its correct place.

Notes

1. See a report by S. Hosokawa in the IASPM Newsletter, *RPM*, 5: 14–15.
2. See also Fletcher (1966) on the gang milieu out of which Merseybeat emerged.
3. With Teddy Wilson and his Orchestra, 30 June 1936, Brunswick 7699.
4. A similar view is put in Gendron (1986), one of the better critiques of Adorno's theory of popular music.

3

'Over the rainbow'? Technology, politics and popular music in an era beyond mass culture

Walter Benjamin

Walter Benjamin shared many of Adorno's basic attitudes; indeed the two men influenced each other considerably. Benjamin often expressed regret at the passing of 'traditional' art and the social ties and functions which had made it possible. At the same time, though, he was much more open to the 'democratic', 'progressive' possibilities offered by new technological developments and the changed social context of cultural production. Partly this resulted from his relative lack of interest in Adorno's theory of mediation by the social totality – for which his colleague criticized him. This left him free to consider specific factors, relationships and techniques in a theoretically less encumbered (if sometimes dangerously speculative) way. Partly it resulted from a preference in his subject-matter for concrete cultural and social detail over Adorno's tendency towards abstraction of social process: for instance, he offered something like a phenomenology of the 'shocks' inherent in modern city life; he discussed actual and potential production practices within modern media, derived from his enthusiasm for Brecht's 'epic theatre'; he focused less on the totalities of aesthetic form than on the fluidities of technique, the conditions of production, and the variable nature of reception.

Benjamin wrote nothing about music.[1] But his arguments can be generalized for all mass cultural forms; indeed, taking more recent popular music developments and music theorizing into account, we can see him at the head – implicitly and sometimes explicitly – of a 'Benjaminian' tradition, pointing perhaps 'beyond mass culture'. Not surprisingly, then, the 1930s debate between Benjamin and Adorno on these subjects (see Bloch *et al.* 1977) can be regarded as a touchstone for later disputes, its premises and positions not yet superseded.

In Benjamin's thought (1973a; 1973b; 1973c;),[2] the place occupied by Adornian 'autonomy' is taken by 'aura' (roughly, the mysterious but absolutely unique 'image' and associations of the individual art-work). Sometimes he explains the disintegration of aura in the modern world by reference to social changes, but more often he stresses the role of technological developments – especially the new importance, quantitatively and qualitatively, of mechanical reproduction. This not only affects the distribution, function and meaning of existing works but also stimulates new artistic techniques, new modes of production and new social relationships, shifting art from the sphere of ritual or disinterested contemplation to that of everyday life and political struggle.

Benjamin's most extended analysis of this is focused on film (Benjamin 1973b: 219–53). But his argument contains ideas which can be applied with striking results to recorded music. Film technology, according to Benjamin, affects production, form and reception. Production becomes much more of a *construction*. Materials (actors' performances, for example) are *edited* together, by camera and producer. They are *estranged* from the totality; detached, collaborative *technique* replaces integral, unselfconscious expression. In the form there is an emphasis on *montage* or, more widely, a kind of *analytical critique* of reality, which proceeds via 'optical tests' (close-ups, different camera angles, slow motion, and so on) to manipulate its material, and, through an 'unconscious optic', to reveal or re-present details of everyday life never normally noticed. For recorded music, the pressure towards collaborative, 'constructed' manipulation of sound materials in the studio production process hardly needs stressing. Similarly, Benjamin's description of cinematic form provokes immediate comparisons with the potential of recording and mixing techniques (mike-positioning, rebalancing, dubbing, and so on) for musical 'montage' and an 'analytical' revelation of new sound details and relationships (for instance, Elvis Presley's 'voice' – that is, the vocal 'image' we hear on his records – seems to me precisely a product of this kind of process). At the same time, whether 'collaboration' *always* implies 'critical estrangement' is, for music as for film, a question to be answered rather than a necessary conclusion from the premises. Similarly, examples of 'analytical montage' (the Beatles' 'Penny Lane'? the Specials' 'Ghost Town'? the whole aesthetic of 'scratch' and 'dub'?) must be set alongside tendencies to use new techniques to revive an old aesthetic, to 'mix *down*' rather than separate *out*, in order to synthesize an all-embracing individual vision (Phil Spector?).

As for reception, Benjamin sees the film audience, detached from the moment of production, as being in the position of a *critic*, identifying with the analytical work of the camera rather than with the experiences of the characters. The transparency of technique and the ubiquity of the reproductions turns everyone into an *expert*, hence a potential *participant*. At the same time, the film offers itself for 'simultaneous collective experience' and the reason why critical and affirmative attitudes can fuse is because 'individual reactions are predetermined by the mass audience response they are about to produce . . . The moment these responses become manifest they control each other' (Benjamin 1973b: 236). Benjamin explains the fact that film reception seems to be not only critical but also 'distracted', the form not only a succession of 'shocks' but also a wrap-around cultural environment, by means of an analogy with architecture, 'prototype of a work of art the reception of which is consummated by a collectivity in a state of distraction' (ibid: 241). Architecture, he argues, has always been assimilated not by attention but by *habit*. New tasks for perception can only be carried out in the same way 'under the guidance of tactile appropriation' (ibid: 242). Thus in the film 'the public is an examiner, but an absent-minded one' (ibid: 243).

This approach has enormously suggestive potential for analysis of listening, for it fully accepts the significance of new perceptual attitudes and situations while by-passing or at least putting in question the usual, too easy Adornian assumptions of passivity. There are problems, too. It is clear that architecture is not altogether the same as a film or a song: for instance, both the latter make use of *performers* – more crucially, *stars*. There is a tendency to refocus identification on the 'personality' of the star – and indeed Benjamin recognizes the appearance of 'false aura'. A second obvious problem is the striking blank where normally we would expect to find discussion of *content*. Is content irrelevant to the effects of the new technically mediated forms? While Benjamin recognized the problem – for example, he discussed Fascist appropriations of the new reproduction technologies – it is doubtful whether he fully accepted its theoretical source: namely his virtual conflation of mass and class. Indeed, for Benjamin the 'rise of the masses' as a historical and cultural theme tends to take the place occupied in most Marxist theories by the revolutionary role of the proletariat. Sometimes the two slide together uncomfortably, with little attempt to differentiate class groupings, levels of consciousness or political motivations. At other times Benjamin is aware of what is, precisely, the problem here: how to *align* the potentials of the new technically determined modes of production and reception with a progressive perspective. His answer is: 'look at Brecht' (see esp. Benjamin 1973b: 15–22; 1973c: 1–13; 85–103).

Benjamin portrays the Brechtian drama as taking a traditional 'apparatus' (theatre) and transforming it through the use of techniques derived from the modern media: montage, interruption, critical quoting of everyday social 'gesture'. Theatre becomes an experimental, analytical experience, in which the audience, detached from the narrative (the famous *Verfremdungseffekt*), is prevented from identifying, forced to evaluate, to think – hence to participate. What is interesting is that Benjamin foregrounds *technique* rather than the traditional questions of form and content. Thus he slices through the old argument between 'formalism' and 'realism' by inserting what we may call a notion of *intervention*. An artist's contribution now, he says, must be assessed by reference to his positioning within the process of production. Using the methods offered by the new technical media, he must become a self-aware participant in the total apparatus of production. He must work towards an *Umfunktionierung*, as Brecht called it – a transformation of the apparatus – which will result in new fusions and relationships between media, genres and techniques, new, more collective production processes, and a new, more participative role for audiences. Content – however radical – can always be appropriated by the existing cultural powers; for Benjamin, then, cultural politics must become more of a running guerilla war, in which any appropriate materials, tactics, techniques and relationships may be used. The quality of a cultural practice then becomes a matter of its *effect*, in the moment of its impact.

This certainly offers a fruitful way to see, say, the impact of early rock 'n' roll, which one intuitively senses as 'radical', yet which from the start, and increasingly as time went by, made use of traditional elements of musical and lyric form and content, and subsisted within the nexus of capitalist production processes. In that early 'moment', rock 'n' roll *was* an important intervention, though carried through at varying levels of conscious awareness. There were, in the context of the established musical apparatus, new relationships of words and music, voice and instrument, white youth and black proletariat; new, more collective composition methods; a new involvement of the audience (primarily through the bodies of listeners, but also through a new wave of do-it-yourself music-making). And these were made possible by the new technical processes (amplified sound, radio transmission of styles across social boundaries, studio instead of written composition, and so on). Quickly, staff writers and producers took over, rehierarchizing production, reaestheticizing the form and re-placing consumers in their seats; but that first moment was real, and the effects, Benjamin would have argued, must be analysed *there*.

It can easily be pointed out, by way of criticism, that Benjamin neglects unduly both the effective autonomy of artistic forms and traditions and the power of the actual (capitalist) social relations of production, in the wider society as well as the particular apparatus. The latter exert immense pressures. The former, likewise, are not 'neutral', are often not easily reorganized or reinterpreted, and are always marked by the objective force of their history and material limitations. Rock 'n' roll was, for these very reasons, a compromised form from the first. But if the situation must be represented as a multi-faceted negotiation rather than the simple, voluntary intervention which Benjamin sometimes seems to describe, he did nevertheless offer a way of analysis which speaks the language of the new pattern of determinants characteristic of late capitalist societies.

Another common criticism of Benjamin – made initially by Adorno – is directed at his tendency towards technological determinism – as though the new media can be seen as a direct, unmediated cause and a straightforward good; this, at times, leads to an over-simple historical picture. He certainly does tend to separate new techniques and technologies out from the total matrix of forces playing on production and reproduction, and to exaggerate their as it were naked power; and he does underestimate the capacity of the capitalist media industries to channel the use made of them to suit their own interests, nullifying radical potential. His analysis of mass consciousness is over-optimistic, while his picture of a shift from 'auratic' to 'democratic' art is over-stark. But if the situation Benjamin describes is *too* open, its constitutive relationships too direct and insufficiently mediated, Adorno's net, by contrast, is *so* tightly drawn, its equations so perfect, its circle so complete, that any change, critique or differentiation of meaning or response is all but impossible. If Benjamin overprivileges technique, Adorno does the same to form. Benjamin's romanticizing of mass experience is matched by Adorno's nostalgia and elitism. The former's idealistically active audience confronts the latter's picture of passive consumers, which is no more than an abstraction.

Of course, both men are right (and wrong). In present conditions the question of the end of the traditional conception of art and the nature of its replacement are still open. The main types of development taking place in the 1930s, and extended much further since, are *both* an immense strengthening of the possibilities of uniformity and control, *and* a broadening and democratizing of opportunities. What we are presented with is a *range*, from almost completely 'dependent' work at one end (exaggerated by Adorno, neglected by Benjamin), to relics of auratic art and new types of critical practice at the other (the effectiveness and interrelationships of the two a matter of dispute).

But when all qualifications have been entered, Benjamin's position is important for three main reasons: he took the potential of new media seriously (as Adorno did not); he recognized a new kind of 'autonomy' for cultural activity, defined in terms of its status as a *practice* and an *intervention*; and he saw that the new modes of production and reproduction would generate new kinds of perception. It is for these reasons that his approach seems the more fruitful of the two in understanding the situation in advanced capitalist societies during the last twenty or thirty years, when Adorno's conception of artistic totality, mirror-image of an increasingly global, oppressive industrial totality, presents a theoretical cul-de-sac; when, by contrast, we are actually bombarded by an increasingly heterogeneous mix of musical methods and messages, often seemingly cut free from traditions and sources, shifted around at random; when listeners do seem to some extent to have learned, gradually, new perceptual skills, through several decades of habituation, enabling more active comparison of styles, a greater variety of uses and a more 'ironic' relationship to the stream of musical products; and when the main opportunities for critique and subversion lie not in head-on 'romantic' protest but in exploiting temporary spaces, in the cracks and at the margins, within the monolith itself. If musical politics now involves a constantly shifting 'war of position', Adorno helps us to understand the enemy, but it is Benjamin who is more able to offer the tools to carry on the struggle.

Forces and relations of production (I): towards a historical dialectic

Benjamin's approach has been developed further by Hans Magnus Enzensberger. In a classic article (Enzensberger 1976), Enzensberger argues that in late capitalist societies the media systems, like the structures of social control, are 'leaky': it is impossible, for instance, to monitor which records are played, how they are used, what is put on a cassette.[3] Furthermore, the electronic media are by their nature democratic. Access is easy and universal, and, unlike reading books, needs no great educational 'capital'; copying is simple; even production is relatively straightforward (anyone can speak, or sing, into a mike). Equipment is such that it is very difficult to prevent autodidactic 'tinkering'. Similarly, 'information' (styles, source-material, technical skills) from *anywhere* is easily and universally available. Moreover, the technology is by its nature reversible: a radio receiver is potentially also a transmitter; a cassette player (*sic*) can also record; even a gramophone record can be used as a factor within a new productive enterprise, as the practices of rap and scratching demonstrate. Even though capitalist organization of the media prevents full exploitation of these potentials, their tendency is to destroy both conventional ideas of history (that is, class-specific ownership of a 'heritage') and the concept of the self-sufficient work of art. In a striking phrase, Enzensberger suggests that 'artistic productivity reveals itself to be the extreme marginal case of a much more widespread productivity' (ibid: 46). Even the involvement of the media in what Henri Lefebvre calls *spectacle* (reality as a permanent theatre of consumer products and images) contains – despite its basis in commodity-fetishism – a potential adumbration of the utopian. The underlying desire, which it disguises but feeds on, is 'for a new ecology, for a breaking down of environmental barriers, for an aesthetic which is not limited to the sphere of the "artistic" ' (ibid: 36–7).

Benjaminian ideas also appear in the work of Peter Wicke and Chris Cutler, this time applied specifically to the sphere of popular music. Wicke argues that the rise of 'the mass' as a cultural phenomenon has qualitative effects, encouraging socialization of production, collectivization of reception and a new social and aesthetic meaning to the music itself (Wicke 1982). And the technical qualities of the mass media play a crucial role in this, becoming 'an independent constituent . . . of the total operation of musical production' (ibid: 236) as well as guaranteeing

> the mass as the specific social character of the recipient. Such mass forms of music now exist, less because a large number of recipients have the same musical needs than because these needs become similar (transcending all ethnic, national and social barriers), since the individual here can be a recipient of music only in association with others (ibid: 233).

It is in rock music, Wicke suggests, that this development is seen most clearly. Here

> the reproduction now functions as the original, the live performance is measured against the recording, and technical equipment is seen not as an external aid to reproduction but as a characteristic of the musical original, employed as part of the artistic conception (ibid: 236).

Similarly, 'the musical reference to a "community", to the great masses of young people behind the music – to the consciousness of mutuality crystallising from it . . . – is a crucial and distinctive social and aesthetic factor' (ibid: 235). Easy-to-learn performance and production techniques, together with readily accessible models in recorded form, change the way music is made. At the same time, listener response is grounded not on individuality – the private feelings privileged in bourgeois art – but on

> mass forms of musical practice which are based on the musical activity of many people *interacting* at the same time and in the same way – forms which structure bodily movements and processes, and which enable bodily experience to become an aesthetically mediated pleasure (ibid: 228).

Interestingly, the musical techniques – modal pitch relationships, 'motoric' attitude to rhythm, easily grasped proportional relationships of phrases, repetitive/variative structures – can be linked with historical mass music forms, and, via Afro-American sources, with African music, in which reference to 'community' is an 'intrinsic constituent' (ibid: 235). But in rock these aspects are given their particular shape by, and centred on, a collectively understood manipulation of amplified sound.

Of course, Wicke stresses, the social meaning inscribed in the music is at odds with the social organization of its production by capitalist business. Even so, his discussion of the contradiction between progressive forces of production and reactionary elements in the relations of production arguably distinguishes between rock and the older 'bourgeois hit' too starkly, for he tends to play down the survival of older elements in rock production, form and performance, as well as neglecting divergences of social use and interpretation, and differences of content. Technologically mediated mass experience is not necessarily in itself progressive, and we need to remember the importance of conflict, within the form and the practice, and of a continuous *articulative* effort on the part of producers and listeners.

Chris Cutler's theoretical alignment with the Benjamin tradition, like Wicke's, is implicit rather than explicit.[4] Nevertheless, he clearly echoes Benjamin and Enzensberger in his stress on the democratic potential of electronic media, and on the leading role played by technological developments in general within the changing practice of cultural production. Indeed, there is again a danger of assigning such developments a too simply determinative role: Cutler refers to the *innate* qualities of these 'internal forces', and the role of the 'external forces' (the relations of production, together with the accompanying ideological/expressive superstructure) seems to be solely to realize their potential.

With the benefit of his experience as a working musician, Cutler describes the part played by new technology in the growth of cheap, do-it-yourself recording, the rise of independent production and distribution networks, and the increased ease of access to production facilities. His discussion of the recording process brings out its *constructed* and its *collective* qualities. Because of its potential for empirical testing and manipulation, it privileges group production and obscures the composer/performer boundary. Because it frees performance from time, assembling it bit by bit, it encourages demystified production: 'Tape runs forwards, backwards and at many speeds. It can be cut up and glued together. Moreover, recording is a medium in which improvisation can be incorporated – or transformed through subsequent work – into composition.' (Cutler 1984: 287).[5]

What gives this discussion an additional interest, though, is that it is incorporated into an ambitious overarching historical schema, which aims to 'explain' nothing less than the whole development of world music. This schema comprises a series of three modes of production, each dominated by a particular medium of reproduction (ear, score, and recording). Each is associated with a particular social mode: these are 'folk' society (a rather unspecified repository for all pre-bourgeois forms); bourgeois society; and (potentially) socialist society (for the potential of the electronic media is seen as coming to fruition only in an egalitarian and classless setting). There are similarities with the historical model that Benjamin puts forward ('folk' epic → bourgeois literature → mechanical reproduction), but Cutler focuses even more clearly on the determinative power of the medium. Thus, the 'folk mode' arises from the processes of oral transmission and biological memory; this means that the relationships between music and musician, musician and community, musical content and collective expression, are direct, non-contradictory and non-alienated. Composition and performance are the same; anyone can take part; music-making is not objectified into 'works' but is the result of improvised variation of collectively owned resources. Notation is a negation of the folk mode. It emphasizes the eye, not the ear; it therefore encourages the 'rational' calculation of complex, unique structures and effects and the manipulation of hierarchies of textural parts, formal units and performing roles. It objectifies the work, storing it in tangible form, and is therefore potentially personal property (and commodity). It leads to division of labour (between composer and performer, for example), individualism and specialization, and production *for* a market rather than *by* a community. It is obvious, argues Cutler, how suitable these characteristics are for the needs of bourgeois society. Finally, recording – 'negation of a negation' – returns us to the ear, registering sound rather than notational schemes, turning performers into composers and composers into performers, and necessitating improvisation and empirical collective production. Thus 'all the main characteristics of recording echo those of the folk mode' (ibid: 287), though qualitatively transformed (for instance, *any* sound is available). However, for the present, these characteristics are largely contained within the stifling constraints of the music industry's commodity forms.

This is very neat – perhaps too neat. Though Cutler seems to regard the three modes as, in the end, ideal types, in practice his discussion of the relationships between reproductive media and musical practices – which is genuinely important – is presented as an abstract schema. We get oral transmission *as such*, notation *as such*, recording *as such*: not concrete practices which manifest particular forms of oral transmission, notation or recording. Thus no attention is paid to the immense variety of types *within* the modes (figured bass as against Wagnerian orchestral score, for example; or esoteric ritual song, in which accurate memory is vital, as against collective-variative improvisation of epic); or to the fact that many musical practices overreach the extent of a mode (thus, improvisation remained important in much notated European music until the middle of the nineteenth century; studio-based musicians quite often use forms of notation, when it suits their purposes). The 'folk community' is idealized, with no recognition of the huge variety of musical practices (and social forms) involved (think of the differences between the music, and social function, of, say, West African *griots*, American Indian ceremonial songs and European medieval ballads); in very, very few – if any – of these cases is there *no* class differentiation (and thus hierarchies, divisions of function, and so on); in none would it be true to say that musical production occurs 'naturally' rather than as the result of learned skills and conventions.

Cutler tends to treat forces and relations of production as somehow separate and only brought into 'equivalence', so to speak, later, when the 'potential' of the former meets 'favourable' conditions in the latter. In fact, however, the *dialectical* interplay of the two means that real productive forces only manifest themselves in forms dictated by real social relations. This is why there are so many forms of oral transmission, notation and recording, associated with different societies, periods and social classes. There can be non-commodity notated music (eighteenth-century court symphonies; some 1960s avant-garde 'happenings') and it can produce non-hierarchical, relatively improvisatory performance ('shape-note' singing in the southern United States). Orally created music can be commodified (performances by 'traditional' singers, sold through concerts) and it can assume forms showing certain types of hierarchy and functional specialization (West African drum orchestra music; Balinese *gamelan* music). Recording technology can be used to produce extended, unique, individual visions (Mike Oldfield's *Tubular Bells*); and, with the advent of 'portable studios', a musician can produce a complete piece on tape at home, then teach it to the band, just like a bourgeois composer, rather than entering into collaborative work.

Similarly, while reproductive media certainly impose constraints and channel musical practice in particular ways, they themselves have to 'negotiate' with traditions of musical content and practice, which possess a certain level of autonomy and in turn shape the form taken by the media. Iterative structures common in orally transmitted music survive in notated music (sets of variations; cumulative dance-forms). Triadic harmony, which may have originated in oral practice (improvised parallel singing), was for good reasons highly developed in notated music but remains fundamental to most recorded music. There exist performer-composers not only in oral cultures and in recorded popular music but also in the traditions of notated music (Liszt, Paganini, not to mention Scott Joplin and Jelly Roll Morton).

The basic point is that far from media changes giving rise to simple shifts in musical practice, media, content and social relations form a very complex interrelationship which renders any schema based on abstract historical antitheses very questionable. The problem becomes acute with the transition from notation to recording. The antithesis necessary for Cutler demands that all residues of bourgeois forms be abandoned as reactionary; at the same time, the new mode also has to 'echo' the folk mode (supposedly killed by notation). Unless its practices are to arise *totally* spontaneously out of the 'innate' qualities of the new media, it is hard to see how this is to occur or what the music will be like. The problem is solved by an appeal to the 'folk' qualities of black American musical traditions, which have played such an important role in the development of twentieth-century popular music. Slavery and white racism, Cutler argues, guaranteed the survival of a folk mode *in the midst* of capitalist society – at the same time as subjecting black people, as victims of this society, to an experience enabling them to represent a more general alienation characteristic of life under industrial capitalism. Their music, therefore, was 'ready-made' for the arrival of the electric media. There is an important kernel of truth here. Black music *was* different in many respects from almost all other Western music of the time. In some of these respects (such as improvisation, or blue tonality and pitch inflection) it *was* more suited to transmission on recordings than in notation. And there are senses in which this music can be seen as representing wider experiences, of workers particularly, within twentieth-century capitalist society. That is a significant conjunction of factors. But by the late nineteenth century, most black music forms had been deeply penetrated by bourgeois influences: materials and techniques from white sources, notation (used by many black musicians), individualized modes of production and expression. In fact these forms provide particularly striking examples of the process of *struggle* – crossing the lines of development of media, content and practice, and relating them to the positions of different groups – which is a more accurate picture of the *general* history than any simple structure of antitheses.

Cutler's insufficiently dialectical treatment of the forces/relations nexus reaches its biggest problem in his discussion of the recording form itself, which has to be *both* the 'ultimate' musical commodity and to offer creative liberation. How can its *innately* progressive potentials be contained in a form which has been developed through the operation of the market, and which, in Cutler's argument, represents a culture completely external to its users, completely hegemonic (not resistible in present circumstances), and having 'no need of artistic value . . . [having] become, effectively, an instrument of class oppression' (Cutler 1984: 291). The first answer is that the commodity form of commercial recordings has a 'distorting' effect and that there is a deeper 'real content' 'lying behind' the distortions. The idealism of this approach is obvious, and it is not pursued very far. The second answer is more developed. If within commercial music the power of exchange-value is total, Cutler argues, then progressive musicians should work 'outside'. This leads to a system of values whose chief criterion seems to be lack of popularity (that is, of commercial success), whose musical politics is governed by a continuous effort to be 'challenging' and 'difficult' so as to outwit the equally continuous capacity of the industry to exploit innovation, and whose approach to production is based on a 'folk spontaneity' model which sees 'real' music-making as arising 'naturally', independent of the influence of existing codes, roles and practices. The resulting picture looks strangely like a kind of *modernism* – a romantic-technological modernism – which ends up valuing innovation almost for its own sake. Not surprisingly, perhaps, Cutler's lineage of influences includes not only Captain Beefheart, Syd Barrett (of Pink Floyd) and various 'folk' traditions but also Schoenberg, Eisler, Varèse, John Coltrane, Sun Ra and Charles Mingus.

What has happened, in fact, is that Cutler has been forced to try and squeeze together a neo-Benjaminian theory of productive forces and a picture of productive relations which is positively Adornian! This inevitably results in a kind of Adornian modernism, in which 'progressive' form acts as social critique, modified by a quasi-Benjaminian view of technical mediation, which ultimately recreates these modernists as a new 'folk'. From another point of view, what has happened is that an older Left position, whose model of an anti-commercial, genuinely 'popular' culture is 'folk' music (regarded as a useful source primarily because of its potential for politically progressive lyric *content*), has been rewritten with an emphasis on the progressive potential of new, electrically mediated *form*, and its capacity to recreate community as an 'echo' of the 'folk'. Within musical politics, this is an important move; and it brings with it, as we have seen, real insights into the significance of musical media. But by pushing the argument into an abstract utopianism, Benjamin's stress on concrete *technique*, on the needs of the specific moment and the free selection of materials and methods to meet those needs, has disappeared.

Another way of seeing Cutler's position, especially his historical schema, is as a conflation of Marx and Marshall McLuhan; 'mode of production' as organizing concept gets mixed up with the Canadian communication theorist's 'medium is the message' philosophy, in which consciousness, cultural forms and social organization all derive primarily from the effects of the various media. It is worth taking a brief look at McLuhan himself (1962; 1964; 1967), partly because his ideas have been adopted explicitly by some writers on popular music but also because in the period of his greatest fame (the mid- and late 1960s) some of these ideas sedimented themselves into the common assumptions of quite widely, if usually implicitly, held views on culture and technology.[6]

At one level, McLuhan brought together a variety of existing studies of cultural modes and forms in oral and in literate societies. He then identified typical elements in each of the two cultural categories, and linked them to the nature of the prevailing communication medium (speech/writing). Thus, oral culture is said to be full, rich and immediate, and to result in collective social experience, a wholeness of awareness and a mythic rather than linear sense of time. By contrast, literacy (more particularly print, which carries writing's homogeneous, mechanical, repeatable, linear qualities to an extreme) is narrow, flat, partial, detached, and results in private experience, a single point of view, a split between 'heart' and 'head', and an 'objective', linear sense of time. Literacy is linked with the device of perspective in painting, individualism in literature and philosophy, personal expression and rational construction in music; also, more widely, with the development of social uniformity, political centralization, empirical science and assembly-line production. McLuhan then goes on to argue that the electric media are restoring many of the characteristics of speech: immediacy, aural and tactile rather than visual qualities, ambiguity, multiple points of view, non-linear montage, and collective experience. This takes place in the context of a 'retribalization' process, an emerging 'global village'.

So far, so good – or at least, it is an arguable case. There are clear echoes of Cutler, and even, in some aspects, of Benjamin and Enzensberger. But McLuhan goes beyond the designation of *links* and proposes that communication technology and culture are related as cause and effect: the medium is the message. Further, the particular form his determinism takes demands a new epistemology. For McLuhan argues that the way our cognitive apparatus works is determined by our 'sense ratio', the balance between inputs to the various senses (aural, visual, tactile, and so on). Changes to this ratio are most effectively induced by the operation of media, which McLuhan defines as extensions to the senses. The alteration in our perception of reality then produces particular social and cultural forms. Thus, for example, alphabetic writing, and still more, print, is said to privilege sight quite strikingly at the expense of the other senses, and the effects of this on the way we think and perceive reality – through a linear, mechanical, single-point-of-view consciousness – then have the cultural consequences described earlier.

We can disregard the epistemology. It is never convincingly argued for; the neurological and anthropological evidence renders it very doubtful (see Miller 1971: 92–120); it is patently there in order to support what is ultimately an idealist position, for the half-hidden premise of McLuhan's argument is that there is an ideal human psyche, an essence, which is characterized by balance and interplay of senses, which may once have existed – in oral cultures – but which was destroyed by literacy (a second Fall). This is in fact a version of the familiar conservative 'critique of mass culture', strongly marked by the influence of F.R. Leavis, G.K. Chesterton and McLuhan's own Catholicism, and by his constant search for a reborn 'organic wholeness' of spirit.

Nevertheless, elements of this ideology, as well as more general aspects of McLuhan's cultural-historical argument, have penetrated some writing on popular music, sometimes in a fairly unreflective way, sometimes as part of carefully constructed theories. An example of the former is Karl Dallas's contribution to *The Electric Muse* (Dallas 1975). Dallas uses McLuhan explicitly in support of his suggestion that rock is a kind of folk music. He justifies this argument not through reference to rock's mass public but because its quasi-oral modes of composition and dissemination result, he says, in collective authorship, close links between musicians and audiences, constant variation of materials, and a spontaneous, 'Dionysian' approach to performance. Also, the electric media (by their nature, regardless of their commercial organization) unify and at the same time decentralize the musical repertory and community, and make possible improvisatory musical styles. Like Cutler, he sees the historical source as the conjunction of electric media and black American 'folk' forms, and, also like Cutler, he insists that the new music is quite distinct from earlier written popular music.

> The electronic popular music of rock is so different in form and function from the old print-based pop of 'moon and June', and so akin to the old pre-literate oral forms of folk music, that most of the assumptions made today about the relations between the two are misguided, based on theories devised at a time when the complete destruction of folk culture by the industrial state seemed only a matter of time. Now that the state itself is disintegrating around us, while folk culture goes on from strength to strength, they need to be re-stated (ibid: 95).

The kernel of truth in this is almost washed away by the wishful thinking.

John Shepherd (1977; 1982), by contrast, has used McLuhan to work out a carefully constructed theory. Broadly, he argues that consciousness, hence cultural forms, are largely conditioned by the media through which reality is perceived and organized. The 'worlds' of pre-literate and literate people, characterized by oral-aural immediacy and wholeness, on the one hand, and, on the other, by what Shepherd calls the 'industrial world sense' (roughly a synonym for the outlook of McLuhan's 'typographic man'), are quite different. Shepherd's description of these 'worlds' is much the same as McLuhan's. Strangely, Shepherd seems to have shown little interest in the effects of the electric media; indeed, his account of the present-day situation assumes an even tighter grip by the 'industrial world sense', the system created by literacy and print being generalized as a ' ''symbolic-technological filter'' which regulates the processes of communication vital to socialisation and the creation of consciousness' (Shepherd 1982: 149–50).

Having established his basic historical schema, Shepherd goes on to his most original contribution, an analysis of how the two 'world-views' are 'encoded' in music, in each case the musical structures and the structures of society and of social consciousness forming 'homologies'. Briefly (leaving out much detail), the oral world-view is encoded through such characteristics as the embedding of music in everyday life; direct, often improvisatory, unreflective composition; use of traditional repeated units; prevalence of monophony; prevalence of pentatonic tonality (which encodes social mutuality); inflected pitch relationships; 'dirty' timbres; and irregular rhythmic patterning, often stressing rhythmic interplay. In music reflecting the 'industrial world sense', by contrast, we find consciously manipulated musical structures, individually composed and divorced from social life; developing, through-composed forms, depending on analytic memory; major-minor tonality and harmony (which encode the centralized, hierarchical structure of capitalist society); 'idealization' and 'abstraction' of sound, through cultivation of 'pure' timbre and exact pitch; and pronounced regular rhythmic patterns (which, together with the 'pull' of harmonic progression and the vertical synchronization of parts, encode an objective, spatialized sense of time). It is obvious how close these are to the characteristics attributed to speech and to print, respectively. Indeed, as Shepherd points out, the developments that took place in post-Renaissance Western music would have been *impossible* without music notation, with its propensity for large-scale, visually organized construction, abstraction of symbol from sound, co-ordination of multiple events and voices (through bar-lines, for instance), and 'spatialized' chord structures and progressions.

It should be stressed that, as compared with McLuhan's total determinism, Shepherd suggests a *dialectical* relationship between communication technology and socially constructed consciousness (though how exactly the dialectic works is not clear, and in practice the influence of media is taken as predominant). Moreover, when Shepherd comes to analyse twentieth-century musics (Shepherd 1982), he tries to see how different musical languages, reflecting different relationships to the 'symbolic-technological filter', could be associated with the different *social* positions of particular groups. Dispossessed and relatively powerless groups – for example, American blacks or white working-class youths – articulate their various perspectives, as victims, on the dominant reality through musics which accept the basic rhythmic-harmonic framework derived from the tradition of notated music but at the same time work against this in various ways, notably by superimposing on the framework musical techniques typical of oral cultures.

Some of Shepherd's associates have taken the argument further, in various directions. Trevor Wishart (1977), for example, stresses the abstracting, analytic properties of notation, which reduce the infinity of sound to a small number of discrete, systematically permutational elements, limit our very *perception* and *conception* of music to what can be written down and rationally described, and result in an idealist account of the relationship between the 'real' music in the score and the performance – an inevitably less than perfect representation. Wishart goes on to emphasize the importance of the electric media in breaking the hegemony of notation, for they enable us to capture the actual sounds, in all their inflectional complexity – freed from the 'filtering' effects of notation – and in experiential rather than spatialized time. 'The tape-recorder and gramophone have . . . enabled this new, direct experientially-based musical tradition to extend to millions of young music-lovers, far beyond the realms of any scribal domination and certification of "musical competence" ' (ibid: 150).

Wishart and Virden (1977) also suggest that in the twentieth century a fundamental opposition between 'literate' music styles (from concert music to Tin Pan Alley songs) and 'oral' styles (quintessentially Afro-American musics, but also popular styles derived from these) is associated with the opposition between those who dominate and control the social system and those who are its victims. That is, class stratification and musical language stratification can be correlated. This produces a broadly dichotomous scheme, analysed in terms drawn from work in the sociology of language on the class differentiation of verbal codes. Thus 'abstract' is opposed to 'concrete', 'explicit' to 'implicit', 'elaborated code' to 'restricted code', 'extensional structure' to 'intensional structure', and these types are taken to be related to differing kinds of social experience mediated or formed by a literate organization of reality, on the one hand, and an oral organization of reality, on the other. The quintessential form of the latter type is taken to be the blues. Blues is defined, without qualification, as based on a pentatonic, inflectional musical language, hence as antithetical to the functional-tonal language of bourgeois tradition. Its influence has been spread by the 'sympathetic' arrival of the electric media.

> Despite the opposition of the dominant culture, the music of those *within* the culture but not *of* it, the blacks, found resonance with the experiences of others who felt alienated from the established order. The black basis of today's 'popular' music is the musical expression of a generation in conflict with the values of its elders (Wishart and Virden 1977: 164).

Similarly, while Wishart and Virden want to admit counter-historical trends to the dominant tonal tradition – in what they call 'genuine folk musics' – these are understood as almost completely separate from and opposed to that tradition. There is little dialectic, then: on the one hand, there are 'those who live, in a more or less besieged manner, in a close commonality which divorces itself from the values of the prevailing culture' (ibid: 163); on the other, those who are 'alienated from the possibilities of an immediate life of the unselfconscious body' (ibid: 157). The political aspects of this dichotomy have been further pursued by Graham Vulliamy (1976; 1977).

We have here a substantial body of work stressing – to make the lowest claim – the important *links* between musical media and the structures of society, culture and consciousness. Now the existence and significance of such links is undeniable (though the existence of *homologies* – as Shepherd describes them – is a different question, which must be left to a later chapter). Specific media certainly impose limits and constraints, and they channel, even force, production in particular directions. It is difficult to write down a Jimi Hendrix guitar solo, and still harder to play it from such a notated version. It would be equally difficult to create a Beethoven symphony without notation. Non-literate music-making almost demands repetitive or traditional frameworks, and – as counter-balance? – these stimulate improvised nuance and inflection; yet transcribed into notation, with the nuances missing, it tends to look banal. Similarly, notation, on the one hand, through-composed forms with precisely synchronized rhythmic/harmonic moves, on the other, seem, almost, to imply each other; and the results, in performance, can sound relatively abstract and 'dead'. Even in notation, the differences in musical language between orally transmitted 'folk' song, printed bourgeois song and recorded rock song come through: they hardly need comment, except to say that they do fit many of the stereotypes of the neo-McLuhanite model (see Ex. 3.1).

The different media regimes, moreover, do have social effects. Certainly, notation encouraged specialization and division of musical labour, stimulated professionalism and gradually reduced the importance of amateurism. The latter development can almost be taken as an index of the spread of musical literacy. We know something of the ways in which 'buskers' and amateur street performers were progressively controlled and eventually almost eliminated from the cities in the nineteenth and early twentieth centuries. At the same time, orally

Lord Bate-man was a-den(a) no-ble lord,
A no-ble lord ___ of high de - gree; he shipped himself on board of ship, Some for-eign coun - te-ries he would go see.

Ex. 3.1a

It's the Sol-diers of the Queen my lads, who've been my lads, who've
Chords: Eb   Bb7

seen my lads, In the fight for Eng-land's glo - ry lads, Of its
Eb   Bb7   Eb   D7

world-wide glo - ry let us sing And when we say we've
Gm   Bb7   Eb

al - ways won, And when they ask us how it's done, We'll
Bb7   Eb   Bb7

proud-ly point to ev' - ry one of Eng-land's sol-diers of the Queen!
Cm D7 Cm C C7   Fm   Eb7 Ab Bb7 Eb

Ex. 3.1b

'Soldiers of the Queen' (chorus) written and composed by Leslie Stuart, 1895.
Printed score by known individual (which might or might not be subject to idiosyncratic performance). Major key with simple modulation and slight chromaticisms. Rhythmically regular and
repetitive. Pitch shape of tune based on chord changes. Articulation nuances would be restricted
by need to fit harmony and rhythm.

(*Left*) 'Lord Bateman' (verse 1) sung by George Wray, 4 August 1904, recorded and transcribed by Percy Grainger (Source: *Journal of the Folk Song Society*, 3, 1908: 195–9).) Idiosyncratic performance of communally owned song (with many tune variants in subsequent verses). Modal (mixolydian) with pitch inflection (F/F#). Much rhythmic variety and irregularity. Nuances of articulation related to delivery of words.

Ex. 3.1c

'Jumpin' Jack Flash' (verse 1) written and composed by Mick Jagger and Keith Richard, 1968. Transcribed from 1968 Rolling Stones recording (Decca F12782) by RM. Unique recording of self-composed song (using repetitive riff framework and melodic clichés derived from blues, and displaying tune variants in subsequent verses). Modal (mixolydian/dorian) with much pitch inflection (especially Db/Db); harmony used as a drone, then modally. Much rhythmic variety and irregularity, with much syncopation. Nuances of articulation related to delivery of words.

transmitted rural music was declining also, under the impact of urbanization and the industrialization of agriculture. We can go on to observe that since the middle of the twentieth century there has been a big revival of informal street music, produced in non-literate, often amateur performance and through the public dissemination of recordings (see Prato 1984); this has, of course, gone along with a wave of amateur music-making, centred on the guitar and on non-literate modes of production, which in the rock 'n' roll, skiffle and 'beat group' periods (the late 1950s and the 1960s) swept across the whole of Europe and North America.

We do not have a complete history of such changes in media and social practice. But it is easy to map out some of the important 'moments' (though they cannot always be dated precisely or uniformly across regions and social groups). One would be the take-up, by former illiterates, of broadsides; these had a printed text but, almost always, simply stipulated the use of an orally transmitted tune. A second would be the spread of printed music into bourgeois homes in the nineteenth century; not surprisingly, the musical language drew heavily on existing notated styles – opera and domestic song. This was soon followed by the growth of a song-writing industry for music hall and variety theatre. Bourgeois musical experience was largely privatized and domesticated; working-class musical experience – formerly centred around collectively shared localities (streets, pubs) – shifted to framed public spaces which eventually became constituents of a national and international musical commodity market.

Another important moment is the American music publishing 'war' between rival organizations in 1939–41. The dispute between ASCAP (the Tin Pan Alley songwriters' organization) and American radio allowed a new category of composer (represented by BMI) into the market. These composers, producing largely in the 'hillbilly' and 'race' genres, often used different methods, codifying or 'transcribing' what were essentially performances rather than producing prescriptive scores; and their methods suited the needs of the emergent recording industry exactly (see Whitcomb 1973: 108–9, 206–12). When performers in this industry, such as the Beatles, started composing their own songs – sometimes writing them, more often producing them directly, using oral, experimental, collective methods – another significant move had been made; and a second phase in this process may be associated with the advent of relatively cheap, accessible electronic equipment (synthesizers, mixers, rhythm and effects boxes of various sorts), which enable 'amateurs' to produce music without playing instruments at all in the traditional sense.

It is thus not easy to refute the idea that cultures and outlooks dominated by oral modes, literacy and print, or electronic media are in many respects distinctive. And the differences feed through to specific practices like music. Establishing these broad relationships is one of the real achievements of McLuhan and those influenced by him, and, at a time when he has gone out of fashion, it is worth stressing the importance of the 'specificity of the medium'. To follow the argument beyond this level, however, is more problematic. We have already noted the dangers of abstractionism in considering media modes, and stressed the importance, in the *real* history, of dialectical interpenetration, resulting in tensions, struggles and compromises between characteristics of different modes, between varying practices in the same mode, and between media form and musical content. The important questions are always, first, what *form* oral production, notation and recording take in this precise situation and second, in what social context it is operating.

For example, it can be argued that between the orally produced blues of the solitary rural Southern black and the equally orally produced collective 'gospel song' of black Southern churches there are some rather crucial sociological differences, which typically manifest themselves in clear musical contrasts (secular/religious; personal/group; solo/choral; rhapsodic/iterative; free rhythm/ strong pulse; and so on). Orality does not seem to be the most important factor here. It is, anyway, easy to idealize the 'egalitarian amateurism' of oral cultures. In almost every society we know something about, except perhaps the very simplest, there are individuals who specialize in music or who are regarded as more skilled; in this respect, notation brings about not a total change but an added stimulus, and even without it, there can develop – as in blues or in British 'folk' traditions – an idea of particular songs being attached in some way to individuals: 'that's X's song'.

Similarly, one could argue that the saturation of nineteenth-century bourgeois homes with printed music resulted, in some respects, not in a mass of passive reproducers but in an intensely *active* music culture, with a high regard for the immediacy of performance and the 'spiritual' value of musical communication. The same may be true in respect of the working classes and mass-produced broadsides. The commodification and rising class status of music hall song is more easily explained by referring to the penetration of culture by market relations than to the influence of musical literacy; the increasingly extensive and homogeneous market demanded more songs more quickly than oral methods could supply. But this would also account for the fact that within this system many singers – Marie Lloyd, for instance – retained performing styles heavily influenced by oral traditions; they often did not read music – as, notoriously, the accompanying orchestras had to remember. Music hall composers too sometimes had little musical literacy. Felix McGlennon's account – probably not untypical – of his composing methods reminds us that some categories of nineteenth-century printed song originated in quasi-oral ways:

> I used to hum a tune and strum it on a child's dulcimer, painfully seeking out the names of the notes. Then . . . find a piece of music that ran to the same metre, and with that for my model . . . divide my 'composition' into bars. Gradually, I acquired a rudimentary knowledge of music, and substituted the piano for the dulcimer . . . I can with its aid commit my melodies to paper, and that is all I need (quoted in A. Bennett 1986: 9).

It is important to remember that in one sense, music, being a *performed* art, always has an 'oral' dimension, even when notated; writing a score certainly affects how the music is conceived, but not absolutely, for performance *may* restore some inflectional, intuitive elements. Interestingly, Shepherd and his 'school' tend to focus their discussion of musical literacy on the extreme representatives of notational abstraction, prescription and calculation, the Austro-German tradition from J.S. Bach through to Schoenberg; less extreme practices would modify the picture and soften the obsession which, ironically, they share with the very traditions in musicology and aesthetics that they attack.

A good example would be the nineteenth-century Italian 'opera industry', which, under pressure – musical and social – from the high status in its traditions of *sung performance*, made relatively informal use of notation (see Rosselli 1984). This music, incidentally, was a vital influence in British and American bourgeois domestic song, an influence which can in fact be traced right through to the years after the First World War, in such singers as Al Jolson.

Western music as a whole, since at least the late Middle Ages, is best seen as a 'total system'. Diachronically there are no simple antitheses; rather there is a continuum with certain quantum jumps, often marked by – among other factors – changing relationships between oral and written inputs or by new kinds of notation. Examples would be the abandonment in the later eighteenth century of figured bass and of optional parts in favour of completely written-out orchestral scores; and the writing out of vocal ornamentation by Rossini, followed by other nineteenth-century Italian opera composers, instead of leaving it to be improvised – though this did not necessarily mean that singers followed their instructions! Synchronically the system is characterized by cross-influence; by 'colonial' extension (into lower classes, and into extra-European regions) and 'colonial implants' (American blacks); and, contrariwise, by upward-moving subversion and renewal. These processes have involved constant interplay between oral and literate sources and techniques in so-called folk, popular *and* art traditions (see Maróthy 1974).[7]

There is a danger in all McLuhanite positions of a simple essentialism: an intrinsically 'natural', 'healthy' musicality is corrupted and destroyed by literacy. And this often results in a simple 'return' theory of history in which oral, literate and electronic stages represent an arch shape. But real (as distinct from potential) musicality is *not* 'natural' – it is learned. And there *is* a historical progression in musical practice. This is dialectical, both in the sense that it is marked by many kinds of interplay, as we have seen, and in the sense that at each stage there is retention and extension of existing elements, as well as negation of them. Thus, in important respects both literate and electronic stages represent (at least potentially) an extension of democratic access to kinds of musical knowledge and creativity – just as both also (potentially) increase consumerist passivity. Both bring into being an increase in the socialization of production, through division of labour and its necessary co-ordination (potentially alienated, potentially collectivized). This is not to deny the differences; it is simply to stress both the connections – which link them within what Raymond Williams calls a Long Revolution – and the importance of the word 'potential'.

This point can help us understand the contradictions within recorded popular music: the fact that there *is* no simple return to oral techniques; that the record form carries a vast range of content types (including 'literate' ballads related to bourgeois traditions); that production methods also differ widely, often using written components as well as 'oral' techniques; that the modern recording studio is actually *more* suited to producing precisely synchronized rhythms and textures, and complex structural processes, than is notation (as well as being suited also to other things). We need to know much more about specific cases of production and their effects on musical form. What differences follow, for example, from the young Elvis Presley starting out from printed song-copies but slowly transforming them in lengthy sessions in Sam Phillips's Sun studio, as against

Lennon and McCartney taking mostly orally worked-out ideas to George Martin who then might transform them through literate methods – for instance, the addition of written parts? We need much more investigation into the exact similarities and differences between oral and recording techniques, and their effects. Clearly, listening to a Robert Johnson record now, in Britain, is very different from dancing to him playing live in a black bar in Mississippi in 1936; and there are probably consequential differences in the music itself, too (for example, Johnson would at the very least be constrained by the time-limits imposed by the record form – as all musicians, even to some extent on LPs, are; thus, in some ways a Duke Ellington concert, in a 'bourgeois' concert hall, using written parts, might turn out a more 'oral' experience than the same piece encapsulated on a twelve-inch record). But what *exactly* are the differences, and the connections? They can patently not be completely summed up as a 'retribalization' by the 'electric age'.

We can certainly say that in an important sense a record is *finished* – finite, objectified – in a way that oral performance is not; indeed, in this sense it is, ironically, recordings rather than scores which represent an extreme form of reified abstraction (with the resulting potential alienation of producer and consumer). The immediacy of musical 'speech' is frozen into electric 'print', producing an 'acoustic publication'. We could argue, then, that recording comes at the culmination of one era as much as at the start of another, and that the blanket concepts of 'mass media' and 'mechanical reproduction' need opening up. Maybe there is a confusing conflation here of 'mechanical reproducibility' and what has been called 'electronic producibility': the capacity to transform, extend and decentralize production itself. After all, the former applies to print as well as recording: the differences between score and record, though startling in degree, are simply in the extent and speed of dissemination, and the degree of mediation, affecting directness of access. Similarly, as Benjamin found with film, mass dissemination does not guarantee innovative production. The conjunction between the record-commodity and the new production media is historical but not necessary; it is possible, for instance, to attach electronically produced music to the context of the bourgeois concert, as avant-garde composers have shown.

Given the prevalence of the commodity record form, this distinction will remain, and it provides a more fruitful way of looking at present contradictions than diagnostic analyses of recorded music into 'oral' and 'literate' elements. In this situation, moreover, the distinction between mass as collectivity and mass as aggregate becomes crucial. So long as the new productive potentials take *this* form – which cannot guarantee and may contradict the thrust of the content – progressive, collective effects will depend vitally on the nature of the musical content and on the mode of its reception and use. The concept of 'retribalization', despite its ideological distortions, is referring to something actual (to do with an instantaneous commonality of awareness, and with certain contents and techniques possessing 'collectivizing' tendencies and associations; but it obscures the point that the important task is to investigate the *precise* ways in which these characteristics operate, sociologically and phenomenologically, in differing contexts, social, musical and political.

Forces and relations of production (II): towards a socio-musical theory of the electric technologies

It should be obvious from the argument so far that when we come to the deepest level of the McLuhanite theory – where *links* are construed as *causes* – big problems arise. As Raymond Williams has pointed out (1974),[8] technical invention is always *sought*, in relation to existing or foreseen social practices. However, this intentionality is not exclusive; innovations can be taken over and used for other purposes; they may have unforeseen uses and effects, which may change the original intention. Thus 'determination is the setting of limits and the exertion of pressures, within which variable social practices are profoundly affected but never necessarily controlled' (ibid: 129–30). For example, the early history of broadcasting is marked by a series of technical inventions and developments inspired at first by military or commercial motivations, but then increasingly by awareness of entertainment potential. In general outline, this technology was foreseen and worked for; indeed, it was part of a whole nineteenth-century complex of research and innovation within 'communications' including telegraphy, electric power, the telephone, photography and moving pictures – which in turn grew directly out of, and depended upon, needs expressed in the trajectory of industrial capitalism. But the specific form this technology was shaped into, in the 1920s – the form of broadcasting ('centralized transmission and privatized reception') – served specific functions in a specific, and new, social situation. This was not inevitable, nor was it 'inherent' in the technology; it was the result of active intervention by governments, industrial interests and cultural arbiters. The domestic receiver tuned, along with thousands of others, to a remote transmission crystallizes a historically specific social-technological form (see ibid: 15–31).

Similar points can be made about records in the same period. Originating in the same nexus of communications technology research, the 'phonograph' and 'gramophone' were at first seen as potentially useful more for commercial activities (office dictation), and pedagogical and archival purposes, than for the reproduction of music. But they also fitted into a nineteenth-century history of the development of instruments for mechanical reproduction: musical boxes, barrel pianos and organs, orchestrions, pianolas; and once the embryonic businesses saw the possibilities of mass dissemination, the necessary mass production technology, cheap playback equipment, and a global distribution network were developed with remarkable speed. By 1914, urban (and many rural) listeners virtually anywhere in the world could be supplied via the subsidiaries and agents of a small number of producers in Western Europe and the United States; world sales of records were probably over 100 million (see Gronow 1983: 54–62).

As with radio, record consumption was largely privatized, at least in the industrialized countries. Indeed, in many ways we can see radio and gramophone in the 1920s and 1930s as parallel avenues for the dissemination of a variety of musical forms to the home and the 'framing' of these forms in the domestic setting. Gramophones were literally 'part of the furniture'; radio incorporated musical performance within a mix of 'public' discourses (news, religion, comedy, theatre), transmuted by the privacy and comforts of the home. Both were symbiotically connected to Tin Pan Alley, whose output of basically 'literate' songs, drawing on bourgeois traditions and stressing individual sentiment, cemented the arrangement (through intensive 'plugging'). When, in 1924–5, electrical (as against acoustic) recording was introduced, in response to the competition presented by radio's better sound-quality, it was intended to offer greater 'verisimilitude' (that is, closer approximation to the, as it were, public 'presence' of live performance); yet one of its effects was the development of 'crooning', which depends on the microphone, and this tied in perfectly with the intimacy, privacy and domesticity of home music-listening – indeed crystallized it.[9]

To some extent the history of records since the 1930s can be seen in terms of a struggle between this dominant model – mass transmission and individual reception, with the concomitant effects on the musical content – and the possibilities of alternative institutions, arrangements and uses. There was some upheaval around the middle of the century. New kinds of music (rhythm and blues, rock 'n' roll) appeared, which seemed unsuited to the bourgeois living-room; they used electric instruments, were loud and encouraged energetic dancing; they started to use the studio to produce recorded sounds which were not just attempts to reproduce live performance, and at the same time they seemed simple enough to encourage imitation outside the institutional context altogether. New, small, independent companies appeared, to supply records of this music, facilitated by the development of magnetic tape, which potentially decentralized recording, making it cheaper and easier. The rise of TV threatened much of radio's traditional programming, and led to a search for new audiences, among them a 'pop audience'. There was a real possibility here of a whole new pattern of musical communication.

By the late 1950s, however, a new symbiosis, recognizably related to the old dominant model, was in place. It adapted the new musical forms and a different mix of technology (some established aspects, some new) to its own conceptual-ization of the new social context (characterized by a newly important youth market), regulating the changes in its own interests. This was epitomized – in the United States – by Top Forty radio (followed by similar developments in Britain and other European countries). A unity of music, social functioning and media apparatuses was recreated, as listening was returned, via the mediation of DJs and 'playlists', to an institutionally defined pattern. The symbiosis was cemented by payola.

> The driving rhythms of rock fit snugly into the unity and consistency of Top 40. For if it was one thing that Top 40 compounded, it was unity – all components (commercials, public service announcements, the excitement) were compatible with the music. The Gestalt was greater than the sum of the parts (Eberley 1982: 219).

Just as the radio and gramophone had a pre-history before being moulded into mass music disseminators, so magnetic tape was invented as long ago as 1899, but did not become practicable for recording until after the Second World War. It was first seen as an *alternative* to records. Soon, however, its usefulness as a *source*, or *intermediary* replacing direct mastering, became obvious. It seemed then to fit neatly into the existing organizational structure: its advantages were cheapness, ease of use and a potential for editing different takes into a 'perfect' master; in other words, it was seen, predictably, as one more tool in the search for faithful reproduction of the best standards of performance. What this view did not foresee, of course, was the decentralization and democratization of recording which tape made possible, nor the possibilities tape introduced for specifically 'studio sound' and 'electronic produceability'. In the same way, the original ideology of domestic radio did not foresee radios in cars and in the streets, and the LP, introduced as a way of avoiding breaks in symphonic movements, was not 'meant' for lengthy progressive rock pieces, let alone extended disco sequences.

Clearly, then, established patterns of socio-technological organization, though powerful, are not necessarily exclusive or permanent; there are always potentials for other arrangements, and the existing structure, when it came into being, was not inevitable – it was actively constructed and imposed. It is obvious that early broadcasting *could* have been organized differently – for instance, through decentralized production facilities and collectively orientated listening. To some extent, this potential has borne fruit more recently, in the growth of local radio, on the one hand, and of listening in the workplace and in public urban areas on the other. Similarly, early music-recording actually was accessible to do-it-yourself production – cylinders could be erased and reused in the home – and cylinder-use was orientated more around existing public leisure sites, through coin-in-the slot phonographs, than the domestic context. These patterns were swept away by the development of mass-produced discs, but again their characteristics have re-emerged more recently, through the appearance of cassettes, cheap recording equipment, juke-boxes and discos.

Even against the predominance of established structures, alternatives have sometimes emerged, proposing new uses for existing technology. 'Pirate' stations broadcast 1960s rock to British youth, against the BBC monopoly; American Top Forty radio was preceded by a far less regimented period, in which the new musics and new presentation styles were first breaking through into the existing system; American FM radio in the later 1960s beamed specific styles at specific, 'subcultural' audiences, at first progressive rock, then a wider range. Public uses of recorded music (in jukeboxes, since the late 1930s; in shops open to the street; in clubs and discos; in workplaces and public spaces) have become important. A new musical practice has grown up based on the 'copying' of records by live bands in pubs and clubs. Though 'copies', these performances, *because* they are performances, inevitably produce different effects, both in the music and in the social meaning, from the originals; for instance, they arrange records into 'sets', which may even mix styles and genres. They also set up an important dialectic between mass product and local re-production – what Bennett calls 'primary' and 'secondary' popular culture (1980: 153–218). Methods of using records as a source of production have developed – in disco DJ 'performances' (often using mixing techniques); in the similar but more elaborate 'dub' techniques evolved in reggae, where they are used live as well as in the studio; in the improvisatory techniques of 'rapping' and 'toasting' over backing tracks; and in 'scratching' and 'sampling' techniques (see Toop 1984). Of course, in most if not all these cases, commercial imperatives have been involved. Either they are dependent on moves within the overall structure of the industry – changes in regulations, entrepreneurial gambits – or they bring commercial benefits – increased record sales, new markets for equipment. Still, they do establish a certain *heterogeneity* within the social-technological structure, which may then allow differential practice.

Nevertheless, there is no doubt that the main overall thrust of developments in music technology since the war has been heavy investment in complex, expensive equipment, directed towards increasingly sophisticated production systems, on the one hand, and towards constructing and supplying a mass market for increasingly sophisticated playback systems, on the other. This has had strong reinforcing effects on traditional patterns of specialized, centralized production and private, perhaps passive, home listening. A highpoint in this history came in the late 1960s and early 1970s, with the appearance of extremely capital-intensive, often custom-built studios, demanding new skills and contributions from engineers and musicians, together with a musical focus on the hi-fi stereo LP, requiring a high level of investment in personal time and money. But the trend is continuous, manifested now by computerized mixing, digital recording, compact disc, video-tape and disc. Still, throughout this development there have been unforeseen 'spin-offs' or 'fall-out' from the planned trajectory, which have provided openings for alternative practices: new instrument design, use of micro-technology to produce cheap, portable recording and mixing equipment, transfer of studio 'effects' (like phasing, filtering and echo devices) into forms suitable for use in live performance, and so on. One of the most interesting of such phenomena is the cassette. Seen by the industry as an alternative to the disc, and as a means of extending that market into new, portable applications (in cars, for example), it is nevertheless a two-way medium – like the early cylinders – and can be used for rerecording, crude dubbing and mixing, and even simple reproduction of amateur music-making. Cottage-industry copying is easy and relatively cheap, obviating the need for expensive record-mastering and pressing technology. In the developed societies these potentials have been relatively little used as yet, though punk do-it-yourself ideas led to a certain amount of 'Xerox rock' (see Laing 1985: 118–19); but in Third World countries they help to explain why the cassette has become the main medium for music distribution. Here it can bypass the (often cosmopolitan) choices of state broadcasting institutions; taxi-drivers often play locally produced cassettes in their cabs, for instance. It may, at the ultimate, even threaten to destroy the property-form of recorded music altogether, for 'bootlegging' and piracy are easy and unstoppable (see Wallis and Malm 1984). In this context, widespread campaigns from the industry for levies on blank cassettes signify not only worries over loss of record sales (it is often the same conglomerate profiting from the cassette sales as supposedly losing the record turnover) but also a determination to return listening – and in Third World countries, production – to institutionally regulated channels.

Actually, given the current tape technology – in recording and in cassette copying – together with relatively cheap mixing decks, programmable synthesizers, drum-machines and rhythm-boxes, and 'effects' units which can be connected to instruments, it can be argued that the extent to which the record industry institutions are *needed* has been, potentially, much reduced. A high proportion of what studios can produce *could* be done informally, or 'on location', or even live. At the same time, the structures predicated on the mass market are hardly likely to disappear. An appropriate politics for the current situation, then, would 'walk on two legs' (acknowledging that they are interconnected). It would attempt to work through the mass market, looking to construct that audience into positions where progressive social and aesthetic effects could occur. This would need continual efforts to – using Benjamin's terms – remake the apparatus. Simultaneously, it would encourage decentralized, grass-roots activity, using the full range of available technology, and opening up its democratic potential.

This is certainly a more promising strategy than anti-technological purism. The effects and constraining characteristics of the electronic technologies, in their specific social-historical forms, have become virtually inescapable. We expect popular songs to take forms, use vocal and instrumental techniques, and include sounds conditioned by the characteristics of microphones, amplification, multiple tracking, non-written composition methods, and so on. This affects our very conception of what music is, our imaginary soundscape. For it is above all the kinds of *sound* with which we have become familiar that define the music culture we live in. We mark out the differences between genres and styles partly by reference to contrasts in the way this stock of techniques and sounds is used. There is no escape from this world: acoustic instruments and unamplified, 'pure'-toned singing can now not be heard except as contrasts to more recent kinds of sound, just as live performances are inevitably 'checked' against memories of recordings.

This has been described by Bennett as the development of a 'recording consciousness' (Bennett 1980). In 'a society which is literally wired for sound' (ibid: 114), this consciousness defines the social reality of popular music, and live performances have to try to approximate the sounds which inhabit this consciousness. Even when they fail, or it is impracticable, an audience's collective memory takes over and it 'hears' what it cannot hear, in the 'sketch' provided by the band. Similarly, musicians learn to play, and learn specific songs, from records, and so 'recording consciousness' helps to explain the ubiquity of non-literate composition methods: 'sheet music is just for people who can't hear' (musician quoted in ibid: 139). The structure of this consciousness has been produced by various elements, among them experience of editing techniques, reverberation and echo, use of equalization to alter timbre, high decibel levels, both in general and in particular parts of the texture (notably, strong bass-lines), and, most interestingly, the 'polyvocality' created by multi-mike or multi-channel recording. Mixing different 'earpoints' produces a 'way of hearing [that] is an acoustic expectation for anyone who listens to contemporary recordings. It cannot be achieved without the aid of electronic devices. It has never before existed on earth' (ibid: 119).

What Bennett does not point out is that within 'polyvocality' there is a *range* of effects, stretching, at one theoretical extreme, from montages of totally separate voices or sounds to, at the other, a completely blended mix-down; and different positions within this range, embracing different 'balances' of 'foregrounds' and 'backgrounds', changing 'perspectives' within stereophonic 'panoramas', dif-ferent 'layerings' and 'dissections' of the musical 'space', are connected to different aesthetics, and these may imply different 'politics'. The standard pop mix of foregrounded solo vocal and balanced, blended backing was challenged by punk's chaotic 'muddiness' which forced the singer to yell, or obliterated him. Phil Spector's 'wall of sound' ('one mike over everything') invites the listener to immerse himself in the quasi-Wagnerian mass of sound:

> he buried the lead and he *cannot stop* himself from doing that . . . if you listen to his records in sequence, the lead goes further and further in and to me what he is saying is, 'It is *not* the song . . . just listen to those *strings*. I want *more* musicians, it's *me*' (musician Jeff Barry, quoted in Richard Williams 1974: 91).

This can be contrasted with the *open* spaces and more *equal* lines of typical funk and reggae textures, which seem to invite the listener to insert himself in those spaces and actively participate.

The existence of this kind of *range* reinforces the point, already made, that however important the effects and constraints of technologies, these are inseparable from specific *contents* and specific *social functions*. Recording certainly encouraged the switch to non-literate composition methods. But when this started, in the United States, it had to draw on *particular* repertories, genres and styles (which happened to be in black music and white country music); it took place in conjunction with a restructuring of the record industry and a growth in the record market which gave the musicians an increased freedom to use their own material and develop the new techniques; and the resulting music was defined as well by the way it was marketed to particular audiences through the particular structure of the American record and radio industry (see Hirsch 1971). Thus it did not, to put it crudely, lead to a wave of popularity for lengthy improvisations in the style of Indian classical music, sweeping the country through formal concerts aimed at a family audience. In the same way, the *studio*, while not a 'neutral' resource, gives rise to a *variety* of musical directions, depending on intention, convention and market. Elvis Presley's early records, with their novel use of echo, may have represented a watershed in the abandoning of attempts to reproduce live performance in favour of a specifically studio sound; but the effect is used largely to intensify an *old* pop characteristic – 'star presence': Elvis becomes 'larger than life'. Similarly, multi-tracking of vocals, which can be used in such a way that it 'destroys' or 'universalizes' personality, is in fact widely used as a way of *amplifying* a star singer's persona, 'aura' or 'presence'. One of the main points of Geoffrey Stokes's fascinating account of the making of a Commander Cody LP (1976) is the tension there is between the *band's* recording aesthetic (they see themselves as a live band, ragged, spontaneous, exciting) and the recording aesthetic of the *producer* brought in to get them a hit (he wants something more precise, co-ordinated, polished).

Which purpose the studio is used for depends on larger, social pressures. Tape is equally suitable for 'polyvocal', highly edited montages of sound *and* for repetitive, 'soul-less' tape-loop techniques, used for sequenced effects and rhythm tracks. Synthesizers, likewise, can be used to create programmed repetitions of limited, known effects and to imitate 'natural' sounds; or they can be used to explore an infinity of new sound-possibilities. The choice will depend on purpose, market constraints and existing conventions and connotations. In the same way, electric guitar 'distortions' (fuzz, wah-wah, feedback), while 'inherent' in the technology (and to some extent no doubt discovered by accident), developed in practice by drawing on existing instrumental traditions (notably the vocalized effects of black guitar playing, which have a long history), and by linking with a body of social meanings settling around the communicative 'expressiveness', 'honesty' and 'authenticity' of rock music. The 'guitar hero' was not a simple product of the technology but of the way that technology was used within the social and aesthetic context of 'progressive' and 'heavy' rock.

In fact, technology and musical technique, content and meaning, generally develop together, dialectically. Each makes demands on the others, but at every stage there is an area 'left over' from the constraints of the immediate relationship, pointing to 'pre-historical' residues or to unforeseen possibilities. This is especially clear with the electric guitar. Amplification began in response to guitarists' demands for their solos to be heard through the sound of big bands. Electrification then facilitated an expansion of certain traditional guitar solo techniques (fast runs, inflection and glissando, vibrato), while demanding certain new playing techniques in the process, which then resulted in new effects (sustained tone). Exploitation of possibilities for tonal modulation led to demands for extra technology in this area (wah-wah, fuzz, and so on) and, within a context of particular aesthetic values, for bigger and better amplification (for example, bigger bass amplifiers, so that electric basses could match louder guitars). But this trajectory of solo playing could not prevent the same resources being used for quite different effects, for instance the crashing rhythm chords of Pete Townshend, developed subsequently in punk. Similarly, the overwhelming bass riffs of heavy metal may be compared with the use of the same high-capacity amplifiers to produce effects of bass-line *clarity*, in funk and reggae.[10]

Once established, particular musico-technological crystallizations can take on definite connotational or ideological references; and these can be hard to shift. Because of its history in rock music, the electric guitar itself signifies 'passion' and 'sexuality', almost inescapably. Similarly, synthesizers, because of particular usages, have acquired connotations of 'modernity', the 'future', 'space-exploration', 'rational control'. This contrast is so embedded now that it can be played upon. In the context of the synthesizer bands prevalent in popular music in the early 1980s, the work of committed *guitar*-based performers, like Big Country, U2 and Bruce Springsteen, was actively taken to signify commitment to the 'classic' values of rock tradition. Such ideological pressures can be very powerful. In the 1950s and early 1960s, the equations of 'acoustic' and 'folk authenticity', 'electric' and 'commercial sell-out', were common; Bob Dylan fell foul of them when he 'went electric' in 1965. For the politics of popular music, such 'constellations' of meaning and practice are anything but 'academic'. Interventions cannot start *ab initio*; they have to begin from an awareness of the relationships that currently exist. Radical work can only hope to succeed if it plays, by modification, inversion, rearticulation or contrast, off an acknowledgement of the strength of existing manifestations of technology and cultural form.

The social relations of production are also subject to a variety of pressures, adopt a variety of patterns and are open to reform and struggle. It is not the case that new, more democratic, participative relations follow inevitably from the introduction of electric technology. There is certainly increased specialization and rationalization of function, which leads to a definite intensification in the *socialization* of the production process. At the same time, tape technology's ease of access and decentralization of skills, together with the necessity it imposes for *collaboration* between studio functions, tends to encourage collective work. There is an implicit tension between these two tendencies; the question becomes, always, to what extent the socialized production process will be bureaucratic or collective in form.

Most accounts of studio recording that we have suggest a great range of patterns, varying according to historical period, social and institutional context, musical aims and individual motivations (see, for example, Martin 1979: 240–60). Varying, too, as between different *stages* in the recording process: Stokes's account, for instance, describes some parts (setting up instruments and mikes; vocal overdubbing; mixing) in terms suggesting intense specialization of function and alienation of individuals, while others (playback, for example) are marked by genuinely collective discussion (between musicians, producer and sound engineer). Kealy's discussion of the sound engineer's role (1979) emphasizes the growing importance of this collaborative dimension, as the engineer necessarily becomes involved in aesthetic questions while musicians need to understand what the machinery can do. In the elaborate independent studios that began to appear in the late 1960s, there is often an ideology about of a collective artistic autonomy, in which musicians, producers and mixers interweave and switch roles. Nevertheless, this can then bring about not democratization but new hierarchies; the *auteur* remains, merely changing his position and identity. Similarly, descriptions of Phil Spector's production methods suggest a collective approach to song-writing and a collaborative approach to decision-taking in the studio, but indicate that subsequently Spector's iron will – represented by the 'formula' he has in mind – takes over and moulds everything into *his* vision (see Richard Williams 1974: 62, 64). The collaborative methods of the Beatles, in the studio and to some extent in composition beforehand, did not prevent conflict between the apparent creative 'leaders' (Lennon and McCartney) and their 'subordinates', which eventually contributed to the break-up of the group. To put the possibilities into the form of an extreme contrast, the same technology can be used by groups deliberately organized in a collective way, such as Chris Cutler's Henry Cow, and to realize Mike Oldfield's megalomaniac visions, where, by performing all the production tasks, he rationalizes the process within himself in a parody of the role of the bourgeois composer-conductor.

Moves aimed at an *Umfunktionierung* of the apparatus, as Benjamin and Brecht suggested, are clearly in order here. But they are inseparably bound up with interventions on the levels of musical technique and content – without which they have no function – and with attempts to build on and develop the 'popular musical competence' of a putative *mass audience* (rather than, for instance, proposing pseudo-artistic alternatives), for without that the production work will exist in isolation instead of encouraging participation and response. Thus the tendency of music video to glittery escapism, to what Alan Durant has called a musical *portraiture*, which 'may fix currencies of sounds, but . . . may also close eyes to music seen more broadly as practice' (1984: 115),[11] needs to be countered not only in more democratic use of cheap video production equipment but also in the cultivation of more subversive and open visual styles.

But intervention of any kind depends upon *control*. And it is the continued importance of the question of control that makes the social relations of music production and distribution a vital area for popular music research. There are the beginnings of a useful literature,[12] but so far little sign of attempts to apply to music what seems to be the most sophisticated general theoretical position in this sphere – that represented by Raymond Williams's 'cultural materialism'.[13] Williams's insistence that 'culture' cannot be hived off to a 'superstructure' but is itself constituted by material processes, is vital. It means that the sphere of culture is marked by complex but fundamental, irreducible and autochthonous relations between specific productive forces and relations, and this explains how the place of this forces/relations nexus within the wider social formation displays not only links, homologies and causalities but also complex mediations, structural asymmetries arising from varied functions, uses and inputs, and the possibility of contradiction. Thus the structure of relations responsible for the making, circulation and use of, say, a piece of recorded music cannot be mapped *entirely* onto the structures responsible for other kinds of commodity, 'cultural' or otherwise, still less onto those constituting an abstract model of capitalist production as such – even though, obviously, important links, similiarities and pressures exist. It is precisely the degree of disparity which indicates the opportunities for independent reorganization of music apparatuses (that is, without a general social upheaval), and at the same time which sets their *limits*.

Williams's position recalls Benjamin's insistence that the primary focus of attention for progressive cultural producers should be their position within their own production apparatuses. This becomes the more important in 'post-modern' societies, where the 'consciousness industries' assume an increasing *economic* importance. Furthermore, both writers suggest fruitful ways of thinking about productive *forces* within the specific sphere of cultural production. Both reject the all-too-common assumptions which associate 'forces of production' solely or primarily with obvious technological instruments, and systems of economic organization. Productive forces are 'all and any of the means of production and reproduction of real life', including not only particular modes of technical or industrial production but also 'certain mode[s] of social cooperation and the application and development of a certain body of social knowledge' (Williams 1977: 91). For music, therefore, we must consider not just 'technology' (instruments, media, systems of dissemination) but additionally modes of social co-operation and bodies of social knowledge. The former, as we have already seen, have effects on the ways in which oral, written and electronic media are actually *used*; the latter are manifested in historically determinate forms of *technique*, *codes* and *repertory* – think, for example, of the 'world library' made available by recording – and also, perhaps, in a certain relatively autonomous development of 'communicative competence',[14] which may even exert a primary determinative influence. Within this ensemble of forces, complex interactions take place, internally and in relation to general modes of social organization.

One more element should be added to this ensemble. If, as I have argued at several points, musical meaning is co-produced by *listeners* – if, indeed, acts of 'consumption' are essential, constitutive parts of the 'material circuits' through which musical practice exists – listening, too, must be considered a productive force. As Marx puts it, 'consumption produces production . . . because a product . . . , unlike a mere natural object, proves itself to be, *becomes*, a product only through consumption' (1973: 91). How would this relate to the new modes of reception described by Benjamin?

From listening to composing

Benjamin's study of Baudelaire thematizes the emergence of the urban crowd in the mid-nineteenth century (Benjamin 1973a): the new quality of 'everyday life', the 'shocks' of mass existence. In the Parisian arcades, the *flâneur* strolls, assimilating the stream of objects, people, movements, to his own pace and experience. 'Abandoned in the crowd', he is intoxicated by the new scale of 'consummativity': 'the pleasure of being in a crowd is a mysterious expression of the enjoyment of the multiplicity of numbers' (ibid: 55, 58) – and not only numbers of people, but also of stimuli, visual and aural. By the twentieth century, with the growth of mass reproduction, these conditions are universalized. Benjamin's spectrum of responses seems to run from distracted listening-in-habit through the *flâneur*'s controlled perambulation, to the heroic or didactic assimilation of the 'shock-effect' into artistic forms. (The latter may be equated with the methods of modernist and critical-Brechtian art, while *flâneurism* perhaps foreshadows the ironic sign-consumerism of post-modernist strategies.)

These conditions now permeate everywhere. In the remotest rural habitat, jumbo jets cover the sky, TV images flicker, the radio airwaves bring a 'surreal' flow of programming, and commodified mass-produced food, furniture, clothes and tools integrate peasant, middle-class commuter and dropout alike into the tentacular megalopolis. In a sense, the 'environmental' experience of music – Benjamin's absorption of post-auratic art into the banal here-and-now of 'real life' – is the other side of the coin from the rationalized production of the *series*: the mass of *copies*, predicated on a homogeneous, planned production–consumption circuit, is complemented by the mass of *types*, spilling out from those circuits, from their privileged sites and sequences, into a heterogeneous montage. Reception lives within this dialectic, governed potentially by both sides, but always liable to turn one into the other, frustrating intended effects.[15]

Musical *flâneurism* may be increasing, particularly as public dissemination spreads, along with the multiplicity of music sources ('strolling' through the home hi-fi collection?) and the ubiquity of non-musical urban sound-sources. A striking latter-day equivalent of the *flâneur* is the Walkman-user. Hosokawa argues that by making listening more mobile, incidental and contextualized than ever before, Walkman-practice becomes a means of reading, or producing, or interacting with the 'text' of the urban space (Hosokawa 1984). Its meaning is intimately bound up with the architectural context, with associated body movements ('walk acts') and with the 'theatre' of Walkman interactions. New definitions of 'text' and 'context', 'activity' and 'passivity', are proposed. The musical roots of Walkman-practice lie in street performance, on the one hand, and all kinds of portable technology, on the other, including that used for production (by amplified street bands, for instance) and that used for reproduction (transistor radios, car hi-fi systems, and so on). Earlier sources may be found in the 'mobility' of much early twentieth-century black music. Open-ended rent-party piano sessions and unplanned 'jams' for heterogeneous combinations of players seem to exist as part of the urban nightlife itself, articulating a musical geography of the cities.

Adorno (1976: 51) and Eisler (1948: 20–22) have pointed out how the ear, unlike the eye, is always *open*; this means it is at once always 'active' *and* an unguarded, 'passive' receptor. Furthermore, it receives stimuli from any direction – the ear does not have the eye's requirement to be *pointed* at the source of information – and it retains an archaic sense of 'participation' in its surroundings rather than any desire to master them by focusing on separate objects. There is a sense, then, in which the ear always tends to be less selective, and less subjectively organized than the eye; the aural equivalent to 'instrumental looking' (possessive scopophilia) is unclear, for the ear is more 'environmentally' organized, more 'other-orientated'. Of course, this 'anthropology' of hearing is always manifested in varying, historically determinate forms: for listening as for the other modes of perception, 'the *cultivation* of the five senses is the work of all previous history' (Marx 1975: 353). Thus, one significance of the emergence of the written score was undoubtedly its ability to project visual, hence more clearly subjective control of sound-objects. Similarly, an important function of the bourgeois concert form is precisely to act as a means of *limiting* music, in time and space, of *framing* sound-stimuli in a clear producer–consumer spatial hierarchy and an equally clear transmitter–receiver communicative chain. The social arrangements of the concert – professional performers, bourgeois listeners, entrance by ticket, aesthetic function – and its spatial arrangements – orchestra at the front, audience sitting, in rows, facing the sound-source, composer either conducting or absent, a controlling deity – are inseparable; and they are not 'natural', nor even 'settled' for long, but part of a continuous process of historical change (see Durant 1984: 30–40; Small 1980: 25–30; 1987a; 1987b : 49–79).

Nevertheless, when the conditions of the 'soundscape' change, in the late nineteenth and twentieth centuries, the physical potentials and limitations of the ear make it easy to understand why 'environmental' modes of listening could emerge with such power. Murray Schafer has described the emergence of the modern dense, lo-fi urban soundscape (1973; 1980). He stresses the interaction of sound-environment and concurrent musical forms and timbres.

> In a lo-fi soundscape individual acoustic signals are obscured in an over-dense population of sounds . . . Perspective is lost. On a downtown street corner there is no distance; there is only presence. Everything is close-miked. There is cross-talk on all the channels, and in order for the most ordinary sounds to be heard they have to be monstrously amplified. In the ultimate lo-fi soundscape the signal to noise ratio is 1 to 1 and it is no longer possible to know what, if anything, is to be listened to (Schafer 1973: 25).

Many domestic environments – with TV and audio equipment, electric gadget noise and external background sound competing with the inhabitants – are not dissimilar, let alone parties, clubs and discos!

The barriers against this development are not great; sound is more suited to wrap-around mixing than are visual images, or even speech (which tends to be heard, in our culture, as 'inner writing'). However, there is no question of a simple *return* – to a pre-concert, pre-aesthetic, music-as-life philosophy. To what, exactly, would the return be? The socio-spatial arrangements of music and of the soundscape before the specialist concert appeared were manifold. In any case, the new urban sound-environment possesses aspects which are radically new: decibel level; sound type; complexity of mix and trajectory; speed and heterogeneity of change. Similarly, the musical effects do not suggest a simple transition, but are full of dialectical movements and interpenetrations. For instance, the many kinds of popular music concert, disco and club performance would need a complicated analytical categorization; the 'distracted' environment of many club settings and the hushed concentration typical of singer-songwriter concerts might represent two extremes. The aesthetics of the 'live' recording – indeed the whole ideological debate surrounding the 'live'/'canned' dichotomy – would also repay attention.

The coming of the loudspeaker seems to represent a watershed. Its ambiguity enables it to move either towards a consolidation of univocal, single-directional specification of meaning, in abstraction from all context, or towards a 'mobile environmentalism', which would obscure the very distinction between 'text' and 'context', 'art' and 'life'. It contributes both to fantasies of time-capsule escape from everyday life (for example, domestic hi-fi set-up as pseudo-concert arrangement) and to post-auratic temporal and spatial flow (for example, carrying the portable transistor round the house).

Even given such contradictions, the effects of the new modes and situations of listening on the music itself, and its meaning, have been pronounced. All music, existing and newly produced, is unavoidably affected, its meaning becoming more obviously contingent. New collisions arise all the time, both between synchronically coexisting songs and styles, and between historical points of reference. Internal quotation and allusion, ironic mixes of style, revivals of older songs and styles, have become common in the 1970s and 1980s. More than ever, musical meaning is generated within a *field*, not a discrete work; and the non-autonomous aspects of this field lead one to think in terms of a complex system of socio-musical *ecology*.

In addition, the new conditions have fed back on to the production of the music itself. The increasingly positive valuation of repetition which can be sensed in post-1950 popular music, whether within a piece or as between pieces, can be related to the rise of non-auratic, 'field' listening. For Henri Lefebvre (1971a: 19), 'everyday life in the modern world' is a privileged site for the crucial fact of recurrence. The question of how to *end* a song now becomes pressing. The answer, often, is not to end: the harmonically inconclusive or artificially abrupt finish, or – quintessentially – the *fade*. As Sean Cubitt points out (1984: 210), this refers us

> to the activity of the auditor, with whom lies the only available fulfilment . . . [It] pledges that the performer . . . has an existence beyond the recording . . . This refusal of completion refers us, not back into the song, as is the case with the classic aesthetic object but outwards to the ways in which the song is heard.

At the meta-song level, the prevalence of pre-taped sequences (for shops, pubs, parties, concert intervals, aircraft headsets) emphasizes the importance of *flow*.

The effect on radio pop programme form – a stress on continuity achieved through use of fades, voice-over links, twin-turntable mixing and connecting jingles – makes this an important factor in the musical production itself. Not only are the meanings of individual songs affected by their positions in the flow, they are recorded in line with norms of dynamic and frequency range, duration and musical structure which will enable them to fit into the context (see Durant 1984: 106–7).

Finally, as these flows themselves collide in the wider listening environment, it may be possible to discern behind the apparent diversity of styles current in 1970s and 1980s pop, a new kind of 'systemic consistency'. This is not readily apparent to conventional analyses (which would look at harmonic structures, voice quality, lyric themes, and so on) but is linked, precisely, to the characteristics of the soundscape of everyday life: norms of (electric) sound; of (polyvocal) rhythm/texture mixes; of (short, often 'cross-talked') phrase-lengths. A song must fit the minimum requirements, but also mark its own presence, sometimes forcibly.

But what does all this have to say, if anything, about the *political* effects of the music's activity, about the directions of *control* governing its circulation around the networks of the megalopolitan ear? Are the older cultural questions – of manipulation *versus* self-direction, for example – simply cancelled? What we find is that such problems are relocated – pushed back to the level of the politics of everyday life itself (on this, see Chambers 1986; and on its specifically musical aspects, see Chambers 1985).

Thus, as well as the feedback of listening onto meaning and even production, what is also interesting is the *uses* to which the products can be put, *beyond* listening (in the conventional sense): hearing turning into interaction, and even, perhaps, into production. There are only glimpses; but they fit into a history, going back to the very beginnings of mass musical reproduction (through sheet music), in which the attempted 'closures' effected by specialized, centralized production are complemented by the opening-out offered by 'popular' assimilation: copying or parodying the stars, reproducing (reworking) famous originals, releasing aesthetically self-sufficient tunes into the flux of the street. Even faithful reproductions are the product of experiential ownership; and this experience may then stimulate variants or even new work (see Bennett 1980: 191–218). Analogous processes may operate for listeners, too. Music-users (listeners, urban pedestrians, dancers) often *sing along*, identifying with the vocal, appropriating the song, making the performance their own; forgotten or indecipherable lyrics may be replaced by substitutes – anything so long as the rhythmic-melodic articulation is maintained. The result may be more interesting than the original. Gino Stefani makes *appropriation* the chief criterion for his 'popular' definition of melody (Stefani 1987a). Melody, he argues, is music 'at hand'; it is that dimension which the common musical competence extracts (often with little respect for the integrity of the source), appropriates and uses for a variety of purposes: singing, whistling, dancing, and so on.

Here a modern musical ecology comes into relation with much older popular traditions, characterized by a continuous sifting, reworking and juxtaposing of heterogeneous musical sources to form new practices, a 'music of your own', as

János Maróthy calls it (1981). The very sound-levels of the pop-mediated soundscape have partly to do with corporeal appropriation. Rhythms are registered differentially by particular bodies, according to resonances and activities; thus the music's effects are activated by body-strategies as much as the reverse. This reaches a peak in Walkman practice. 'When we listen to the "beat" of our body, when the walkman intrudes inside the skin, the order of our body is inverted . . . the body is opened' (Hosokawa 1984: 176–7).

At times, modes of interaction can become more formalized. A visit to Japan set Charles Keil speculating just how important domestic 'sing-alongs' and 'play-alongs' to recordings might be in Western countries (Keil 1984). In Japan, he finds more public versions of such practices: men singing with records, then turning the sound down and continuing alone, into a mike; traditional-style dancing to music combining a recorded orchestra and live drummers; street musicians using their own percussion in conjunction with a megaphone-amplified cassette; and *karaoke* ('empty orchestra') bars, in which customers – in an atmosphere of conviviality and group support – use mikes and mixers to supply imitations (appropriations?) of missing lead vocals on specially produced tapes of the customer's choice. Keil interprets this as a personalization of mechanized processes. More recently, a further addition is the possibility to record the *karaoke* performance on video, against a pre-taped, appropriate visual setting. In either case, co-ordination of body movements with vocal expression is important (see Herd 1984: 82–3).

The practices of appropriation mentioned here are glimpses (no more) of the possibility of a new form of composition, inscribed within a new cultural ecology. This might – ultimately – supersede the category of art. It would be, in Enzensberger's words (1976: 36–7), an 'aesthetic which is not limited to the sphere of "the artistic" '. Composition in this sense comprises the (part-speculative) fourth stage in Jacques Attali's historical schema for a political economy of music (Attali 1985). According to Attali, 'repetition' (mass reproduction, his third stage) is in crisis. Overproduction leads to a devolution, even a universalizing, of cultural power among users, because the fantastic accessibility of music threatens all traditional 'uses' and communicative codes with destruction – music, all music, is just *there*. Attali's utopia is a situation in which 'production' and 'consumption' fuse in an autonomous creativity; here one would be able to make heard one's own voice, to compose one's own life, to create for oneself, outside any system of 'values'. Listening would then become truly part of productive practice; it would be, in Barthes' words (quoted in Attali 1985: 135), 'to put music into operation, to draw it towards an unknown practice'. In such 'pointless production', music would take on aspects of *carnival*, referring not to aesthetic values but the rhythms of the body, not to communication but collective creation, not to response but pleasure.

Reaching that state depends not simply on musical practice but on the politics of everyday life as such. In the repetitions, spontaneity and trivial details of everyday life, Henri Lefebvre has argued, the quotidian and the epic meet; and though the thrust of capitalist developments since the war has been towards rationalizing and commodifying even this last site of the irrational, it retains an extraordinary power, the desire of action and creation signified by all things and identified by none . . . residual and irreducible, it eludes all attempts at institutionalization, it evades the grip of forms. Everyday life is . . . the time of desire . . . extinction and rebirth (Lefebvre 1971a: 182).

The repetitions and trivialities of modern pop work through – in however compromised, reified forms – aspects of the epic/everyday dialectic. To the extent that its all-pervasiveness offers the means to wrench it away from its origins in exchange-circulation and appropriate it for daily practice, it offers a glimpse of an irreducible human reality.

Popular music's investigation of 'everyday life' (in its specifically modern sense) can be traced back certainly as far as early music hall song – to Sam Cowell, for example (see Gammon 1984); it is apparent in lyric content and in the deliberately cultivated banalities, 'hooks' and repetitions of the music. And the calculated images of conviviality which characterized the social relations of the halls, together with the love of parody,[16] represent an early attempt to mediate the spontaneities and vulgar irreverences of older popular traditions with the demands of capitalist enterprise (see Bailey 1986b). Popular music has drawn on this strategy ever since, just as its listeners have moved between distracted acquiescence and *flâneurist* irony. At the same time, of course, music hall also evolved a contrasting mode, in which a quasi-auratic cult of the star offers escape from the everyday into fantasy; the *lions comique* were the first focus (see Bailey 1986c). There are occasional examples of a 'shock' strategy, as perhaps in W.G. Ross's 'Sam Hall' with its celebrated 'damn yer eyes' refrain (see A. Bennett 1986: 5–6). And if we add contemporary industrial songs of protest, and possibly some other music hall acts of a surreal, life-overturning quality (Little Tich, Dan Leno), we have the outline of the three modes forming the matrix within which twentieth-century popular music has worked, together with their attendant functions: the everyday (distraction/participation/conviviality); the auratic (image/fantasy/narrative identification); the critical (shock/protest).

The interrelations and interpenetrations of these three modes define the arena for musical politics today. The manifold permutations and hybrids, affecting production and consumption, are matched by the varied opportunities for types and points of intervention. Within this matrix, any overall historical trend would in a sense be a description of the course of the argument between Adorno and Benjamin – from mass culture to a possible beyond – as well as a map of the changing state of musical practice.

Notes

1. Though the composer Hans Eisler, who collaborated with Brecht, did apply a similar approach to music. See Eisler (1978; 1948), though the latter is theoretically complicated by the – apparently quite extensive – contribution by Adorno. For a study of cinema sound drawing on aspects of Eisler (1948), see Levin (1984).
2. See especially 'the work of the art in the era of its mechanical reproducibility' (1973b: 219–53); 'The author as producer' (1973c: 85–103); 'what is epic theatre?' (1973b: 15–22; 1973c: 1–13). Arato (1977) and Paetzoldt (1977) offer useful summaries and critiques of Benjamin's argument.
3. For a critique of this article, see Baudrillard (1981: 164–84).
4. See Cutler (1984); and Cutler (1985b: 126–69, where Cutler 1984 is substantially reprinted, and *passim*).

5. On electronic technology in popular music see also Bacon (1981); Crombie (1982); Mackay (1981); Souster (1975).
6. For an example of the application of a McLuhanite view to popular music, see Laing (1969: 34–7).
7. There is a well-argued critique of the reification of notation by Shepherd and others in Green (1988: 130–6).
8. See also Williams (1981: 108–18). For similar arguments in respect of cinema, see Heath (1981c); and in respect of music, Durant (1984: 98–115); Frith (1986); Struthers (1987).
9. On the 'domestication' of popular music in this period by the BBC, see Frith (1983b).
10. For further examples amplifying this point, see Durant (1984: 211–22).
11. See also Frith (1988c: 205–25), which contains useful bibliographic references on music video.
12. For Britain and the USA, see, for example, Bailey (1986a); Barnard (1989); Bennett (1980); Chapple and Garofalo (1977); Denisoff (1975); Eberley (1982); Ehrlich (1985); Ewen (1964); Frith (1978; 1983a; 1986; 1987a, 1987b, 1988a); Gillett (1975, 1983); Goldberg (1961); Hardy (n.d.); Harker (1980); Hirsch (1969; 1971; 1972); Kealy (1979); Nanry (1972); Peacock and Weir (1975); Peterson (1982); Peterson and Berger (1971; 1975); Rogers (1964); Roth (1969); Sanjek (1988); Stokes (1976); Waites (1981); Whitcomb (1973; 1975). For France, see Hennion (1981); Hennion and Vignolle (1978); Hennion and Meadel (1986); for the Netherlands, see Rutten and Bouwman (n.d.); for West Germany, see Zeppenfeld (1979); for Hungary, see Szemere (1983). For more general works, see Gronow (1983); Blaukopf (1982), which contains studies of Canada, Sweden, Italy, Hungary, the USSR and Austria; and Wallis and Malm (1984).
13. See especially Williams (1977); for other useful theoretical work in this general area, see Hall (1977); Wolff (1981).
14. A phrase used by Jürgen Habermas; for a summary of the argument, see Held (1980: 267–95).
15. On listening in the era of 'electronic reproducibility', see Mowitt (1987).
16. Still alive in British 'folk' practices: see I. Russell (1987).

Part two

Taking a part:
Towards an analytical framework

4

'Change gonna come'? Popular music and musicology

The musicological problem

Musicology is 'the scientific study of music'. It 'must include every conceivable discussion of musical topics', being

the whole body of systematized knowledge about music which results from the application of a scientific method of investigation or research, or of philosophical speculation and rational systematization to the facts, the processes and the development of musical art, and to the relation of man in general . . . to that art (*Harvard Dictionary of Music*).

Musicology, then, is clearly a science which, above all others, should study popular music.

With a few exceptions (mostly recent), it has not done so. As a general rule works of musicology, theoretical or historical, act as though popular music did not exist. Sometimes it is explicitly condemned, as light, crass, banal, ephemeral, commercial or whatever; and sometimes it is patronized: all right in its way (for other people, that is) but not worth *serious* attention. Occasionally it is admitted to academia but shuffled sideways: very important but really a matter for sociologists rather than musicologists. And now and then it is actually taken seriously but misunderstood, through the application of inappropriate criteria, either negatively (Adorno) or positively (as when the Beatles are compared to Schubert, a comparison which tells us very little except about the process of *legitimation* being operated).

What is the explanation for this state of affairs? There are many fairly obvious reasons, ranging from the self-defensive elitism typical of craft mentalities to the long-established mistrust for any connection between music and commerce. But the underlying reason concerns *value*, hence *criteria*. Both condemnation and neglect, on the one hand, and misunderstanding, on the other, are motivated by hierarchically understood differences of 'cultural class' (which usually mediate social class differences as well). Both contemptuous and condescending musicologists are looking for types of production, musical form, and listening which they associate with a *different* kind of music – let us call it 'classical music' for now – and they generally find popular music lacking.

As will become clear later, it is not my intention to argue that musicology *cannot* understand popular music, or that students of popular music should abandon musicology. Nevertheless, it is true that the bundle of methods, assumptions and ideologies which came to constitute 'mainstream musicology' in the later nineteenth and the twentieth centuries renders it a less than useful resource in many ways. There are three main aspects of this problem.

The first is a terminology slanted by the needs and history of a particular music ('classical music'). This has two sides. On the one hand, there is a rich vocabulary for certain areas, important in musicology's typical corpus, and an impoverished vocabulary for others, which are less well developed there. Examples of the former are harmony (chord types, chord functions and relations), tonality, certain sorts of part-writing (counterpoint, homophony, and so on), and certain conceptions of form (motive, development, episode, and so on). Examples of the latter are rhythm, pitch nuance and gradation outside the steps of the diatonic/chromatic system, and timbre. On the other hand, terms are commonly ideologically loaded. 'Dissonance' and 'resolution' immediately suggest certain *harmonic* procedures, and a string of associated technical and emotional associations. 'Motive' immediately suggests Beethovenian symphonic development technique. Compare 'melody' (something graceful? Mozart?) and 'tune' (you whistle it in the street). 'Accidental', 'semitone', 'third', 'fifth', 'dominant seventh', and so on, can hardly be used without producing images relating to the processes of functional-tonal music. 'Syncopation' has the connotation of a *subversion* of the rhythmic norm (the regular beat) – though in many non-European musics this would not be appropriate. 'Drone' straightaway suggests something primitive, folkish. 'Ternary' (the basis of Tin Pan Alley ballad form) nevertheless brings to mind eighteenth-century minuets and operatic arias or nineteenth-century piano pieces. And so on.

These connotations are ideological because they always involve selective, and often unconsciously formulated, conceptions of what music *is*. If this terminology is applied to *other* kinds of music, clearly the results will be problematical. In many kinds of popular music, for example, harmony may not be the most important parameter; rhythm, pitch gradation, timbre and the whole ensemble of performance articulation techniques are often more important; 'dissonance' and 'resolution' may be produced by non-harmonic means (stop-time in rhythm and blues, for instance); 'motives' may be used not for 'development' but as 'hooks' or 'riffs'; drones may be an important and complex structural device (for instance, 'bottleneck' guitar variations on a single chord, in many blues songs).

The second aspect of the problem is a methodology slanted by the characteristics of notation. We have already seen (in Chapter 3) that notation inevitably imposes pressures and channels practice. The typical musicological corpus is notated, and is the product of those pressures and practices. Again there are two important aspects to the resulting 'notational centricity', as Philip Tagg calls it (1979: 28–32). In the first place it means that musicological methods tend to foreground those musical parameters which can be easily notated: discrete pitches within the diatonic/chromatic system; organized combinations of such pitches (chords) and of melodic parts using those pitches (counterpoint); mathematically simple durational relationships; through-composed structures (involving relationships of phrases, sections and movements, and thematic relationships and developments); combinations of voices and instruments (texture; orchestration). Conversely, they tend to neglect or have difficulty with parameters which are not easily notated: non-standard pitch and non-discrete pitch movement (slides, slurs, blue notes, microtones, and so on); irregular, irrational rhythms, polyrhythms, and rhythmic nuance (off-beat phrasing, slight delays, anticipations and speed-ups, and the complex durational relationships often involved in heterophonic and 'loose' part-playing, and overlapping antiphonal phrases); nuances of ornamentation, accent, articulation (attack, sustain, decay: what electronic musicians and sound engineers call the 'envelope') and performer idiolect; specificities (as opposed to abstractions) of timbre; not to mention new techniques developed in the recording studio, such as fuzz, wah-wah, phasing and reverberation. It is possible to develop forms of notation which will cope better with these parameters; many ethnomusicologists have tried to do so, especially for gradations of pitch and rhythm. But they are usually so complex as to be difficult to read and work with; in any case, mainstream musicology has shown little interest.[1]

These problems affect analysis directly, but they also have significant indirect effects. Notation-centric training induces particular forms of *listening*, and these then tend to be applied to *all* sorts of music, appropriately or not. An important part of conventional musicological training is in the skill of score-reading-with-'inner-hearing'. But what is 'heard' is strongly guided by what has been really – predominantly – heard in the past (notated music, in which the parameter biases noted above apply) and by the score's propensity, in its very layout and in the nature of the act of scanning, to privilege acts of aural abstraction, synchronization, blending and arranging in hierarchy. A training in harmony focused on producing imitations of J.S. Bach's chorale arrangements left me with a seemingly ineradicable tendency to concentrate hearing, real and inner, on the functional-harmonic properties of the bass (important in Bach's style but not necessarily in, say, rock harmony,[2] or in soul and funk bass lines). It needs a considerable act of sociological sympathy to grasp that other listeners may actually hear different things, or hear them in different relationships.

The second aspect of 'notational centricity' is its tendency to encourage reification: the score comes to be seen as 'the music', or perhaps the music in an ideal form. In one stroke, this downgrades the vagaries of performance, the productive significance of variants, and the influence of performance context; practice is frozen into symbol. Not surprisingly, the resulting habits of mind are then applied to non-notated music too. In a sense, the recording – to the extent that it too 'freezes' performance – does continue to legitimate this approach: though this is to obscure the dialectic of objectification and practice going on there (after all, the recording stores performance, not symbols, and it is only usable analytically in real time). In any case, the musicological mind tends to regard the recording as a source for extracting the 'fundamentals' of the music, its 'framework', and condensing them into a score, either real or mental; my own training, for instance, makes it very hard for me not to 'see' harmonic progressions in notated form as I listen, and these are then (perhaps unwarrantably) foregrounded.

It should be stressed again that notation is not as such determinative of practice. We should distinguish between the *practices* of 'classical music' – which encompassed a variety of notational forms and of relationships between score and performance – and its *musicology*, which, as we shall see in a moment, derived its methods and assumptions from a *particular* practice, manifesting an extreme notational centricity.

Clearly the application of notation-centric methods to popular music may be problematical. Of course, as we saw in Chapter 3, many forms of popular music have been and are notated. To that extent, the difficulty is not an absolute one, and it can be legitimate to make use of such scores as exist. Nevertheless, in most forms of Afro-American and white country music, in most Western popular music since rock 'n' roll, not to mention Third World hybrids, the 'non-notatable parameters' are of great and often predominant importance. Conversely, the 'notatable parameters' are often reduced in importance, or used in different ways (chords used in parallel, in a kind of 'thickened heterophony', rather than functionally; 'part-writing' transformed into polyvocal, quasi-pointillist, often largely percussive textures; diatonic tunes used as vehicles for, *obliterated* by, vocal persona; and so on). In these contexts score-derived thinking seriously distorts what is going on.

Even in notated popular music – Tin Pan Alley ballad, music hall, vaudeville and minstrel songs, ragtime and nineteenth-century dances – the published sheet music, almost always for piano or voice and piano, sometimes 'simplified', acted to some extent as a prognostic device or a beside-the-fact spin-off. For most listeners, the primary 'text' was the performance, usually in a specific, unpublished arrangement, made for live playing or for recording. Thus the particular performers involved would be more important than the composers – certainly this was the case for music hall and Tin Pan Alley songs – and the performed variant represented 'the music' more than the score did. Even here, then, notation-derived thinking, while by no means irrelevant, is at best partial and at worst can distort actual musical practice, affecting understanding and valuation. In all these cases, it is misleading to extract pieces, as completed objects, from socio-musical practice, where their meaning and function are defined. Even recordings do their *work* in particular contexts where they are heard. As Bennett points out (1980: 108–11), popular music is defined, internally categorized and analysed in terms of diverse social practices as much as in terms of discrete compositions.

The third aspect of the 'musicological problem' is an ideology slanted by the origins and development of musicology itself. This took place in intimate relationship with the development of a particular body of music and its aesthetic. Musicology is not historically neutral; it has not 'always been there'. It arose at a specific moment, in a specific context – nineteenth-century Europe, especially Germany – and in close association with that movement in the musical *practice* of the period which was codifying the very repertory then taken by musicology as the centre of its attention. That movement produced the idea of a body of music, a 'tradition', which we would think of now as 'classical', centred on the work of the Austro-German 'great masters' from Bach and Handel to Mahler, Richard Strauss and Schoenberg, and forming the core of the emerging bourgeois concert repertory. It found its philosophical grounding in the aesthetic and historical theories of German idealism.

The construction of a 'classical' repertory went hand in hand with the construction of a new audience (see Weber 1975; Dahlhaus 1967), and both were legitimated by a historical-aesthetic vision stressing the gradual emergence of music as an autonomous, transcendent form with cognitive value (it opened a window on Truth, rather than simply providing social pleasures). Sometimes the connection between practice and musicology was explicit. The nineteenth-century revival of J.S. Bach was both an exercise in scholarship and in aesthetics; the cult of Beethoven attracted – and was built up by – musicologists and historians, on the one hand, and practitioners and listeners, on the other; the 'historical concerts' which became common in the mid-nineteenth century had didactic as well as aesthetic functions. The result, typically, was an evolutionary sense of history (progress being usually defined in terms of structural complexity, 'intellectual' level and expressive capacity), intertwined with the notion of a *canon* of 'good music'.

Subsequently, the musicological corpus has been expanded; but even today, pretensions to scientific comprehensiveness have not destroyed the centrality of a concept of 'art' music which is derived from a particular historical practice. Similarly, methods have been considerably modified – for example, through the influence of positivist historiography, cultural historians and hermeneutics – but still, for the core of musicology, the main assumptions remain strong: works are autonomous; art has transcendent qualities; the individual, the genius, the 'great man' (*sic*) should be the focus of historical explanation; listening should be detached and contemplative, and analysis therefore text-centred. What has happened is, of course, the result of a reciprocal relationship between musical practice and what Foucault calls discursive formation, the hierarchy of values and legitimations in the one reflecting and producing that in the other, the whole complex intimately connected with social class structure. (At the simplest level, idealist and formalist notions of 'art' clearly perform the useful function for the bourgeoisie of removing the sphere of culture out of the immediate context of social meaning, argument and struggle into the pure realms of the Absolute, while conveniently insisting on this class's ownership of the 'highest' values.)

Actually, it could easily be argued that this approach is less than completely suitable even for 'classical' music – hence, for instance, the misleading tendency to 'universalize' the Bachs, Handels, and Beethovens out of their historically specific roughnesses, to undervalue the Liszts, Chopins and Tchaikovskys (who are hard to 'universalize') and to 'whitewash' a composer like Mozart, whose music was widely regarded in his lifetime not as manifesting 'transcendent grace', 'absolute beauty' or somesuch but as breaking the bounds of 'form' and constituting a threat to social order. When we come to popular music, it is obvious that such an approach is likely to create great problems. Indeed, a tentative definition of 'popular music' – or, to be more precise, of tendencies which typically exert popular pressure within the musical field – would probably stress precisely such factors as ephemerality (that is, contemporaneity), socially significant form and technique, performance rather than fixed text, the experiential rather than the abstract.

The musicological approach – some examples

Terminology; methodology; ideology: the effects of these three interlinked aspects of the 'musicological problem' run so deep that they can be found even in the work – often very useful work – of scholars sympathetic to, and knowledgeable about, popular music.[3]

Alec Wilder's imposingly thorough survey of Tin Pan Alley and Broadway songs from the first half of the century, *American Popular Song* (1972), can, because of its very choice of subject, claim a certain degree of legitimacy for its main aim: to discuss the *texts* (the sheet music), relatively free from wider considerations. Similarly, the undoubted importance of harmonic structure in this repertory makes his focus on that parameter defensible. Nevertheless, the resulting approach is dangerously one-sided.

Wilder's criteria for assessment are *innovation* and *honesty*. The first he is clear about:

> while many of them [popular songs] deserved their popularity they simply do not possess the innovative quality with which I am concerned and which this study is all about. In the choosing of songs I have set up arbitrary qualitative rules which often may seem academic to the point of snobbishness. So I must repeat that my primary concern is to demonstrate how a popular art form can rise to the dignity and grace of a non-popular art form, and to contend that popularity does not automatically presuppose or demand pedestrian or 'hack' invention (ibid: 389).

There are at least two problems with this. The first is that 'innovation' is defined almost entirely in terms of melody and harmony, where it is assumed to operate through *surprise* (that note was unexpected, that chord gave a buzz of broken conventions, that progression was unpredictable) and through *complexity* (thus the often elaborate chords of Cole Porter and George Gershwin come out well, as do the distant modulations of a song like 'Body and Soul'). Why this should be so is not explained. The second problem is that, whatever else these songs may be, they *are* popular songs. The fact that there does not seem to be any necessary relationship between their popularity and the presence or absence of 'innovation', as Wilder defines it, needs to be accounted for, particularly the popularity of those lacking in 'quality'. Wilder (ibid: 92) asserts that

> to [Irving] Berlin, as well as to many other song writers, a *good* song and a *hit* song are synonymous. Therefore, it is doubly remarkable . . . that Berlin wrote so many songs which deserve to be praised for musical reasons rather than because they were hits.

The second sentence is an inadequate solution to the problem posed in the first. Not surprisingly, Wilder has some difficulty accounting for the success of the 'musically uninteresting' 'Alexander's Ragtime Band'. Indeed, the incipient elitism of this approach is not far below the surface: paradoxically, given his own stress on harmony, Wilder claims that 'very few non-musicians hear any harmony, good or bad' (ibid: 230).

The only other principle put forward which might serve as an explanation for this state of affairs is in fact Wilder's second criterion. This is the quality of *honesty*, and it is reserved for less 'innovative' songs. But nowhere is it clearly defined. It seems to be something like 'unpretentious craftsmanship'; but what, in the context of popular music, is this, exactly?

To get further than this, Wilder would surely need to pay much more attention than he does to the context within which these songs had their effects – both the social context and the wider musical context of contemporary practice constituted by a variety of styles (blues, jazz, dance-band, show) and performing situations (nightclub, movie, theatre, radio, and so on). Similarly, he would need to place substantial weight on the importance of *performance*, and the variants and charismatic appeal it might convey. Ironically, some of the most interesting moments in the book are when Wilder does remark on common performer variants; often he prefers these to the sheet music versions – but this point, potentially of cardinal significance, is always treated as a passing detail. After all, the popularity of these songs was associated not with the published texts but with particular *performances* and *arrangements*. Wilder's good-tempered aversion for the 'mass produced song' – a derivative of the industry's own cynicism (he was a song writer himself) – certainly provides good material for a refutation of Adornian critiques of Tin Pan Alley; but only on the same musicological ground as the critiques themselves use, that of 'quality'. This is its limitation – and explains why the book ends at the onset of rock 'n' roll, refusing to join in 'grotesquely extravagant tributes to the creations of untutored amateurs' (ibid: 29).

Charles Hamm's *Yesterdays* (1979) deals in part with the same material as Wilder, but within the context of a complete history of American popular song – or rather, a particular stratum of that song: for as we have seen already (p. 5 above), Hamm's criteria of 'popularity' severely restrict his selection of subject-matter. And, despite the invaluable data and analysis contained in his narrative, this is where problems begin. Part of Hamm's definition insists that a popular song is 'a piece . . . in physical form' (ibid: vii) and this leads inevitably to a focus on *texts*. One result is a pretty rigid demarcation between the mass-selling commercial products and the wider sphere of (especially lower-class) musical practice – not only in the sense that the latter is largely excluded from the discussion but also in the sense that its influence on the former, the industry products' influence on *it*, and indeed the whole interplay between the two in musical and social practice, are played down. Thus, for example, Tin Pan Alley publishers 'had little or no knowledge of the Anglo-American and Afro-American music that was the native musical language of many millions of Americans . . . Tin Pan Alley did not draw on traditional music – it created traditional music' (ibid: 325). (What about the coon and ragtime songs? Or the fact that many songwriters spent time in lower-class haunts to pick up ideas and generally feel the pulse of the market? 'Ta Ra Ra Boom Deay' was born in a St Louis brothel.) At the same time, commercial songs 'remained practically unknown to large segments of American society, including most blacks . . . and the millions of poor, white, rural Americans' (ibid: 379) – but what about dance-band record-ings – black and white – of Tin Pan Alley tunes in the 1920s and 1930s? The increasing ubiquity of networked radio, on which these songs were pervasive? Not to mention a statement like Little Richard's: 'I came from a family where my people didn't like rhythm and blues. Bing Crosby – "Pennies from Heaven" – Ella Fitzgerald, was all I heard' (quoted in ibid: 391).[4]

It is almost as if the history of popular music is taken to be represented by a series of 'important' songs, extracted from the wider musical context which gave rise to them – much as historians of 'classical' music used to construct their histories simply out of a selection of 'great' works. One result is that *indirect* influence is played down; thus, James Bland's minstrel songs are disconnected from any links with Southern black folk music because his 'musical environment . . . was the minstrel stage, not the plantation' (ibid: 276) – but what of the pre-existing network joining plantation and minstrelsy? Moreover, the emphasis on a core of best-selling songs means that other trends and influences are minimized. Charles Harris's and Paul Dresser's turn-of-the-century songs are fully discussed, but the many 'coon' songs are not, and ragtime song is cursorily treated. This enables Hamm to deny the importance of black input in shaping the new, specifically 'American' style of early Tin Pan Alley (whereas Wilder insists on this). Similarly, the whole jazz and swing context to Tin Pan Alley song of the 1920s and 1930s is marginalized, treated as at most an adjunct in the dissemination of the songs, not as an active ingredient in a music culture. The resulting historical continuities in Hamm's narrative are *real*; but they are only one part of the picture. What is striking – and in need of explanation – about this picture, then, previously and in subsequent years, is precisely the *interplay* between the 'industry' and the wider musical culture, including its 'oral' and lower-class components.

The methodological focus on *texts* means that sometimes important distinctions of category or meaning are missed or simplified. Thus 'rock' becomes all one category; so does Tin Pan Alley song between the wars (ibid: 465ff., 337–9). Now there is a sense in which this is true (especially if you look at texts); but the effects, meanings and cultural associations of, say, early rock 'n' roll and Californian 'acid rock' can hardly be elided, nor those of 'hot', 'jazz age' numbers from the early 1920s and 'smooth', 'sophisticated' Broadway songs of the late 1930s. Elsewhere (1980: 115), Hamm describes punk as nothing more than a continuation of rock musical traditions (but what a continuation!), and is forced to describe the effect of the most successful musicians in terms of mystification: the Beatles 'were successful because they were enormously talented in using familiar musical elements to create songs of such apparent simplicity that one wonders why other musicians could not or did not do just what they were doing'.

The general problem here is a lack of concern with *practice* – how all these texts worked as *culture*. Hamm is aware of the importance and effects of informal networks of musical dissemination,[5] but he does not draw the implications of this into his method. This leads to a familiar music-historical approach which centres on great men's texts, treating them in terms of the influences to be discerned and the development of an integrated personal style. Stephen Foster, for example, is described this way, and, despite the insights, we are left wondering about the reason for his particular stylistic fusion. What did it mean to Foster and his audience? What was the nature of its appeal? As with Wilder, this kind of focus also makes it difficult to explain the impact of simple, unexceptional songs – and this despite the fact that one of Hamm's criteria for defining popular song is simplicity: it must be easy to grasp (see, for example, Hamm 1979: xvii, 11 258–9, 341).

Within the focus on texts, the main stress is on structure and harmony. The appropriateness of this approach varies; but when Hamm (ibid: 395–6) comes to rock 'n' roll, where it is patently less appropriate than for earlier periods, the musical analysis becomes sketchy – the vocabulary and the methods are simply not there. Similarly, aspects of rhythm and timbre coming into pre-rock 'n' roll popular song from black sources are described as exotic flavourings (ibid: 358, 372, 385) – which in turn is why Tin Pan Alley song can be described as relatively little influenced by black music.

The textual focus leads, too, to a neglect of *performance*, which is treated, often, as an adjunct, merely a means of disseminating pre-existing musical objects: all that changed was the 'sound' (!).[6] For Berndt Ostendorf (n.d.: 4–5), this provides an explanation of Hamm's denial of important black influence in Tin Pan Alley song:

> Charles Hamm looks for provable, textual evidence of cultural transfer or adoption, his tracking device being musicological analysis . . . on the basis of scores . . . But is not the score . . . the European grid which fails to capture much of what makes 'Africa' swing? Hence whatever surfaces in notation has undergone the preventive censorship of what one might call the imperialism of Western literacy . . . The late nineteenth century was an age of 'productive misunderstanding' . . . among America's ethnics . . . [and] the problem becomes infinitely . . . complex when we consider that . . . stolen 'texts' or 'scores' could be changed by performance; black stuff could be whitened, white stuff blackened . . . [7]

And in a fascinating argument, Ostendorf (n.d.: 15–20) suggests that turn-of-the-century Tin Pan Alley song was actually *dominated* by ethnic outsiders, a kind of black/Jewish alliance of the dispossessed and oppressed. He quotes Lewis Erenberg (1981):

> Staffed by songwriters of immigrant and at times black origin, Tin Pan Alley brought syncopating out of the red light districts and into the larger society. Many of the songwriters were Jews . . . Irving Berlin was one; he was the son of an orthodox cantor who had lost much of his authority in success-oriented America. He was at home in the streets, that marginal land between his own culture and the culture of his new society. The streets presented a world of constant experience and action, there was excitement at every turn and where the choices and sights could provide feelings of constant experience of the self uprooted from a stable past. Working in the city's dives, he took his speech and rhythm from the city streets, from Yiddish intonations, and from Italian, Yiddish, black and Irish voices and caricatures he found around him.

Pointing out that 'many of these Jewish and other immigrants did not share the scruples of the host society against blacks', Ostendorf argues that Jewish songwriters like Berlin and singers like Sophie Tucker, Al Jolson, Eddie Cantor and Jimmy Durante acted as mediators of black culture, routing it through their own sense of marginality. In this situation, the key characteristics were improvisation, interaction with the audience, an ability to switch moment by moment between multiple codes.

The sheet music does not necessarily tell the whole story, then. Moreover, the developments it reveals may not have only one cause or meaning. Thus the growth of more chromatic harmony which Hamm rightly describes in Tin Pan Alley song of the 1930s may represent a *confluence*: an evolution in *composers'* harmonic language, on the one hand; the desire of *performers* to expand the microtonal aspects of the melodic line, on the other. All those chromatic chords certainly play a functional harmonic role; but they also allow the potential for a lot of note-bending and sliding. Much of Duke Ellington's music, combining complex chromatic harmonies and bluesy improvising soloists like Bubber Miley and Johnny Hodges, was *built* on this principle; but it also applies to many singers of Tin Pan Alley material – Billie Holiday for example, or many Jewish singers, whose ethnic musical heritage can certainly be aligned with the microtonal elements in black vocal technique.

Wilfrid Mellers's books on the Beatles and Bob Dylan (1973; 1984)[8] pay much more attention to performance than Charles Hamm's work; indeed, he stresses the analytic centrality of what is heard, and warns that 'written notation can represent neither the improvised elements nor the immediate distortions of pitch and flexibilities of rhythm which are the essence (not a decoration) of a music orally and aurally conceived' (Mellers 1973: 15). Both books are essentially dissections and interpretations of the recorded outputs of their subjects. Nevertheless, in the Beatles book music quotations do play a central role. Moreover, these are not transcriptions of what has been recorded but extracts from the published sheet music – despite the fact that Mellers recognizes such publications to be 'after-events' supplying an often incorrect approximation of the recording. The problems which ensue are obvious. Important elements (drums, for example) are excluded; vocal nuances (for instance, rhythmic articulation and pitch inflection) are simplified out; and texture and sound are misrepresented through piano arrangement layout.

In the Dylan book, Mellers accepts the distorting effects of these problems and abandons notation. This is an important advance – though it brings its own problems, for it now becomes quite difficult to talk clearly and in depth about harmony and melody at all. Moreover, though the renunciation of scores seems to move Mellers's attention away from the notatable parameters and towards a greater interest in 'performed detail', this also brings into clearer focus the paucity of analytic vocabulary for the non-notatable parameters. So these details can be only vaguely described: 'wavering' microtones, 'teetering' irregular rhythms, 'cawing' vocal timbre, and so on. Similarly, discussion of a Beatles song like 'I Wanna Be Your Man' can only talk of 'nervously driving rhythm', 'continuously misplaced vocal accents', a 'raucous voice' (ibid: 39).

In the Beatles book, Mellers insists on the necessity for, and the appropriateness of, the 'accepted terminology' of the musicological tradition (ibid: 15–16). But this terminology acts like a sieve, letting anything foreign to its sphere of competence escape, and, moreover, setting its own observations within a powerful ideological context. Thus, when the second strain of 'Things We Said Today' is described as having 'tonal movement flowing from

B♭ by way of a rich dominant ninth to E♭: the subdominant triad of which then serves as a kind of Neapolitan cadence drooping back (without the linking dominant) to the grave pentatonic G minor' (ibid: 47), nothing in the description is *wrong*, but we are straightway pressed into a world constructed by *functional harmonic movement* (dominants, Neapolitan cadences). In fact, what happens at this point in the music seems to me to have more to do with implicitly *anti*-functional tendencies: on the one hand, the techniques of 'barbershop harmony', which in turn derive from methods using *repeated circles* of chords, and, on the other hand, the use of *parallel* harmonic side-slips originating in guitar playing.

Not surprisingly, both Wilfrid Mellers's books privilege the areas of tonality, melodic contour and, especially, harmony. This is, still, the case in the Dylan book, but it is particularly striking in the earlier work on the Beatles, where almost any analysis can be taken as an example of the way harmonic progressions are automatically seen as the most interesting, the most interpretatively important, aspects of the music. Thus the tonality and harmony of 'I Saw Her Standing There' receive detailed description, while the rhythm is just 'fairly complex, with rudimentary African affiliations . . . [and] a certain corporeal energy' (ibid: 34–5), and the vocal timbre – very important I suspect to the song's effect – is unmentioned. Similarly with a song like 'The Word'. This has 'tonic and subdominant triads accompanying a love-call rising upwards in parallel thirds, then descending. The tonic minor triads formed by the voice part are underpinned by false related tonic major triads in the guitars, giving the song a runic wildness; and false relations between triads of D major and B flat major occur too, syncopated, in the descending answering phrase' (ibid: 65). But there is no mention of the heavy, syncopated bass line, the stabbing backbeat accents on guitar and piano, or the fact that many of the phrases, vocal and bass, are *riffs*: together these account for a large part of the driving, invigorating effect of the song. Again, the 'surreal' effect of 'Strawberry Fields Forever' is attributed almost entirely to its unusual harmonic progressions, with some contribution from its irregular phrase lengths and speech-rhythms (ibid: 84). But surely an equally large role is played by the *sound*, both of the vocal and of the instrumental/electronic backing, which goes unremarked.[9]

A partially valid defence of Mellers's approach would be that in the context of rock the Beatles do use comparatively complex harmony and do draw more than most on Tin Pan Alley harmonic methods. What is necessary is to see the Beatles as standing *between* different musical methods and traditions, and for this a methodological overweighting of harmony is no less misleading than culture-centric interpretation: for example, the tonality of E major may have specified 'Eden' to Schubert, in line with eighteenth-century theories of key-associations, but it is doubtful whether, as Mellers's analyses sometimes suggest, it does to the Beatles, Bob Dylan or their listeners.

The Beatles are taken to be the most interesting rock group because their music is 'the best'; in what sense this is the case is not precisely specified, but it seems to have less to do with musical skill than with the honesty to experience attributed to their texts. Similarly, it is assumed that it is valid to take Dylan's songs as self-contained, individual statements with a definite, decipherable meaning and an autonomous reality. Now there is no doubt that both the Beatles and Dylan were 'originals', who had widespread influence and possessed great talent; at the same time, it is open to question whether this kind of 'concentration on the text' is sufficient, or in some cases appropriate, for *any* popular songs. Is the individual song the only, or even the basic unit of meaning – rather than larger discursive categories (genre, style, performers, album, radio programme, and so on) and the context provided by social practices (dancing, partying, driving, discussing)? Does the song's meaning exist outside precise conditions of consumption, and can it be linked solely to the intentions of an individual *auteur* without detailed consideration of the conditions of production? Certainly the Beatles and Bob Dylan created personal *oeuvres*; but their development was intimately intertwined with the general history of popular music from the late 1950s on, and with changing structures of the music industry and of the audience.

There is very little of that context in these two books: influences on the Beatles (rhythm and blues, acid rock, Dylan) and on Dylan (rock 'n' roll, the Beatles, the Rolling Stones); technological changes; details of production (to what extent can the Beatles and Bob Dylan be held compositionally responsible for their recordings?); the political and social situations (the cold war, Vietnam, 'Social Democratic consensus', the counterculture, Swinging Britain, and so on); the cultural market (youth consumption, and so on). That makes it impossible to situate the significance of the music within the context of its popularity; it becomes semi-transcendent. For instance, the change in the Beatles' audience (from rockers and teenyboppers to countercultural freaks), and the *decline* in popularity suffered by Dylan in the 1970s, are not mentioned, still less related to changes in the music. Which means that, for instance, Dylan's post-*Blonde on Blonde* development can only be described in terms of a self-justifying personal odyssey.

The purpose of this discussion of three notable authors, whose work has made a significant contribution to our understanding of popular music, is not criticism for criticism's sake; it is to try to reveal the ideological underpinnings of the assumptions shared by all those trained in the traditional musicological disciplines. As a rule, musicological writing on popular music is related, ideologically, to the general 'mass-culture critique' position. Wilder's elitism is clear: of 'Body and Soul' he writes, 'the miracle is that the public not only accepted this song, they've gone on accepting it for forty years' (Wilder 1972: 428). By contrast, there is not a trace of snobbery in Charles Hamm's writings. Indeed, his respect for measurable popularity and for mass musical pleasures marks him perhaps as a populist. But the ties binding this inversion to its origins are revealed by the historical and analytical method, with its tendency to separate written form from performance and both from cultural practice, resulting inevitably in a model of popular song as the music of 'ordinary' people, defined by its *simplicity*. 'After the Ball' or 'She Loves You' certainly look simple on the page; but whether the cultural phenomena represented by their performance, dissemination, emotional effects and audience appeal are best described as 'simple', sociologically, semiotically or aesthetically, is another matter.

In yet another variant, Wilfrid Mellers might be described as a kind of 'enlightened Leavisite' (he was a student at Leavis's Cambridge, and later worked for *Scrutiny*). He extends the Leavisite method – cultural critique and moral seriousness allied to close scrutiny of texts – in an 'enlightened' way, in the sense that he is prepared to recognize the possibility of 'creativity' surfacing *within* the products of the commercial culture industries. He accepts that

> in a machine-made world we must expect to find two contradictory types of art which do their best to cancel one another out. One kind gallantly (and precariously) keeps flying the flag of the human spirit; the other exploits mechanistic techniques to prostitute the spirit for material gain (Mellers 1964: p. 239).

But he goes on to argue that the distinction is not absolute nor correlated totally with a distinction between 'art' and 'commerce'. Simply transferring pop stars from 'mass civilization' to 'minority culture' does not overturn the concepts, however. What is misleading is the reified opposition of concepts – as though 'the creative spirit whenever and wherever we may meet it' (ibid: 234) was always just there, to be either fulfilled or repressed, rather than different *kinds* of creative or (better) productive practice being characteristic of different societies and cultural values. Thus for Mellers the only salvation for commercial popular music is if it becomes something else (art, folk, ritual, . . .). But Beethoven's heroic humanism was not separable from his sense and exploitation of market freedom, any more than the Beatles' most heart-stopping love-songs were separable from their relationship with the leisure consumerism of post-war youth.

Towards a new musicology

In a not dissimilar critique of musicological methods, Charles Keil describes Western musical analysis, by virtue of its dependence on notation, as *syntactic* (Keil 1966b). It centres, he argues, on the hierarchic organization of quasi-linguistic elements and their putting together (com-position) in line with systems of norms, expectations, surprises, tensions and resolutions. The resulting aesthetic is one of 'embodied meaning'. In contrast to this, he says, non-notated musics – and *performances* of written music to some extent – foreground *process*. They are much more concerned with gesture, physical feel, the immediate moment, improvisation; the resulting aesthetic is one of 'engendered feeling' and is unsuited to the application of 'syntactic' criteria. Andrew Chester (1970) posits a similar opposition of 'extensional' and 'intensional' musical practices.

> Western classical music is the appdigm of the *extensional* form of musical construction. Theme and variations, counterpoint, tonality (as used in classical composition) are all devices that build diachronically and synchronically outwards from basic musical atoms. The complex is created by combination of the simple, which remains discrete and unchanged in the complex unity . . . If those critics who maintain the greater complexity of classical music specified that they had in mind this *extensional* development, they would be quite correct . . . Rock however follows, like many non-European musics, the path of intensional development. In this mode of construction the basic musical units (played/sung notes) are not combined

through space and time as simple elements into complex structures. The simple entity is that constituted by the parameters of melody, harmony and beat, while the complex is built up by modulation of the basic notes, and by inflexion of the basic beat. All existing genres and sub-types of the Afro-American tradition show various forms of combined intensional and extensional development (ibid: 78–9).

Other writers have mounted similar arguments. We have already noted Philip Tagg's discussion of 'notational centricity' and its inappropriateness for popular music analysis. John Shepherd has also attacked musicological distortion of popular music (Shepherd 1982). Bennett, too, agrees about the distorting effects of notation and notation-centric analysis for many kinds of popular music, and he argues further that, certainly for rock music, 'the composition' and 'compositional technique' may anyway be less important analytic categories than the culturally defined criteria of musicians and listeners themselves, which are often extra-musical: 'types are culturally produced categories which could be applied to diverse compositional patterns' (Bennett 1980: 111; see also ibid: 106–14). Antoine Hennion goes so far as to deny the possibility of a musicology of popular songs altogether, because, he says, they have no objective meaning or form, only taking these on empirically, in specific modes of production on the one hand, in social contexts of consumption on the other (Hennion 1981: 221ff.; 1983). They must therefore be analysed *there*, and there only.

In part, Hennion's method is an ethnography of the production process. In the light of the problems with musicological terminology mentioned earlier, his descriptions of studio practice in the musicians' own terms pay dividends, as Tagg points out (1983: 311):

> a 'dry' acoustic guitar track is mixed 'up front' while the drummer asks for a 'wet, muffled' sound and the producer wants the Fender piano to be 'heavier' (*'plus poilu'*) and more 'explosive', not so 'rickety tin can'. Then the singer wonders whether the end of a particular phrase should be left musically 'in the air', the guitarist asks if the others want him to play 'jazz' or 'wham bam' (*'paf-paf'*) and if the engineer can 'boost/inflate/thicken' (*'gonfler'*) his sound by adding an extra octave or fifth through the harmoniser. The producer thinks a certain synthesiser timbre should have less 'buzz', be less 'mechanical' but still sound 'synthetic'. The keyboard player applies 'breathing' (*'respiration'* – crescendo + diminuendo) to each note but the singer finds that too 'gurgly-gobbly', not 'majestic' or 'symphonic' enough, though she admits that it should still sound 'crazy' and 'neurotic' to fit the lyrics *'quand le mec devient fou'*. Sounds are further described by musicians, singer, producer and sound engineer as 'American', 'hard and heavy', 'tense and speedy' (a rock number), 'sensitive', 'cool', 'ironic', 'throbbing with pain', 'violent but discrete', 'crackly', 'sea green', 'beyond the tomb', 'vampirish', 'drooling organ', 'majestic with a hangover', 'police siren', etc., etc.

But there are dangers here. By *sticking* at the level of ethnographic description, Hennion cannot get any deeper, analytically, than this; he cannot – and does not try to – link the terms and criteria of musicians and audience with an independent account of what actually happens in the music, so he is not able to *explain* how the music works and has its effects. By associating musicology *as such* with 'classical' music and completely separating that sphere from the sphere of popular music, he throws away any chance of musical analysis.

There is in fact a common tendency for the 'critique of musicology' to go too far. This is particularly true of the 'popular' versions which have become widespread in the popular music culture itself. Typically, these display either a retreat into sociology – the music interpreted solely in terms of the social categories into which the industry or the fans can be fitted – or an aggressive 'insiderism', which stresses that interpretation is 'intuitive', 'anti-academic' and intrinsic to the music culture itself. Underlying these attitudes is generally an assumption that popular music, especially recent genres, is *completely* different from 'academic' music, an antithesis; often this assumption is grounded in a naive revolutionism, which sees rock music as representing a decisive *break*. Now I, too, have been emphasizing the methodological implications of popular music's difference, but such totalizing views are misleading, resting on an inadequate historical knowledge or on an undialectical notion of the musical field. Between recent types of popular music and historical traditions of popular, so-called folk, and even bourgeois music stretching back at least as far as the sixteenth century, there are innumerable links and parallels. In a fascinating study, Van der Merwe has documented many examples connecting techniques of traditional African musics, of 'folk' styles in Britain, and of the offspring of both in America (Van der Merwe 1989).[10] There is, evidently, a kind of subterranean stratum, in which the strength of traditions and the rearticulatory force applied to 'extraneous' materials impose major continuities.

Thus some blues and rock bass patterns can be traced back to sixteenth-century dance music. The *passamezzo moderno*, one of the most popular harmonic formulae in the Renaissance period, divides into two complementary strains thus: I | IV | I | V ‖ I | IV | I-V | I ‖; and it appears in, for example, the Beatles' 'I Saw Her Standing There' (Ex. 4.1), having never died in the intervening

'I Saw Her Standing There' (verse 1), as sung by the Beatles (1963)

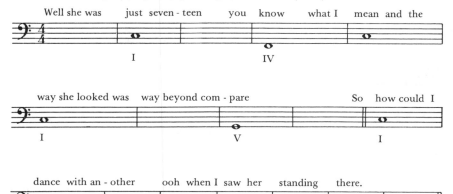

Ex 4.1

'Don't Let Me Be Misunderstood' (opening), as sung by the Animals (1965)

Ex 4.2a

'When A Man Loves A Woman' (opening), as sung by Percy Sledge (1966)

Ex 4.2b

centuries. Van der Merwe, indeed, sees the twelve-bar blues harmonic sequence as developing out of the *passamezzo moderno*; this is both plausible and a shock to the conventional view, which sees the likely source as nineteenth-century hymns. Similarly, the descending scalar bass-lines so popular as 'grounds' for passacaglias and sets of variations in the sixteenth and seventeenth centuries survive in twentieth-century popular music (Ex. 4.2).

In the eighteenth century – at least in written music – patterns built on scalic basses or on I-IV-V chord sequences were supplemented and to some extent eclipsed by circle-of-fifths patterns (e.g. VI-II-V-I). These have also remained popular (Ex. 4.3).

Melodically, the typically arching shapes of pop ballad tunes go back to the beginnings of bourgeois song (Ex. 4.4). And rhythmically too, how easy it would be to turn many sixteenth-century dances into punk songs (Ex: 4.5).

These few examples – chosen almost at random – stand for a major network of relationships. Ways of forming melody, cadencing and organizing tension and resolution which are found in seventeenth-century opera, eighteenth-century concerto and nineteenth-century *Lied* retain their influence still, however modified and contested, in 1980s pop. This is not to minimize the *differences* between historically distinct examples nor to collapse – against the thrust of previous arguments – distinctions of meaning and use, in the cultures as well as in the musics; but at the level of musical materials and conventions there seem to be some large-scale continuities. To be more precise, beneath the flux of syntactic, semantic and cultural change and contradiction, there is a level which preserves major conventions; and indeed, such continuity may be more solid at this 'popular' level than at levels higher in the socio-cultural structure, with their greater propensity to change. It has exerted a continuous 'upward' influence on 'art' composers – just as, we must remember, the pervasive importance in much 'art' music of orally transmitted performance practice (including traditions of improvised variation and ornament) has modified notational abstraction and kept alive there at least some of the dimension of 'engendered feeling'. One might see this level of continuity as a kind of 'permanent critique' of the historical vicissitudes taking place 'above' it.

At the same time, as was argued in Chapter 1, those vicissitudes have *altered* the 'popular' layer – and vice versa. The field has been in continuous dialectical movement. Thus popular music should not be seen as an *antithesis* but as an *alternative position on the same ground*. János Maróthy (1974) provides a rich

Jerome Kern 'All The Things You Are' (1939)

Ex 4.3a

'Caravan Of Love' (opening), as sung by The Housemartins (1986)

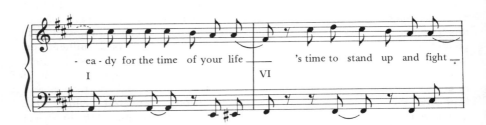

etc.(repeated harmonic riff)

Ex 4.3b

Moniot d'Arras: 'Ce fut en mai' (thirteenth century)

Eubie Blake: 'Memories Of You' (1930)

Ex 4.4

Hans Neusidler: *Gassenhauer* for harp (publ. 1536)

etc.

Ex 4.5

cross-section of this dialectical activity, from the late Middle Ages to the early twentieth century.[11] Popular musicians have taken over 'high' techniques and pieces, and – often through orally based performance methods – have transformed them. Gammon describes how nineteenth-century instrumentalists in rural Sussex played written bourgeois pieces with an almost Afro-American rhythmic flexibility (Gammon 1985: 117–18); while 'jazzing the classics' has a lengthy twentieth-century history. Often aspects of the different 'spheres' develop in parallel. We have already noted traditional musicology's impotence in the face of twentieth-century popular music's radically increased interest in *sound*; but 'art' music in the same period, from Debussy to Stockhausen, has manifested a similar interest (with which musicological analysis has fared no better). The roots of this must lie deeper therefore than pop/art, oral/literate, illegitimate/ legitimate antitheses would recognize – perhaps, to adapt an argument of Adorno, in a common 'phantasmagoric' riposte to widespread 'rationalizing' tendencies elsewhere in musical style. Finally, 'art' composers have always lived in the same musical field as those in the popular stratum, often in close contact with it – Bach with the Lutheran chorale, Beethoven with the popular heroic music of revolutionary France, Elgar with the turn-of-the-century march, Mahler with the Viennese waltz.

The 'critique of musicology', then, should take aim not at 'art music' or musicology themselves – separating popular music off from them, and from the whole idea of the scientific analysis of music – but at a particular construction of musicology, based on a particular subject, conceived in a particular, ideologically organized way. Once the musical field as a whole is freed from the distorting grip of that ideology, the ground is cleared for a useful musicology to emerge. The metaphor should be not one of opposed spheres, or of decisive historical breaks, but of a geological formation, long-lived but fissured and liable to upheaval: the task is to *remap the terrain*. Indeed, the greatest promise of a reformed musicology lies not so much in its study of popular music – though that is important – but, as one consequence of such study, in an inevitable reorganization of *the whole of Western musical history*. The need then becomes the identification, within the musical field as a whole, of different historical *levels* – at each of which a different pattern or focus of change, continuity and contradiction may be found. That in turn demands the development of an appropriate language for diachronic analysis (stability, shift, rupture, synthesis, influence, and so on).

Raymond Williams distinguishes between long-lived 'general forms', the origins of which correspond to important moments of social development, and – developing within these – a variety of 'specific forms'. The former become

> a quite general cultural property, in the end belonging more to the sociology of our species, at a certain level of cultural development, than to the specific sociology of a given society at a certain time and place . . . [they show] markedly longer . . . phases and rhythms than the specific conditions of practice of any particular society or period. Yet these markedly longer phases and rhythms – these deepest forms – can no more be abstracted from general social development than they can be reduced to merely local conditions (Williams 1981: 150–1).

Forms based on triadic chord sequences; solo song forms organized in regular phrase-lengths: these may be two such 'general forms', each beginning in the late medieval and Renaissance periods, each being subject to a variety of 'specific' developments, 'popular' and 'non-popular'; and the 'phase' we are discussing here is of course that associated with the biography of capitalism.

To this complex model of musical practice – but linked with it – we can then add Gino Stefani's conception of a distinction in musical *discourse* between 'popular' and 'cultivated' codes of 'musical competence'. Stefani insists that the common use of the 'musical mother-tongue of the Western world' has resulted in a unified music culture. To understand that culture requires 'analysis and description of popular constant characters, of common musical codes', which in turn needs 'a theory of general musical competence, where cultivated and popular codes can find their place and be compared'. 'Popular' and 'cultivated' codes not only give rise to different bodies of music but also work on the same body of music, and on the same musical materials, using them for different effects, for different purposes. 'Popular competence', for example, 'is not simply a reduced version of cultivated competence, but a rich and complex production of sense, although transverse when compared to ruling ideologies. Transverse because popular culture is subaltern, clandestine, oppressed by upper, "cultivated" culture' (Stefani 1984: 18–19).

A musicologist of popular music stands, inescapably, in the midst of all this, drawn to the 'cultivated' side by his training, to the 'popular' side by his subject-matter. Rather than pulling to one side, with the traditional musicologists, or the other, with the 'total critics' of musicology, it will be better to *look both ways, living out the tension*. Given the 'fractured unity' of the musical field, that is the way to a faithful reflection in one's method of the reality of the practice and the discourse. Negatively, this avoids (potentially) capitulating to the myths and ideologies of either side; positively, standing in the margin, two-sided as it is, it offers a golden opportunity to develop a *critical* musicology which could provide a vastly increased analytical power.

Franco Fabbri has asked the question (1982b: 7):

> How much do we improve our comprehension of popular music if we call the introductory fuzz guitar part in 'Satisfaction' an 'ostinato' rather than a 'riff'? . . . one might wonder if this sort of linguistical Trojan horse is still necessary . . .

Indeed, it might also be dangerous, for

> terms, vocabularies, metalanguages do not simply reflect the ideologies of genres, of musics; they are the concrete verbal means through which those hierarchies of values, those ideologies are constructed. So the improper use of any 'foreign' metalanguage for the analysis of a given set of musical events . . . would result in the acceptance of the values for which that language is a vehicle of expression (ibid: 7).

However, the opposite is also true: 'the use of an "internal" metalanguage would only confirm the ideological myths of the genre, and would not prove to be critical'. The answer is a method which is both self-reflective and explicit about the values implicit in its own terms; a cross-critical use of both 'internal' and 'academic' criteria is

> the only way to create a musicological metalanguage for popular genres which has to be, at the same time, ideologically clear and as comprehensible to those who spent part of their lives studying baroque music, as to those who started their scientific interest in popular music from 'inside' (ibid: 9).

Stephen Blum has made a similar point (1975: 208–9):

> the question 'what does it mean to know a music?' entails that the inquirer attempt to achieve a measure of critical perspective upon the social circumstances and processes which have produced his own education . . . The contextual variables which determine the epistemology of a musician or a scholar, as an agent who participates in more than one social group, must themselves limit the techniques and options available for further intellectual (and musical) activity, including any interaction between one's own (socially produced) modes of operation, and those exercised by 'informants' in a foreign culture.

Without such a 'third-order knowledge', as Bourdieu calls it, there is no 'escape from the ritual either/or choice between objectivism and subjectivism' (Bourdieu 1977: 6). The musicology of popular music is likely to subside, at best, into a 'progressive liberalism' which treats popular genres simply as additions to the musicological corpus, with no effect on how the whole field is viewed, or assimilates them to traditional methodologies and criteria, by way of legitimation. In the latter case, the old power relationships remain, the dividing line merely shifted; in the former, there is a pluralistic disregard or denial of tensions, contradictions and power imbalances, a simple broadening of the field from 'above'.

Jazz is the classic case of the legitimation of a once disreputable music. In recent years, much ragtime research has trod a similar path. The key to the approach is that this is 'art', and the analytic and aesthetic criteria developed in classical musicology can be applied. This affects *how* the music is heard and interpreted, and also *what part* of the corpus is privileged for study (written rather than 'folk' ragtime, 'artistic' rather than 'commercial' jazz).

'Liberal pluralism' is associated particularly with the social history of music, a growing area in recent years (see, for example, Dahlhaus 1967; Raynor 1978; Weber 1975).[12] Most work, however valuable, has treated popular music as an extra or as a context: the focus is, explicitly or implicitly, still on the 'great music', but it is now assumed that this is better understood against the background of the contemporary social organization of musical life and of its *Trivialmusik*, or in relation to the 'second-rate', conceived as a separate, additional sphere. *The New Grove Dictionary* (Sadie 1980) – 'bible' of musicology in the English-speaking world – makes much of its vastly expanded coverage of popular music compared to earlier editions; and this is indeed significant. But the approach is simply aggregative; popular music appears, but has no *effect* on everything else – it stays in its own compartments. The method is to demarcate 'popular music' (defined, very loosely, in terms of commercial success and widespread 'comprehensibility') and to treat this, or at least its Anglo-American mainstream, in a lengthy, separate article. Related genres (blues, jazz, and so on) are given their own articles, and some aspects of popular music styles are also covered in larger entries devoted to particular countries or cities. There seems to be an implicit assumption that 'art', 'popular' and 'folk' styles can and should be segregated, with various 'ethnic' or 'regional' variants (rhythm and blues, for instance) being located in between these major categories in separate compartments. Thus the 'Popular Music' article discusses music hall but not 'workers' song'; it can say that 'the decades after the Civil War were not important ones for American popular music' (ibid, Vol. 15: 104) – this of the period when the progenitors of blues must have been forming; and it maintains that rock 'n' roll and rock are not themselves part of popular music but somehow separate genres. The article on Great Britain, having hived off the subject of 'popular music', deals only with 'art' and 'folk' traditions (and the section on 'folk' music, a particularly striking example of the reification of musical categories, discusses only *rural* song and dance); the article on the United States says a little more about 'popular' genres but not much; while those on Germany and France contain nothing, that on Japan a couple of sentences. Similarly, Nashville rates only ten lines, the entry for San Francisco says nothing about popular music in the area, that for New York (nineteen pages) devotes a page to jazz and a few words to musical comedy, and that for Liverpool only one short paragraph on the 'beat-group cult'.

The strategy behind this approach seems to be a conception of the musical field as divided horizontally into layers; the concerns of lower layers rarely cross over into higher spheres. Thus, for instance, hi-hat and ride cymbals are given three lines at the end of a three-page article on cymbals, while the term 'rim-shot', explained in the entry for drum, is not discussed as a popular music technique. The articles on electronic music and synthesizer have nothing to say about popular music, and explanations of such terms as 'chorus' and 'slide' (that is, glissando) do not mention the important popular music usages. 'Riff' and 'walking bass' are defined as jazz terms (very briefly) but their use in other styles is not considered. Vital popular music terms like 'vocal', 'hot', 'cool', 'laid back', 'lick' and 'back beat' have no entries. There is no attempt to include 'folk usage' of terms: for instance, most rock musicians use 'riff' as a synonym, almost, for 'musical idea'. Similarly, the article on the ballad, while containing an account of the 'traditional' ballad which is exemplary, dismisses British and American broadside ballads in one paragraph, has nothing about ballads in other street-song traditions, dispatches what it calls the 'English sentimental ballad' of the nineteenth century in two paragraphs, and deals with twentieth-century usage thus: 'In recent years, particularly since World War II, the word "ballad" has been used to refer to pop songs with sentimental or narrative texts and (usually) a slow tempo' (ibid, Vol. 2: 76). The most striking examples of all are found when we move to the level of the most fundamental musical terms. The article on harmony does not mention popular music (nor jazz nor non-European traditions for that matter); that on melody, after nine pages of discussion, includes a single paragraph which mentions the Beatles, George Gershwin and Cole Porter, and pentatonicism in rock; while the entry on rhythm, astonishingly, is completely unaware of popular music's existence.

A rather different species of pluralism appears in some American musicology (see, for example, Chase 1981; Hitchcock 1974). Here the particular cultural history – with its populist elements, its distrust of European pretensions, its reference point in the experience of the 'common man' – has to some extent discouraged elitism, encouraged consideration of both 'cultivated' and 'vernacular' musics, and resulted in a historical method in which they rub together much more. But here the problem is that this very pragmatism, this celebration of democratic pluralism, is liable to miss the *relationships* between the components of the field, in particular the tensions and power inequalities represented there. In so doing it tends to ratify the status quo; a melting-pot theory of 'to each his own' can easily result in a taxonomic rather than a dialectical approach.

By contrast, a *critical* stance recognizes the need to 'walk round' the entire topography, holding this map in the mind so that there is ultimately a committed point of view which is nevertheless aware of a structure of mutually critical perspectives analogous to the structure of the musical practice itself. Methods applying to diverse musics a point of view deriving from one perspective, and methods which simply aggregate varying perspectives, are equally unsatisfactory. The musicologist has to recognize the existence and the interaction – within a society, within a history – of different musical problematics. By 'problematics' is meant characteristic sets of concerns, attitudes, problems addressed and sound-sets conceived, allowed and heard. These come into existence somewhere in the space constituted, synchronically and diachronically, between production and reception; thus, they are conditioned by, at the least, received conventions; how producers 'make us listen'; how listeners hear; and ideological predispositions (for example, the formalist assumptions of traditional musicology). In this sense, a problematic is close to the 'principles of articulation' discussed earlier; in fact, problematics are the products of such principles, for the latter work by actively constructing materials and conventions held or available in common within a musical field or history, into a particular ideological form. Clearly, then, what is at issue for any 'critical musicology' is the exact nature of the relationship between particular musical problematics and the wider cultural, social and ideological forces. And it is to this problem that subsequent chapters are addressed.

Notes

1. For an example of how notational centricity can affect a whole analysis, see Dena Epstein's (1982) scathing attack on the argument – usually based on examining printed texts and transcriptions alone – that 'Negro spirituals' come from white sources. For a description by an ethnomusicologist of the problems associated with using staff notation for unsuitable music, and of other forms of notation, see Hood (1982: 61–122).
2. On the non-functional nature of much rock harmony, see Winkler (n.d.); Björnberg (1985); Bobbitt (1976).
3. Before criticizing others, I should confess my own faults in this respect in my earlier book, Middleton (1972).
4. For examples of interplay between published sheet music and lower-class practice, see Oliver (1984). For the tradition of interaction between urban popular styles and white rural musical culture, dating back at least to the mid-nineteenth century, see, for example, Wilgus (1971).
5. See his quotation from Edmund Wilson's *The Twenties. From Notebooks and Diaries of the Period*, Hamm (1979: 378–9).
6. See Hamm (1979: 384–5) on the big bands of the 1930s.
7. See also Ostendorf (1982).
8. See also Mellers (1964, Part 2; 1986).
9. Actually the sound of 'Strawberry Fields' is mentioned elsewhere in the book (Mellers 1973: 192) but only as an example of the Beatles' use of recording technology; it is detached from the discussion of the song, playing no part in its interpretation. For critical discussion of another example from Mellers (1973), see Shepherd (1982: 147).
10. Note, too, the prevalence of 'blue notes' in English 'folk' music: see Lloyd (1967: 52–4).
11 Lee (1970), though restricted to Britain and by no means as sophisticated theoretically, also contains useful material.
12. For a critique of 'liberal pluralism' in music education, see Green (1988: 102–20). Green advocates a self-aware, critical pluralism similar to the position put forward here.

5

'I heard it through the grapevine'.
Popular music in culture

Since music comes to us through the 'grapevine' of culture, it is, as we have seen, vital to study it 'as culture' and 'in culture'. But what is the nature of this relationship? The concern of this chapter is to look at some examples of 'culturalist' approaches to popular music. My aim is twofold: to draw out what is most useful in these approaches, and to assess the validity of their concept of culture – usually defined in a quasi-anthropological way as 'whole way of life' – together with their picture of music's specific role. There is, we shall find, a tendency to reduce the music/culture relationship to a deterministic, functional or structural homology. This in turn encourages a stress on the notion of 'authenticity', since, given homologous systems, honesty (truth to cultural experience) becomes the validating criterion of musical value.

Folkloristics

An apt place to start is with 'folk music', for here 'authenticity' plays a central role. Folk music is usually seen as the authentic expression of a way of life now past or about to disappear (or in some cases, to be preserved or somehow revived). Unfortunately, despite the assembly of an enormous body of work over some two centuries, there is still no unanimity on what folk music (or folklore, or the folk) *is*. The Romantics, who originated the concept, often thought of 'the people', in the sense of a national essence. Or – and this later became more common – they thought of a particular part of the people, a lower layer, or even class. Often this became limited to a particular part of the lower class, the country workers or 'peasantry'. As the complexity of social stratification and interaction became clearer, and increased, various conditioning criteria, such as 'continuity', 'tradition', 'oral transmission', 'anonymity' and uncommercial origins, became more important than simple social categories themselves.

Charles Seeger identifies three main approaches to the definition of folk music current now (Seeger 1980). The first is associated with a schema comprising four musical types: 'primitive' or 'tribal'; 'elite' or 'art'; 'folk'; and 'popular'. Usually, though with varying interpretative nuance, folk music is associated with a lower class in societies which are culturally and socially stratified, that is, which have developed an elite, and possibly also a popular, musical culture. In the second approach, defining criteria are sought in cultural processes rather than abstract musical types. Foremost among folk music processes are said to be *continuity* and *oral transmission*; and these are seen as characterizing one side of a cultural dichotomy, the other side of which is occupied by *written* culture. Under this definition, folk music is found not only in the lower layers of feudal, capitalist and some oriental societies but also in 'primitive' societies and in parts of 'popular' cultures. The third approach (less prominent as yet) is characterized by a rejection of all rigid boundaries, preferring a conception simply of varying practice within *one* field, that of 'music'. This, it will be clear, is the nearest of the three to the approach advocated in this book; yet it remains important to understand the rationales of the other two.

The first of these, confining folk music to a distinct social location, probably remains the most common. Cecil Sharp gave it classic expression in Britain in the first decade of the twentieth century, removing the concept of folk song from vague 'national traditions' and restricting it to what he saw as the culture of country workers, isolated, uneducated, uncontaminated by commerce, reading or 'art' (Sharp 1972: 1–5). In A.L. Lloyd's hands, this folk expands to include the urban working class; but the nub is still the same: 'primitive' song had spoken for the whole of society but when social differentiation made this impossible, folk song split away to express the specific situation of the lower class.[1] This view has run into trouble in recent years, when increased social mobility and the effects of the mass media have resulted in a multiplicity of new hybrids and audiences, and made the old boundaries difficult to police, and when, within historical analysis, the problems with isolating lower-class culture from 'high' and commercial 'popular' cultures have become clear. Hence the emergence of the second approach identified by Seeger. The trouble with this approach is that, as shown in Chapter 3, the oral/literate distinction will not stand up, at least, not as a simple dichotomy (see Seeger 1949–50). The result is either a system of ideal types, such as that of Redfield (1947), or a naive empiricism in which folklore is defined in terms simply of a list of all the things that are folkloric – that is, it is what the folklorist says it is (see, for example, Dundes 1965: 1–3).

Whatever their approach, most folklorists now would agree on the importance of *interaction* between what they take to be folk music and other musics; and they would largely agree that folk music itself is rarely homogeneous but is subject to social and geographical specification, historical change and cultural layering.[2] But the questions to which this gives rise – what kinds of interaction? how much? what do they mean, how do they work and why do they happen? where do these processes leave the concept of 'folk music'? where do we draw the line between 'folk' and 'non-folk'? – receive no agreed answers. In reality, it is surely unprofitable to attempt to draw a single, categorical line at all.

But this does not mean we can make no use of the discoveries, materials and methods of folkloristics. I shall concentrate on four aspects which are potentially the most useful to us. The first of these is the object of study itself, however it has been defined. The musical texts, types and processes which in practice have been assembled and studied are – depending on one's theoretical perspective – *part of* popular music, or are located in a space *adjacent* to popular music, or have been *influential* on popular music. Whichever is taken to be the case, students of popular music therefore need to know about them.

The second aspect is methods of study. Comprehensive discussion is impossible here; but some methods and concepts stand out for their potential relevance, notably those having to do with questions of dissemination and those having to do with methods of analysis.

The third aspect is the politics of folk. Whatever the definition, folk is always seen as 'real' music, not imposed on or sold to people but produced by them, expressing their participation in an unalienated culture. This ideology impinges on commercial popular music in two ways. 'Authentic' folk music is presented as an 'Other', with which popular music can be adversely contrasted; or its values are seen as surviving, or recreated, within certain favoured forms of popular music, usually forms associated with specified groups or subcultures.

Lastly, there is the sociology of folk music. Again, variations in definition do not affect the widespread agreement that in some way or other folk music reflects 'folk society'. And again there are two main ways in which this affects the study of commercial popular music. First, where 'folk' and 'popular' *meet*, clearly important sociological consequences must follow. Second, we can ask whether the general notion of *homology* between music and society stands up, and if it does, whether it can be applied to popular as well as folk music. Does popular music too function within a 'whole way of life'?

The object

It is impossible to write a history of popular music or an analysis of virtually any nineteenth- or twentieth-century genre without an awareness of what is commonly regarded as folk music. At the very least, the latter is often seen as *giving way* to the former, as 'traditional' societies modernize, isolated folk enclaves are assimilated into capitalist cultural relations, old-fashioned rural populations are urbanized, and commercially organized practices supersede folk practices. This is precisely the way that many popular music historians visualize the emergence of popular music. But many also would want to refer to the *influence* of folk sources on popular genres. This applies particularly to rhythm and blues, Country music and rock; but also, via the indirect influence of ragtime and jazz, to Tin Pan Alley song – and, in earlier periods in Britain, to such genres as music hall song, the ballad operas of the eighteenth century and many of the urban popular songs and dance-tunes of the sixteenth and seventeenth centuries. There are also various twentieth-century 'folk revivals' – not to mention the multiplicity of 'neo-traditional' styles and hybrids developing in 'Third World' countries.

However, this apparently simple picture is betrayed by the problems that attach to the conceptual distinction of 'folk' and 'popular'. It is commonplace among scholars now to criticize the view of folk music associated above all with Cecil Sharp.[3] Lloyd (1967: 13–93) devotes a good deal of space to an attack on Sharp's romantically idealized 'folk' – a construct which had been developed simply as an antithesis to the threat of industrialization. This 'folk' never existed – certainly in European culture; in fact, as far back as we can see, the culture of the common people of Europe has been marked by a myriad of subcultures and functional categories, and has been inseparable from the culture of the whole society, contributing to and drawing on the practices of other groups (see also Finnegan 1977: 30–41; Burke 1978: 3–64).

Lloyd argues that the creators and transmitters of folk songs were not ignorant and cut off from learning but tended to be the *most* educated of their class; that songs were created not communally or anonymously but by particular individuals, whose names are often unknown simply because of historical distance, lack of cultural legitimacy or absence of property rights in their work; and that creation was not 'spontaneous' in some mystical sense but the product of deliberately exercised skill. Similarly, he establishes that, while oral transmission was central, the roles of manuscript, printed broadsides and songbooks, and travelling professional performers were important as far back as the Middle Ages. This brought the influence of commercial products, together with interchange between country and city, lower classes and bourgeoisie. Folk music, it follows, has *changed* – continuously, but in particularly striking ways at moments of *general* social upheaval, when interclass contacts and intracultural movement were at their greatest. For Lloyd, then, the 'authenticity' of folk music should be sought not in a particular social origin but in its 'realism', its reflection of changing, historically determinate social conditions.[4]

Significant work has been done on the ways in which the Sharpian conception distorts the songs that were collected (see, for example, Gammon 1980; Pickering 1982: 3–7; Harker 1985: 172–97). Texts were censored and bowdlerized. Tunes that were modal (therefore supposedly 'old') were preferred to those in a major or minor key, as were those that were thought to be uninfluenced by harmony and sung unaccompanied. Songs judged unsuitable (because they were of the wrong type, got from print, of commercial origin, or insufficiently old) were omitted from publications, rejected when offered by singers, or ignored as 'corrupted' elements in the culture. In any case, the class gulf between bourgeois Victorian or Edwardian collector and lower-class singer was unlikely to result in performances typical of the usual performing context or in full representation of. the repertory. Some singers were puzzled. Samuel Willett wrote to Lucy Broadwood, 'Madam, I do not know if there is sufficient rusticity in the above song to answer your purpose; if not my powers of discrimination are too limited to work out the process of winnowing you suggest in your letter' (quoted in Gammon 1980: 68–9).

Gammon has sketched the historical context to this process of ideologically motivated mediation (ibid: 75–83). It was a conjuncture defined by the nationwide spread of urban musical culture, especially music hall songs; the 'threat' posed to the established order by a more visible, active and organized working class; the need felt for a 'national' English music which would at once unite the society and stand comparison with other 'national' traditions; imperialist rivalries and the love-hate relationship between the English bourgeois musical establishment and German music. Out of this web came the project for a revitalized workers' music culture, and for this an uncorrupted national traditional music was needed. This 'folk-song' could be taken up as raw material in concert music by composers such as Vaughan Williams, Grainger and Butterworth, and it might help push back the spread of the 'vulgar' music of the urban masses.

The urgency of the project, together with its organizing ideology, is well caught in composer Hubert Parry's address (1899) to the inaugural meeting of the Folk Song Society:

> in true folk-songs there is no sham, no got-up glitter, and no vulgarity . . . and the pity of it is that these treasures of humanity are getting rare, for they are written in characters the most evanescent you can imagine, upon the sensitive brain fibres of those who learn them, and have but little idea of their value. Moreover, there is an enemy at the doors of folk-music which is driving it out, namely the common popular songs of the day; and this enemy is one of the most repulsive and most insidious . . . It is for . . . people who, for the most part, have the most false ideals, or none at all – who are always struggling for existence, who think that the commonest rowdyism is the highest expression of human emotion; it is for them that the modern popular music is made, and it is made with a commercial intention out of snippets of musical slang. And this product it is which will drive out folk-music if we do not save it. For even in country districts where folk-songs linger, the people think themselves behindhand if they do not know the songs of the seething towns . . . But the old folk-music is among the purest products of the human mind. It grew in the heart of the people before they devoted themselves so assiduously to the making of quick returns . . . [it is] characteristic of the race, of the quiet reticence of our country folk, courageous and content, ready to meet what chance shall bring with a cheery heart. All the things that mark the folk-music of the race, also betoken the qualities of the race, and are a faithful reflection of ourselves. We needs must cherish it . . . in that heritage may lie the ultimate solution of the problems of characteristic national art.[5]

However, while this intervention had the specificity of its historical moment, it was not completely unprecedented. Dave Harker has shown that the *construction* of 'folk song' by bourgeois collectors, editors and publishers, as a category operating not within lower-class culture at all but within bourgeois culture, has been a long-standing practice, part of an active ordering and defining of the national culture in the interests of hegemony (Harker 1985).

This practice did not stop with Sharp. While the revisions of Lloyd and others enabled them to widen the boundaries of 'folk song' and to liberalize its definition, it did not follow that the concept of 'folk' was dead – far from it. Certainly the achievement of these folklorists has been enormous. We now know that industrial workers *made songs* – and that they continued and adapted older, rural practices and materials, and took over and 'folklorized' commercial products. We have learned something about the contexts in which these songs were used (see Lloyd 1944; 1967; Green 1972; Cohen 1981; Korson 1938; 1943; McColl 1954; Raven 1977; Harker 1980). Other scholars have concentrated on (and reprinted) broadsides and other printed material (see, for example, Palmer 1974; Vicinus 1974), and have studied the assimilation into folk tradition of Tin Pan Alley songs (see, for example, Cohen 1970). The same impulse has carried work not only into historical areas but also, especially in the United States, into the new field of 'urban folklore' in today's cities or urbanizing countryside. For some scholars, the folk becomes simply a group of people united permanently or temporarily by shared common experiences, attitudes, interests, skills, ideas, knowledge, and aims. Those shared attitudes are elaborated, sanctioned, and stabilised by the group over a period of time. Any such group or any communally shaped culture trait might be the subject of folklore study (Linda Dégh, in Paredes and Stekert 1971: 54–5).

This opens the way to studying the *continuity* and *communality* of *any* musical practice – though so far, actual work has been largely on examples of *transition* between rural and urban cultures or of the *urbanization* of rural music. This, for instance, is largely the way the histories of hillbilly/Country music, Afro-American music and 'ethnic' American musics in general have been treated by folklorists.[6] One clear conclusion to emerge is that recordings, far from threatening the existence of these musics, have encouraged their continued vitality; and in the process they have helped to articulate ethnic and subcultural identities – not only of blacks and 'backward' Southern whites but also American Jews, Poles, Finns, Mexicans, Irish and many more. It may be that studies of this process could provide models for the more general investigation of how materials from 'folk' sources, entering the orbit of mass cultural production, can bring with them, or be conferred with, the capacity to symbolize the cultural values of a 'folk' or subcultural group (various youth groups, for instance).

Nevertheless, as noted already, the 'folk' concept itself has not been relinquished by most urban and industrial folklorists. As a result, there is a tendency to look for practices that are in some way *close* to what is seen as folk music of a traditional type ('survivals'), and to restrict analysis to a historical period rather than contemporary material. So the Golden Age of 'folk' myth is still there, even though it has been moved or extended, and it is still seen as under attack from today's corruptions. A 'liberal' such as Alan Lomax – who considered that workers 'have not, as certain scholars expected, ceased to make and sing folk songs in "urban" twentieth-century America. Living in city slums, working on huge industrial projects, watching TV, they continue to come forth with fresh song ideas' (Lomax 1964: 117) – nevertheless attacks modern urban society and mass media for destroying the variety of the cultural 'gene pool', resulting in a 'cultural grey-out'; and all the familiar, stereotyped dichotomies – between rural and urban, oral and literate, tradition and innovation – reappear in his description (Lomax 1968: 4–6). But in the modern world he criticizes, the characteristics traditionally ascribed to folk music – orality, community of response, continuity, variation of formulae and received material – are all around us (along with other, different characteristics, admittedly); why not use the accumulated techniques of folklore to study these?

Similarly, Lloyd, having attacked Sharp's concept of folk, himself sticks with the 1954 International Folk Music Council definition of folk song (derived from Sharp!):

Folk music is the product of a musical tradition that has been evolved through the process of oral transmission. The factors that shape the tradition are: (i) continuity which links the present with the past; (ii) variation which springs from the creative impulse of the individual or the group; and (iii) selection by the community which determines the form or forms in which the music survives.[7]

Given that to construct the oral/literate contrast as a dichotomy is specious – and in practice Lloyd, as we have seen, admits the role of print – the first sentence loses both its status as a rule and its exclusiveness to 'folk' music. There is nothing in the whole definition which *in principle* could not be applied to the history of Beethoven symphony performance – or to the performance histories of music hall, the songs of Irving Berlin or rock 'n' roll. So in order to maintain a 'folk' category, Lloyd is forced to hang on to older criteria – lack of commercial motive, unselfconscious, amateur composition – and apply them to the definition even of industrial songs. In the process he romanticizes his 'worker' just as Sharp romanticized his 'peasant'. He merely moves Parry's distinction between 'folk' and 'popular' a short distance across the cultural map, 'sordid vulgarity' and 'snippets of slang' being replaced by the 'mumbled withdrawals or frantic despair of the pops' (Lloyd 1967: 10). Thus music hall songs could not be 'folk songs', and this applied even to those (in North-East England, for instance) made for workers by ex-workers, and even though *miners* creating songs out of the same materials – many of them of commercial origin – *did* apparently produce 'folk songs'! 'Folk-revival' and 'folk-protest' singers such as Joan Baez or Bob Dylan, let alone rock performers like the Rolling Stones, 'belong to the insubstantial world of the modern commercial hit'; American country singer Johnny Cash and English 'folk' singer Harry Cox are *categorically* different; pop is 'poor fare', reflecting 'panic' and 'emptiness', while real folk offers 'more nourishment' (Lloyd 1967: 410; 1970: 11; 1982: 15).

When Lloyd is discussing the pre-twentieth-century period, and even early twentieth-century America, he is quite happy to describe cross-influence and fuzzy boundaries between categories, but this flexibility ends when he reaches more recent times: now he sees only a 'loss in profundity, a gain in brilliance, a general simplification for the sake of quick acceptance' (Lloyd 1970: 10). But, as Harker asks (1985: 248), 'why do not continuity, variation and selection represent the conditioning factors for all artistic production, amateur or professional?' In what sense is the 'dialectic . . . between the collective and the individual, between tradition and innovation, between what is received from the community and what is supplied out of personal fantasy, in short, the blending of continuity and variation' (Lloyd 1967: 16–17) not characteristic of *all* song-making? In what ways can a song like 'Blowin' in the Wind' or 'Satisfaction' – not so much the initial recording but the song-processually-at-work in society – be held not to conform to the IFMC criteria of 'folkness'? Only by means of quite particular (and loaded) notions of time ('continuity'), creativity ('variation') and above all community (rooted in old romantic conceptions of *Gemeinschaft*) – notions which would arbitrarily exclude the activities of the many small and part-time professionals, and amateurs, who recreate these songs week in week out for club and pub audiences. In the end, Lloyd can only define folk song by assertion (the old technique of 'if I say it's folk, it is'); and, according to Harker (1985: 249–50), he was not above amending history and texts to make them fit.

The crux of Archie Green's definition of 'folk' (1972: Chapter 1) is the need for a song's popular acceptance and continuous, varied life in a community – hence 'tradition' in an active rather than a romantic sense. 'Folkness' can be an attribute of a process or an activity rather than of a society or an individual – so that the latter can be 'folk' in some respects and not in others. This is fine – though it seems to be describing the dialectic between generality and particularity, collective and individual characteristics, which is inherent in all social life, and could be applied to most *popular* songs – but in practice, sensing the self-destructive potential of his definition, Green retreats. Other criteria are important too, he argues – notably *solidarity* and *collective feeling*, which are apparently typical of the mining communities he is describing. He has problems with songs collectively known but associated with only *one* singer; Green becomes uneasy with his insistence on active variation through transmission and mentions the alternative that a song confined to a single singer might be 'folk' if it is *asked for* by the community, that is, if it is 'in the consciousness of that community' (ibid: 84). Where do we stop? Lloyd has a similar problem, and responds by fudging the doctrine of variance so that 'industrial folk song' can include 'super-variants' and 'invariants', that is, versions or even song-originals that *do not change* (!). Few *'popular'* songs vary as little as this.

Such muddles over the folk/popular boundary have the result that in some work in this area, often some of the best work, the distinction tends to, as it were, involuntarily disappear; the pressure of reality renders it more or less redundant. Sometimes the 'folk' label is still present – but against the grain, so to speak. This is the case with Oliver's study of black American music on 'race' records in the 1920s, and its sources and antecedents; he wants to keep a distinction between 'folk' genres and performers, on the one hand, and professional, commercial production, on the other, but in practice the book is forever blurring the distinction, historicizing previous myths of black music, and destroying 'folk' stereotypes (Oliver 1984). At other times the label just disappears. For instance, Slobin's discussion of the evolution of American Jewish ethnic popular music from the 1870s stresses its eclectic sources (not only European 'folk' and traditional synagogue styles but also European opera, American operetta and Tin Pan Alley) and its function in the urbanization, Americanization and proletarianization of immigrant Jews (Slobin 1982). This is a description of a 'subculture', not a 'folk'. Similarly, Keil's analysis of polka in Milwaukee focuses not so much on its relationship to European 'folk' roots as on the relationship of ethnicity and class in the American city; and, realizing the implications, he quite rightly goes on to denounce the folk concept himself (Keil 1982).

Keil has pursued this denunciation elsewhere (1978; 1979a), arguing that the invention of the 'folk' concept serves to protect the ruling class from the threat and suffering of proletariats by first exoticizing them and then absorbing their cultures into its own. In fact, he says,

> there never were any 'folk' except in the minds of the bourgeoisie. The field is a grim fairy tale . . . 'high art' versus 'folk art' represents a dialectic that is almost completely contained within bourgeois ideology. One requires the other . . . Can't we keep 'the folk' concept and redeem it? No! and no! again. You can't because too many Volkswagens have been built, too many

folk ballets applauded, too many folksongs used, too much aid and comfort given to the enemy (Keil 1978: 264–5).

If the *concept* must be abandoned, what of the *processes* which, at least in the more liberal definitions, have been covered by it? Cannot these be 'redeemed'? The crux is the dialectic of *continuity* and *active use* (recreation/selection/variation). In an analysis of 'commercialization and tradition in the Nashville sound', Ivey points to people's apparently *general* need to 'traditionalize' part of group experience (Ivey 1982). He attacks that view of the 'Nashville Sound' which sees it as a sell-out of Country music's 'folk' traditions, arguing convincingly that within a particular production nexus (Nashville, 1957–*c*.1975) there developed practices (certain musical textures and instrumentations; certain social practices in the recording studio) which among a close-knit group of performers acquired the force of a living, active 'tradition'; the pop clichés, often overdubbed later, were a *gloss* on that. Only afterwards can we get a clear impression of this 'tradition'; it was a 'great era in the adaptation of one minority music to the forces of a national popular culture' (ibid: 138). Of course, this approach can be applied to *all* musics – and that is the point.[8] From this perspective what is wrong with folkloristics is the way it has always elevated questions of *degree* (how much continuity? how much variation? how large and how solid the community? and also, where on the literacy spectrum?) into qualitative distinctions, which reserve these characteristics for privileged areas. By dissolving the 'folk', then, we can bring popular musics of all sorts within the scope of an approach which analyses the cultural networks of musical production in their universality *and* their historical variety. And in that case, there is no reason why the same process of generalization should not apply to *methods*.

Methods

Two broad areas stand out: that of transmission, and that of form. What can be said is mostly a matter of what *could* be done, for little attempt has been made so far to apply folkloristic methods in these areas to popular music.

If we take the core of any useful conceptualization of transmission to lie in notions of *continuity, commonality* and *variance*, it is clear that these are still applicable. But in the era of electronic dissemination, when the media forms fix continuity at the same time as the rapid flow of products ensures variance, they move into the meta-folk regions of 'popular memory', 'popular communication' and 'popular learning'. Which songs do people remember and why? How do musicians learn songs, and how do they construct repertories? What brings people together, with musicians, around certain songs, and has this anything to do with the coexistence or evolution of variants – of styles, rhythmic formulae, tune-types or whatever? Of course, while record and tape have *not* – as often prophesied – had the effect of stopping re-creation (the continual appearance of 'covers' and new versions demonstrates that) or of destroying the continuity of tradition (as shown by revivals in the charts, nostalgia programmes and 'golden oldie' presentations on radio, and long-lived 'subcultural' and minority styles), it is true that the nature of memory and tradition has changed. They become much more heterogeneous and fluid, the inputs mediated and turned over faster, the 'unit of continuity' probably much shorter (traditions measured in years or even months rather than generations). And this will make the much needed empirical investigation of this area more complex, affecting the structure of both repertories and audiences. Similarly, the folklorists' distinction between 'active' and 'passive bearers' will have to be applied in new ways. Perhaps the chief 'passive bearer' now is the recording itself – though it is clear that, even leaving live performance aside, recordings often also work as active intermediaries: how many bands learned Chuck Berry songs not from his records but the Rolling Stones' cover versions?

If the processes of transmission can be looked at in this way, it would not be surprising to find that the musical products can, too. One of the most productive areas of folk-music research has been the classification of tune-variants and 'tune-families'; often a seeming multiplicity of melodies turns out to reduce to a small number of 'models' or sets.[9] Some headway has been made on the methodological problems (the choice of quantitative or qualitative analysis, the ranking of parameters for usefulness, the question of how 'deep' the 'real' structure lies, and so on), and there is little doubt that important 'tune-families' could be located in the popular music repertories, which in any case would probably reveal links with 'folk' families. Peter van der Merwe has made a start on this (1989); and Hatch and Millward have drawn attention to some important family relationships (1987).[10] It seems likely that intensive research would reveal that beneath the breathless pace of popular music turnover lies, on another level, a considerable degree of coherence and stability, which ultimately will help to characterize historical periods, distribution of forms and types, and patterns of cross-influence, conflict, continuity and disjunction. At the limit, we may find that in *some* respects the structures of twentieth-century popular songs fit into very long-lived patterns which are characteristic of a large cultural area.

If – often – 'different tunes are the same', it is also true that 'the same tune is different' (Burke 1978: 124–5; see also ibid: 124–48 *passim*); and in fact tune-families are often formed through processes of variation. There are two aspects to this, the variants associated with an individual (an *idiolect*) and those associated with a context or locale (a *dialect*, or to use a term of the folklorist Carl von Sydow, an *ecotype*). Ecotypes can be associated with geographical distinctions (think of 1960s Merseyside versions of rock 'n' roll or Motown songs) or sociological ones (Beatles numbers performed by the James Last Orchestra), or functional ones (a Jimi Hendrix single was not the same as a concert version of the same song). Individual variance is more complex. As with 'folk' and 'traditional' musics, we can think of a scale, running from 'faithful copies', at one end (the Rolling Stones' early versions of rhythm and blues and soul records would be examples), to radical transformations done for deliberate aesthetic or ideological reasons, at the other (here, Sid Vicious's version of Sinatra's 'My Way' would be an obvious example). In between would come Elvis Presley's reworkings of blues songs, the Beach Boys' use of Chuck Berry riffs, Cream's version of 'Rockin' and Tumblin' ', and so on – not to mention performers' successive versions of their own songs. Thus, as with 'folk' songs, the value and meaning of popular songs can be only partly assessed on the basis of any single version; their subsequent life 'in tradition' must also be taken into account.

Another way that tune-families arise is through the use of stock structures, and of stock phrases and motifs which 'wander' from tune to tune. Partly because of the nature of oral composition, 'folk' songs often draw on a pool of collectively owned, pre-existing schemes and materials. Analysis of such techniques has been applied more to verbal texts than to tunes; and no doubt popular song lyrics would reveal stock themes, situations, phrases and word combinations. Given the composition methods characteristic of popular music production, it would be surprising if similar structural patterns could not be found in tunes. Analysis of structural 'laws' and schemas merits extended discussion in the next chapter (though see also pp. 45–9 above); but there is one folkloristic method – the so-called 'oral-formulaic theory' – which is particularly relevant here.

This theory was developed by Milman Parry and Albert Lord (see Lord 1960), starting in the 1930s. The aim was to explain how the enormously long unwritten epics of Yugoslav bards (and, by analogy, the Homeric epics also) could be composed in performance, apparently spontaneously. The secret lay, it was argued, in the use of formulae: stock adjectives, phrases, lines, verses, characters, plots; composition then consisted of the combination, rearrangement and variation of these formulae. The stress of this theory on composition as performance and performance as a site of variative activity makes it most obviously applicable to musical styles of an improvisatory kind – though one can imagine even some Tin Pan Alley composers sitting at the piano and working in a similar way.[11]

Analysis of Jimi Hendrix's recording of 'Gipsy Eyes'[12] in terms of the relationship of formula and variant reveals that the entire performance is put together from variants of five stock ideas. These are familiar from other recordings in the same style (provisionally termed a 'hard rock'/'psychedelic rhythm and blues' synthesis).

1 Drum lick A, which starts the performance off (note that the rock term 'lick' means – significantly – something like 'a stock pattern or phrase'). This alternates bass drum, on the beat, and hi-hat cymbal, off the beat; it is a staple pattern in rhythm and blues (see Ex. 5.1a).
2 Drum lick B, which follows on from the first and subsequently alternates with it. This is a typical *rock* rhythm. Its basic form, using drums and/or cymbals, appears in Ex. 5.1b.
3 A complex of riffs on guitar and bass guitar, all centring on the tonic and emphasizing it – often it alternates with the note below. For a few of the variants, see Ex. 5.1c.
4 A basic melodic falling pattern, using the notes of the pentatonic scale. The first vocal phrase is an example (Ex. 5.1d). This generates all of the vocal and much of the lead guitar work as well. Again it is a typical rhythm and blues formula (cf. Muddy Waters).
5 A characteristic electric guitar effect, the attacked single note with long decay and glissando fall. Common in rock (and varied in timbre and electronic treatment in all sorts of ways), it derives again from rhythm and blues – this time guitarists such as B.B. King.

The combinations and variations of these formulae are many and highly imaginative. But the basic formulae are so simple that the recording could well have been worked out 'in performance'.

Not surprisingly, given formulae are often much repeated within a song. In

Well I   re - a-lised   ? ___   ?   ?   I love you gip-sy eyes. ___

Ex 5.1

this sense, repetition within a song can be regarded as a localized instance of formulaic method within a style. Repetition, again, is an aspect of popular music of such importance that it demands separate discussion in a later chapter. What can be said here, however, is that, as in 'folk' music, the presence of repetition may be connected both to the nature of oral composition and to the need of audiences for periodic 'rests' to help assimilation of perhaps lengthy performances. Repeated phrases and riff structures help create a framework against which variation can take place; they also invite in and make comfortable a perhaps heterogeneous, perhaps distracted audience. Thus 'hook' lines offer a route through the song to both producer and listener; in a similar way 'folk' ballad singers often insert a 'filler' – a 'redundant' repeated line at the same point in each stanza. While repetition is a feature of *all* music, of any sort, a high level of repetition may be a specific mark of 'the popular', enabling an inclusive rather than exclusive audience.

Politics

The politics of 'folk' centre, through all interpretative nuance, on the 'authenticity' of the music. Its value – particularly when set against other, less favoured kinds of music – is guaranteed by its provenance in a certain sort of culture with certain characteristic processes of cultural production. Thus the supposed 'purity' of folk society (or in liberal accounts, of the essential processes of folk creation) goes hand in hand with the 'authenticity' of the music. As we have seen, both are myths. Culturally they originate in the romantic critique of industrial society; politically they derive from the bourgeoisie's attempt to make such critique comfortable, providing an ideologically functioning fantasy which can be used to counter the threat of real workers' culture. The judgement of 'authenticity' is always directed at the practice of someone else. Either it removes this practice from its own mode of existence and annexes it to the system of an imperialist cultural morality, or it scapegoats undesirable ('inauthentic') practices and casts them beyond the pale.

However, just as within the discredited concept of 'folk' hide real processes which may still be identified – *continuity* and *active use*, together forming *tradition* – so from the debris of 'authenticity' we may rescue a useful notion: that of *appropriation*. But this refers to possibilities which are universally available. Thus János Maróthy defines the 'folkloric' itself in terms of appropriation: the making, from *whatever* materials, of 'a music of your own' (Maróthy 1981). At the ultimate this would lead to Attali's *composition*. Whenever there is division of musical labour, the question arises of the response to production of those further down the production chain (whether disseminators, performers, re-creators, participants, or listeners): shall it be appropriation, acceptance, toleration, apathy, or rejection? With cultural stratification, hence alternative musics, the question becomes more pressing: wherever this music has come from, shall I make it mine, shall I reject it as alien, or shall I just consume it with more or less enthusiasm? Really authentic music is appropriated music, that is, it is integrated into subjectively motivated social practice.

'Folk' is too weak a term for such a broad concept. The materials for the process may come from 'folk' and non-'folk' sources alike. Moreover, there is no simple dichotomy between activity and passivity, appropriation and manipulation; rather, there is a spectrum, stretching from new production, at one end, to a (hypothetical?) Pavlovian automaticity of response, at the other. Positionings on the spectrum can only be assessed in context. Thus, for instance, music *use* (listening, dancing, and so on) is no less part of 'social practice' than is production; and if completion of structure and effect takes place there, if constitution or reconstitution of meaning is going on there, this practice may be thought of as 'subjectively motivated'. Where such practice is orientated around the existence of a social group, however ephemeral, partial or geographically diffuse, all the essentials of traditional 'folk' culture are present, in generalized form. A rough sketch of the spectrum might look something like this:

Studying popular music

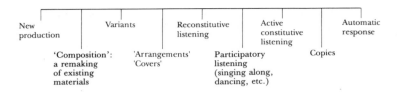

By contrast with this reformulation, many attempts have been made to retain the traditional ideology of 'authenticity', moving it across into new areas. Critics, fans and musicians have joined in these attempts to construct their own preferred music as a 'pure' alternative to the 'commercial manipulations' of the mainstream, and almost every variety of Afro-American and Country music, jazz, rock, and now 'roots' or 'world' music styles has been construed as a new 'folk' genre (see, for example, Malone 1982; Palmer 1982; Baraka 1982; Belz 1967; 1972: esp. 3–15; Landau 1972: 21, 130; Laing 1969: 80). As approaches to musics which unavoidably have to operate in cultural fields characterized by stylistic conflict, ideological contradiction, alienated work/leisure relationships and commercial mass dissemination, such descriptions are simply not accurate. At the same time, as Frith has pointed out (1981), they read as sociological facts what are in reality ideological experiences (see also Frith 1983a: 48–52); feelings of 'community', 'creativity' and 'honesty' are read into the music so that it is made to match participants' own cultural desires. This is not to say that these musics could not be, and were not, *appropriated* by certain listeners (and musicians) in such a way that they really produced effects subsequently described in terms of folk myths. But this is true of other musics as well (possibly of all musics); moreover, the mythologized styles have also been used in other ways – their value and validity could never be simply measured off against a pre-existing touchstone of 'authenticity'. In fact, there are always limits to appropriation; it can never be complete. Within cultural production in capitalist societies, musical objects, however integrated into particular social practices, always carry the marks of their (contradictory) origins and of other (real or potential) existences. And this then raises the whole question of how they relate to particular social locations.

Sociology

Whatever their disagreements, folklorists almost always take it as axiomatic that 'folk' music and 'folk' society are intimately linked. For Sharp, 'peasant society' produced 'peasant song' (1972: 20). Folk music, he wrote,

> is the product of a race, and reflects feelings and tastes that are communal rather than personal . . . The racial character of a ballad or song is due, therefore . . . to communal choice . . . they reflect the popular taste, express the popular ideal, and are stamped with the popular approval (Sharp 1972: 41).

He does not explain how this 'reflection' comes about or how to recognize it. Similarly, Green argues (1972: xii) that the miners' songs he discusses 'reveal miners' values' (but how?). Commercial products could be accepted in the mining communities; but these, while made as commodities, could apparently also carry collective cultural values: 'miners heard the ring of truth in discs intended merely to ring coins into cash registers' (ibid: 34) (but how do you recognize this 'ring of truth'?). Lloyd, needing to accommodate a broader historical dimension, develops a (relatively vulgar) Marxist version of the theory (Lloyd 1967). The nub is still the same – but reflection is now governed primarily by *economic factors*, is explicitly related to *class*, and is mediated by *change*: songs are

> born into a tradition that fits a certain society . . . folk song is the musical and poetic expression of the fantasy of the lower classes . . . as the life of the common people is changed, however slowly, through the movement of society, so their folk music alters too (ibid: 72, 24, 58).

But how is the 'fit' between the musical tradition and the society defined? How do songs express class identity? And how is the course of change in song governed by changes taking place elsewhere in society?

Lloyd's historical schema centres around four 'moments' of change. The transition from 'clan' society to a class of small individual producers and serfs results in a shift from collectively organized 'variative' singing, often with ritualistic functions, to the symmetrical, strophic solo song of 'classic' European folklore (this theory is taken from Maróthy). Dating is hazy: sometime between the fall of the Roman Empire and the Middle Ages. The rise of the bourgeoisie, and the influence of its culture on that of the lower classes, results in a squarer, robust, common-chord-based kind of tune. This dominates the period *c*.1550–*c*.1750. Then the rise of capitalist agriculture and the resulting pauperization and disruption of rural lower-class life produces a new sort of tune: longer, tonally unstable, meandering, highly ornamented – reflecting uncertainty and crisis. This phase lasts roughly from 1750 to 1850, and is overlapped by the emergence of 'industrial folk song' (*c*.1800–*c*.1914; with a revival after 1945), which, of course, reflects the industrial revolution and the development of an urban working class. The industrial songs draw on rural song traditions and on the written music of the towns, but they are harsh, direct, less poetic in expression, the texts reflecting industrial reality, poverty, protest and class consciousness.

This periodization is plausible (and is not seriously at odds with the schema of 'situational crises' proposed in Chapter 1); but the mechanisms by which change takes place and which govern the homology of music and social life are vaguely defined, epistemologically naive, and – mechanical. There is little sense of negotiation taking place *within* culture, as classes struggle over the articulations and meanings of musical and lyric materials, old and new. Similarly, the nature of 'expressive fit' is not seen as a problem; we know it exists because Lloyd's intuitive interpretation says it does. 'Folk song' for Lloyd cannot be understood except in an awareness of the whole society, so simple class determinism has to be partially modified; but there is little awareness of a dialectical working out of this tension – rather a hazy and uneasy compromise between class reductionism and cultural *Zeitgeist*. Of course, these problems are inevitable given that folk music itself has already been defined in terms of its *difference* from other musical practices; it is the *real* voice of a (preconstructed) class.

In more recent periods, when 'folk' styles come to exist in much more fluid social situations, when they change more rapidly and take on new functions and audiences, these problems become even more acute. Yet urban and industrial folklore tends to retain reflectionist assumptions. Most analyses of Country music, and of urban black styles, tie them to working-class American culture, white or black respectively. The question they almost never tackle is the most obvious one: how do these musics come to appeal to *other* social groups – in the case of Country music, to *Northern* workers, to middle-class listeners, to non-Americans?

Assessment of the theory of homology in the general field of modern popular music will be best undertaken in the context of a discussion of youth and subcultural theory. What can be said now is that the work of folklorists will be of little help there – partly because of a tendency to take the sociological datum of class, group or community for granted (as a thing, with a prior analytical existence) rather than considering whether the experience of class, group or community may not be articulated and constructed, in a more processual way, *within* cultural forms and practices; and partly because of the temptation, even in progressive conceptions, to relapse into an ahistorical functionalism, in which the characteristics of 'folk' practices are thought of as static, conservative and 'different'. Folkloristic sociology is always defensive, and it defends an ideology. As Alan Lomax puts it (1959: 950), 'folk' 'musical styles may be symbolic of basic human value systems which function at the unconscious level and evolve with glacial slowness because the basic social patterns which produce them also evolve slowly'; as a result, 'from the point of view of its social function, the primary effect of ["folk"] music is to give the listener a feeling of security . . . [and] the work of composers in the folk world is . . . limited by this stylistic security-bringing framework' (ibid: 929, 930). Whose security is being protected here?

A case study: 'folk blues'

A brief case study may demonstrate how the four aspects considered here – definition, methods, politics and sociology – come together in the treatment of a specific form. 'Folk blues' (or 'country' or 'rural' or 'downhome' blues) was constructed as a distinct discursive category in the early decades of this century, mostly as a result of the activities of record companies, marketing 'old-fashioned' music to rural Southern 'folk' and newly arrived urban dwellers. The field-collecting of folklorists, such as John and Alan Lomax in the 1930s, contributed, too, as did the work of subsequent blues scholars, from Samuel Charters and Paul Oliver down to David Evans, Jeff Todd Titon and William Ferris. Pretty well all those involved were white – and, doubtless, bourgeois.

The music from which this category was constructed had originally been part of a much more heterogeneous, fluid musical field cultivated and enjoyed by black (and some white) people, and including other kinds of secular song and dance, ragtime, early jazz, religious song, and theatre, minstrel and Tin Pan Alley song (see, for example, Oliver 1984; Russell 1970). These people seem mostly to have defined blues functionally – it was 'good time music' – or experientially – blues was a feeling – rather than by reference to any formal characteristics or folk stereotypes. At the same time, many of those characteristics (pentatonic melody, blue tonality, typical chord progression and stanza patterns, call and response) could be found in *other* forms and contexts too: in hillbilly and Country music, gospel song, ragtime, jazz and Tin Pan Alley hits. And in that wider context the 'blues' label was applied, at different times and by diverse groups, to many different products, ranging from white ballads to Ellingtonian mood pieces, from W.C. Handy's Tin Pan Alley music sheets to a 1920s dance craze, from semi-pornographic urban party music to 'downhome' hollers. So for blues to become *one* thing, with a 'folk' label attached – or at least for that one thing to become the primary, original, authentic form – necessitated considerable ideological struggle. The evidence is now strong that blues was not born in the 'folk' mists of pre-history but developed at the same time as, and in interaction with, the songster repertories of the late nineteenth and early twentieth centuries, ragtime, early jazz, and the first major black successes in commercial entertainment; that it developed in an urban as much as a rural context; that professional performance, and dissemination and codification by records, played vital roles. It was necessary to ignore all this – to extract and privilege one part of the repertory, to idealize it, to write the history backwards, *from* the 'survivals' *to* the (reconstructed) origins, and to 'museumize' the music (for 'folk blues' was always about to die out).

So far this is a familiar story of folkloristic distortion, which brought with it the predictable myths of 'authenticity': the so-called 'mouldy fig' mentality insisted that *real* bluesmen were old, illiterate, blind, toothless, and ideally had a colourful or criminal background. Revisionists appeared, too, who extended the category to include previously forbidden styles: urban blues (defined as 'folk' in contrast to contemporary white pop or soul music); black music as a whole ('folk' in contrast to white commerce); even rock 'n' roll (influenced by blues, hence . . .). But the misunderstanding went further. Even if we accept the 'folk blues' repertory as a real one, it was in important aspects misanalysed.

Admittedly, in certain respects this music was produced, and sounds, like 'folk' music is supposed to be produced and to sound. Dissemination through oral tradition was central; performers were not formally trained, had no systematic music theory and were amateur or semi-professional; composition relied heavily on standard forms and patterns, on collectively used formulae in words and music, and on variation of these patterns and formulae; performance was mostly for defined social contexts and functions (dancing, an accompaniment to drinking, and so on) and for relatively homogeneous, local audiences. Not surprisingly, then, scholars have been able to apply standard methods to analyse processes of transmission (see, for example, Evans 1982b) and of formulaic construction (Titon 1977) (though in itself this means little, since, as we have seen, such methods could be applied very widely in popular music). Moreover, if we turn to the society within which this music was current – it being taken for granted by the scholars that this 'folk' music reflected a 'folk' mentality and functioned as part of a 'folk' culture – it looks in many ways like a 'folk' society is supposed to look. As Keil writes (1966a: 75), in the late nineteenth and early twentieth centuries, after Reconstruction had been broken and given way to segregation, the relatively homogeneous, isolated, illiterate, static communities of 'share-cropping and tenant-farming Negroes in the rural South are not far removed from the folk society as an ideal type'. The nearest blues scholars come to doubt is probably Titon's observation that downhome blues songs . . . do not sound like the folk songs of singers like Leadbelly . . . yet . . . early downhome blues is best regarded as folk music . . . despite the dangers of the implication that if downhome blues is folk music, then downhome black Americans must constitute a folk group (Titon 1977: xvi).

If we pursue those doubts, and look more closely at both music and society, problems with the analysis arise. Folksingers are supposed to reflect collective, rather than overtly individual, feelings. Yet, however much blues singers reworked collectively owned themes and devices, the result always comes out sounding highly personal. Songs are associated with individuals. The repertory is characterized by a large variety of styles and a high rate of style-change, and these styles and changes are connected with individuals. Abbe Niles spoke of blues having to do with 'the element of pure *self* ' and W.C. Handy wrote of the function of blues as being to 'express . . . personal feeling in a sort of musical soliloquy' (quoted in Levine 1977: 222). To Robert Palmer (1981: 75), the singer's 'involvement becomes both the subject and substance of the work', while Laurence Levine writes that

> The blues was the most highly personalised, indeed the first almost completely personalised music that Afro-Americans developed. It was the first important form of Afro-American music in the United States to lack the kind of antiphony that had marked other black musical forms. The call and response form remained, but in blues it was the singer who responded to himself either verbally or on an accompanying instrument. In all these respects blues was the most typically American music Afro-Americans had yet created and represented a major degree of acculturation to the individualised ethos of the larger society (Levine 1977: 221).

The rural bluesman was typically a wanderer, often a social misfit or problem, and regarded by many with distrust, equivocation or even as a demonic figure. Standard themes in his songs concerned loneliness, alienation and travel; and performance techniques generally suggested great emotional involvement. To some extent, then, we can regard him as an exception, an outsider, a marginal figure who breaks folk norms. Given the irony that the development of changed styles in the cities actually manifested an *increase* in 'folk' characteristics (group performance, often in quasi-ritualistic forms, explicit call-and-response, stress on creating solidarity rather than expressing personal anguish, more homogeneous styles), there is point in Keil's observation that 'if . . . juxtaposition of the blues spectrum with [Redfield's] folk-urban continuum offers any insight, it is that blues expression tends to reveal a mirrored or reversed reflection of its immediate social milieu' (Keil 1966a: 76). In a sense, then, the 'folk' bluesman was to some degree a *critic* – a licensed critic, since he was also often regarded as a culture hero; he revealed an area of experience neglected by the everyday 'folk' world, his individualism contrasting with its drive for conformity imposed by the reality of segregation and oppression, and making him its conscience or memory. The point is made clearer by a comparison between blues and other contemporary musics in the same society – black religious music, the songsters' ballads and dances, or white hillbilly music – which seem to conform much more to 'folk' stereotypes. This does not tell us anything about the nature or use-

fulness of concepts of 'folk' music. What it does tell us about is the relative autonomy of cultural forms, and the variation in the amount and mode of such
autonomy, in relation to different forms and their use by different groups, in
different contexts, in a society.

However, the particularity of blues – its social critique – would have been
impossible if it had not been able to draw on elements existing in the culture. If
we place the picture of apparently isolated, homogeneous rural black
communities in the larger context of the whole society, as it developed from the
Civil War through to the 1920s, its incompleteness becomes obvious. Tenant
farmers and share-croppers, however serf-like in some ways, had entered into
market relations and, along with other black workers, were increasingly drawn
into the capitalist cash economy. The turbulence of Reconstruction, the
beginnings of capitalist agricultural development in the South, economic crisis
and high unemployment all resulted in large-scale black mobility. For many
blacks, there was some choice of work: day-labour, permanent agricultural
employment, tenancy or share-cropping – or industrial wage-labour in the
sawmills, on the levees or on railroad construction. Especially after about 1900,
urban jobs increasingly drew blacks to cities within the South and up
North – and the promise of a 'freer', more individualistic life. In short, a new
and dynamic stage had been reached in the conflict between Southern
'feudalism' and Northern industrial capital.

On the ideological level, the effects of Emancipation and Reconstruction – the
promise of individual freedom, defined by American (bourgeois) norms – must
have been written deeply into the black psyche.[13] In everyday social life they had
largely to be repressed. But the discontented blues singer did not forget; his
'unflinching subjectivity . . . in the context of its time and place . . . was
positively heroic. Only a man who understands his worth and believes in his
freedom sings as if nothing else matters' (Palmer 1981: 75). As the reaction to
Reconstruction tried to rebuild a new version of the old status quo of slavery
days, the contradictions were acute; for historic reasons blacks were at the sharp
point of these structural contradictions – and within black culture the blues
singer represented one point where they were most sharply focused.

This allegedly 'feudal' society, then, was less like that of the European Middle
Ages than that of 'rural' England in 1820. In both cases, affixing a 'folk' label, to
society or music, is of no help whatever. Within what is clearly a major
situational crisis in the wider society, blues appears as, if anything, a proto-
proletarian form. At the same time, simple functional theories of adaptation go
too far in the opposite direction. Szwed argues that

> Blues arose as a popular music form in the early 1900s, the period of the
> first great Negro migrations north to the cities . . . The formal and stylistic
> elements of the blues seem to symbolise newly emerging social patterns
> during the crisis period of urbanisation . . . By replacing the functions
> served by sacred music, the blues eased a transition from land-based,
> agrarian society to one based on mobile wage-labor urbanism (Szwed 1969:
> 118, 119).

By contrast, we need to see blues as offering the possibility, within a cultural
form, for some people in some contexts to *negotiate* a particular response to the

contradictory forces in the society at this time. For a complete picture, we would need to take account of the society's other musical practices and genres, their differences from, and overlap with, blues; and in the study of that complexity and that history, any remnants of 'folk' theorizing would be finally washed away.

Ethnomusicology

In many ways musical folkloristics can be regarded as being subsumed within the anthropology of music (ethnomusicology). Ethnomusicology shares many of the characteristics of the folkloristic approach – stressing the importance of performance, cultural location and social function, and of oral as well as written material – but applies them more generally. A 'culturalist' viewpoint is common: in John Blacking's words (1976: 31), 'If some music can be analysed and understood as expressions of human experience in the context of different kinds of social and cultural organisation, I see no reason why all music should not be analysed in the same way'. Many ethnomusicologists are clear that this perspective should be applied to popular music, and Adamo has explained the methodological gains which would ensue (1982: 6). He lists the 'cardinal points' in the specific 'scientific culture' which ethnomusicology has developed:

(a) the interpretation of music and musical behaviour in terms of cultural patterns and rules which can be analysed in their structure;
(b) the interest in the relationship between patterns and rules at the musical level and all the other patterns and rules of the biological and social life of music makers;
(c) the tendency towards interdisciplinarity and to a systematical approach, which arises from studying musical phenomena from as many points of view as possible.

In practice, however, most ethnomusicologists study the music of 'primitive' societies, of the oriental high cultures and of 'folk' cultures; popular music, let alone Western 'art' music, has hardly been touched (though see Finnegan 1989). This is partly because other disciplines have been perceived as attending or likely to attend to them, and it is partly because methods and attitudes developed early in ethnomusicology's life are not easily given up; but mostly it seems to be yet another result of the colonial quest of the Western bourgeoisie, bent on preserving other people's musics before they disappear, documenting 'survivals' of 'traditional' practices, and enjoying the pleasures of exoticism into the bargain. If it is suggested that for objective research a 'foreign' culture is necessary in order to produce analytical 'distance', most Western ethnomusicologists could easily find this among the popular music subcultures of the developed societies. Moreover, the subcultures often decay very quickly and are in great danger of disappearing! The primary motives for ethnomusicological exoticism, then, obviously lie in value-judgements about 'authenticity' in musical culture.

This is not to say there is nothing of use to us in mainstream ethnomusicology. We can point to certain directly relevant bodies of research.[14] Similarly, strongly developing theoretical work in certain areas – for instance, on aspects of *performance* and concepts of *change* – could be profitably applied to popular music.[15] What is most germane to my argument in this chapter, however, is the widespread influence of *homology* theories, and it is this I want to pursue.

Most of ethnomusicology's subject-matter comes from societies which, on the face of it at least, are culturally well integrated, so it is not surprising to find most ethnomusicologists taking it almost as axiomatic that there are close structural links between music and culture as a whole. As John Blacking puts it (1976: 54): 'Music . . . confirms what is already present in society and culture, and it adds nothing new except patterns of sound.' David Coplan, however, while quoting Blacking to the effect that 'the creation of musical structures is a problem of synthesis that reflects the creation of societies', insists on the 'dialectical relationship between the creation of styles and performances and the course of social life'; he sees performances as 'metaphoric' rather than just representational, the metaphoric acts not merely interpreting and classifying experience but participating in, enacting and realizing it (Coplan 1982: 116, 123). Clifford Geertz goes further (1973: 142–69; 360–411). He regards the various cultural processes and social structures as possessing specific modes of existence and integration; they are interactive but not mutually determinative; they may be interconnected but not through any innate homology, rather through the active experiences and interpretation of participants. Tendencies which are felt as reinforcing each other – which are 'isomorphic' – produce 'cultural integration', but this tends to happen only when there has been a long period of stability. Subversive, discontinuous or contradictory tendencies can coexist with them – and such contradictions can be the source of change. Thus Geertz's model of culture is of an *octopus*: 'confluences of partial integrations, partial incongruencies, and partial independencies' (ibid: 408) which are interconnected but rather indirectly. This is a useful corrective to reductively tight models of cultural homology. However, it is so flexible that it risks ending as a weak empiricism; moreover, it is incapable of *explaining* connections – except as the product of individual interpretative choices, which, somehow, just happen to result in social and cultural patterns. The most persuasive position is somewhere between total correlation, on the one hand, and meccano-set pragmatism, on the other. As Lévi-Strauss puts it (1972: 79):

. . . between culture and language [or music] there cannot be *no* relations at all, and there cannot be one hundred per cent correlation either. Both situations are impossible to conceive. If there were no relations at all, that would lead us to assume that the human mind is a kind of jumble – that there is no connection at all between what the mind is doing on one level and what the mind is doing on another level. But, on the other hand, if the correlation were one hundred per cent, then certainly we should know about it . . .

This can be tested against two ethnomusicological cases, associated with Alan Lomax (1959; 1962; 1968) and Charles Keil (1966a) respectively: the first concerning 'simple', 'primitive' societies, the second a 'subculture' in a developed society.

Lomax's earliest writing in this area seems to conceive the homological relationship as operating through symbolism: 'Only when . . . behavioural patterns . . . are taken into account can . . . formal elements . . . be properly understood, for they are symbols which stand for the whole' (Lomax 1959: 929). In later work the relationship takes a more functionalist turn, with the 'working hypothesis . . . that each [expressive] system supports and reinforces the same central message in its own way' . . . 'the chief function of song is to express the shared feelings and mould the joint activities of some human community. It is to be expected, therefore, that the content of the sung communication should be social rather than individual, normative rather than particular.' At the same time, the approach is, in a stricter sense, structural: 'every cultural system has an internal congruence reflected in its expressive and communications systems' (Lomax 1968: x, 3, 120).

Lomax's initial study takes a relatively narrow range of subject-matter and applies a relatively narrow focus. He is primarily concerned to show that in the performance of 'traditional' song (he calls it 'folk song') singing style reflects the social structure of gender relations. Analysing singing style in Spain and southern Italy, he finds its roots in the oppression of women. A culture of sexual neurosis, jealousy and deprivation has psycho-physiological effects on muscles, face and vocal chords (they are taut, tense, constricted), and this in turn leads to the high-pitched, nasal, strangulated, highly melismatic solo style of the vocal music. To some extent the logic of this argument derives from its large behavioural (as against symbolic) component: the link between culture and music is seen as partly physiological. At the same time, this very approach – with its tendency to a naturalistic view of style and an arbitrary isolation of one factor – ignores the extent to which style is a *coded* distillation of a *complex* of cultural factors.

This mistake is no doubt why difficulties inevitably arise when the approach is applied to popular musics in more differentiated societies, where there is greater contrast of codes and conscious playing with codes for ideological or aesthetic purposes. A comparison of the sexual mores of hillbilly society – the music of which tended towards a nasal, high-pitched singing style – with those of Southern black society – which typically cultivated more relaxed, open-voiced song styles – might bear fruit, and it would be interesting to compare early, 'nasal' Bob Dylan with post-*Blonde on Blonde* 'relaxed' Dylan from the same point of view. But it seems doubtful that, say, the ultra-relaxed style of 1930s crooners represented a society of sexual equality; that the high-pitched strangulated, melismatic singing of many soul singers symbolized a turn to quasi-Islamic gender relations; or that the conjunction of the medium-voiced, relaxed vocal approach of reggae and the typical male chauvinism of Rastafarian ideology means that music and culture cannot be related. What, moreover, do we make of 'liberated' women singers who, from Janis Joplin to various punks and feminists, have deliberately adopted harsh-toned, aggressive singing styles?

Lomax's later book extends the boundaries of both subject-matter and analytic focus (Lomax 1968). It reports on the ambitious project he calls 'cantometrics': a computerized attempt to quantify all aspects of song style (not just performance style but also melodic range, content and elaborateness, rhythmic variety, textural forms, and so on) across a global map of 'song-areas' (confined to 'traditional' song), then to quantify other cultural traits for the same areas, and then to relate the two models. The list of relevant culture traits is broadened to include not only sexual mores and gender relations, but also level of production, level of political organization, level of class stratification and level of social cohesion. Lomax's discussion of gender relations is more satisfactory here, simply because it pays more attention to social structure – through a concept of 'complementarity' – as against sexual psychology. High complementarity denotes a relatively high female contribution to social and economic life, and is said to be reflected musically by the existence and extent of *polyphony*, and of *tonal blend* (playing down the individuality of voices in the interests of cohesion), as well as in (relaxed) voice production. Conversely, as social cohesion declines, and individual male assertiveness grows, *solo* singing increases, and with it raspy, nasal, narrow vocal tone.

Lomax goes on to develop this approach more broadly, arguing that *general* social structure, as represented on a cohesion/individualism scale, is reflected, too, in the extent of melodic elaborateness and rhythmic variety (both of which increase as individualism increases) and also, more interestingly, in the social structure of vocal performance. Lomax's scheme for the latter takes the following pattern:

interlock: equal but distinct simultaneous melodic parts, no leader; primitive gathering societies, no hierarchy;

social unison: everybody sings the same; simple tribal societies, conformity stressed, leaders have little authority;

overlap: overlapping call and response; more complex tribal societies, leader's authority 'embedded' in collective approval;

alternation: call and response; more stratified societies, leader's control unquestioned and supported;

explicit solo: one voice only; highly stratified or individualistic societies.

We are left to work out the meanings of other possibilities: for example, choral homophony (voices blended into chords), or the myriad sorts of combination of solo-plus-backing-singers common in popular music.

The link construed here between music and culture concerns a continuity in actual social structure – that is, it is behavioural as well as symbolic. That common-sense correlation, though, needs to be modified by a recognition that musical performance is a *specific* social situation, and the musical effects of social relationships are mediated by that specificity. For example, the culturally coded acoustic aspects of unison, heterophonic, octave or harmonic singing constitute a *musical* resource with its own 'rules'; and they interact with a range of different melodic and rhythmic processes. Vocal counterpoints in the Supremes and in the Beach Boys are structurally similar, in Lomax's terms, but clearly not identical in meaning. The same is true of the vocal unisons indulged in by Slade, Bill Haley's rock 'n' roll band and Band Aid's 'Feed the World'. Without this kind of semiotically mediated account, it will be impossible to explain the variety of vocal textures in rhythm and blues vocal groups, doo-wop, Motown, the Beatles, the Who, and so on, let alone the fact that a single song can *switch* between them. Moreover, meanings are not absolute but are constructed in conditions of 'discursive relativism'. The unison chorus singing of the music hall audience could be interpreted as reflecting a 'simple tribal society' only by comparison with, say, the part-singing common in the refrains of contemporary bourgeois ballad performance. An unaccompanied solo can, with the complicity of its audience, include them implicitly in a 'social unison', by comparison with the explicit socially complex textures of other musics. Instrumental appropriations of vocal textures raise further questions (not to mention recording techniques associated with 'chorus' and 'harmonizer' devices, and double tracking of voices); for instance a single (keyboard or guitar) instrumentalist can 'mimic' a variety of solo and polyphonic vocal structures. In short, the continuity between the social structure of musical performance and the wider social structure is not necessarily or wholly direct, but is subject to semiotic manipulation.

Having said that, the intuitive assumptions that 'polyphonic music says "we" ', as Adorno puts it (1973: 18), while solo song reflects 'the "little world" of the isolated Ego' (Maróthy 1974: 18), and that the many in-between stages, combinations and interactions can be analysed in social terms, may be accepted as pointing to a basic material resource on which musical codes always draw. The rest of Lomax's theory raises more doubts, for he simply correlates 'complexity' of mode of production, of political organization and of social stratification with 'complexity, density and specificity of the [musical] message' (Lomax 1968: 122); this includes melodic elaborateness and rhythmic variety, melodic interval size (the more complex the society, the narrower the typical intervals), the 'wordiness', explicitness and precision of enunciation of verbal texts, and the 'rationality' of performance. Apart from the immense difficulties, descriptive and epistemological, of defining complexity – of music and of society – there is no obvious reason for this correlation, and, whatever the definitions, there will be many exceptions; Lomax's dubious suggestion that, in the hands of Bob Dylan and the Beatles, rock 'n' roll changed from being forceful and repetitive to a more rational precisely enunciated style, and that this led to its acceptance in the complex society of urban middle-class whites, is an indication of the kind of question marks that are raised and the kind of generalizations that inevitably appear. The assumption that everything fits and that the possibility of internal conflict can be discounted is supported by a quantitative approach to data, the interpretation of which is carried out in the safety of the analyst's study, far from its cultural source. The resulting circular arguments are characteristic of many theories of homology. A style is described as 'typical' of a culture but the culture has already been identified and delineated through an awareness of this and other 'typical' traits; the homology is pre-formed in the analyst's mind.

Homology theories, applied to relatively homogeneous, stable cultures, can be fruitful; or rather, the evident reproductive efficiency of the culture conceals the *arbitrariness* of its internal structure, elides the gap between 'culture' and 'society', and enables 'homologies' to appear 'natural'. In more differentiated, dynamic societies this can no longer be guaranteed. A classic ethnomusicological analysis of a culture located in such a society is Charles Keil's *Urban Blues* (1966a).

Unlike Lomax, Keil, as he himself admits, has comparatively little to say on an analytical level about the music. His assumption is that the meaning of urban blues is largely defined by its position in Afro-American culture, particularly the beliefs, behavioural patterns and historical awareness of 'blues people'. Keil sees the ideology of 'soul' and its associated behavioural practices as central; among the most important constituents, his description of black culture mentions the following:

(i)   the influence of religion, the role of the black preacher, organizational patterns associated with the black church and church service;

(ii)   call-and-response patterns, apparent in conversational formulae, ritualized greetings, religious services and sermon structures, and comedy routines; Keil relates these (rather vaguely) to particular kinds of social structure, notably a sort of interactive conception of solidarity and cultural identity: the right response is necessary for group membership;

(iii) a striking awareness of, and emphasis on, common experience and traditions; whatever the reasons (slavery and discrimination), black culture *is* different;

(iv)   related to this, an awareness of, and emphasis on, 'folk roots', for example, 'soul food' (typical items of black Southern diet);

(v)   specific male and female roles, too complex to go into here but related to the historical development of black family structure in conjunction with the pressures of ghetto life;

(vi)   an emphasis on resilience, strength through suffering (keep on keepin' on) and a resulting valorization of *effort* (as much as, or even more than, achievement);

(vii) a valorization of strong feeling, integrity, honesty (tell it like it is), as against outward form or 'beauty';

(viii) explicit expressions of sexuality, manifested in everyday conversation and body movement, dance styles and representations of male–female relationships.

If we listen to typical urban blues performances – say, those of B.B. King, who is central to Keil's book – this list could be correlated with musical characteristics as follows:

(i)   typical elements of lyric vocabulary; vocal patterns, both structural (incremental repetition for example) and intonational (rhythm, phrasing, melodic contour, rhetoric), borrowed from sermon techniques; singer's didactic, representational and inspirational role; performer–audience relationship modelled on preacher–congregation relationship;

(ii)   musical call-and-response, between singer and audience, and singer and instrument(s);

(iii) a very specific repertory with strong historical roots; styles which emphasize familiar and repeated elements and formulaic structures; function of performances and of performer's charismatic role in confirming group solidarity;

(iv)   'downhome' musical elements: a felt continuity, in musical technique, with life in the South and even with 'that slavery shit' – this music has 'paid its dues';

(v)   most lyrics are concerned with sexual themes, and performances dramatize the situations and relationships; men identify with a singer like King (successes *and* problems), women form relationships with him; the problems are cathartically played out;

(vi)   the music is valued for evidence of hard *experience* (expressed through the singer's personal authority and representativeness), and *work-rate* (manifested in expressive explicitness, vocal effort and bodily exertion);

(vii) a stress on personal statement and truth to self: this is B.B. King – the *real* B.B. King – speaking; the blues form and its characteristic phraseology are felt to represent cultural integrity: this is *our* life he's singing about; blue notes, pitch inflection, 'dirty' sounds and vocalized tone (on instruments) are felt to denote honesty: getting down to where it's really at;

(viii) lyric themes and vocabulary; sensuous vocal tone, paralinguistic effects and performance movements; strong connections between the musical style and (rather erotic) dance styles, and (without going here into the complex question of exactly how 'sexuality' is represented in music) with a general sense of erotically understood rhythm.

In many ways this is a more sophisticated approach than Lomax's. Many of the homologies are seen not as innate but as 'associative', that is, as products of historically informed social learning, cultural activity and conscious manipulation. There is a certain space between 'culture' and 'society', so that it is even possible to think of some of the meanings of the music – solidarity, black consciousness, group cultural identity – as referring to *desirable* social qualities rather than operative ones. Nevertheless, some of the same problems arise. Keil assumes a priori that music's principal roles are expressive and functional, and this strongly 'culturalist' angle is related to the fact that within his picture of culture there remain distinct elements of circular thinking: though in his case evidence for the proposition that musical and other patterns are bound into a single cultural unit is drawn less from quantified data and more from an uncritical acceptance of the 'folk view'. New problems arise, too. They stem from the fact that the blues form and culture exist not in one of Lomax's 'traditional' societies but in a particular part of a dynamic, highly stratified and culturally pluralistic capitalist society. How can such tight homologies be maintained in that situation? There are four problems here:

1 Black culture, though 'different', has never been isolated, and its music has been formed within, and in interaction with, a wider style pool. As we become aware of cultural traits and musical influences passing across social boundaries in both directions, interpretation of blues solely by reference to a tightly delimited picture of black culture becomes less convincing.

2 A specific extension of that point touches on Keil's relative neglect of the role of wider economic and institutional structures and processes in the formation of the music. The forms the music has taken, its modes of dissemination, its technology and its accessibility are inseparable from the operations of white capitalism and its black progeny – and hence from social patterns of far wider provenance than the black ghettos.

3 Within black society, musical tastes are not uniform; in particular, not all blacks are 'blues people'. If individuals from the same cultural context do not see their situation expressed in blues, what does this tell us about homology theories?

4 The converse of the previous point: urban blues have been enjoyed – more, culturally appropriated and integrated – by white people, within the United States and, even more problematically, outside. If the meaning of blues derives from its position in black culture, how can we explain a musician like Eric Clapton (who modelled himself on B.B. King)? How can we account for

the growth of a young white audience for blues in the 1960s, or for the seminal influence of blues on almost all post-rock 'n' roll popular music styles?

That the kinds of diffusion just mentioned should affect a music from such a relatively distinctive culture as that of black Americans makes the last point particularly striking. Can anthropology's 'struggle to get beyond the assertion that traits of each society form a unique configuration and lose their meaning when abstracted from it' succeed, without destroying the possibility of homology (Peterson 1976: 12)? Three possible answers suggest themselves:

(i) different social groups using the same music have cultures containing sufficient similarities to make homologies possible in both cases;
(ii) the 'secondary' group hears the music differently from the way the 'primary' group hears it, and so a new homology can come into being;
(iii) the musical form is more or less autonomous, and its essential meanings and deep patterns produce and structure cultural responses; thus they are available quite widely, to any individuals able to acquire the syntactic and interpretative codes.

The first and second positions retain 'culturalist' assumptions; music reflects or expresses experience, or in Raymond Williams's terms, a 'structure of feeling'. The third position, by contrast, assumes a structuralist perspective, in which musical forms offer the categories in which 'experience' can occur. As far as the relationship between blues and young whites is concerned, the first position is not uncommon (see Middleton 1972: 117–41); and certainly it is not implausible to see some similarities in the structural positions and stereotypical cultural profiles of urban black males and white male working-class youth. Each group, it can be argued, constitutes a ghettoized underclass, struggling to define a cultural identity against dominant/parental norms; each is commonly regarded as 'tribal', living in the present, irresponsible, irrational and hedonistic. To some extent these positions are imposed; to some extent they are deliberately worn as a badge of difference. However, this approach has to gloss over some rather striking dissimilarities – young white blues fans are *not* soul brothers – and it fails to come to terms with the fact that many white blues enthusiasts are middle-class, their musical taste coexisting with qualities which would not usually be associated with ghetto proletariats. The links become rather stretched. One helpful move might be to make a distinction between different kinds of homology. On the one hand, there might be 'behavioural' homologies (connecting, for instance, social structures of performance to those current elsewhere in the culture) and 'positional' homologies (arising out of the structural position of a subgroup *vis-à-vis* the larger society); these would be relatively easy to construct. On the other hand, we might find 'associative' homologies: the network of connective meanings built up within black culture over generations, which no culturalist theory could plausibly transfer to young whites.

The second position has not, to my knowledge, been systematically argued, though implicitly it lies behind much commentary – for example, suggestions that young whites heard blues as a 'protest' music and therefore used it to express their own rebellion. This position is more common in cases when the musical style is reworked to some extent (acculturated), so as to *enable* it to fit a not entirely similar cultural context. Thus Dave Laing suggests that in 'white blues' the focus of the style is switched; it moves from the singing to instrumental aspects, especially the guitar solo.

> White blues has, in effect, torn blues away from any dependence on local reference, both outside the song (in a shared general culture) *and* within it. The guitar solo in a B.B. King song takes its emotional colouring and resonance from the details of the personal crisis described in the lyrics. But when Cream played blues songs, the guitar solo had no point of reference outside itself to relate it to any individual situation or emotion. Intensity was all (Laing 1969: 158).

This approach has to confront the question whether there are any *limits* – within the musical form – to reinterpretation; and it is noticeable, too – the quotation from Laing is an example – that the analytic focus often drifts away from culturalist assumptions (text reflecting context) to a semiological perspective, which sees the process of producing meanings as internal to the musical practice.

This takes us to the third position, which can assume a variety of forms, ranging from a rather reductionist insistence on immanent meaning to the view that meanings are produced within the conjunction of text and reader, in the act of listening. Here the operation of *difference* is crucial: meanings are constructed through the mutual differentiation of units of musical practice and cultural interpretation. Thus, it would be possible to see an awareness of the 'linguistic' distinctiveness of blues, within a wider network of *shared* codes in Western music as a whole, as producing a particular structural position for white blues fans within Western culture; hence – to give a concrete example – one would see their conception of the cultural meanings of, say, blues singing ('realistic') or blues rhythm ('erotic') as arising from the structural differences between these practices, and singing and rhythm in mainstream white popular song, with their 'received' connotations ('sentimental', 'polite', respectively).

Whatever the position, it seems likely that in practice there are, inscribed in the musical form and in its cultural history, *limits* to the transmutation of meaning and hence to the re-construction of homologies; 'culturalist' social actors are not free to express themselves by inventing or interpreting *ab ovo*, and 'structuralist' texts are not free to wander infinitely away from the cultural contexts within which their meanings have been defined. It seems likely, too, that in the relationship of form and what can provisionally be called 'experience' (however that relationship is conceived theoretically), the two must 'dock' – rather than the one completely producing the other or the conjunction being purely one of juxtaposition. The docking may be relatively loose; but the parties must meet within certain *limits of tolerance*. It is possible that these limits vary according to degrees of cultural coherence and homogeneity; thus they may be relatively narrow in situations of cultural stability or constraint, relatively wide in situations of cultural flux or conflict. Assuming for the moment that the docking is engineered by processes of *articulation* – rather than by structural determinism, on the one hand, or (individual or collective) subjective expression, on the other – we can say that the *scope* of these processes is likely to be socially and historically variated, according to objective social pressures and patterns.

Subcultural theory

Within the wider context, urban blues can be seen as a *subculture*. But, while analysis of urban musical subcultures has drawn to some extent on anthropological work,[16] the main body of theory has focused on youth groups rather than ethnic communities; and a more important inspiration has been the long-standing interest of American and British sociology in deviance: 'street' cultures, working-class subcultures, bohemian, criminal and *lumpen* groups.[17] Another sociological source is the work on *uses* of mass cultural products which has developed since the 1950s. As early as 1950, David Riesman described the existence of *two* youth audiences for popular music, a majority, which passively accepted commercially provided styles and meanings, and a 'subculture' which actively sought a minority style (hot jazz at that time) and interpreted it in accordance with subversive values. Thus 'the audience . . . manipulates the product (and hence the producer), no less than the other way round' (Riesman 1950: 361); and this has social repercussions, for when a member of this minority audience

> listens to music, even if no-one else is around, he listens in a context of imaginary 'others' – his listening is indeed often an effort to establish connection with them. In general what he perceives in the mass media is framed by his perception of the peer-groups to which he belongs. These groups not only rate the tunes but select for their members in more subtle ways what is to be 'heard' in each tune (ibid: 366).

In Britain in the 1960s, these and other approaches came together within the embrace of the emerging discipline of cultural studies. The new subcultural theory, confronted by the apparent buying-off of traditional working-class radicalism in the Macmillanite rush to classless affluence, saw youthful deviance as one of the few remaining sources of popular discontent or protest. This brought yet another academic field into the picture, the sociology of adolescence – which was already making the connections, economic and expressive, between the new pop music and young people, and was constructing a theory of the new youth *class*: the 'teenager' had arrived.[18] One of the first objects of the subcultural theorists was to demolish this view of the classless nature of youth popular culture.

Riesman, as we have seen, had disputed the existence of a unitary youth audience. And even in the mid-1960s, when many considered that universal consumerism was transforming the old social categories, it was not difficult to find evidence of continued differentiation and stratification within youth culture. This is not to deny that in an important sense post-rock 'n' roll pop music was young people's music, its social meaning inseparable from that fact; nor that in this period the connection between young people's class, on the one hand, and their tastes or styles, on the other, became much more fluid, with a good deal of cross-over, social and musical. But the rise of 'adolescence' as a cultural category refracted rather than shattered the class-cultural formations. 'Adolescence', the 'teenager' and 'youth' are ideological concepts not natural phases; they signified differently for different groups in specific social-structural locations, and their connections with particular musical styles functioned differently, too. Moreover, as Simon Frith has pointed out (1978: 46–51; 1983a: 215–18), to see the meaning of pop as wholly or even primarily a response to the needs of 'adolescence' as such is to neglect the material context within which such a response could have meaning, a context constituted by specific and variegated relationships to work, school, leisure practices, family and community. The early Beatles could not have meant the same to a working-class, and working, adolescent boy dancing to a performance in the Cavern in Liverpool as they did to, say, a middle-class adolescent schoolgirl listening to the records in a suburban London bedroom.

This is one way in which the pop music/youth culture equation begins to unravel. But it also neglects the external relationships, of both music and young people, to the wider society. Iain Chambers describes how, in that context, the figure of 'the teenager' had, from its emergence in Britain in the early 1950s, served as a motif on which widespread current preoccupations could be focused (Chambers 1985: 1–17, 31–3). The pressure to 'modernize', the awareness of an increased pace of change – and worries about its social effects – the emerging discourse of consumerism, the association of all these with the pull – desirable but feared – of 'Americanization': this complex knot of feelings was fixed onto its most readily available representation – the 'teenager', with his 'American' music, disrespect for morals and traditions (real or imaginary), hooliganism, hedonistic consumerism, trivial, fashion-ruled culture and apparent threat to the settled relationships of the old class structure. If the music's significance is bound up with the phenomenon of 'youth', then, that concept is standing for a body of meanings of far wider social relevance.

In fact, the new subcultural theorists were so suspicious of the 'youth culture' discourse – feeling, rightly, that it was part and parcel of the whole 'social democratic' thesis of 'classlessness' – that they were less interested in the external relations of the subcultures than in their internal structures. One criticism of their approach, as we shall see, is that the network of commercial youth culture products was regarded either as mere 'raw material' for subcultural adaptation or as simply the dominant cultural consensus, against which more 'authentic' subcultures reacted. The classic statement of the position is the collection of studies produced by the Birmingham Centre for Contemporary Cultural Studies, *Resistance through Rituals* (Hall and Jefferson 1976), and I shall take my description from this, especially the key essay, 'Subcultures, cultures and class – a theoretical overview'.

Culture here is taken to be the patterns in which social groups organize their response to their experiences. In class societies these experiences differ for various groups, and so, therefore, do their cultures; moreover, these cultures are related, and unequally ranked, in terms of the dominance or subordination of the classes: that is, in terms of the operation of the processes of hegemony. It is against this perspective that youth subcultures are located. They exist *within* a 'parent' culture; thus they share many aspects of the parent culture's structural position in society, and of its 'characteristic' experience, problems and cultural traditions. At the same time, their distinctive 'focal concerns' (activities, values, material artefacts, territorial locations) set them off to some extent from the parent culture. Thus working-class youth subcultures are seen as inhabiting a 'double articulation' – first, to the parent culture, second to the dominant (bourgeois) culture – and it is in terms of this intermediatory position that their cultural practices must be understood. The middle-class counterculture is in a rather different position because its parent culture *is* the dominant culture. This explains many of the particular features of countercultural values and practices, as well as the relative ease with which these were 'incorporated' by the dominant order, their significance defused.

But how, precisely, do subcultural 'articulations' manifest themselves in details of cultural practice? The key idea put forward is this. Within the 'negotiations' surrounding the operation of hegemony the working class has gradually built up specific modes of resistance, of 'winning space' for partly autonomous activity (resulting in typical institutions, leisure pastimes, sports, neighbourhoods, etc.); young members of the class participate to some degree in these modes but they may also develop *new* modes of response. Working-class youth subcultures confront the same problems as the parent culture but 'solve' them in a way that produces a *distinctive* identity, determined by class *and* generation. Operating on the level of culture rather than formal politics, these 'magical solutions' enable young people to live out their place within real situations through an 'imaginary relation'.

Mostly they make use of already existing cultural materials. Some of these are available within the parent culture; others are provided by the institutions or, more crucially for us, the consumer products (clothes, music) offered by the dominant culture. What is important is the *use* made of these institutions, values and objects. They are taken over, transformed, reinterpreted, inserted into new contexts, combined to form a new *style*. And the principle governing the choice, combination and interpretation of objects is that of *homology*, the process whereby the group's 'focal concerns, activities, group structure and collective self-image' are brought together into a distinctive and coherent ensemble, in which members can see 'their central values held and reflected' (Hall and Jefferson 1976: 56). The theorization of homology proceeds through a takeover of the anthropological (more specifically, the Lévi-Straussian) concept of *bricolage*. In this usage, *bricolage* refers to 'the re-ordering and re-contextualisation of objects to communicate fresh meanings, within a total system of significances, which already includes prior and sedimented meanings attached to the objects used' (ibid: 177). This theoretical framework is, it can be seen, a way of holding together a sense of the *coherence* of subcultures, on the one hand, and an awareness of the 'second-hand', collage-like quality of their styles, on the other. In practice, though, as we shall see, analyses can diverge according to their relative emphasis on stylistic bricolage – flamboyant 'surfaces' as 'political' gestures – or on homology – the internal order of the whole subcultural structure.

Good examples of the Birmingham School approach are provided by their treatment of the teds and of the skinheads. Faced by the post-war destruction of their neighbourhoods, communities and employment opportunities as a result of urban redevelopment and economic change, young working-class South Londoners in the early 1950s responded, argues Tony Jefferson, with an aggressive defence of street territory and gang identity (a modification of older working-class patterns) but also with newer, generationally specific 'solutions' (Jefferson 1976; n.d. for longer version). Foremost among these was dress. The Edwardian suit was taken over from an upper-class style, this move denoting, according to Jefferson, the buying of status – one of the few methods available to a near-*lumpen* group. Subsequently, this suit was modified (narrower trousers, 'bootlace' tie, garish colours, and so on), combined with characteristic hairstyles, and thus reinterpreted in the light both of traditional working-class approval of 'flash' and of an American urban romanticism transmitted by contemporary films. Thus the teds reworked existing attitudes and materials, combined them in new ways, and created a coherent *style*, which reflected on the cultural level a way of coping with economic and social problems.

Similarly, the skinheads, confronted by the same kind of problems a few years later, responded with attempts at a 'magical recovery of community'. As John Clarke shows (1976: for a longer version, see Clarke n.d.), a reworking of older working-class values (a tough, male chauvinist masculinity; racist scapegoating; the importance of collectivity) was again involved; at the same time, however, these values were directed into new channels: gang fighting, football violence, a stylized 'proletarian' appearance (cropped hair, half-mast jeans with braces, big 'working' boots). This appearance, Dick Hebdige points out, drew to some extent on 'rude boy' styles of contemporary West Indian *lumpen* youth (Hebdige 1976a; for a longer version, see Hebdige n.d.a.). Once again, then, the axes of class and generation define the conjuncture within which the new style developed – while that of race also makes an appearance.

What is striking about both these accounts, however, is the absence of music. If subcultural styles can be described without mentioning the musical tastes of their members, this suggests that subcultural theory may not (always?) have the key to understanding the musics. In the case of the teds, rock 'n' roll arrived in Britain in 1956, some two years *after* the subculture became visible. It was retrospectively grafted onto the stylistic ensemble – though by this stage the style had been diffused, partially in diluted forms, much more widely through the country and among working-class youth. Of course, this does not rule out the possibility of 'homology' – though George Melly's famous description of rock 'n' roll as 'screw and smash music' (1972: 36) tailor-made for the teds seems too restrictive, eliding one subcultural usage with the music's own available meanings; but it does suggest that analyses of rock 'n' roll purely in terms of the ted subculture or of the teds' use of rock 'n' roll in terms of an integral subcultural function are on insecure ground.

The role of music in the skinhead subculture is even less clear. In the first place, it was far from central – 'following' football occupied that position – but in any case the preferred music altered over time, starting with some rhythm and blues styles (notably Tamla) and Jamaican ska, moving (as the culture spread, was consumerized and – admittedly – diluted) through the football-chant-influenced records of Slade and the 'glam rock' of T. Rex and Gary Glitter, and settling, in a late 1970s 'revival', on 'hard punk' and 'oi' music. The only common factors here are that these are all dance music styles, and that they were brandished as alternatives to the despised complexities and (unproletarian) 'prettiness' of hippie, progressive and post-punk 'romantic' styles. This is hardly sufficient of a peg on which to hang a subcultural theory of skinhead musical tastes.

One contribution to *Resistance through Rituals* which does centre on music is Iain Chambers's essay on black American music and its appropriation by white subcultures (Chambers 1976). Chambers argues that American capital divided its working class on racial lines and that Afro-American music reflects the experience of an ethnic fraction of the class. Thus he frees the music from the grip of predominantly ethnic interpretations, aligning it with the typical Birmingham emphasis on class; at the same time, he insists that its subversive meanings are able to arise because it is the 'strategy for living' of a particular, culturally defined group. For Chambers, the tension resulting from this dual articulation provides the space within which appropriation of the music by other working-class groups can occur: young Southern whites, and, even further afield, British subcultural groups. Such appropriations, he admits, are often superficial; they are mediated by institutional pressures; and the new context can lead to variants in the musical style.[19] Nevertheless, 'embedded in black culture, in black music, are oppositional values which in a fresh context served to symbolise and symptomatise the contradictions and tensions played out in British working-class youth sub-culture' (ibid: 166).

This is an intriguing argument, and probably the furthest a culturalist explanation of the appeal of black music to whites can go; though Chambers is not clear exactly *how*, in the music itself, the specifics of the *new* context are articulated – a style is, somehow, 'worked up in a living social and cultural context' (ibid: 164). Moreover, the picture is very general. No attempt is made to explain the *variety* of black styles, of white preferences, of subcultural appropriations and of appropriating social groups (middle-class as well as working-class), or the complex relationships between all these.[20]

For such attempts we can turn to the work of two other Birmingham School members, Paul Willis and Dick Hebdige.[21] These represent the contrasting directions – focusing on 'homology' or on 'style' – referred to earlier.

For Willis (n.d.: 6),

> Experience is not atomised . . . and people live their expressive lives as a symbolic whole . . . What we are confronted with is a whole way of life interpenetrated by a whole symbolic system, not a series of discrete bits of behaviour alongside a series of discrete cultural artefacts.

The relation between experience and symbol is organized and can be analysed on three levels, which Willis calls the indexical, the homological and the integral. The indexical level is that governed by quantifiable aspects: for example, which music people listen to, where, when, and so on. Analysis on this level can tell us nothing about the *significance* of the listening activity; indeed, the details may, from the point of view of the listeners, be arbitrary – made up simply of what surrounds us. Nevertheless, Willis regards the 'indexical field' as important. It is where the 'tyranny of the commodity form', the 'slow drip of conventional daily habit, supported by institutions, state agencies and the systematic practices of others' produce a 'one-way determination of meaning'. But, significantly, he is not particularly interested in this activity (which is where, one might think, most consumption of popular music takes place). He regards it as the 'realm of ideology', and contrasts with it a different practice (by implication, then, non-ideological, fully self-directed and autonomous) in which 'the collective activity of human groups can roll back somewhat the one-way determination of their own meanings and sensibilities'.[22]

That practice, according to Willis, operates at the homological level. Here we find particular types of music, 'differentially sought out and pursued by, rather than simply randomly proximate to, a social group' (Willis 1978: 191). These types can be made 'to reflect, resonate and sum up crucial values, states and attitudes for the social group involved' (Willis n.d.: 11) – musical meanings being socially constituted – though this process is somewhat limited by the 'objective possibilities' inherent in the internal structure of the form and in historical influences. Particular interpretations depend on objective 'resonance' – for potential meanings are only activated when 'rubbed against the real life experience of a particular group' (ibid: 16).

Homological analysis is synchronic. But the relationship between group life-style and cultural item comes into being, develops and (usually) ends on a dia-chronic level which Willis calls the integral. Within the history of a subculture, he argues, determination of meaning can proceed in either direction: lifestyle influences choice or production of (for instance) music; music affects lifestyle. When determination is two-way, ever-tighter homologies ('integral circuiting') develop, and this process can be powerful enough to 'drag in' other, less obviously related forms and practices, mediating their significance. What this level of analysis should also tell us about is the way the inital homology comes into being in the first place; but Willis has little to say about this.

To flesh out his position, Willis presents two case studies of late 1960s groups, the (working-class) 'bike boys', or rockers, and the (middle-class) hippies.

The rocker culture is designated as conservative, masculine, physical and aggressive; and as valorizing concrete activity (rather than thought), the 'now' (rather than a linear time-sense), and chauvinist sexuality. To a large degree, these values are mediated by the activity of motor-bike riding: its speed, violence, physical excitement and need for control. The preferred music is rock 'n' roll, principally the early heroes such as Elvis Presley and Buddy Holly, but stretching to the early Beatles and Rolling Stones. This style had been deliberately selected, in Willis's view, for two reasons. It was historically distant; it had a *unity* and, as the 'classic' pop music from a Golden Age, an *authenticity* which, in the sixties context, could reflect cultural *difference*. In addition, it had associations with 'youth', 'sex' and 'violence' acquired in the 1950s (these associations represent historical 'objective possibilities'). Musically rock 'n' roll could resonate with rocker culture in several ways. First, its strong, regular beat mirrors the love of movement and physical activity. Second, the 'single' form mirrors the love of speed and of *control* of technology (as against the LP's lengthier time-scale and imposition of itself as an environment). Third, the music's aggressiveness mirrors the rockers' 'masculinity'. Fourth, the privileging of rhythm, especially the regular beat, subverts 'bar form'; at the same time harmony and cadence are unimportant, and so is melody which is replaced by discontinuous short units; the result is a stress on repetition, a neglect of sequential progression, a 'stream-like quality', which mirror the predominance of the body and the implicit rejection of industrial, bourgeois, 'rational' time.

Now, there is clearly quite a bit in this correlation. At the very minimum, it is not surprising, given the rockers' behavioural practices, that their musical taste ran to short dance pieces with a strong beat, and we would not expect to find them listening in attentive silence to Ravi Shankar or late Beethoven quartets. Nevertheless, several quite specific criticisms of Willis's argument must be made.

First, many aspects of the music (such as texture and vocal style) are not mentioned. For those that are, the analysis is sometimes of doubtful accuracy. For instance, it is hard to accept that harmony is unimportant, replaced, as Willis says, by a 'kind of anarchy'. Progressions still structure the chorus form, cadences divide the song into choruses, and sometimes there are even Tin Pan Alley middle eights. Similarly with the alleged disappearance of melody: what about the early Beatles' tunes, and how did the rockers respond to Elvis's ballads?

Second, the analyst's *interpretation* (admittedly representing – accurately? – that of the culture) is offered as a description of *objective* possibilities; but is, for example, rock 'n' roll always and necessarily 'aggressive'? In fact, Willis has some difficulty in assimilating the Beatles and Buddy Holly to this label!

Third, Willis's interpretation of rock 'n' roll has to assume an ideal type: yet this is imposed on what is actually quite a wide diversity of styles – Elvis, Buddy Holly, the early Beatles and the Stones can hardly be said to form a 'unity'; at the same time, this 'corpus' is *not* distinctly set off from other pop music: there are many continuities with other styles current in the 1960s, and its 'authenticity' is just as compromised and uneven as that of the whole field.

What this adds up to is that the connection between this music and the rockers is much looser than Willis suggests. Many other people were listening to it, and probably interpreting it differently; other styles were influenced by and contiguous to it; its subcultural sojourn was not an isolated phenomenon but part of a complex history. In fact, that level of meaning in the rock 'n' roll/rocker relationship which we can be reasonably sure about – organized around the connotations of 'youth', 'dance', 'sex' and 'violence' – had been the product of a *historical* accretion of meaning, and that process had taken place within a much wider social arena than that occupied by any subcultural group (even if the teds did contribute to it), just as its effects were much more widely available.

When he turns to the hippies, Willis's procedure is much the same and is open to similar criticisms. Again the connection between music and subculture is drawn much too tightly; the 'purity' of both subcultures is a fiction, their 'opposition' to dominant culture exaggerated.[23] As Shepherd argues (1982: 167–73), both groups are articulating *contradictory* positions within contemporary capitalist society. Their musical styles display *tension* between oppositional tendencies and an acceptance of basic categories associated with the norms of the dominant culture (notably functional-harmonic tonality). Thus, despite distinct virtues in Willis's approach – notably the richness of ethnographic detail, the insistence on the importance of user-interpretation, the emphasis on the multiple and contradictory possibilities within the commodity form, and the potential (albeit underdeveloped) of the concept of 'objective possibilities' – it is flawed above all by the uncompromising drive to homology. There is a relative neglect of the subcultures' relationships with their parent cultures, with the dominant culture and with other youth cultures, and the stress on internal coherence leads to circularity of argument. A striking example is the relationship in the rocker culture between a supposed antagonism to industrial time-discipline and the music's alleged subversion of 'sequential temporality'. Willis argues that inter-mediation is involved, producing dialectical circuiting, and this is indeed possible. But from the point of view of analytic methodology, it is impossible, without some perspective based *outside* the circle, to prove that it is not a 'fabrication', or to say anything about the music's 'objective possibilities' that could not be said from a position of total interpretative relativism, let alone to establish with which pole – music or culture – the circle started.

Willis himself is aware of this problem, acknowledging the

> difficulties in determining the structure and form of the sensibility, values and attitudes of particular social groups – not least because these things are never experienced directly but in media and through cultural items in a way which . . . helps to constitute the social group in the first place, and which are themselves likely to be objects of study in the second stage of the analysis (Willis 1978: 192);

but, as can be seen, his acknowledgement accepts the circularity rather than offering any solution. Certainly it does not begin to address the fact that, as Murdock and McCron point out (1976), much the same social location can be associated with a *variety* of subcultural styles (teds, rockers, skinheads, for example) – all of which appear to the analyst to form equally elegant and plausible homologies. It is this problem that lies behind the exaggerated political significance Willis gives to the rocker and hippy subcultures. Difference is read as radical opposition, internal contradictions and variants are missed out, continuities (with the dominant culture, with the commercial music sector, with the wider network of youth culture) are neglected. Certainly style is politically important, in showing 'the possibility of the revolutionary in the small, detailed and everyday' (Willis 1978: 182); but in a complex, differentiated society it is never pure, never static and never just subcultural.

An approach which tries, implicitly, to overcome that limitation can be found in Dick Hebdige's *Subculture* (1979). Hebdige remains committed to the idea of homology, but that, together with the whole Birmingham emphasis on culture as class expression, is fused – and comes into some tension – with a wider analysis of post-war cultural history (see, for example, Hebdige 1981a) and with the influence of semiological methods.

In Hebdige's early writings on the mods (1976b; n.d.b), lifestyle and music come into alignment in the form of a 'magical' solution to problems arising from the mods' class position. An admiration for the black urban hustler's 'cool', his sharp dress, hedonistic consumption and command of the night hours is correlated with musical choices centred, typically, on esoteric American dance records in rhythm and blues or soul styles. Upper working-class youngsters in semi-skilled manual or dead-end office jobs, the mods seemed to conform to the demands on them for smartness and for consumption but, Hebdige argues, they inverted and reinterpreted these by taking the minutiae of appearance to obsessive, eccentric extremes, by incorporating consumer objects (clothes, pills, scooters) into a new subcultural network of meanings, and by focusing these meanings and investing their real energies on an 'underground' leisure existence – a mode of 'living on the pulse of the present' – ruled by dance, music, non-stop pleasure, 'speed' (the various pills) and style. This imaginary world, organized around the mod's 'desire to . . . draw himself closer to the Negro', and set against his contempt for the greyness of 'straight' existence, represented at once a compensation for work-time tedium and subordination and an appropriation and parodistic reworking of some of the straight world's values and artefacts, notably a subversive use of commodities.

By the time of *Subculture*, Hebdige's general approach was changing, but his account of the mods is not significantly different. The argument is still that 'the positive values of the mod's relative exclusiveness, his creation of a whole supportive universe . . . provided him not only with a distinctive dress, music, etc. but also with a complete set of meanings' (Hebdige 1976b: 94). 'Somewhere on the way home from school or work, the mods went "missing": they were absorbed into a "noonday underground" . . . of cellar clubs, discotheques, boutiques and record shops which lay hidden beneath the "straight world" against which it was ostensibly defined. An integral part of the "secret identity" constructed here . . . was an emotional affinity with black people . . . an affinity which was transposed into style' (Hebdige 1979: 53).

In both accounts Hebdige has little to say about the mods' music, beyond the obvious points that on the whole it was black and ideally it was relatively little known (in order to be exclusive). If we listen to a classic mod record – the Who's 'My Generation' – how much help is the subcultural approach in understanding the song? How clear, how important, is the homology? The musical style is clearly derived from Afro-American sources and this may have to do with the mods' 'emotional affinity with black people'. (On the other hand, *most* pop music since rock 'n' roll has been influenced by Afro-American sources.) The sense of being an 'underground', against the 'straight world', may have given rise to feelings of persecution and aggression which could explain the incoherent, stammering vocal and 'aggressive' instrumental sounds. (But similar techniques occur in some non-mod pop.) The frantic energy of the song may have to do with the mod's use of 'speed', whereby the 'dynamics of his movements were magnified, the possibilities of action multiplied' (Hebdige 1976b: 91). (On the other hand, frantic energy pervades many pop styles.) The importance of repetition (solo vocal phrases, vocal backing riff, chordal riff) might suggest the mod 'living on the pulse of the present'. (But repetition is a common pop technique anyway.) The feeling that instruments are being 'maltreated' may be linked with the mod's 'inverted', subversive use of commodities; in live shows the early Who physically damaged their equipment. (At the same time, 'illegitimate' treatment of instruments is part of the Afro-American tradition and characteristic of most pop styles influenced by that tradition.)

These aspects seem to fit the idea of a homology quite well – but, as we saw, on reflection they tend to lose their specificity to mod subculture (which may be why the song achieved much wider popularity). Moreover, many of them do not emerge from the perspective of subcultural theory anyway, but from some kind of semiological interpretation (in which a wider field of musical signification, with its internal structure of meanings and differences, is important). At the same time, we can ask whether the links mentioned exhaust the meaning of the song. It seems unlikely. Conversely, certain other mod values stressed by Hebdige – the dandyism, the subdued 'cool', for instance – seem to be missing. This slackness of 'fit' becomes even slacker if we add into the equation the much larger category of mod music which, far from being produced by an avowedly mod band (as the Who were in 1965), was appropriated from a quite different, non-mod context: American rhythm and blues. This music was rather different in style from 'My Generation': certainly it lacked the latter's aggressive hysteria.

Two years after *Subculture*, in a radio programme, Dick Hebdige himself analysed 'My Generation' (1981b).[24] He made some of the links suggested above; but his central proposal is that the aggression and incoherence constitute a 'musical metaphor' for the seaside mod/rocker disturbances of 1964:

> Mod, it's implied in the song by a series of formal echoes or correspondences, is improvisation within a tight framework: the tailored suit, the 4/4 beat of R & B, the . . . pulse of work and pleasure. But the pressure of constraint . . . of 'clean living under difficult circumstances', the accumulated pressure eventually takes us to the point where the contradictions can no longer be contained, where the pose can no longer be held'

– hence the 'explosion' at the end of the song. Hebdige also tackles the problem of apparently contradictory mod music styles. The 'cool' self-assurance, the controlled ordinariness, of Dobie Gray's 'The In Crowd' – another mod classic – are related to the *imaginary* world of mod, to the culture's success rather than its failure: this record was taken to reflect 'those moments when mod *worked*'. The argument here, however persuasive, derives almost wholly from content analysis of the lyrics – which reproduce typical mod themes of consumerism, image, cliquishness and male chauvinism; the only comments on the music relate to the 'worldly' tone of Dobie Gray's vocal style and the appropriateness of the 4/4 beat for dancing. Moreover, if two such contrasting songs can both be aligned with (contrasting or contradictory) aspects of the subculture, it suggests that either the credibility of the analytical method or the coherence of the subculture itself – the exclusiveness of its 'whole supportive universe' – is being stretched.

In all these accounts there is a feeling of a latent desire to leave the rigours of homological analysis and class expression behind in order to enjoy the transient details of the stylistic *bricolages* themselves. And in *Subculture* – a brilliantly observed, phantasmagoric survey of the metropolitan surfaces of youth culture in the 1960s and 1970s – this results in a real tension. The broader picture – generation and race become at least as important as class, and the wider cultural/institutional complex is given a much larger role than in Willis – attenuates some problems but brings others. The specificity of class location becomes vague and the exclusiveness of the subcultures themselves is put at risk. At the same time, the metropolitan focus militates against understanding the wider spread of subcultural styles. The picture of black music, which occupies a central position, is not without its romanticized aspects. Methodologically, the use of semiological analysis marks a big advance; Hebdige comes to see subcultural styles less as expressing a group's material position in society than as intervening in existing processes of signification. Yet what becomes problematic now is precisely the relationship between such interventions and their localized social base. In the information-saturated society we inhabit today, 'semiotic guerilla warfare' is not the sole prerogative of young male subcultures; these are an (admittedly spectacular) part of a more generalized practice of symbol manipulation. The question is, what is sociologically and politically specific, and important, about *these* semiological forays? Writing under the dominating influence of punk, with its ambiguous class base, its stress on the manipulation of style for its own sake, its self-aware cultivation of the bizarre, the surreal, the semiotic fracture, Hebdige does not answer this question. But if 'punk style contained distorted reflections of all the major post-war subcultures', in 'cut-up', safety-pinned forms (Hebdige 1979: 26), this does not automatically make of it a theoretical touchstone for general subcultural analysis.

At the same time, Hebdige still insists on the importance of 'expressive circularity' between music and subculture; and this means that he is forced to argue that punk, which one might see as a *refusal* of homology, 'signified chaos at every level, but . . . the chaos cohered as a meaningful whole' (ibid: 113)! As musics and subcultures

> assume rigid and identifiable patterns, so new subcultures are created which *demand* or *produce* corresponding mutations in musical form. These mutations *in their turn* occur at those moments when forms and themes imported from contemporary black music break up (or 'overdetermine') the existing musical structure and force its elements into new configurations (ibid: 69, emphasis added).

At what point, on what level, by what mechanism, does the semiotic 'play of difference' within the music discourse meet up with and get focused upon the 'experience', the 'demands', the 'central values' and 'focal concerns', of a particular group? In a sense, part of Hebdige's solution to that problem is to say very little in detail about music; in general, its significance stays at the level of the symbolic appeal of black music as a whole – which is a reasonable overview but leaves unanswered the central question of how different musical styles articulate specific subcultural identities. Hebdige's main solution, however, is through a plunge into post-structuralist theory (ibid: 117–27).

The idea of *polysemy* means 'each text is seen to generate a potentially infinite range of meanings' (ibid: 117), making any homology, out of the most heterogeneous materials, possible. The idea of *signifying practice* – texts not as communicating or expressing a pre-existing meaning but as 'positioning subjects' within a *process* of semiosis – changes the whole basis of creating social meaning. 'Experience' is constructed *in* the text, in ideology (so the problem of the link between 'text' and 'experience' disappears). Subcultural styles are seen as 'deconstructing' existing meaning-systems and proposing new 'positions' (so the problem of where the position 'really' is disappears). Different subcultural strategies are identified, using different kinds of signifying practice; thus the teds and the skinheads constructed a coherent ideological position through the manipulation of homologous contents, while the punks, by contrast, attacked the basis of meaning itself, in a 'modernistic' assault on the received 'linguistic' systems.

This is all very well – though it jettisons the level of *real* (as distinct from ideological) social location, which had been important earlier in Hebdige's book. But:

(i)   what has now happened to Willis's 'objective possibilities'? If the range of potential meanings is infinite, what governs particular choices, why black music rather than any other, and, in this completely arbitrary world, how do we assess motivation and expressive value?

(ii) the *Tel Quel* post-structuralist theory, on which Hebdige draws, is orientated largely by a neo-modernistic enthusiasm for avant-garde disruption of formal conventions; radical effects occur through subversion of linguistic norms, which disrupts the ideologically fixed positions offered in everyday discourse. However, does this not mean the end of subcultural styles as political protests – or even, perhaps, as social movements at all – in favour of the formalistic impotence which Adorno identified as characteristic of radical modern art?

Questioning culturalism

The post-structuralist – not to mention the structuralist – critique of subcultural theory centres on its culturalist humanism, in which already formed individual consciousnesses and social classes originate their own homologous cultural forms. For post-structuralists, culture is not a 'way of life' growing out of experiential raw material but 'a system of representations dependent on a certain subject position, constructed by signifying practices' (Coward 1977: 78). There are unresolved questions here – notably over the status of human agency, the mechanisms of cultural change, the relationships between culture on the one hand, society and economy on the other, and the possible need for some conception of the *real*, if any practices of valuation and politics are to survive; nevertheless, this perspective at least has the virtue of taking seriously the specificities and relative autonomy of individual cultural practices.

Subcultural theory – like many branches of folkloristics and cultural anthropology – has relatively little to say about music as music. Often its significance is taken to operate at the level of a general symbol (its 'blackness', its 'subversiveness', its exclusiveness, and so on); the details of its structure, the conditions of existence of its characteristic genres, the particularity of the acoustic as such, pass unnoticed. This does indeed seem to be its role in some subcultures: not central so much as a background, knitting the cultural fabric together; but the music itself cannot be fully analysed in terms of that role. In cases where subcultural identity *is* centrally focused on music – the culture of Northern soul, for example – subcultural theory has paid little attention.[25] Similarly, on the rare occasions when a subculture has *started* from music, coalescing round it rather than integrating an existing style into an already formed or forming ensemble – as was the case with punk – subcultural theory again has problems, since now the connections with the wider music discourse (in this case, rock history) and the music industry become crucial, and the theory is not equipped to tackle these (see Laing 1985: xi).

Other problems arise, too. How should we understand the situation – from the point of view of musical meanings – when a subculture *changes* its musical taste (as the skinheads did)? Or when it embraces *different* styles at the same time, one appropriated, the other produced (as with the mods)? For subculturalists, the nature of the relationship between subcultural interpretation and the music's other existences, where 'objective possibilities' and 'preferred readings' are laid down, is important but unclear. This is no doubt compounded by the relative 'openness' of musical codes – they are hard to 'fix' permanently – and at the same time the heavy ideological investment going as a result into fixing dominant meanings. The fairly imprecise meanings which music styles seem to have for most subcultures have the effect that subcultural ownership of these styles is very hard to protect. This 'openness' extends – unusually for songs – even to lyrics. Alan Durant (1984: 182–211) has described the crucial role in pop music lyrics of pronouns and other 'shifters' (words where reference varies according to who is speaking, when and where). These at once foreground the music's accessibility to concerns over group identity and expression ('I', 'you', 'my', 'our', and so on); explain how the music is amenable to appropriation of these references (identity is localized and pinned down); but also ensure that the music's *possible* references 'cut across any simple, general structure of subcultural dissent' (ibid: 187) (who is the 'my' of 'my generation'?). To understand these songs fully, then, it would be necessary not only to investigate specific fixings of meaning but also to follow the operations of the 'text' into that sphere where the construction of its 'openness' can be analysed.

That is the business of the next chapter. What can be said here is that the culturalist neglect of music's specificity, together with the 'whole way of life' orientation which accompanies this, helps to explain many of the problems with subcultural theory. The theory neglects particularities and overemphasizes structural coherence, especially in class-determined forms; thus cross-overs, ambiguities and changes in group taste are often missed, along with the role of fashion, maverick enthusiasts and trend-setters. Girls are another absence – their alternative uses and valuations of music would threaten the coherence of subcultural analyses, just as the absence of unspectacular subcultures (Irish music enthusiasts; old-style dance-band fans; and so on) is necessary to protect the over-simple equation of style and politics. The importance of mainstream commercial pop, where music is a 'background' or a 'game' rather than a coherent part of a 'serious' culture, is played down – despite the fact that the subcultures' own self-definitions and styles are generated in part through a symbiotic relationship with media-disseminated images and broad cultural and social trends.[26]

The culturalist perspective – however valuable its insistence that musical functions and meanings are culturally mediated – is too unfocused, too all-inclusive. Culture is everywhere, it is true; for *Homo sapiens*, everything – all activity in and experience of the world – is culturally formed and grasped.[27] But it does not follow that culture is every*thing*. It is better to see culture as a 'system of shared meanings' (Geertz 1973: 5), a network of 'webs of significance' (Burke 1978: Prologue); it is 'the complex unity of those practices that produce sense' (Mulhern 1980: 32).[28] Culture, then, is not a particular *area* at all – either the whole or a part – but a particular way of grasping (all) social practice. The cultural *level* pervades all human activity – but differentially, and in a variety of signifying modes not reducible one to another – while other levels – the social, the economic, the political – are not absent from even the most specifically cultural forms and practices (see Williams 1981: 12–13, 206–10, but also *passim*).

Thus we must insist, on the one hand, on 'the complex density of mediations involved in the production and reproduction of pop music' . . . which identifies it 'as a cultural practice . . . organised through multiple points of cultural power and . . . potentially susceptible to a whole range of social pressures arising from class, gender, race, age, locality and education', and, on the other hand, on the way that 'economic, political and social "elements" are displaced, translated and condensed into the specificities of musical production'. Similarly, 'the specific operations of musical "languages" or "codes" [and] . . . the potential social connotations of such music are structurally interrelated but ultimately separate moments' (Chambers 1982: 33, 34; 1979: 13, 33).

The relationships between music, culture and society are far from simple, then – and musical value becomes a much more difficult question now than can be covered by a mere notion of 'honesty'. As the relationship between musical and other practices assumes its proper complexity, simple concepts of 'authenticity' fail (on authenticity, see Frith 1988b). Such concepts assume, always, that there is 'our' music and 'their' music. One is 'false', the other 'true to experience'. One is corrupt, manipulated, over-complex, mechanical, commodified or whatever; the other is more natural, spontaneous, traditional – and perhaps a radical alternative or even a protest. It is difficult not to connect this conceptualization to older schemas with roots in the Romantic period and their sociological offshoots in patterns of the *Gesellschaft/Gemeinschaft* sort. In these traditions, such ideological couplets as black/white, nature/culture, body/mind, aural/visual, collective/individual are pervasive. The most self-aware writers fall victim to the attraction of this romanticism. We have already noticed that Hebdige is not free from the mythologizing of black music. He also, as he admits, sees working-class subcultures in the context of a historically rooted romanticism of the street, the bohemian, the outcast, the bizarre, the surreal. Charles Keil, having attacked the romanticizing exoticism of the folklorists, has in recent years turned the focus of his attention from ethnicity to class, but in his studies of 'peoples' music' – polka, ju-ju, Greek rebetika, Afro-American – he takes up a not dissimilar position himself. 'Not so long ago', he writes, 'this planet was peopled with a variety of classless, artless, unscientific and relatively ahistorical-apolitical societies whose cultures were genuine' (Keil and Keil 1984: 11). Then came 'a Fall', bringing 'class' and 'art', with its individualism and abstraction. Now, healthy musics are found only among the proletariat, a 'robust organism' where culture is embedded in 'the thick life processes of the community' and is 'created by generations of intense and shared experience' (ibid: 8). Indeed, the essential qualities of the styles go back thousands of years, and their 'primordial qualities' show the way towards the revolutionary classless society of the future.

Of course, the problem is made more difficult by the fact that to some extent the cultures are involved as well as the scholarship. Working-class subcultures were at least dimly aware that the appeal of black culture was an exotic one, and they often saw their own musics as more 'real' than the commercial mainstream. Punk and the counterculture were quite conscious of their own status as bohemian alternatives. Some black musicians have come to *assert* their own 'primitivism', while even with 'folk' revivalists the romantic nostalgia is not always unacknowledged. The 'tribal' objects of ethnomusicology's gaze can rarely escape post-colonial nationalism's need for 'traditions', and it seems that even the urban popular music-makers who are succeeding them often feel the lure of a claim to 'authenticity'.

This should not surprise us. Romantic primitivism is embedded in the development of capitalism itself: ideologically, in capitalism's need for an Other, to refresh its 'spirit' in non-productive time, to energize and justify its own contrasting drive to 'civilization', and at the same time to prove its liberalism; economically, in capitalism's need for 'raw materials', natural, human and cultural, to feed the expanding machinery of commodification. As capitalism penetrates and colonizes Third World cultures, their musics are dragged into this dialectic, an intensifying search for anti-capitalist remnants delivering them up to the bourgeois appetite. As capitalism moves to complete its grip on the First World societies, commodifying its peoples' thought and cultural practices, attempting to turn all use into exchange, a similar search for oppositional or revolutionary residues ensues. Cultural workers and intellectuals (popular musicians and popular music scholars) are not independent of these movements.

However, as an ideology for scholars, romantic primitivism is clearly unsatisfactory. It 'enslaves' its objects of study, just as the capitalist culture industries exploit them: blacks, workers, the young, are refused permission to make, define, use and interpret music as they wish but must have their practices idealized. It places an antithesis (approved/not approved; authentic/inauthentic; ultimately, natural/cultural, that most treacherous of ideological pairs) where there should be a dialectic. It utopianizes a part of what is inherently imperfect (human life), postponing self-analysis and productive activity *here*.

What is perhaps signalled here is the end, in the sphere of culture, of the abstract 'revolutionary subject' whose political demise has been widely remarked. Peasants, workers, oppressed minorities, bohemians, *lumpen* sub-cultures: all have been tried; there are no revolutionary subjects left to wheel onto the stage. If the primary field of conflict is now constituted by the signs and fragments of everyday life, these older categories, while not rendered irrelevant, become more like definitional shooting-stars across the map of (musical and other) self-activity. One struggle, as we saw in Chapter 3, is for *possession* of that activity – and there is little reason to think that this will take place within the strict boundaries of any class, subcultural, ethnic or gender claims to ideological truth or exclusive identity in musical styles. But analysts, too, should look carefully at their own work and the 'native' musical traditions which lie behind its historical formation. They, too, are part of the culture within which popular music exists. As Gabriel García Márquez has written, 'The interpretation of our reality through patterns not our own serves only to make us ever more unknown, ever less free, ever more solitary'.

Notes

1. See Lloyd (1967: 55 fn.) for a concise expression of this view. For a more general account within the same perspective, see Herzog (1949–50).
2. Burke (1978: 23–64) is good on both aspects. For a stimulating discussion of twentieth-century developments and the questions that follow, see Seeger (1977a). For another excellent theoretical overview, see Pickering and Green (1987).
3. Sharp's views have still been propagated in recent years, however; see, for example, Karpeles (1968; 1980).
4. Green (1972, Chapter 1) puts forward a similar view. He also accepts the role of recordings in dissemination, as well as print.
5. See also Sharp (1972: 161–80); Kidson (1912).
6. On Country music see, for example, Green (1965); Malone (1982; 1985); Wilgus

(1971); Wolfe (1981). On Afro-American music see, for example, Evans (1982a); Ferris (1978); Keil (1966a); Oliver (1970a). For a bibliographical and discographical survey of the whole field of 'ethnic' American musics, see Cohen and Wells (1982).

7. *Journal of the International Folk Music Council,* VII (1955: 23). For Sharp's original argument, see Sharp (1972: 21–41).

8. For a conception of 'tradition' as a universally present processual field, see Seeger (1949–50).

9. For classic investigations of two such sets, the first diachronically organized, the second synchronically, see Bronson (1969) and Seeger (1977b). For extensive work on these lines, in the area of Anglo-American 'folk song', see the writings of Bronson, Samuel Bayard and Philips Barry.

10. Similarly, Jackie Bratton has discovered important links in the texts of Victorian and 'traditional' ballads: see Bratton (1975).

11. Lord maintained that whether a 'text' was orally composed could be assessed by quantitative analysis of its formula content. If this is correct, computerized analysis of the formula content of the Tin Pan Alley repertory might do more for our knowledge of its composition methods than biographical anecdotes, which often mystify and in any case cannot reveal the reality of mental processes.

12. On *Electric Ladyland Part 2,* Track 613 017 (1968).

13. See Jones (1965: 50–68), though without necessarily accepting all the historical detail.

14. On African musics, see, for example, Jones (1959); Tracey (1948); Nketia (1979); Blacking (1976); Merriam (1959; 1962); Keil (1979b); Chernoff (1979); Berliner (1978); Feld (1982). On the dissemination and acculturation of African musics in the Americas, see, for example, Borneman (1977); Courlander (1970); Oliver (1970b); Merriam (1955); Waterman (1952); Roberts (1973). In general, work on Central and South America is less accessible since it is often not in English, but for a bibliography see Fairley (1985). Roberts (1979) discusses the influence of 'latin' music on North American popular music and jazz. For a useful introduction to the 'traditional' musics of Africa, the Americas and Europe, see Nettl (1965). For studies of the urbanization of 'traditional' African and South American (and some Asian) musics, see, for example, Coplan (1980; 1982); Kauffman (1972); Kubik (1974; 1979–80; 1981); Rycroft (1961–2); Nketia (1957); Baily (1981); Cohen and Shiloah (1985); Béhague (1973); Stigberg (1978); Ware (1978); Nettl (1972); Herd (1984). The development of new styles in Africa and the Americas is surveyed in Roberts (1973); Collins (1985). A path-breaking world survey by an ethno-musicologist is Manuel (1988).

15. On performance, see, for example, Schüller (1982); Keil (1966a: 114–42 and *passim*); Fairley (1989). On concepts of change, see, for example, Blacking (1977a); Merriam (1964: 303–19); Nettl (1978, Chapter 1); Hampton (1979–80).

16. It could make more of such work – for example, Mary Douglas's (1970) studies of symbolic and social structures and Victor Turner's (1969) work on ritual, 'communitas' and 'liminality'. For an application of these approaches to contemporary culture, youth groups and pop musicians, see Martin (1983: 45–52, 154–60). On the liminality of American ethnic groups, see Ostendorf (n.d.: 15–21). On the liminality of minstrelsy (blacking up, and so on), see Pickering (1986: 89–90).

17. For a summary of the literature, see Brake (1980: 29–85).

18. For discussion of this literature, see Frith (1978: 19–27, 37–9); Frith (1983a: 181–96, 202–4). Its assumptions permeated journalistic writing of the 1960s but also spread into studies of pop music with more radical perspectives: see, for example, Laing (1969); Middleton (1972).

19. Ironically, however, the variant Chambers identifies – up-front vocal with instrumental backing replacing the more equal and collectively organized interactions of voice and instruments in black styles – is almost the opposite to that picked out as typical by Dave Laing (see pp. 153–4 above). This is not a casual difference but

symptomatic of the fact that in each case there is, for black source and white appropriation, too narrow a conception, both of the musical styles and of the network of cultural practices and influences within which the musics were located. Black music has never been *just* working-class, *just* oppositional; institutional mediation has never been *just* white-directed; white appropriations have not taken *just* one form, and so on.

20. There is an interesting comparison in the equally varied styles, meanings and interpretations of American minstrelsy in nineteenth-century Britain; see Pickering (1986).

21. Especially Willis (1978); Hebdige (1979). I shall also refer to Willis (n.d.); Hebdige (n.d.b; 1976b).

22. Elsewhere, however, Willis (n.d.: 23) argues that 'one-way determination' is not total ideological manipulation because it can only really work 'when the consciousness is already in the grip of a basic homology, and . . . this basic homology must, in the first instance, come from the authentic life interests of the actors'. Subcultural theory in general has difficulties over the relationship between commercial provision and subcultural use, and between 'ideology' and 'expression'.

23. Cf. Chapter 1 above, pp. 27–32. Amusingly enough, popular music history itself provided a refutation of Willis's purism, in the growth – already visible in the years when he was writing – of a 'heavy metal' subculture. This brings together rockers and ex- or proto-hippies around a musical style deriving both from hard rock traditions with roots in rhythm and blues and ultimately rock 'n' roll, and from the virtuoso, guitar-based, improvisational tendency (Clapton, Hendrix, and so on) in progressive rock. How could both rockers and middle-class students relate to a style so obviously indebted to traditions each group was supposed to despise? See Chambers (1985: 122–4).

24. For a different – but not totally dissimilar – reading of 'My Generation', in the context of mod subculture, see Laing (1969: 148–56).

25. But on 'Northern soul' see Cosgrove (1982).

26. For discussions of these problems, see McRobbie (1980); McRobbie and Garber (1976); Frith and McRobbie (1978); Coward (1977; 1984); Martin (1983: 150–2); Chambers (1981: 41–2; 1985: 128–38); Frith (1983a: 218–19, 225–34).

27. For anthropological evidence on this – indicating that the physiology and neurology of the species developed not before but at the same time as, and in conjunction with, the first 'cultural' activities – see Geertz (1973: 33–83). There is *no* pre-cultural 'human nature'; the 'instincts' were culturally formed – a point of some importance when, for instance, the allegedly 'instinctual' aspects of popular music, such as rhythm, are discussed.

28. See also Eco 1979: 21–8.

6

'From me to you'.
Popular music as message

Communication, code and competence

At the level of popular assumption, the belief that music produces sense, or conveys meanings, is unquestioned. And it slips very easily into the idea that there are analogies between music and language. Thus we hear such statements as 'I don't *understand* what punk rock is trying to *say*', 'the Rolling Stones *repeat* themselves', 'Bruce Springsteen just doesn't *get through* to me', 'the Beatles *articulated* what a whole generation felt', and so on. Yet such unquestioned assumptions mask a number of questions. First, what *kind* of meaning is music supposed to convey – affective, cognitive, referential? Then, how is the process supposed to work? Certainly all music, 'in so far as it is a cultural activity . . . is communicational activity' (Stefani 1973: 21). What is required is to specify the attributes of the processes governing *musical* meaning, and, at a second level, to specify them in particular contexts.[1]

The language analogy may be partly, but only partly, useful. While many semiological concepts originate in linguistics, there are strong arguments that music inhabits a semiological realm which, on both ontogenetic and phylogenetic levels, has developmental priority over verbal language.[2] Such arguments not only suggest the possibility of a specifically musical 'thought' derived from the operations of sensorimotor intelligence; they also imply the existence of a musical 'language of feeling' connected with symbolisms of the unconscious and movement patterns of the body. If verbal language is a very particular development from this pre-verbal semiotic stage, then verbal translations of musical thought and feeling, while unavoidable and not entirely invalid, are problematic (see Volosinov 1973: 15). Unfortunately, the science of music semiology, where such metalinguistic modelling should become more rigorous, is young and underdeveloped; moreover, it has paid virtually no attention to popular music.[3] It will thus be necessary here not only to suggest ways of applying music-semiological principles to popular music but also to discuss those principles themselves.

The concept of *code* is central – both in the sense of the mode of organization governing the internal structure of a system, and the mode of relationship coupling a syntactic to a semantic system, a *signifiant* to a *signifié*, expression plane to content plane (see Eco 1979: 32–8; Stefani 1973: 23–4). Existing models of musical communication, though a useful starting-point, often understate the plurality of codes involved and the multiplicity of variables affecting every component: sender, channel, context, message and receiver.[4] If 'encoding' and 'decoding' are to be conceived not as abstractly predictable but as culturally situated (that is, participant-orientated), the question of *competence* is crucial. And since competence varies – participants use and respond to codes in different ways – this directs maximum attention to the question of *pertinence*, that is, to finding those levels and types of coding which actually signify.

There is a *range* of codes operating in any musical event, some of them not even strictly musical but emanating from general schemes governing movement, gesture, rhetoric, affect, and so on (see Stefani 1973: 25–8). Theatrical, dance, and linguistic codes may be involved as well. Then, too, since music is a multi-parameter system, the strictly musical codes are several, organizing pitch, chord structure, rhythm, timbre, and so on; and these may not always reinforce each other but may be out of phase or contradictory. Additionally, codes may vary in *strength*. That is, the patterns they organize may be familiar and predictable – heavily coded – or they may be rather ambiguous and unpredictable – subject to weak or newly invented codes. At one extreme, pieces may create their own individual codes (this is more typical of avant-garde music); at the other extreme, a piece may be so tightly bound to socialized conventions as to be 'about' its code.

Eco (1979: 129–37) describes the first type as 'undercoded': individualized aspects of a piece – seemingly uncoded – are received within a general sense of 'understanding'. Examples of the second type, by contrast, are 'overcoded': every detail is covered by a network of explicit codes and subcodes. Historically this distinction is associated with the growing divergence, from the nineteenth century, between increasingly 'autonomous', aesthetically-orientated 'art' music and more 'conventional', functionally-orientated 'popular' music. It would be a mistake to couple the distinction with a rigid art/popular categorization, however; rather there is a variable ratio of the two types throughout the musical field, and there are examples of undercoded 'popular' works (*Sergeant Pepper*) as well as examples of overcoded 'classical' works (many parts of Puccini operas; Mendelssohn's *Songs without Words*). Nevertheless, the two trends do seem *differentially* tied to the two conventional categories. The history of nineteenth-century 'art' music is defined to a considerable extent by individual, innovatory works which were often not at all easy for contemporary audiences to decode. Most popular music, on the other hand, seems relatively highly coded or overcoded: controlled not only by tight, explicit general codes (for instance, a harmonic code governing chord vocabulary and sequence) but also, within these, by more specific codes as well (thus many styles use particular, conventionalized chord-progressions, such as the twelve-bar blues).

Another way of putting this would be in terms of Eco's distinction between 'text-orientated' and 'grammar-orientated' styles or cultures (ibid: 137–9). A text-orientated style builds up (often incomplete or ambiguous) codes from a repertory of (undercoded) texts; a grammar-orientated style derives (often overcoded) texts from a pre-existing system of rules and conventions. Arguments over the aesthetic status and semiotic functions of popular songs may well derive partly from conflicts between these two impulses in our culture, and within popular music production itself. At the same time, it would seem that most popular songs attach preponderantly to a grammar-orientation, and this has important implications for the status of the individual song (as against that of the originating system).

Nevertheless, it is the songs – the individual messages – that are given to the analyst. Codes never appear as such; they are a postulate, an operational device, necessary for explanation of the semiotic process. This postulate is the level which Saussure called *langue* (1960). Saussure described the *langue/parole* relationship in linguistics by comparison with that between a musical score and its performance. This is misleading, since a score is an individual product rather than a postulate representing socially systematized conventions; it is an aspect of *parole*, an intermediate stage comprising instructions for a performance-act. The musical *langue* must be sought at a deeper level. Nevertheless, it is tempting to find some *langue*-like elements in individual popular songs (not any scores that may exist but the songs themselves). Divergent performances of a Tin Pan Alley 'standard', of a collectively known blues, or of a 'classic' rock song, might be understood as selective activations of a socially owned framework. Variants of overcoded formulae, common to many songs, might be seen in the same way. It is even possible that extensive repetition of a phrase or figure within a song could be seen as the establishing of a conventionalized 'rule', which is then 'pulled' in specific directions, made to 'speak' in a particular moment, by, say, the detailed vocalization. On the whole, however, when comparing music and verbal language, it is better to see these frameworks as an extra level in the process, perhaps analogous to poetic, rhetorical or proverbial formulae.

For popular music, we might think of the following levels of code (cf. Nattiez 1976: 76–87; see also Barthes 1968: 17–22):

langue: a general Western music code, governing the territory, roughly speaking, of functional tonality (starting, that is, about the sixteenth century and still largely current today);

norms: e.g. the mainstream conventions *c.* 1750–*c.* 1900, or those governing the post-1900 period; within these

sub-norms: Victorian, jazz age, 1960s, etc.; and

dialects: e.g. European, Euro-American, Afro-American; within these

styles: music hall, Tin Pan Alley, Country, rock, punk, etc.; and

genres: ballad, dance-song, single, album, etc.; within many of these

sub-codes: e.g. within rock, rock 'n' roll, beat, rhythm and blues, progressive, etc.; and

idiolects: associated with particular composers and performers; within these

works and performances.

At many of these levels, there are relationships with 'non-popular' musics. Many of the codes are not necessarily wholly 'popular'; as we have seen before, the 'popular'/'non-popular' code is an *ideological* one, cutting across all the intramusical codes mentioned here. Very often, articulation processes are concerned with this boundary (was the 'ballad' of the Victorian period a 'popular' form or not?); but also they are concerned with the intramusical code-boundaries, crossing codes, recombining them, applying the 'wrong' code for decoding, and so on.

Stefani's model of the musical code hierarchy – perhaps the best available – adds even further levels (Stefani 1987b). His intramusical levels, which he designates as *Musical Techniques* (MT), *Styles* (St), and *Opus* (Op), and which subsume all those listed above, are grounded on *Social Practices* (SP) and below them on *General Codes* (GC). The SP level comprises codes concerned with the relationships between all the social practices of a culture, including those of musical life. Whereas the MT level is open to those versed in this particular cultural practice, that is, all speakers of the 'musical mother tongue of Western people', the SP level is open to all the members of the social group concerned. The GC level covers all basic categorization schemas, applying to music and other modes of symbolization: sensorial-perceptual schemas (high/low, and so on); logical schemas (same/different, and so on); formal/textural schemas (rounded/pointed; smooth/rough, and so on). This 'anthropological' level is theoretically open to all members of the human species.

Stefani's model can be applied both to coding and to decoding. The maximum 'signification effect' would occur when music coded on all levels was interpreted with full competence, that is, 'densely' on all levels; the minimum effect would occur when a purely GC coding was interpreted simply on a GC level, or, interestingly, when a purely Op coding was interpreted in a purely Op-specific way (something like the situation for many avant-garde 'classical' performances). Obviously many other intersections are possible, too.

Given that the very conditions of interpretation are not *etic* (that is, objective and autonomous) but *emic* (that is, the product of cultural knowledge),[5] it follows that there can be more than one type of competence. Specific usages often centre on specific levels of coding or specific relationships between levels. Stefani (ibid) suggests that in our culture the two most common types are what he calls 'high competence' and 'popular competence', which, in terms of his model, function through 'top-down' and 'bottom-up' approaches respectively (see Figure 6.1).

High competence is Op-orientated and treats music as a highly autonomous practice. Popular competence appropriates music in a more global, heteronomous manner, focusing on GC and SP levels. We could regard the distinction as analogous, on the pragmatic level, to that between text-orientated and grammar-orientated cultures, on the syntactic level. There is a shared area of 'common competence', and there are unexploited areas to the sides into which this, or high or popular competence, could expand.

Popular competence can attach itself to *any* kind of music – though musics themselves coded in an analogous way are the most likely. Similarly, popular *music* can be listened to according to *high* competence principles (as is sometimes the case with professional performers). But a *preponderance* of popular music listening does seem to be of a popular competence type; to that extent, this mode of competence is part of the definition of 'popular music'. At the same time, the fact that the two are not entirely homologous helps explain the *difficulty* of defining popular music (as an object). Furthermore, as we have seen, much popular music does de-emphasize the Op level and focuses more on lower levels;

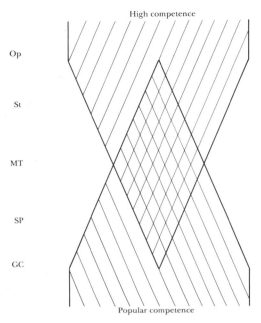

Fig. 6.1

it is grammar-orientated (grammar originating not only within St and MT but also SP and GC). Associated cultural practices tend to centre on social function and context, and on motor and emotional responses, rather than technical and aesthetic matters (for example, dance rather than criticism). Of course, this degree of correlation is historically and culturally specific. If high competence were to become universal – or better, if an expanded common competence were to become universal – 'popular music' as our society understands it would have disappeared, along with much else.

For the popular music analyst, the variability of competence implies that the problem of pertinence be fully taken into account. This affects not only the process of segmentation – deciding which division of a piece into syntagmatic units is meaningful – but also the choice of analytic level, from the auditory surface down to the deeper structures underlying this. The argument here will be that an open-minded synthesis of available methods is necessary. But first, ways of applying some of those methods must be considered.

Syntactic analysis

A music phonology
One of the first attempts to develop a quasi-semiological method of analysing surface structure in music was the application of *information theory*.[6] This, in a sense, however, simply rewrites older assumptions about pattern, expectation, and the relationship of unity to variety, in terms of allegedly quantifiable probabilities; style is defined in terms of measurable 'information', product

of the relative proportions of 'originality' and 'redundancy'. Thus while the method has its uses, it also suffers from severe flaws. Its culture-centric assumption of universal syntactic norms – an ideal balance of originality and redundancy – leads it to an elitist aesthetics; for example, it privileges modes of musical 'narrative' (the tension/relaxation effects associated with forward movement between different events) and neglects the pleasures of repetition (which it necessarily sees as totally predictable, hence boring). Its reductionist analytical method oversimplifies both the interaction of musical parameters and the complex variability of listening acts, while its behaviourist model of communication reduces meaning and choice to an abstract measure of 'stimulus' and blanks out the role of participant input. The question of *pertinence* hardly arises.

Attempts to apply to musical analysis various methods derived from *structural linguistics* began around the same time as interest in information theory (the 1950s). In structural linguistics 'pertinent' units or features are those which are functional in respect of semantic communication. Other units and features that may be present would be described as 'redundant',[7] and this distinction has been generalized for semiology as that between the *emic* and the *etic*. Emic elements are those recognized by a system's user-culture as meaningful. Hence, in theory, a complete description of such elements for a given system would define its extent, and at the same time provide a method of delineating units.

In music, the raw material of acoustic matter is organized in many different ways, within different systems, into 'pertinent' patterns: scales, modes, durational relationships, available timbres, and so on. The quasi-phonological status of this level of structure has been noted by Lévi-Strauss (1970: 21–8) and others (Nattiez 1976: 94–9; Sloboda 1985: 23–31; Stefani 1973: 28–33; Mâche 1971). Since it may be surrounded by non-pertinent components (accidental or non-significant elements, or free variants), its analysis would seem to be vital for the establishing of syntactic structure.

However, for any music, it is not immediately clear what levels or kinds of pertinent unit would be the appropriate focus. Since music, like natural language, is a temporal system, should we concentrate on the *syntagmatic chain* – the way units are joined sequentially to form 'strings'? If so, at what level – the note, the 'cell' or 'motive', the phrase? But *parameters* are important, too, and a timbre or a tempo or a metre can stay the same throughout a piece; the organization here cannot be syntagmatic. Parameters and units can be regarded as bundles of *features*, and it may be that we should focus on these. In phonology, the contribution of 'features' to phonemic structure is seen as organized through binary oppositions: particular phonetic features (voicing, nasality, dentality, and the like) are either present or absent, and marked or unmarked (that is, pertinent or non-pertinent), and the limited number of combinations defines the stock of phonemes. In music, some features may be subject to binary choice (for example, accent (or not) and modality (major or minor)) but most result from multiple choices (for example, pitch-step and duration) and some even from 'cutting' into continua (for example, dynamic level and pitch gradation). The number of possible permutations is very large.

This difference can be looked at from the point of view of the distinction between linguistics and paralinguistics. Paralinguistics covers all aspects of a verbal message which are surplus to the phonological structure, and which are therefore not strictly necessary to communication of the basic message. Many of these aspects are not only 'supra-segmental' – that is, they *cross* segments of structure – but also are articulated within continua rather than according to binary oppositions: voice-quality, pitch-level, speed of enunciation, dialect pronunciations, details of emphasis and speech-rhythm are examples. It is tempting to think of music as possessing a basic 'grammatical' framework plus a 'paralinguistic' superstructure. But how – without introducing an unsatisfactory idealization of the score, and regarding performance as an 'extra' – could we decide where the distinction lies? If we stripped away a notional level of paralinguistic detail, would the remaining 'framework' still 'make sense'? Would the 'basic message' remain, or would it have changed, or lost part of its basic meaning? Even within the study of natural language, the distinction has become less rigid, as scholars have demonstrated that paralinguistic features are often meaningful, culturally acquired and mediated, and rigorously coded. An alternative would be to consider musical systems as a whole as paralinguistic. But then the potential value of the distinction would be lost, as well as the possibility that the application to music of linguistic techniques of segmentation and syntagmatic analysis could be of use.

Commutation

In conventional music analysis, segmentation is generally carried out intuitively. Phrases are distinguished by their 'shape', their 'completeness', their repetition, their closure by cadence or 'breath' (there is an implicit comparison with verbal phrases); cells or motives (= words or morphemes?) are distinguished, again, by repetition but also by their integrity, self-sufficiency and distinctness; notes (= phonemes?) are taken as self-evident.[8] In songs, a close connection is often assumed between words and music, with notes following syllables, motives often correlating with words or word-groups, and musical phrases fitting verbal ones.

Now it may well be that these intuitions could often be rationally justified. But the lack of an agreed formal method of segmentation does leave many obscurities unquestioned. For example, spectographic analysis shows that the concept of a 'note' is actually an imposition on the dynamic, processual quality of all sound; and even if we accept the widespread existence of what has been called *abstraction notale* (Francès 1958: 26–7) – that is, a culturally acquired scalar model into which listeners fit all sounds, even when they are pitch-mobile or slightly divergent from recognized pitch steps – this does not of itself mean that 'notes' are of phonemic status and independence, always and in all musics, nor does it rule out the possibility of dialectical interplay, of phonemic significance, between abstracted notes and subsegmental and suprasegmental features. How, for instance, would *abstraction notale* apply to the pitch sequences of a rhythm and blues or country and western slide guitar solo?

As far as the relationship of words and music is concerned, a song like Little Richard's 'Tutti Frutti' – where the same music sometimes carries different words, the same words are sometimes carried by different music, and word-setting varies from syllabic to melismatic – is enough to suggest that the relationship of words and music in songs is dialectical: each affects the other, but their structural relationship varies along a continuum from complete homomorphism to a radically heteromorphic superposition.

In structural phonology, segmentation is carried out through commutation tests. A given phonetic entity, considered a potential phoneme, is substituted by a different entity. If a change in meaning follows, a phoneme has been located. The same operation can be employed at higher levels, to demarcate morphemes and lexemes. In other words, a change on the plane of content is structurally homologous with a change on the plane of expression.[9] For music, the problem is, of course, that the structure of the content plane is little understood, probably rather ambiguous and amorphous, and quite possibly not homologous with the structure of the expression plane.

One solution might be to use 'endosemantic' rather than 'exosemantic' distinctions. For example, Bright has suggested (1963: 30–1) substitutions designed to discover distinctions in 'internal meaning' (grammatical function); to test listeners' ability to distinguish two similar entities consistently; or to test pairs for equivalence (rather than difference). Picking up the last point, Nattiez also argues for equivalence tests, based on the idea of a stimulus/response (rather than expression/content) coupling, hence on the hypothesis of a *sentiment émique d'identité* in listeners (Nattiez 1976: 231–3). It is not clear whether 'equivalence' is meant to mark variants (hence to define a single phoneme through its constituent 'allophones') or to mark a kind of 'positional' identity, an equivalence of function or level (hence to define distinct units within the same structural class). Nevertheless, an illustration of the general approach can be given (see Ex. 6.1). A represents the beginning of the vocal of the Clash's 'White Riot' (the words 'white riot'). Most acculturated listeners would probably hear the second note of B as *grammatically* distinct from the second of A: it is a different scale step (and suggests a different chord). They would probably hear C as *equivalent* to A, in the sense of being a variant (at the level of a morpheme? – hence an allomorph); the same pitches appear in a different rhythm. The second note of D would probably be taken as a variant (an allophone) of the second note of A; since the major-key system does not recognize eighth-tone differences from scalar pitch as meaningful, and since expressive pitch

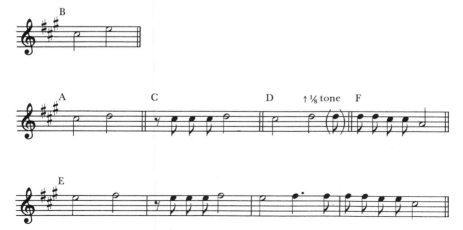

Ex. 6.1

nuance is not typical of punk rock style, the note in D would be assimilated to the A model. Lastly, the whole of E might well be heard as *positionally* equivalent to the whole of A-C-D-F, while distinct in 'content': the internal pitch relationships are similar, the rhythmic structures are identical, and the tonal implications are similar (the same chords are implied). But what about F? Is it grammatically equivalent to the whole of A-C-D (it can sound like a 'consequent' to their 'antecedent')? Is it a variant of C (similar rhythm)? Is it a variant of A (the pitches C# and D are important in both)? Or is it a distinct unit, positionally equivalent to A or C or D (same length)? The confusion reveals the heterogeneity of possible 'emicities', which may vary with the individual, depending on which level and which parameter are the focus of attention. Similarly, from what we know of punk rock style, it seems quite likely that pitch *as a whole* is relatively unimportant in a vocal of this sort; it may be that the hoarse, manic, shouted timbre is the primary emic category and that almost any pitches would serve, all being variants of each other, none particularly distinctive.

Rigorous experimental work with stable groups of respondents, using approaches of this kind, could well produce significant results. But these results will probably always be rough and ready, not only because of the confusion just mentioned but also because of the absence of the dimension of exosemantic meaning.

The only application of commutation methods adapted specifically to popular music analysis is Philip Tagg's technique of 'hypothetical substitution' (1979: 71–7; 99–154 *passim*).[10] For any musical message (usually a melodic phrase or a melody-plus-accompaniment compound) the analyst carries out substitutions of the various constituent elements and parameters, with the aim of discovering how the 'meaning' of the message is changed. As this description suggests, Tagg is mostly concerned with elucidating content, rather than with segmentation as such: his technique is a way of confirming or falsifying interpretations of meaning gained by other means. Indeed, he explicitly rejects use of the term 'unit' for basic constituents of syntax; he prefers 'element' (which can be segmental or non-segmental). Also, he refuses to theorize the quasi-phonemic level of structure, leaving it as a loose and variable assembly of 'components' contributing to meaning at a higher 'morphemic' level. Nevertheless, the technique has the potential to tell us quite a lot about the relative distinctiveness and importance of 'elements'.

Take the beginning of the tune in the Beatles' 'A Day in the Life' (Ex. 6.2a). Any single pitch could be substituted (6.2b). The entire pitch contour could be changed, while keeping the tonality intact (6.2c). Any single duration could be substituted (6.2d). The modality could be changed (6.2e). A change in the accompanying harmonies might take the style toward, say, soul (6.2f), while a substituted metre could change the effect into that of, for instance, a waltz (6.2g). A change in the articulation could destroy the tune's seriousness (6.2h). It is easy to conceive of substitutions of tempo (imagine doubling it); dynamic (imagine fortissimo); lyric (imagine 'My ice cream runs right down my chin'); singer (imagine Placido Domingo instead of John Lennon); instrumentation (imagine tremolando string orchestra; Wagner tubas; gamelan ensemble).

Clearly, all of these substitutions would affect the overall 'meaning'. Equally clearly, the biggest changes would come with substitutions of whole parameters

Ex. 6.2

(for example, tempo, timbre, metre, articulation). By contrast, the substitutions in Ex. 6.2b and d seem to have a much smaller effect. Most listeners would probably agree they 'make a difference'; but they would probably also agree that the differences were not very important or noticeable. Even the total change of melodic contour in Ex. 6.2c, while it affects the grammar, does not seem to affect the overall mood of the tune particularly. In fact, Tagg's technique is only partially successful for segmentation purposes; as he admits, the smaller the unit substituted, the less obvious any change in meaning. The technique is much better at demonstrating, ranking and comparing the distinctive contributions of suprasegmental parameters than those of syntagmatic units.

Tagg's use of the technique in his analysis of the 'Kojak' signature tune is virtuosic, presenting altered versions in the manner of a hymn tune, sixteenth-century counterpoint, bossa nova, twentieth-century atonality, clippety-clop Wild Westism, and many more. But it works best for him when whole parameters are altered (tonality, harmonic language, pitch register, as well as timbre, tempo and phrasing); or – in the case of smaller alterations – when these involve *relationships*, not single events (melodic intervals, pitch shapes or rhythmic patterns). Indeed, the method is really most suited for making distinctions at the level of *style* codes rather than for phonemic or morphemic analysis *within* a given style code (cf. Ex. 6.2f, g). As Tagg himself points out, the relative importance of any given 'element' – and thus the effect of substituting it – varies in different styles and genres. We have already noted the high importance of a particular vocal timbre and performance style in punk rock; choice of timbre would be much less important in, say, medieval dance music. Similarly, the introduction of rhythmic rubato in singing a nineteenth-century *Lied* would be of secondary significance – an aspect merely of 'interpretation' – but in jazz singing (Billie Holiday or Ella Fitzgerald, for example) it is central. Tagg's approach provides an excellent method of delineating and checking such style codes.

As far as segmentation is concerned, the problem is the seeming lack in music of a clear and consistent dividing line between syntactic levels – between significant and non-significant, distinctive and non-distinctive units. Instead there is a continuum. *Any* substitution, however small, will probably be agreed by attentive listeners to 'make a difference'; but what kind of difference and how great? From another point of view, some substitutions may be heard as immaterial, even when it is hard to believe their effect on 'grammatical meanings' is not substantial. How big and what kind of difference does substitution have to make before the substituted element is regarded as a unit? In linguistics this question can be answered; in music it cannot.

A related problem is that the same element, in different contexts, can shift level – can be both phonemic and morphemic, for instance. Just as timbre can be both a constituent feature and a significant category in its own right, so a single pitch can be not only a functional component of a meaningful unit but also meaningful in itself. Tagg mentions examples of single bass notes – drones, for example – of which this is the case. The same can be said of chords. Usually a constituent of a 'meaningful' chord-sequence, a single chord can take on a morphemic or lexical status. A good example would be the prolonged, orchestral E major triad which ends 'A Day in the Life'. Whatever the exact 'meaning' of this chord, most listeners would attribute to it a certain level of significance in its own right.

Underlying many of the problems with commutation techniques in music is the fact that, whereas in linguistics they are built on an assumption that the system in question operates according to relations of *difference*, in music the assumption must be that relations of *equivalence* are just as important, perhaps more so. To the extent that many parameters work along continua, and that units and their constituents often relate to each other as variants, transformations or repetitions, rather than oppositions, substitution techniques will mislead or provide only partial results. The moves by Bright and Nattiez towards concepts of 'identity', 'variance' and 'equivalence' signal an implicit confirmation of this – and suggest that we should look more carefully at the concept of 'equivalence'.

Paradigmatic analysis

In the 1960s, Nicolas Ruwet developed an analytic method – since termed 'paradigmatic analysis' by others – based on the concept of 'equivalence'. Ruwet argued that the most striking characteristic of musical syntax was the central role of *repetition* – and, by extension, of varied repetition or *transformation* (Ruwet 1987). Drawing on Jakobson's description of poetry (1960: 358), he saw music's basic property as the 'projection of the principle of equivalence from the axis of selection on to the axis of combination'; thus the act of paradigmatic selection – making a choice for a given moment out of a class of similar terms – is 'turned on its side', and the similar terms are combined to form the syntagmatic string. This helps to account for the difficulties of segmentation in music – relationships of equivalence *across* segments seem to be at least as important as distinctions marking segment boundaries – as well as the difficulty of associating distinct contributions to meaning with minimal units. Ruwet makes repetition the basis of his method. Anything repeated (straight or varied) is defined as a unit, and this is true on all levels, from sections through phrases, presumably down as far as individual sounds. This means that in principle he can segment a piece without reference to its meaning, purely on the basis of the internal grammar of its expression plane. There are some problems, however. Which parameters are to be regarded as pertinent and on what grounds? What are the criteria for a judgement that two entities are sufficiently similar to be considered equivalent? If intuitive, such decisions would seem to 'solve' the segmentation question before the event.

Ruwet makes certain assumptions: that scores represent pertinent categories of sound-event; that there are valid means of assessing the existence of equivalence (variance, transformation); that among all the parameters which could be affecting segmentation, pitch and duration are the most important. But he reduces the effect of the problems somewhat by applying the technique to *single pieces*: there is no attempt, as there is in the somewhat analogous methods of distributional linguistics, to delineate the make-up of a system – though presumably if analysis of a number of pieces revealed similarities in types of segmentation and unit relationships, that would constitute the beginnings of a description of a code.

Ex. 6.3

In outline, Ruwet's method (1987) is to use the criterion of repetition/transformation, together with evidence provided by caesurae and verbal texts, to segment the piece.[11] Working through the piece several times, the analyst breaks it down into its constituent units on each structural level in turn. Units are assigned to a particular level if they are roughly the same length as each other. Here is how the method could be applied to George Gershwin's 'A Foggy Day'. Example 6.3 shows the complete tune. Example 6.4 shows the complete tune when read conventionally – left to right, top to bottom – while the columns show the paradigmatic relationships, that is the repetitions and transformations of units. Example 6.5 shows the smallest units (Levels III, IV). Repeated units, from the highest to the lowest level (0, I, II, etc.), are represented by letter, thus: A, a, a_1, a. Transformations are represented by superscripts, e.g. A^1. Units

Ex. 6.4

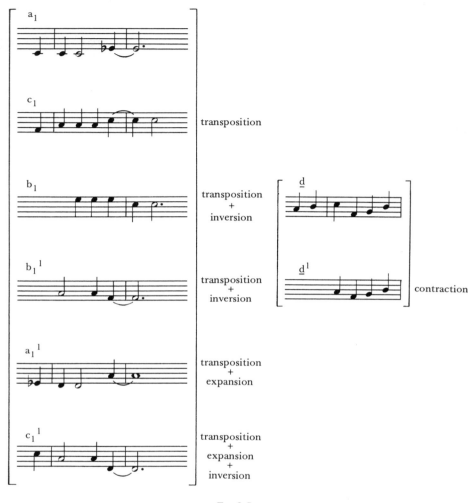

Ex. 6.5

which (for the moment perhaps) are unassigned as to level and appear to be unrepeated are represented by X.

Level 0:   X No strictly repeated units. But using criterion of transformation . . .

Level I: $A + X + A^1 + Y$ (A^1 = A with slight rhythmic variants), or rather $A + B + A^1 + C$ (all units same length, or very nearly).
But $B = b + c$; $C = b^1 + d$ (see next level). Moreover, B and C are equivalent in length and end on held notes. Thus $C = B^1$. Hence: $A + B + A^1 + B^1$.

Level II: A, A^1 = a + b (words assist segmentation here) b = a^1
            (transformation through transposition). Hence A, A^1 = a + a^1.
            Similarly, B = b + c, B^1 = b^1 + d (b^1 = b at higher pitch with slight
            changes in some interval sizes).
Level III: a = x_1 + y_1 (words again assist).
            a = a_1 + b_1 (same length).
            a = a_1 + a_1^1 (transformation through expansion of 3rd to 5th).
            Similarly, b = b_1 + b_1^1 (sequence).
            c = c_1 + c_1^1 (expansion and inversion).
            But all these are variants of a_1 (see Ex. 6.5).
            d = $\underline{d}$ + $\underline{d}^1$ (next level) + e_1.

If the analysis were continued to Level IV, we would find not only $\underline{d}$ (one bar long) but the single notes out of which the bulk of the tune is made. These are also implicitly one bar long, but varied internally through repetition and syncopation (see Ex. 6.6). They can be regarded as 'equivalent' – in the sense of being units on the same level – through durational equality (and similarity of grammatical weight); the rhythmic variants (together with the melodic differences, of course) create transformations of this durational identity.

Are these the minimal units in the tune? And are they phonemic or morphemic? Ruwet's method cannot answer these questions. A good case could be made for Level III units to be considered the minimal significant segments: each contains a melodic leap, which seems to be structurally meaningful in the tune. Indeed, these leaps could themselves be regarded as primary, with the

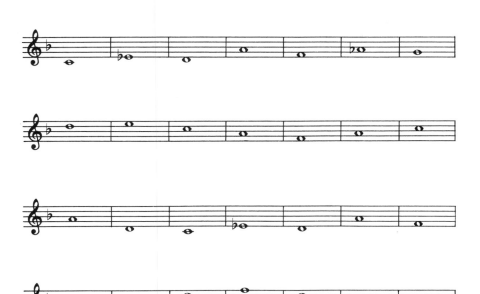

Ex. 6.6

repeated notes and step movements surrounding them seen as 'paralinguistic' ornamentation. The stresses introduced in particular performances might help adjudicate (while also introducing other paralinguistic nuance to pitch and rhythm, which might *complicate* the judgement).

Privileging melodic leaps is to propose a different criterion for segmentation, of course. And this raises another problem with the analysis: there are many such possible criteria. If all upward leaps were regarded as comprising a paradigmatic class, downward leaps another, and all remaining events a third, a different segmentation of the tune would result. Similarly, if one particularly frequent rhythm (♩ ♩ ♩ ♩) were seen as the main principle of equivalence, and all other material lumped together as contrast, yet another breakdown would appear. Even accepting, say, the Level II divisions initially proposed, alternative relationships could be suggested. If type of anacrusis were a primary criterion, units a, c, and b^1 would be linked. Or if overall ambitus of units were important, b^1 would be linked with a (all sixths), while b and c would be a separate class (sevenths). Considering initial and final notes of units as particularly significant would reveal a strong connection between a^1 and c (both start on F, end on D).

Altering criteria can affect the relative weight of levels within the structural hierarchy. Ruwet's method might suggest an overall two-part form at 'Level $\frac{1}{2}$' (AB/A^1B^1 = AA^1); but this articulation is not revealed strongly because the chosen criteria do not show up the two parts as equivalent. A stress on pitch contour, as a *Gestalt*, would show each half describing a similar arch shape (see Ex. 6.7); and this would clearly mark the end of c as a midpoint.

The question of criteria is one side of the problem of equivalence. The other side is the question of 'distance'. It is not only a matter of what means we should use to judge the existence of transformation but also how far we may travel along the axis defined by any given criterion. At what distance does a transformation become a contrast? In the paradigmatic method of musical analysis, equivalence and difference tend to run into each other: even the establishing of difference (A + B) requires an equivalence of duration – the same time-span is *repeated*.[12]

There are no answers within the method to either question. Such questions must be referred to *listeners*, for the answers depend on what is heard and how it is heard. In that sense, the method's 'objectivity' is not only limited (for initial assumptions *are* made, as Ruwet himself recognizes) but limiting. It would make sense to twin paradigmatic analysis with commutation techniques, using each to test the results of the other. Ruwet's method, starting with a single piece, works from the top downwards. Having assumed criteria of pertinence, it then works entirely by reference to the internal grammar of the system. Commutation techniques work from the bottom upwards, within a whole corpus or system,

Ex. 6.7

implicitly or explicitly defined. Their criteria of pertinence are derived from tests of culture users, and refer throughout to meaning or context.

Such a marriage will not solve all problems. Nevertheless, it would increase the likelihood that Ruwet's method will be fruitful in popular music analysis, not only for its general property of checking intuitive segmentation through more formal procedures but also, in this specific sphere, because of some particular properties of the music. Many kinds of popular music place heavy reliance on techniques of repetition and variance – if music is a syntax of equivalence, much popular music carries the principle to a highpoint. At the same time this music tends towards relatively clear, symmetrical segmental structures. The usefulness of Ruwet's method is inversely proportional to the degree of contrast and to the amount of asymmetrical, overlapping units, infringing clear structural hierarchy – so 'free atonal' Schoenberg, on the one hand, Beethoven sonata movements, on the other, are less amenable than the internally regular, stepped structures of many song melodies.

An analysis of Bo Diddley's 'Hey Bo Diddley' (Ex. 6.8) will illustrate this point – as well as showing that the method can be applied not only to written tunes but also to non-notated songs (though here we have, of course, to accept the transcription's abstraction of pitch and duration – which may or may not be valid: strictly speaking, commutational tests should be carried out).

Generative theory
The units located on Level III (a_1, b_1, c_1) or Level IV ($\underline{a}$, $\underline{b}$) of 'Hey Bo Diddley' and Level III (a_1, b_1, c_1) of 'A Foggy Day' would, I think, be termed 'musemes' by Philip Tagg (by analogy with 'morpheme'). By 'museme' he means 'the basic unit of musical expression which in the framework of one given musical system is not further divisible without destruction of meaning' (Tagg 1979: 71); as we saw earlier, he argues that a museme may

> be broken down into component parts which are not in themselves meaningful within the framework of the musical language . . . but are nevertheless basic elements (not units) of musical expression which, when altered, may be compared to the phonemes of speech in that they alter the museme (morpheme) of which they are part and may thereby also alter its meaning (ibid: 71).

The term 'museme' is a good one, and I shall adopt it – though, in view of the difficulties already found in defining minimal units consistently and precisely, the nature and size of the museme need to be regarded flexibly. Tagg, even though he derives the concept from the work of Charles Seeger, where it is rigorously and narrowly defined, does use it in a flexible way – indeed, he does not define its limits at all, beyond what has been quoted above.

Seeger's method (1977c) draws on certain concepts in symbolic logic, and the appearance of several theoretic systems drawing on this and similar sources seems to indicate an important trend. There is an implication in common that the basis of syntactic structures in music lies in metamusical processes of the human mind, either innate or connected with very deep levels of psychological development. And it is in this more general area – where cognitive science, experimental music psychology and artificial intelligence theory come together – that work is

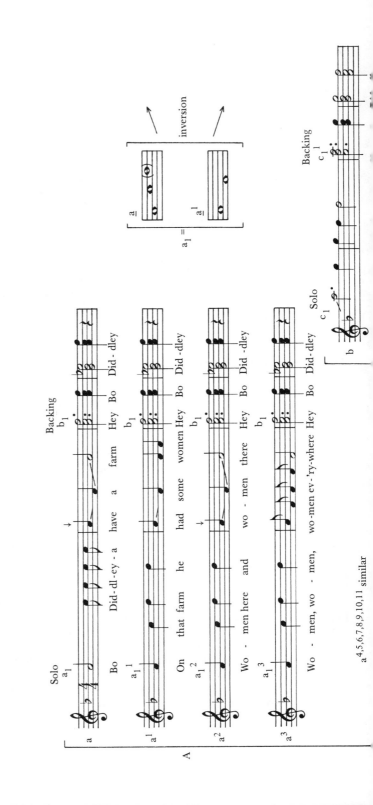

Ex. 6.8

going on which may eventually not only reveal a universal framework underlying the different types of musical structure and sense, but also provide both ethnomusicology and popular music studies with the weapons that will dethrone traditional musicology from the centre of the analytical stage.[13] The processes explored in this work clearly inhabit the lower levels in Stefani's model of musical competence (GC, SP and the lower areas of MT). The notion of 'competence' comes from Chomskyan linguistics, and it is not surprising that the turn to logic and cognitive theory has been accompanied by an interest among music analysts in generative grammar. It is precisely on the level of general cognitive processes that Chomsky's generative 'deep structures' may be presumed to lie.

Chomsky argues that people's ability to understand and produce an infinite number of well-formed utterances within systems theorized as *langue* requires the concept of a 'deep' model of syntactic structure which, through the operation of structural transformational rules, generates the 'surface structures' that are actually spoken. Language competence, then, relates to a power of *abstraction* and an understanding of *function* rather than just learning particular syntagmatic combinations and their meanings. Applied to music, this approach would imply a conception of structure as comprising not just paradigmatic choices and syntagmatic sequences but also a *functional hierarchy* lying 'behind' what is heard. The typical Chomskyan 'tree diagram' makes clear both the abstraction, and the importance of function, since not only can one deep structure generate many surface structures but one surface structure can be interpreted as the transformation of more than one deep structure, depending on the grammatical labelling (see Figure 6.2).

There are several ways in which the concepts of generative grammar could be, and have been, applied to music. Here we are concerned solely with their possible usefulness as an analytical tool – that is, in explaining the perception and cognition of musical structures. It may be that we understand the syntax of popular songs we have never heard before not only through knowledge of phonological, musematic and combinatory codes but also through reference to deep structures into which specific details (notes, rhythms, musemes, and so on) can be slotted.

As a matter of fact, such an approach is not altogether foreign to established music theory. The family resemblance between the concepts of generative grammar and those of the German analyst Heinrich Schenker have often been

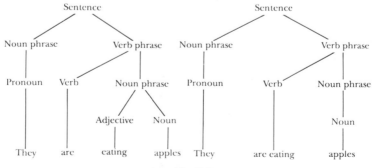

Fig. 6.2

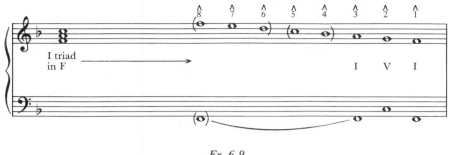

Ex. 6.9

noticed. While a complete exposition of Schenkerian theory is not appropriate here (see Forte and Gilbert 1982; Jonas 1982), it is worth investigating the applicability of the fundamental principles to popular music.

Schenker regarded the basis of all functional-tonal music (the only kind he thought worth attention) as the tonic triad. His deep structures (the level he called *Ursatz* or 'background') comprise a two-pronged 'composing-out' of this triad, harmonically through arpeggiation in the bass (I-V-I, forming a kind of giant perfect cadence), and melodically through the *Urlinie*: a stepwise descent from one of the triad notes to the tonic (hence, $\hat{3}$-$\hat{2}$-$\hat{1}$, $\hat{5}$-$\hat{4}$-$\hat{3}$-$\hat{2}$-$\hat{1}$ or $\hat{8}$-$\hat{7}$-$\hat{6}$-$\hat{5}$-$\hat{4}$-$\hat{3}$-$\hat{2}$-$\hat{1}$).[14] To Schenker, all good pieces follow this pattern (see Ex. 6.9). It is elaborated through subsidiary harmonies and processes of voice-leading (the 'middleground' level of structure), and through various kinds of melodic detail and rhythmic articulation, resulting in the 'foreground' (which we hear). Analysis therefore reverses this movement, reducing what we hear, by means of analytic notation, to increasingly abstract levels of structure. For to Schenker, grasping a piece has to do with the interplay between the details which make the piece unique and the deep structure which it shares with many other pieces (and which, he believed, was grounded in innate characteristics of hearing, reflecting acoustic laws).

There seems no reason why Schenker analysis could not be applied to popular songs governed by functional-tonal processes: nineteenth-century types, for example, or most Tin Pan Alley songs. A simple analysis of Gershwin's 'A Foggy Day' using Schenkerian principles illustrates this (see Ex. 6.10).

This has the merit of revealing, beneath the rich chord-sequences, the importance of basic V-I harmony, and, melodically, the centrality of the notes of the tonic triad (F-A-C), particularly the C-F relationship. On the other hand, it could be argued that the location of the *Urlinie* mainly in the last phrase is arbitrary (indeed, that the fundamental melodic structure of the song has nothing to do with descending scale patterns at all); that the importance of the *motivic* structure discussed earlier is missed; and, similarly, that the importance of *rhythm* in creating structure (particularly the syncopation regularly produced by the tie across the bar-line) is ignored. These points echo some of the criticisms commonly made of Schenker (see especially Narmour 1980), who simply took the nature of the *Ursatz*, and especially the leading role of triadic harmony, as axiomatic. It follows that his theory is anti-historical – all valid musical styles are

Ex. 6.10

Notes Structural pitches are shown as white notes. Structurally important pitches at the middle-ground level are shown as beamed black notes. 'Prolongations' of these (unattached black notes) are related to them by a slur. 'Register transfer' (i.e. an octave relationship) is shown by a dotted slur.

seen as *essentially* the same – while a good deal of music either has to be condemned as invalid or bad, or misanalysed.

Some of the problems are clearly ineradicable. Thus, Schenkerian 'tonalism' could not be satisfactorily applied to much Afro-American and rock music, in which pentatonic and modal structures are important, and where harmonic structure in any case plays a comparatively small role (for example, songs with a drone chord, but with richly inflected melodic structure, such as Sly and the Family Stone's 'Thank you (Falettinme Be Mice Elf Agin)'). It might even be misleading when applied to pop songs which at first sight would seem candidates for Schenkerian analysis. The verse of Wham's 'I'm Your Man'[15] ends in a strong V-I cadence; what is more, the melody line follows a clear $\hat{3}$-$\hat{2}$-$\hat{1}$ pattern. The melody of the chorus could also be assimilated to this *Urlinie* without too much trouble (See Ex. 6.11). However, harmonically the chorus is built on a modal cell (I-IV-bVII), which is treated as a riff. Undoubtedly, the Schenker approach registers something important about the song; but at the same time it distorts the whole structure, which surely is a two-levelled process: sections of riff-based circularity are *set against* sections with cadential closure.

The same tension appears in a song like the Beatles' 'Twist and Shout' – see

Ex. 6.11

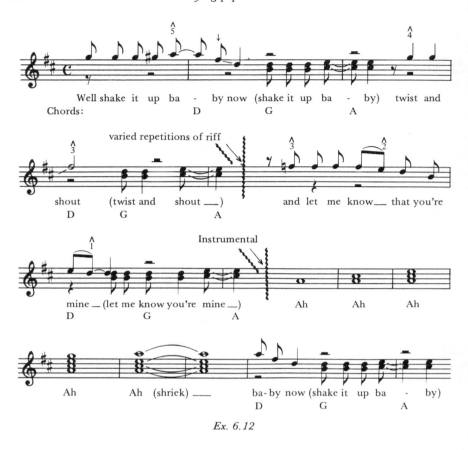

Ex. 6.12

Ex. 6.12.[16] One could find a $\hat{3}$-$\hat{2}$-$\hat{1}$, or perhaps a $\hat{5}$-$\hat{4}$-$\hat{3}$-$\hat{2}$-$\hat{1}$ *Urlinie* in the melody – though it is not so obvious as in 'I'm Your Man' – and the riff is now I-IV-V: potentially functionally tonal. But the harmonically static V^7 'breaks' (the build-ups to a vocalized 'ah'), though giving way to the riff's tonic-chord, create little sense of closure; and the ever-cycling riff produces more of a 'circular' structure than the goal-directed form central to Schenkerian theory.

Nevertheless, a full-blown rejection of the theory for this kind of music is less appropriate than the development of a 'modified Schenkerianism'. If we rewrite the V-I bias in terms of a principle of 'tonicity' – the 'prolongation' of a tonic chord through structures of harmonic difference, which may take many other forms than V – a method which is more flexible but which retains the concept of hierarchy emerges. And if we forget the rigid *Urlinie* forms but keep the approach to melodic prolongation, a link between the conceptual origins of Schenker's thought in earlier European musical practice and important twentieth-century popular music techniques comes into view. For sixteenth-, seventeenth- and eighteenth-century methods of 'prolonging' (elaborating) tonal frameworks through strict and free counterpoint, melodic variation, ornamentation and (often improvised) 'division' bear close comparison with improvisation over chord sequences in jazz, and melodic construction over I-IV-V patterns and harmonic riffs in blues and rock (cf. p. 55 above).

This point is supported by Perlman and Greenblatt's study of jazz improvisation (1981) – not in fact a Schenkerian text, but one which proposes an analogous application of generative grammar to the structure of jazz performance. They see the different chord sequences used for improvisation as deep structures from which an infinite number of surface structures (solos, and even in some cases different written tunes based on the same chords) can be generated. In between, they posit a 'shallow structure', which comprises chord modifications and substitutions, and the cluster of notes available for improvisation; this – 'the array of possibilities that the musician may choose from at any given point' (ibid: 172) – will vary, for a specific chord sequence, between different styles; compare Charlie Parker's vocabulary for a twelve-bar blues with Louis Armstrong's, for instance. Thus the different selections are 'transformations' of the same deep structure. Perlman and Greenblatt point out that, just as in language, these deep structures can be conjoined and embedded to form longer and more complex patterns. The V-I sequence is an extremely common case in point. It can be repeated, exactly or sequentially (that is, conjoined – see Ex. 4.3, pp. 119–20 above); or it can be made to coexist with itself on different levels (that is, embedded), as when 'secondary dominants' are used to form low-level V-I progressions within a higher-level V-I over the whole phrase or even piece (see Ex. 6.13). It is a bedrock of the jazz and popular song repertory, certainly up to the mid-1950s.[17]

This recursiveness is picked up by Steedman (1984), who has worked out a comprehensive set of 'rewrite rules' which will generate all recognizably well-formed transformations used in jazz of the basic I-IV-I-V-I twelve-bar blues sequence. The most important transformations are: (1) the replacement of a chord by its subdominant, or, especially, by its dominant – which, recursively extended, can produce complex sequences such as

$$1\ 2\quad 3\ 4\ 5\quad 6\qquad 7\qquad 8\qquad 9\qquad 10\ 11\ 12$$
$$\text{I/IV/I/I}^7\!/\!/\ \text{IV/VII}^7\!/\text{III}^7\!/\text{VI}^7\!/\!/\ \text{II}^7\!/\text{V}^7\!/\text{I/}\ \text{I}\!/\!/$$

(2) the use of chromatic passing chords (so that bars 7–9 above could be rewritten as $\text{III}^7\!/\flat\text{III}^7\!/\text{II}^7$); and (3) the use of chord alterations (minor chords, diminished

Jerome Kern 'Yesterdays' (bars 9-16)

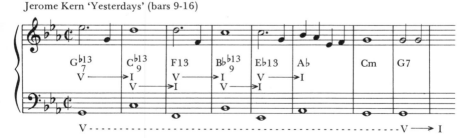

Ex. 6.13

sevenths, and so on). Steedman points out that, slightly modified, the rules could generate non-twelve-bar blues patterns based on I-IV-V (such as 'I Got Rhythm'). Even more interesting, he adds that recursive elaboration of the IV-I rather than V-I sequence could also easily be covered, and this results in a kind of chord-structure governed by fourth rather than fifth relationships – as in Jimi Hendrix's 'Hey Joe':

```
1         2           3 4 5        6           7 8  9          10          1112
♭VI,  ♭III/♭VII,  IV/I/I//♭VI,  ♭III/♭VII,  IV/I/I//♭VI,  ♭III/♭VII,  IV/I/ I//
 └─────┘ └──┘ └─────┘ └──┘
  4th     4th   4th     4th
```

This is important because it results in what Alf Björnberg (1985) has called 'Aeolian harmony', which has become an important category in rock music. By this, he means chords built from the notes of the Aeolian mode, especially Im, ♭III, IVm, Vm, ♭VI and ♭VII. Several different subsets are common, notably patterns built around Im-♭VII-♭VI, and Im-IVm-Vm, and around various sequences (I-♭III-IV; I-IV-♭VII) which Björnberg links with blues, in that they could be understood as deriving from the blues 'minor pentatonic' scale (I-♭III-IV-V-♭VII). The verse of 'I'm Your Man' belongs to this latter category, of course; the category could also be derived from fourth-movements, as we have seen. All the subsets lack the V-I perfect cadence so important in functional-tonal music.

Far from 'modal' and 'fourth-orientated' structures being distortions or surface transformations of Schenker's favoured V-I kernel, it is more likely that both are branches of a deeper principle, that of tonic/not-tonic differentiation. Also, interestingly, twelve-bar blues – which includes both IV-I and V-I – could be seen as articulating a tension between subdominant and dominant branches, a tension which has wound its way through the whole history of Afro-American-influenced styles.

Thus a generative tree for a basic twelve-bar blues would give equal weight to both branches (Figure 6.3). And it becomes clear that the chord structure of a song like the Beatles' 'I Saw Her Standing There' (see Ex. 4.1, p. 117 above), though more extended and complex in its use of the three chords, derives from the same kernel (Figure 6.4). While the opening strain of 'I Got Rhythm' also originates in this kernel (with several chord substitutions), its middle eight derives from a typical 'dominant-branching' tree (Figure 6.5).

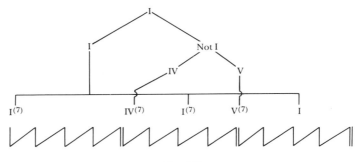

Fig. 6.3

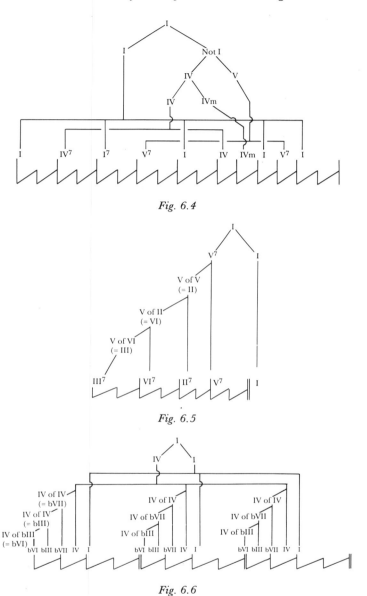

Fig. 6.4

Fig. 6.5

Fig. 6.6

By contrast, a classic 'subdominant-branching' tree is provided by 'Hey Joe' (Figure 6.6), while for other 'modal' types, which undergo *different* transformations at the middle levels of structure, we could turn to The Who's 'My Generation' or Eric Clapton's 'Layla' (Figure 6.7).

It is noticeable that these trees reveal processes of both *distribution* (multiple appearances of the same chord; that is, structures of *equivalence*) and, at branch-points, of binary choice (this chord/not this chord; that is, structures of *difference*).

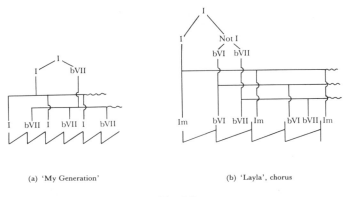

(a) 'My Generation'   (b) 'Layla', chorus

Fig. 6.7

The result is, of course, the same patterns at the surface as are analysed by information theory in terms of probability ratios or by classic semiology in terms of syntagmatic codes; but the understanding of how these surfaces arise and make sense is rather different here. As a matter of fact, elements of equivalence can be found even within the relationships of harmonic difference, for such relationships are concerned not only with 'digital' choice (+ / −) but also with 'analogical' proportion (*how* different are the chords? What harmonic 'distance' is traversed?). It might be argued, for instance, that I-IV sequences traverse less 'distance' than I-V sequences: in the first case, the tonic note is present in both chords, whereas in the second, only the dominant note − already *different* from the tonic − is common. The result, perhaps, is that I-IV is less 'tense', 'more static' − this is Björnberg's conclusion about 'Aeolian' rock harmony in general; at any rate, the contrast provides interesting material for interpretation of the use of the two categories in twentieth-century popular song.

The studies mentioned so far in this section are only a few of the recent attempts to apply the concepts of generative grammar to music. Others concentrate more on melody or rhythm, or try to model a whole syntax − though rarely using popular music material.[18] One important critique of such applications, developed by Nattiez and others, needs to be addressed at this point. The argument made is that in linguistics deep structures are *external* to actual utterances; they are abstractions, linking surface structures to the grammatical system. In music, by contrast − so it is argued − deep structures are *in* the piece: they are *heard*, not abstract; moreover, they and their transformational trees are not systemic but *piece-specific*. Now, this is not entirely true. Piece-specific trees *are* common in the written compositions of the European art-music repertory, but, as we have seen, in popular music there are many deep structures generating whole categories of pieces. Furthermore, if these structures are conceived at a level of sufficient generality (for example, as the *principle* of tonic/not tonic), they are indeed abstractions. Nevertheless, it is true that just above this level, relatively deep structural processes are actually audible; thus Schenker's *Urlinie* and I-V-I pattern are present in the piece, and analysis consists in exposing their structural priority and revealing the relationship of higher-level events to them.

What we need to recognize here is the existence of two types, or moments, of generation. There is a *tree of elaboration*, which distributes the elements of the basic structure around the piece, 'prolongs' them by means of ornamentation and higher-level connectors, and transforms them through variants, substitutes, and so on. This tree concerns the hierarchy existing among the actual sound-events. 'Lying behind' this, there is a *tree of abstraction*. We know that, in linguistics, describing the deep structural kernel depends on meaning – but not so much on semantic content as on semantic *form*, that is, the categories which construct grammatical sense (active subject, action affecting an object, descriptive property of object, and so on). Similarly in music, if we look for the *form* of the signified, we shall find the abstract level of deep structure. One such from will be the tonic/not tonic principle, which has references in general cognition. There are others in the areas of rhythm and melody, as we shall see.

These forms can be thought of as 'gestures': 'cognitive shapes' (with affective and motor connections) which lie behind musical structures and 'explain' different transformations of the same 'idea'. There may even be subsets of the gestures – little investigated as yet – which are rather more precise and music-specific in nature. The twelve-bar blues form, for instance, seems to perform a gesture which is understood even when some components of the harmonic deep structure are unheard. The following example given by Steedman contains only three of the basic chord-events (and those briefly)

$$1 \quad\quad 2 \quad\quad\quad 3 \quad\quad\quad 4 \quad\quad 5 \; 6 \quad 7 \quad\quad 8 \quad\quad 9 \quad\quad 10 \; 11 \; 12$$
$$\flat\text{IIm}^7, \; \flat\text{V}^7/\text{VIIm}^7, \; \text{III}^7/\text{VIm}^7, \; \text{II}^7/\text{Vm}^7, \; \text{I}^7\!// \; \text{IV}/\#\text{IV}^\circ/\text{IIIm}^7/\flat\text{III}^7 \; // \; \flat\text{VI}^7/\flat\text{II}^7/\text{I}/ \; \text{I}//$$

but it would be grasped as a twelve-bar blues by any player or informed fan of modern jazz.

A similar duality of generative moments – 'elaborative' on the one hand, 'abstract' on the other – is characteristic of melodic structures. Schenker's *Urlinie* is, of course, one type in the first category – the category of *noteframes*, as we can perhaps call them – but there are many others.

Zak argues (1982) that the existence of tune-families in popular song can be largely attributed to the existence of modal frames – intonational formulae as much as scale-resources – which migrate among tunes. Moreover, these frames are often relatively hidden and can only be discovered through analysis of the structural tones – a 'backbone' (or deep structure) which he terms the 'Line of Latent Mode' (LLM). The structural tones are defined by metric accents. Thus the Beatles' 'Hard Day's Night', at first glance major-key-with-modal-touches, is revealed through its LLM to have a deep kinship with typical blues melodic structures: it is centred on three of the notes of the minor-pentatonic mode (E♭-G-B♭), with the contradictory major seventh (B♮) set against that. Moreover, the *shape* assumed by these notes – the modal *frame* – as well as the abstract scale they represent, is revealed, too; and this – an initial, repeated circling round the dominant (G), with an excursion to its minor third (B♭), 'answered' by a fall to the 'symmetrical' minor third of the tonic (E♭) – is a common pattern in blues (see Ex. 6.14).

Zak's method, however, is rather over-simple in its location of structural tones. Not only does a purely metric approach fail in the face of rhythmic complexity – syncopation, for example – but it ignores other important factors: tonal priority and stability (thus the tonic will usually be structurally important);

Ex. 6.14

duration (long notes are usually of higher structural importance than shorter ones); repetition (repeated notes increase in importance); pitch profile (notes high in relation to the melodic context stand out structurally); articulation and (non-metric) accent. All these must be taken into account.

Van der Merwe has also written of modal frames (Van der Merwe 1989), and he has described a number of the types permeating and unifying African, European and American song. He introduces the useful concepts of *floor note*, *ceiling note* and *central note*; these refer to functional constituents of a specific note-frame, not the theoretical scale hierarchy. Thus, in 'Hard Day's Night' the tonic virtually never appears. The ceiling note is Bb, the floor note is Eb (since the low C is merely passed through), and G is the central note, around which most of the tune rotates. Perhaps the most important frame discussed by Van der Merwe is what he calls the *ladder of thirds*, common both in blues and in British 'folk' song. This is a pentatonic type, but the structures of tunes using it make it clear that it actually comes into being through piling up thirds below and/or above a tonic or central note. The modal frame of 'Hard Day's Night' is a ladder of thirds, built below and above the central G. Other, related patterns are commonplace in post-rock 'n' roll popular music – and also appear in some earlier tunes (Ex. 6.15). It seems likely that the way these tunes 'make sense' has partly to do with what they have in common, in the deep structures.

There are several other note-frames frequently found in popular music. Tunes in the *chant* category virtually never leave a single note; it is classically represented by Bob Dylan's 'Subterranean Homesick Blues'. *Axial* tunes treat a single note as a central note, around which the whole tune circles. 'Hard Day's Night' (built round the dominant, G) and 'Peggy Sue' (built round the tonic, A) illustrate this category, but classic examples are Marvin Gaye's 'Can I Get a Witness', which throughout the vocal harps obsessively on the tonic and barely leaves the space bounded by the third above and the fourth below, and Roy Milton's 'Do the Hucklebuck', which does something similar with the dominant. *Oscillating* tunes treat either the chant or the axial principle as the basis for a pendulum movement between two structural notes, as in the Rolling Stones' 'Jumpin' Jack Flash' (see Ex. 3.1c, p. 79 above) (incidentally, the accompanying guitar riff is an axial pattern circling round the dominant).

The oscillating principle, shifted to the level of phrase-relationships, gives rise to the *open/closed* frame type. Here the implication of the oscillation is of a question/answer, antecedent/consequent relationship. In 'Hey Bo Diddley' (Ex. 6.8, p. 190–1 above), the solo vocal phrases a_1, $a_1{}^1$, $a_1{}^2$, $a_1{}^3$, and so on, end alternately on the note A (or very occasionally C) and the tonic, F; the effect of this oscillation is of an open/closed structure. If the oscillation applies to whole units, rather than a single note, it produces a new category, the *terrace*. This is familiar in functional-tonal music in the form of the *sequence* (for examples see Exx. 7.7–7.9, pp. 274–5 below); but in Afro-American-influenced styles, it often happens that a whole shift in level, as Van der Merwe calls it, takes place. By *level* he means the note-frame, melodically and harmonically considered; by *shift* he means a wholesale parallel pitch-slide. Thus, in Chaka Khan's 'I Feel for You' (Ex. 6.16a), a tonic triad-orientated frame drops by a tone to a similar frame based on the flat seventh. This is a common structure, but so, too, is that governed by the tonic/subdominant relationship, which obviously derives from

Ben Harney, 'You've Been A Good Old Wagon' (1895)

(a)

(T = Tonic)

Ben Bernie et al., 'Sweet Georgia Brown' (1925)

(b)

No gal   made—   has   got a   shade— on Sweet Geor-gia   Brown, —

Two left feet — but oh so   neat — has Sweet Geor-gia   Brown.—

Buddy Holly, 'Peggy Sue'

(c)

If you knew   Peg-gy Sue —   Then you'd know why I   feel blue with-ou-out

Peg-gy,   my Pe-eg-gy Su - u-ue   Oh well I

love you girl, yes I   love you Peg-gy Sue. _____

Ex. 6.15

The Who, 'My Generation'

Peo-ple   try   to   put us   down —

Just   be-cause   we _____   get   a   -   round.

Ex. 6.15 cont'd

twelve-bar blues; 'Satisfaction' (Ex. 6.16b) is an example. Sometimes terracing is applied to the ladder of thirds; usually this results in a shift to a different band in the pentatonic formation, often a third away, as in 'A Day in the Life' (see Ex. 6.16c).

These structures based on an oscillation principle, but especially the open/closed type, are beginning to move towards what can be called the *binary* category, which, in its classic forms in bourgeois song, is marked by out/back, away/home symmetries in phrasing and harmony, and often an ascent/descent arch-contour in pitch. This type is common in the Tin Pan Alley repertory; 'A Foggy Day' is a good example. We have already noted its arch (or rather double-arch) contour; and, as Schenker analysis revealed, its harmonic deep structure describes the classic open/closed binary pattern (I→V//I→V→I), which is echoed by the tune's open/closed tonal shape (→D//→F) (see Exx. 6.7, 6.10 pp. 188, 194 above).

Tunes of all these types can, at the surface, be segmented into phrases and musemes, of course. But the surface structures are generated by deeper patterns, and these sets of structural pitches and note-frames group the tunes into families, as well as seeming to account for much of their effect and comprehensibility. How to model the relationship between surface and depth? Philip Tagg's generative tree for the first phrase of the *Kojak* signature tune offers a persuasive example (see Ex. 6.17) (Tagg 1979: 186–202). As Tagg points out, and as is usual for generative models, the diagram reverses the actual analytical procedure, representing the analytical reduction in terms of a (hypothetical) process of production – which would be largely unconscious. This model has the great advantage of picturing the deepest level of structure as, so to speak, pre-musical: it describes a movement from an initial motif to a terminal motif, a semantic form or *gesture*. Moving down the diagram, this gesture takes an ever more concrete shape, as paradigmatic choices, syntagmatic combinations and adjustments, and 'paralinguistic' specifications are made.

All the melodic types discussed above can be regarded as having deep structural gestures lying behind them. These can be represented graphically, but are better acted, or 'felt', as kinetic patterns (see Figure 6.8). Obviously there are links between several of these types, and family groups could be formed.

Let us take a further type, not mentioned so far, and apply Tagg's model to it,

Ex. 6.16

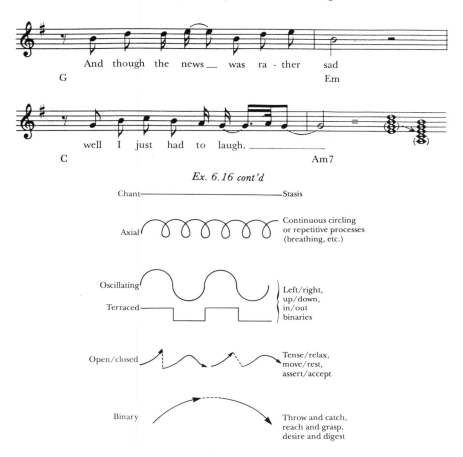

Ex. 6.16 cont'd

Fig. 6.8

in a simplified way. The 'shout-and-fall' type (referred to by some ethnomusic-ologists as the 'tumbling strain') is very common in Afro-American-derived styles, and unites such different songs as 'Shake, Rattle and Roll' and 'My Generation'. Gesturally, it suggests 'affective outpouring', 'self-offering of the body', 'emptying and relaxation'. As the generative trees of the initial phrases of these two songs show (Ex. 6.18), they originate in the same gestural deep structure, and their differences lie not only on the surface but begin at deeper levels, where differing transformations generate different pitch-ideas, different note-frames and different numbers and shapes of museme.

A limitation of Tagg's model is that he seems to see his representation of the gestural level – the initial motif–terminal motif formula – as universal. This formula seems to carry an implicit idea of what musical phrases must be like. A worked-out theory based on such an idea can be found in Asaf'ev, for whom all melodic phrases fall into a three-part shape: *initium – movere – terminus* (Asaf'ev 1977: 258–412). In Asaf'ev, this conception is an explicit attempt to describe all musical movement as goal-directed: 'intonation' is a kinetic process, and all

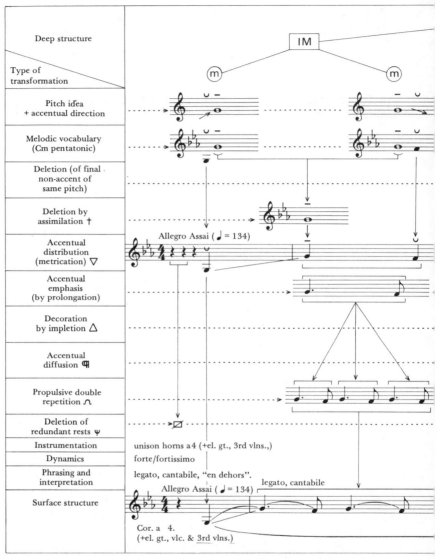

Notes

MP = Melodic (Musical) Phrase

IM = Initial Motif

TM = Terminal Motif

m　= museme

⬜ = zero museme (deleted or non-existent)

† : Two consecutive ⊖ of the same pitch may be assimilated (elided) into one.

▽ : Points of accentuation (⊖) are grouped at regular intervals along the one-dimensional time axis.

Ex. 6.17

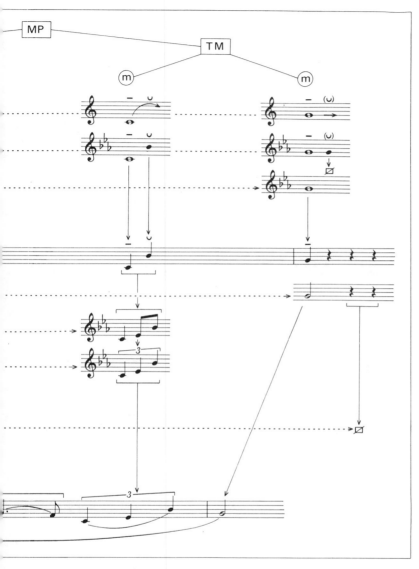

Δ : Larger intervals may be filled in (impleted) with interjacent tones. Intervals may also be circumscribed (decoration by circumscription) or extended upwards, downwards or in both pitch directions (decoration by sublateral, superlateral or bilateral extension).

ꟼ : The dualism of a -∪(∪) relationship can be modified (diffused/mollified) by revoking the tendency to emphasise accents by prolongation, spreading the time values of the component tone beats in the museme over equal durations.

⌒ : The 'ready-steady-go' technique.

Ψ : These crotchet rests at opposite ends of the MP cancel each other out and change the periodicity of the MP from 4 x 4/4 to 3 x 4/4.

Ex. 6.17 cont'd

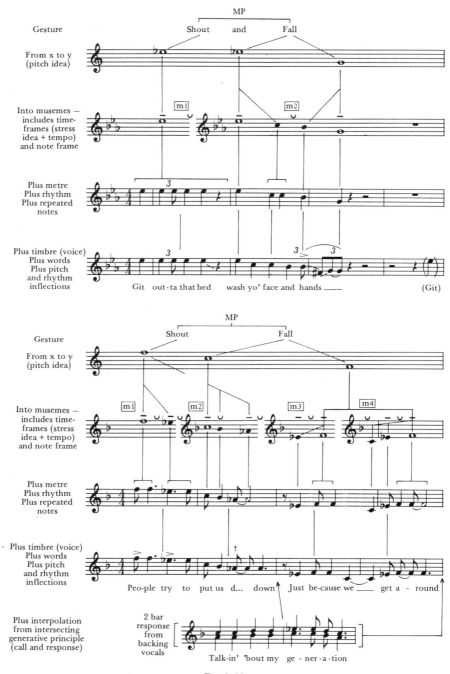

Ex. 6.18

phrases travel a journey from an initial impetus, a release of energy, through to cadencing stability. Now this approach, like Tagg's, has the great merit of stressing the *dynamic* nature of melodic structure, but, while the I-T or I-M-T manifestations of such energy may be central to the practices of bourgeois song, and to popular repertories related to them, they do not seem to be universal. They do not fit the Chant, Axial or Oscillating types very well – for these are much more ongoing – and they do not always fit the Terraced category either. We need to envisage a more differentiated gestural field, with some kinetic manifestations producing cadenced or well-articulated, relatively self-contained phrases, others generating more continuous processes of dialogue or oscillation. While the history of melodic types has yet to be written,[19] it may be suggested that in popular song, a preponderance of I-M-T types (open/closed; binary; arch) in the nineteenth and early twentieth centuries has in recent decades declined in the face of an increase in the use of 'circular' types.

A two-levelled generative structure similar to that identified in the areas of melody and harmony can also be found in that of rhythm. C.S. Lee has described metre in terms of deep structure (Lee 1985).[20] Through the application of rewrite rules analogous to those used in phrase-structure grammars, each metre (4/4, 3/4, 6/8, and so on) generates a large number of different surface rhythms. Thus the generation of the first phrase of 'A Hard Day's Night' (excluding, for simplicity, the syncopation of 'night') could be represented as in Figure 6.9.

As Lee points out, understanding the rhythm of such a phrase involves allocating it to a deep structure; and this depends on the perceived pattern of relative stresses (accents), for, as with some linguistic phrases, the same surface could be allocated to more than one deep structure: for instance, the tree below assumes 'hard' and 'night' have the strongest accents, but if, say, 'day's' were given that position, a different allocation of 4/4 would result.

Metres are analogous to note-frames. Just as discrete pitches, considered as phonological data, are organized in a comparatively few basic shapes, so a 'durational phonology' (a beat; patterns of relative proportion) gives rise to a small number of metrical frameworks.

But, 'behind' this level is a deeper one: the level of 'gesture'. Here we find the basic principle articulated by the opposition stressed/unstressed. As with the

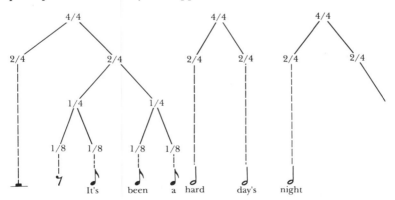

Fig. 6.9

tonic/not tonic distinction, to which it is equivalent, this 'cognitive map' is a way of organizing experience (in this case, time) into a hierarchy: all moments are stronger and/or weaker than other moments, and these relationships often take the form of binary oppositions (strong/weak). Within this basic system, we find a variety of 'kinetic ideas' (equivalent to melodic gestural types), which are often designated by such terms as 'slow waltz', 'medium rock', 'ballad tempo' or 'fast boogie', each with its own 'feel', and which in turn generate the metrical deep structures. The principle of accentual hierarchy seems basic, even universal; such phenomena as the 'even four' of mainstream jazz and the 'pogo four' of punk rock are attempts to point beyond the possible, to an undifferentiated flow of time.

Without much further research on rhythm cognition, the exact process linking deep to surface structures can only be speculatively modelled. The diagrams showing generative trees for 'Shake, Rattle and Roll' and 'My Generation' (Ex. 6.18) suggest gestures emerging as 'time-frames', with a 'stress idea' and a tempo. It is quite possible that these originate at the same stage as the 'pitch idea' (as, in fact, Tagg's model proposes) rather than subsequently. At any rate, they give rise to metrical structures, which in turn are filled with more fully realized rhythmic patterns. The rules governing this process are partly the phrase-grammar rules indicated by Lee, which control possible subdivisions and binary choices, and partly they are rules analogous (and probably cognitively linked) to the prosodic rules which structure stress patterns in speech. The latter are linked, in music, to style and genre codes: thus in boogie-woogie they would give prefer-

ence to the typical long-short (♩ 3 ♪) triplet patterns.

Narmour suggests that these 'prosodic rules' fall into three categories (Narmour 1980: 147–53). Rhythmic sequences are *additive* (the same duration is repeated) or *cumulative* (shorter gives way to longer) or *countercumulative* (longer gives way to shorter). (Other things being equal, long/short is associated with, and heard as, stressed/unstressed; the cumulative and countercumulative categories between them, therefore, generate all the poetic 'feet'.) Narmour associates cumulation with *closure* (relaxation), countercumulation with openness (tension). He argues that all musical structures are governed by a search for rhythmic closure; but this appears to be a Euro-centric restriction, similar to that which sees all melodic motion as goal-directed and cadence-seeking: in Afro-American-derived popular music, *additive* (open-ended, repetitive) rhythmic processes are commonplace.

All the rhythmic processes mentioned so far can be seen in terms of a phrase-structure grammar: that is, they are generated directly from the deep structure through successive rewriting of constituents. But it is very difficult to account for *syncopation* by this method, and syncopation, after all, is of cardinal importance in almost all twentieth-century popular music. Here we need the concept of *transformation*. Just as an active sentence can be transformed into its passive equivalent, so a simple writing of 4/4 can be transformed into its syncopated equivalent (Ex. 6.19a). The analogy is not complete, since the 'meanings' of the two musical patterns would seem not to be identical; nevertheless, they do, so to speak, cover the same semantic topology – but from different angles – for the

Ex. 6.19

syncopated pattern is heard 'with reference to', 'in the light of', as a remapping of, its partner.

Similarly, a simple division of 4/4 can be transformed into a 'latin' equivalent (Ex. 6.19b). The 'backbeat' transformation exemplified in Ex. 6.19a, combined with a 'before-the-beat phrasing' transformational rule, gives rise to the phraseology of 'Satisfaction' (Ex. 6.19c). And so on. Analytically, the usefulness of this method is that the rhythm of the 'Satisfaction' phrase, for instance, is revealed as based on a simple and common gesture – a repeated trochee (‾ ˘ ‾ ˘); and, notwithstanding the obvious importance of the transformations, not to mention the 'paralinguistic' inflections added in Mick Jagger's performance, this might well help explain the phrase's comprehensibility.

Of course, the validity of such a claim depends ultimately on listening behaviour. It is unlikely that 'deep structural' understanding entirely destroys the importance of *surface* listening; to believe so would be to reduce difference to the relationships between a few simple categories. Indeed, all listening (and analysis) may take place against the background of a continuum, ranging from totally holistic modes at one end to totally linear modes at the other. There is evidence that these contrasting modes are associated disproportionately with the work of the right and left brain hemispheres respectively (in fact, the complex interactions between brain areas make this an oversimplification, but the general relationship seems to stand); and that different usages and proportions of hemisphere activity result in different kinds of listening (see Clynes 1982; Davies 1980; Howell *et al.* 1985; Sloboda 1985). Thus the same music could well be understood by different subjects not only as possessing a range of meanings but as actually grasped through different cognitive mechanisms. This suggests the need for a *synthesis* of approaches to the analysis of syntactic structures.

Towards a synthesis

This synthesis can be visualized as the intersection of several continua. First, there is a *generative continuum*. Analysis can be aimed at a variety of levels, from that of the surface to that of the deepest structure. Perhaps we can think of four analytical levels – though in practice these run into each other:

1 General cognitive processes. Here, methods relating to the schemes of sensorimotor-affective organization and symbolic-behavioural logic would be appropriate (for example, principles of same/different, strong/weak, up/down, and of proportion, grouping, contour and gesture).
2 Culturally determined applications of (1), specific to *musical* materials (for example, note-frames, time-frames, patterns of tonal and harmonic relationship). Generative theories come in here.
3 Style-specific syntaxes constructed from (2) (for example, available scales, intervals, rhythms, parameter relationships; preferred formulae, modes of combination). Distributionist, commutational and paradigmatic approaches are appropriate at this level.
4 Intra-opus patterns: the individual piece in all its uniqueness.

The similarity to Stefani's model of a codal hierarchy is, of course, no coincidence. In analysis, the results gained from methods coming 'from below' (levels (1) and (2)) and from methods working at the surface (levels (3) and (4)) should marry up, as in Figure 6.10.

As we have seen, on every level we find the operation of an equivalence/difference dialectic. And this comprises our second analytic parameter: a *syntagmatic continuum*. If we return to Jakobson's discussion of this (see p. 183 above), we find that he describes the principle of equivalence (similarity, analogy, identity) as the *metaphoric* pole of language; it governs the paradigmatic axis. By contrast, he sees the principle of difference (sequential combination, contiguity, adjacency) as the *metonymic* pole of language; it governs the syntagmatic axis. In poetry (and music) we find the 'projection of the principle of equivalence from the axis of selection on to the axis of combination' (Jakobson

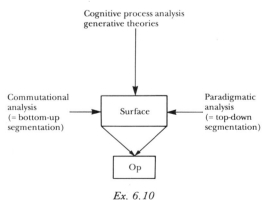

Ex. 6.10

1960: 358); that is, repetition, variation, similarity, association are everywhere. One might argue – on a strictly theoretical level – that whereas ordinary language, because of its denotative function, 'tends towards' an extreme of total differentiation (maximum information), music, because of its self-reflexive character, 'tends towards' an extreme of total sameness (infinite repetition, maximum redundancy). In fact, it would be better to fix these two extremes not to particular signifying systems but to tendencies or dispositions within signifying practice as a whole – to which language and music, respectively, are abnormally prevalent. Thus, in practice, different musics and different language-systems are located at different points on the line between the extremes. Moreover, as we have seen, 'equivalence' and 'difference' in music are difficult to distinguish precisely; they tend to run into each other, through techniques of transformation and variation, and it can even be argued that, with sufficient analytic sleight of hand, *all* differences can be reduced to being transformations of a single generative source. Jakobson himself stresses the varying balance of the two poles, historically and between different systems, media and styles; and he too insists on their interpenetration: 'any metonymy is slightly metaphorical and any metaphor has a metonymical tint' (ibid: 370). Nevertheless, it is safe to say that music *privileges* the pole of equivalence; and it seems reasonable to suggest that for most styles of *popular* music this is even more the case.

If we designate 'extreme equivalence' as a position of monadic unity, and 'extreme difference' as an infinite set, the syntagmatic continuum might be modelled as in Figure 6.11. As the diagram shows, movement from monad towards infinite set can take two routes. On the lower route, increasing difference takes the form of quantities on numerical scales, governed by abstract or logical schemas: either binary switching (+ / – ; 0/1; A/B), or digital selection, which extends the binary system somewhat but keeps the principle of limited series containing restricted sets of discrete quantities (for example, scale steps, durations). On the upper route, increasing difference takes the form of qualitative variation giving infinite ranges of choices along continuous spectra (how much, how great, how far, and so on). From this point of view, repetition represents a variation which never comes, or a binary question which always receives the same answer (A, A, A, . . .); as repetition proceeds, the lack of variation becomes predictable, the binary question becomes weaker, and the music moves

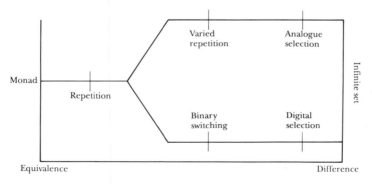

Ex. 6.11

towards monadic plenitude. The infinite set represents difference carried to the point of a rule; to the extent that every sound-event *is* different from all others, it is an omnipresent principle, always pulling music towards a position in which nothing would be heard twice. Gesturally, we could envisage the two extremes as circular, empty, 'mythic', on the one hand, and linear, replete, 'narrative' or teleological, on the other.

The importance of binary choice is familiar in semiology. The role of analogical relationships is less so – perhaps because in linguistics it is largely hived off into the field of paralinguistics – and its importance in music is striking. Eco has pointed out that while the chief requirement for the existence of structure is *opposition*, this can result from relationships between gradations on a continuum as much as from binary choices (Eco 1979: 176–7). Indeed, analogy may be just as deep a mental principle as binarism – or deeper. As part of the human search for similarity and mutuality, it may go back ontogenetically before the childhood stages of learning the manipulation of difference to an infantile and even foetal involvement in unity with the maternal and metamaternal environment. Piaget (1971:106–19) proposes a system of developmental *levels* in the evolution of our mental representational processes, with *metaphor* (ruled by analogy and an iconic relationship between signifier and signified) preceding *sign* (ruled by difference and a conventionalized relationship between signifier and signified). He insists on a 'pre-logical' level, prior to explicit logical systems and governed by 'participation', that is, by the analogical fusion of the individual in the generic. So the importance of analogy and equivalence in music – especially striking in popular music – may have deep roots.

At the same time, the principle of equivalence is, as we have seen, always in dialectical relationship with processes of difference. Some writers have drawn a comparison between the structures of difference producing melodies (Cubitt 1984) or harmonic progressions (Cook 1983) and those responsible for the structures of narrative, particularly in the so-called classic realist text. In both cases, it is easy to feel the involved, identifying listener being 'pulled through' the linear 'diagesis', the 'movement from phoneme to phoneme, from note to note', commonly making the singer 'the object and the trajectory of desire' (Cubitt 1984: 212); in both cases too, difference – disturbance of stability – gives way in the end to *closure*: tension is resolved by cadence or phrase-ending. We should remember, though, that this is no universal category; there is no 'natural' level of 'narrative difference'. Not only does the quantity of syntagmatic differentiation vary between styles, genres and periods; the 'narrative' mode is only one of the categories in terms of which the concrete workings of the syntagmatic continuum in nineteenth- and twentieth-century popular music can most easily be analysed. In contrast to the narrative category, which privileges difference, there is what we can call an 'epic' mode, where the focus is on repetition and varied repetition; and in between comes a 'lyrical' category (marked by symmetrical open/closed and binary structures), in which processes of difference are grasped partly in terms of relationships of equivalence (phrases perceived as *Gestalten*, as monadic wholes, related to each other symmetrically, that is, analogically).

Narrative's coupling of goal-directed linearity and self-confirming, 'possessive' closure makes it, like the realist prose text, easily articulated to typical bourgeois ideological preoccupations. The lyrical mode, then, could be seen as the nearest the bourgeois imagination can come, within the assumptions of 'narrativity', to the holistic, the 'circular'; while the epic (at least in a hypothetical pure state) opens up quite new (yet old) modes of experience. However, the categories never present themselves in a pure state. They interrelate dialectically. In broad terms, most nineteenth-century popular song displays varying proportions of narrative and lyric, most post-rock 'n' roll popular song displays varying proportions of lyric and epic, while there are smaller admixtures of the third mode throughout; the first half of the twentieth century seems to be a changeover period. This means that while it is tempting to correlate the three categories with the three musical strategies suggested at the end of Chapter 3 – narrative: auratic identification; lyrical: utopian critique; epic: everyday/festive – the different areas covered by the two frameworks, and their different modes of internal organization and characteristic dialectical processes, make it hard to map them together in any precise way. (For example, one would have to leave room for the avant-garde strategy of shock/protest, which can be used to disrupt any of the three syntagmatic categories.)

Analysis of the syntagmatic continuum, as we have seen earlier, depends on the answers to such questions as what exactly equivalence *is*; how distinctions are recognized; how difference is measured. In other words, it depends on the criteria of *pertinence*. This brings us to the third analytic continuum, the *paradigmatic continuum*. On the one hand, this covers the line between purely segmental division at one end and purely parametric division at the other; there are many different analytical positions along this line. On the other hand, it covers the spectrum of analytical levels – what length of unit is regarded as pertinent? Positions range from the suggestion by Bennett (1980: 152–3) that for popular music listeners the main unit of meaning is often the *set* (group of performed songs; continuous chunk of radio programming; LP side) to the argument by Orlov that in music the unit is the *unique sound*: 'tones are unique elements of an infinite set. Even those tones that have the same name and hold the same position are not identical and differ in their presentational value if they differ in at least one of several other characteristics' (Orlov 1981: 134).

What is needed is a position of extreme flexibility. Levels of pertinence relate to given cultural contexts – what level or mode of division a listener perceives – and to modes of organization within pieces – there are so many different arrangements of relationships between units and parameters that the same element can have different functions (redundant; distinctive; significant) in different styles. Barthes' concept of *lexies* might be useful here (1975a). He defines these as 'units of reading', and they can be of vastly varying lengths and interpretative significance. The dangers of subjectivism are obvious. But, as Boretz points out (1969: 46) 'interpretation is an *inter*subjective process: we have access to our own assumptions, can report them and compare them with others'.

Stefani argues that the level and type of segmentation will vary, depending on the code in use, and that, above all, this will relate to competence type (Stefani 1973: 28–9). Under popular competence, people's

> segmentations are the opposite of the grammatical categories of composers and theorists (period, phrase, etc.); above all, they do not care at all about respecting the integrity of the work. [Indeed,] . . . people always operate

on *major units*, not on simple elements such as notes, intervals, single durations, etc.

They perceive by 'motivic quantum' – the catchy detail, cliché or 'hook' – which is regarded as

> a brick, a little tool, having already a meaning in itself, ready to be appropriated, reproduced, repeated, combined with other motives, associated with short acts of language, gesture, etc. . . . [and] to work as a part for the whole, as a sample and a signal. In all this there is at work the main principle of popular economics: *the maximum result with the minimum effort* (Stefani 1987a: 25–6).

This does not necessarily mean that the constituent elements of these motives are insignificant, only that they are below the listener's consciousness and their status is unclear.

Eco emphasizes that music, unlike language with its pure system of double articulation, is a system of differential and multiple articulation (Eco 1979: 228–37). A given element, in varied contexts, can function phonemically, morphemically or be redundant or a free variant. Stefani's (n.d.) study of 'the octave' substantiates this thought. At a first abstract level, the octave is a grammatical unit, deriving its syntactic function (and meaning) from its position in a system. At a second level, that of actual musical discourse, particular contexts can result in either the *weakening* of this function – the octave is 'absorbed' within higher syntactic levels, becoming part-'neutralized', a purely phonemic element – or in its *strengthening* – the octave is foregrounded as a musematic or even 'lexical' unit. This foregrounding can take many forms, depending on context. We can find examples of the purely phonemic octave in 'My Generation', where the F-F interval sets the framework for the shout-and-fall, and in the last phrase of 'A Foggy Day' (again F-F). In 'Over the Rainbow' (Ex. 6.20), the initial rising octave seems to be semi-foregrounded, with the semantic task of suggesting *ascent* (over the rainbow); then it is absorbed into the higher-level syntactic unit, as it generates 'transformations'. Of the more completely foregrounded types mentioned by Stefani, 'halo octaves' are

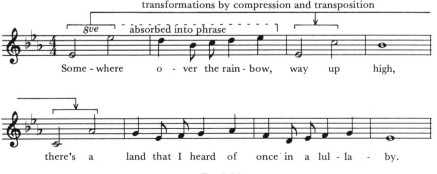

Ex. 6.20

commonly used by arrangers of string accompaniments to ballads; and a 'gestural octave' may be found in the basic riff of Led Zeppelin's 'Whole Lotta Love' (see Ex. 7.24, p. 283 below) – the falling octave here seems to be an essential gestural idea (imagine the riff without it).

The existence of a paradigmatic continuum – that is, the need for flexibility in segmentation – is why attempts such as Keil's to make a clear distinction between an 'abstract', 'logical', 'linguistic' dimension to music and a 'spontaneous', 'expressive', 'paralinguistic' dimension are ultimately misleading (Keil 1966b). In principle (and often in practice) *any* element can be grammatical – or an 'expressive' extra – or both. While the methods of paralinguistics could well be of use to popular music analysts,[21] paralinguistic research has tended to show that its material is *not* an optional extra to a more basic 'cognitive' communicational stream, but that it is coded and may contribute to meaning.

In principle, commutation tests could peel away any 'paralinguistic' stream, revealing the 'systematized' core; but in fact this is difficult, first, because parameters are interrelated (thus, removing detailed variations of accent affects the way pitch relationships are heard), and second, because one suspects the removal process would reveal a *gradient* rather than a clear cut-off point. Besides, the procedure is epistemologically suspect, since it implies the existence of an *Urtext*; but as folkloristics has shown, in performance arts a work is comprised of, precisely, all its variants, and all variants are equal. A better method would be to assemble the variants of a song and find what they had in common. Ultimately what is needed is the development of more rigorous analytical techniques for the seemingly paralinguistic stratum. Only then will it be possible to develop a systematic framework within which the *whole* syntax, its codes, segmentations and internal organization, can be represented. The likelihood is that, as in linguistics, this would turn out to reveal previously unsuspected levels of coding – though, of course, whether the codes are activated, and in what way (whether a paralinguistic parameter is 'phonemic', 'morphemic' or even 'lexemic') – would be a matter for further investigation, within the context of a given use-situation.

The three continua discussed so far must be placed within the context of a fourth – the *processual continuum*. All musical events relate forward (through expectation and implication) and back (through memory), and their function and meaning change as the processual dynamic unfolds. As Eco puts it (1979: 240–1), in some signifying systems, including music, signs have *vectorial* qualities: that is, their sense depends not just on their characteristics and modes of combination, synchronically considered, but also on their *direction* (see also Tarasti 1983). This applies on all levels, not only the surface. A fall-and-shout is different from a shout-and-fall made up of the same gestures. A closed/open sequence would have different implications from the reverse ordering. A note-frame is temporally as well as 'spatially' organized: for instance, does it start and/or end with the tonic note?

Tagg discusses the characteristics of the processual dimension in some detail (Tagg 1979: 183–229). He offers two models, which he terms *centrifugal* and *centripetal*. In the first (very rare), the experiential focal point ('home') comes first, but gives way to a move into new areas. In the second (predominant in Western music), the home–away move is followed by a return home. The centripetal type is certainly common in popular music – it generates all open/closed and binary gestures – but we need also to recognize the development of more one-levelled, open-ended processes. This seems to be largely how Chant, Oscillating and Terraced structures are experienced; riff-based structures in particular often have very little sense of leaving 'home' and no strong 'return', no definite closure. Time, then, is here constructed as 'mythical' (through a 'popular economics of desire'), rather than directed to a goal (either that of an existing location or that of a new horizon).

Semantic Analysis

Much popular music analysis, commentary and criticism is marked by a 'rush to interpretation', centring usually on the area of *connotation*: the feelings, associations, evocations and ideas aroused in listeners by songs. This is a pity, for at least two reasons. Semiotic theory emphasizes that connotation is always built on a prior system of denotation; it is *secondary*.[22] Moreover, while there is no doubt that most music does give rise to connotations in most listeners, there is good reason to believe that semantic processes more directly tied to syntactic structure are particularly important in music. The temptation to skate over this level, often founded on an assumption of the syntactic impoverishment of popular music, should be avoided.

Admittedly, denotation in the sense in which the term is used in linguistics is rare in music. Except in the very few cases of direct imitation of natural sounds (for example, the animal noises in the Beatles' 'Good Morning' or the motorbike noises in the Shangri-Las' 'Leader of the Pack'), there is no system of objective references to concepts and perceptions concerning the 'outside world'. Nevertheless, there *is* a direct and immediate semantic correlation to musical structures, which can be conceptualized in various ways. For a general framework, we can quote Laske (1975a: 172, 190):

> Semantic knowledge is essentially knowledge concerning the construction
> of effective representations of some input . . . the semantic component
> provides a 'frame' within which structures satisfying some interpretation
> can be elaborated . . . [Thus] music-semantic properties are the projection,
> into a musical structure, of sequences of operations underlying its
> generation and/or recognition.

This does not rule out 'meta-musical' dimensions, but it grounds them on a structural semantics implicated in the musical form itself. To avoid any difficulties attaching to the term 'denotation', let us call this ground the level of *primary signification*.

Primary signification
One way of conceiving this level is to say, with Ruwet (1967: 85), that 'the meaning of music can only become apparent in the description of the music itself'. It is certainly clear that words *about* music – not only analytic description but also critical response, journalistic commentary and even casual

conversation – affect its meaning. The significations of ragtime, rock 'n' roll or punk rock cannot be separated from the discourses which surrounded them. But this is only one kind of interpretant – a metalinguistic one. And it is better understood in the terms developed by the French school of experimental music psychology.

Francès distinguishes *signification* and *expression*, but insists they are linked:

> Significative judgements condense into words expressive properties which are sensed in the musical object and which are *sometimes linked to verbal enunciations mingled with them in perception*. Expressivity appears as the raw datum inherent in the structure, signification as an elaboration of that datum tending to reduce it to a concept, to rationalise it, even to explain it (Francès 1958: 272).

Imberty uses the terms *sens* and *signification* (1979: 3–21) – which, rightly, avoids too quick a correlation with the traditional aesthetic pair of 'emotion' and 'cognition'. Significations, he says, are verbal interpretations of *sens*, which is the musical *signifié*; the words have denotations, and these connote the *sens*. There is no *direct* link between the verbal signifiers and the musical signifying process; rather, it *passes through* the verbal signified, and this is why any musical *sens* can give rise to many verbal interpretants.[23]

Another way of conceiving primary signification is in terms of internal reference. Jakobson's theory of syntagmatic equivalence obviously lends itself to such a conception, and he suggests that 'rather than alluding to some extrinsic object, music presents itself as *a language which signifies itself*' (quoted in Nattiez 1976: 212). He sees this 'introversive signification' or 'auto-reflection' as characteristic of the aesthetic functions of all semiotic processes, but argues that it is especially privileged in music.

Auto-reflection takes place on various levels. To the degree that a piece is made up of structures of equivalences, the units so related are referring to each other introversively, in complex ways linked to the amount and type of transformation involved. In addition, though, quotation, stylistic allusion and parody fall into the same category, the reference here being *outside* the piece. Jazz musicians have long indulged in quotations from well-known songs or solos, slipped into an improvisation, and quotation is not unknown in rock – for example, Electric Light Orchestra's 'Roll Over Beethoven' borrows from the work of Beethoven and Chuck Berry. Self-quotation also occurs – the snatch of 'Lucy in the Sky with Diamonds' in the Beatles' 'A Day in the Life' is an example. Stylistic allusion was particularly common in progressive rock – for example, Procul Harum's 'Whiter Shade of Pale' (with its allusions to Bach) and the whole Beatles *White Album* (a compendium of pop styles). Parody in the sense of reworking is also common – for example, the Beach Boys' 'Surfin' USA' (which takes after Chuck Berry's 'Sweet Little Sixteen'); Blood Sweat and Tears' 'Child is Father to the Man' (Erik Satie's *Gymnopédies*); the Beatles' 'Twist and Shout' ('La Bamba'); and many 'classic-rock' pieces by such groups as Emerson, Lake and Palmer. Destructive parody is less frequent; it is fundamental to Frank Zappa's work, however.[24]

In popular music, the same principle – of allusive reference – applied to performers and performances is particularly important. How many male rock singers have paid homage to Elvis Presley? No performance of 'Strange Fruit' can avoid referring to Billie Holiday's. All crooners – to exaggerate only slightly – sound like Bing Crosby. In a similar way, musical events can refer to the genre characteristics of the category to which they belong – Meade Lux Lewis's 'Honky Tonk Train Blues' to 'boogie-woogie', and the 'Blue Danube' to 'the waltz', for example. By extension, this kind of reference can take in the associated cultural setting and its associations: black ghetto bar or rent-party; nineteenth-century European bourgeois dance-hall. The relationship, Gasparov argues (1975: 189–90), is metonymic – the part stands for the whole – and one could consider the process as *indexical*: the signifier 'points to' the larger class (style, genre, activity) of which it is a member.

A third way of conceiving primary signification has been proposed by Eco (1979: 88–90). He suggests that in 'systems that are purely syntactic and have no apparent semantic depth' the primary signification is, so to speak, grammatical. As Stefani puts it (1973: 40), it is 'the value or the positional significate which an element has in a code, in other words, the semantic value of the syntactic function'. Thus, for example, the sound of the note C signifies 'C-ness' (at any octave), a value which can be understood only positionally, that is, in relation to other pitches. Further, the sound will be understood in relation to its scalar and tonal functions (tonic, dominant, and so on), and in relation to its position in the surrounding *melos* and syntagmatic context. Obviously it is this level of signification which gives rise to analytic types of metalanguage. It also relates to Laske's concept of 'semantic frames', conceived as representations of structures capable of interpreting sound data.

All the conceptions of primary signification discussed so far – *sens*, auto-reflection, positional value – have a common thread: content is defined through its *structure*, which is closely tied to the syntactic form; conversely, whatever might *fill* this structure is left blank, or ambiguous, or undeciphered. To the extent that musical meanings have to do less with the significance of discrete sound-events than with systems of internally validated relationships between events, it seems natural to look for a 'structural semantics', which would consider the meaning of units and parameters in terms of their relationships with other units and parameters and in terms of their positions on various 'axes' referring to binary oppositions or continua – axes such as repetition/change, quantity of variation, tonal polarity, melodic type (smooth/jumpy, short phrase/long phrase, ascending/descending), timbre (harsh/smooth, varied/not varied, how much varied), and so on. Such a semantics of structure would be internally consistent and comprehensible on its own terms, but linked to other cognitive and affective structurations through the interpretative 'frames' that are brought to bear (see Eco 1979: 73–142). (We saw earlier, pp. 201, 207, 211–12, how this works on the levels of deep structure.)

There is a striking similarity between this musical model and Lévi-Strauss's theory of myth – which, in the event, Lévi-Strauss has often compared to music. For Lévi-Strauss, myth is a structured system of signifiers, whose internal networks of relationships are used to 'map' the structure of other sets of relationships; the 'content' is infinitely variable and relatively unimportant. Rather than being a means of conceptual representation, like language, myth is seen as a 'science of the concrete': it does not signify, it *is*; it does not deal in representation of the world but in *reciprocal correspondences* – between myths, between elements and codes in myth, and between these and other structures which can be thought of as analogous, and which therefore 'mean' each other. Myth is thus less a means of referring to other domains than a tool for modelling their structure; it is *'bon à penser'*. As such, and as a search for analogy and structural equivalence, it is a method of *reconciling difference*.

Music, too, considered as a structural-semantic system, offers a means of thinking relationships, both within a work and between works, and perhaps between these and non-musical structures. Musical patterns are saying: as this note is to that note, as tonic is to dominant, as ascent is to descent, as accent is to weak beat (and so on), so X is to Y. And, of course, these relationships obtain in different syntaxes, with different associations (connotations). Moreover, the important role in music, as in myth, of equivalence and analogy makes it clear why both can be regarded as 'instruments for the obliteration of time'; the push towards the monadic denies clock time, and grounds its dynamics in a 'synchronic totality', in the 'psychophysiological time' of the listener. This is neuro-mental but also, in the case of music, 'physiological and even visceral': 'any piece of counterpoint includes a silent part for the rhythmic movements of heart and lungs (Lévi-Strauss 1970: 16). In fact it is better to think of a *dialectic* between 'mythic' and 'narrative', 'psychophysiological' and 'objective' temporalities; but, as we have seen, much popular music tends strongly towards a repetitive synchronicity.

Pursuing this line, Tarasti (1979) has applied Greimas's structural semantic method to music, defining *semes* as 'minimal semantic units' which are affixed to *lexies* by organizing them in terms of continua or binary polarities (size: long/short; speed: slow/fast; intensity: loud/soft; continuity: continuous/discontinuous; tension: tense/relaxed; and so on). Over complete pieces, these 'cultural units' (*semes/lexies*) are organized into a variety of typical 'mythic' patterns, often having to do – according to Tarasti – with the reconciliation of difference and with the correlating ('synchronizing') of past and present (then/now, *avant/après*, musical idea/recalled, transformed or contrasted musical idea). A clear example is the Specials' 'Ghost Town'.[25] Here the delineation of 'the present' ('This town is coming like a ghost town') is set off by a snatch of memory ('Do you remember the good old days before the ghost town?'). The two sections are contrasted in most musical parameters: minor tonality/major tonality; mainly chanted and axial melodies/shout-and-fall melodic phrase; stabbing ska rhythm/more flowing rhythms; mainly dark, percussive timbres/rich, continuous timbres; tense/relaxed. Yet, the two sections are introduced by the same musical idea, a rising sequence of diminished seventh chords (itself an archaism, suggesting nineteenth-century concert music or Hollywood thrillers), and this serves to 'reconcile' them, locating them in the same 'mythic' time-frame.

Any piece with a reprise is likely to provide fruitful material for this kind of approach – for instance, many of the progressive rock 'concept albums'. Thus the reprise of the title song on the *Sergeant Pepper* album brings together the original Edwardian 'then' and the updated 'now', modified by the intervening songs, which again include, significantly, 'archaic' and 'exotic' material. But most popular songs are short and rarely more than two-state structures – often less. If pop songs are 'little plays', as has been suggested, they are mostly sketches of situations rather than lengthy dramatic narratives. Thus Philip Tagg's study of Abba's 'Fernando' (1981: 59–63), where an oscillation between 'then' and 'now', expressed through exotic/familiar, tense/relaxed contrasts, could easily be explored in 'mythic' terms. (Here, as in 'Ghost Town', it can be argued that reconciliation of difference leads to political quietism, and that this is one of the typical problems with the 'mythic' status of music.)

It must be re-emphasized that in this approach the interpretative principle is wholly a structural one: the significance of particular units lies not in what their substance happens to be but in their relationships (by contrast, equivalence, proportion, analogy, and so on). Nevertheless, much of Tarasti's inspiration comes from the Prague semiotic school, particularly from Mukarovsky; and in *his* theory structure is seen as having important connections with social function. For Mukarovsky, a work's overall significance and integrity are governed by a 'semantic gesture'; this is the 'integrating principle of its structure', and it operates on all levels (see Tarasti 1979: 35; Nattiez 1976: 159–65). In music, it seems to be created mostly by the structural articulation of time, as this affects patterns of rhythmic, harmonic and melodic relationships in the context of particular tempos; and it often holds across rather large style categories, with the details of *substance* being filled in, in many different ways in different pieces.[26] Thus an open/closed principle seems to govern the 'bourgeois song', operating on melody, harmony, phraseology and rhythmic stress; while a principle of open-ended repetition is similarly pervasive in many pop dance-songs.

As these examples suggest, it is the overall 'semantic gesture' which generates the harmonic, melodic and rhythmic 'gestures' or 'cognitive shapes' discussed earlier, and of course these in turn produce the more musically concrete generative trees. But in Mukarovsky's theory, the semantic gestures are linked to the work's social function. Thus, for the two examples given above the links might be (i) to solo performance, in concert, drawing-room or even recording, for a listening audience; (ii) to collective participation, in disco, party or dance hall.

This is only one kind of exosemantic link. For Lévi-Strauss (1970: 341), when, after all internal, reciprocal correspondences have been accounted for, one seeks their 'final meaning', the answer is that 'myths [and music] signify the mind that evolves them by making use of the world of which it is itself a part'. In other words, musical structures reflect the structures of thought: 'when the mind is left to commune with itself and no longer has to come to terms with objects, it is in a sense reduced to imitating itself as object' (ibid: 10). The dangers of mentalism are at least partly assuaged by Lévi-Strauss's recognition that sensorimotor and physiological processes are involved, too: musical structure relates, he says, to 'the periodicity of cerebral waves and organic rhythms' (ibid: 16); it 'makes the individual conscious of his physiological rootedness . . . [it] hits us in the guts' (ibid: 28).

It is worth stressing that we are here still on the level of primary signification – and the operative principle is still auto-reflection or correspondence, rather than denotation. A diagram may make this clearer. While, in linguistics and general semiotics, the denotatum is usually pictured as on the reverse side of, or lying underneath, the signifier, with connotation and metalanguage taking place at

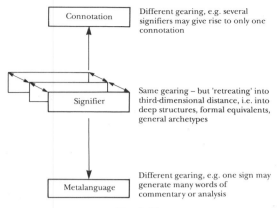

Fig. 6.12

other levels, correspondence involves the operation of *parallel systems*, at the *same level* (Figure 6.12).

Exosemantic correspondences are often thought of as 'natural' in some way; and in a sense this is right: correlations are objectively given. Nevertheless, the correlations have to be noted, the equivalence picked out; inputs have to be mentally structured *that* way. And in this movement between one structure and another – a movement of translation or transformation – the relationship commonly becomes at least partly stylized and conventionalized. Music is often felt to 'symbolize' awareness of time (through tempo and rhythmic structure) and space (through pitch-height relationships, and intensity and textural contrasts). We think of pitch going 'up' and 'down'; sounds being 'closer' or more 'distant'; rhythm as being 'in time', 'late', 'out of phase', and so on. Connotations relating to other senses are often attached (thus 'high' sounds are 'light', 'bright', 'clear') and so are emotions (usually related to tension/relaxation schemas); and images of movement are usually involved, too: we have already met many 'gestures', and equations of musical rhythms and body rhythms (walking, breathing, heartbeat, and so on) are commonplace.

These relationships undoubtedly have their grounding in Stefani's General Codes – his *anthropological* level. Thus they are always culturally mediated. Symbolic representations of movement, space, time and feeling are *musical* representations – they are not 'real' – and are organized in line with the internal requirements of musical structure. Moreover, they have been filtered through the articulating grid formed by the norms of a *particular* music culture. In some cultures there is, for example, no correlation of the pitch range with a high/low spatial metaphor.[27]

Correlations (that is, correspondence or analogy) articulated through conventions (that is pertinence criteria): this is precisely Eco's definition of the iconic sign – or rather of the *function of iconicity* (ECO 1979: 178–217). And we are moving towards the area of denotation, as it is more usually understood. This is a fuzzy boundary area. But two points at least seem reasonably clear. First, there seems to be a kind of 'synaesthesia' within mental functioning through which the structures of inputs from a wide variety of sources are assimilated to each other and to general patterns of brain activity. These general patterns may be innate or they may be those cognitive-affective schemas which, Piaget argues, develop in the learning human. Such schemas are, according to Imberty (1979: 41–125), rooted in the structures of the *'vie intérieure'*, the drives of the unconscious. Second, the conventional distinction between cognitive and affective schemas – between 'ideas' and 'emotions', 'mind' and 'senses', as Lévi-Strauss has it – is misleading (see Francès 1958: 337–45; Stefani 1973: 39–40). *Musical* emotions are specific; they *take the form of* basic musical structures – especially those drawing on kinetic and gestural patterns – which at the same time can be grasped cognitively. These patterns in turn relate to the more general schemas of the *vie intérieure*, hence also to other, analogical manifestations of these in other media. Thus, while a 'state of emotion' undoubtedly has a neuro-physiological correlate, within culture it is inseparable from the conventionalized forms it takes, which are organized according to the rules of syntactic sense operating in music and in other signifying systems. We feel musically according to the same structures which organize our musical understanding, and for popular music studies, where assumptions of syntactic impoverishment and the predominance of sentiment and visceral excitement are common, this is an important point.

There are strong arguments for thinking that the level of 'unconscious iconicity' or 'inner gesture' which underlies the more culturally conventionalized relationships may be rooted in fundamental patterns of neural activity (see, for example, Pribram 1982; Clynes 1977). Since such patterns have affective and physiological correlates, as we have seen, it is not surprising that inner gesture often gives rise to outer gesture. Lomax points out that kinesic research reveals a constant, high level of synchrony between speech and body movement in conversation, between music and movement in performance. This is a communicational baseline: an unconscious level of interconnectedness without which more conscious patterns of contact would not work. It is both *inter*personal – often correlating the gestures of performers and members of large audiences – and *intra*personal – synchronizing the aural and kinesic gestures of an individual. And for Lomax (1968: 171–4) it too is both universal and fundamental, probably deriving from mother/foetus synchrony, and accounting, perhaps, for the 'prelinguistic' impact of music and dance. Similarly, Keil's call for a 'bodily aesthetic' of music, focused on the link between sound and gesture (Keil 1966b), is at the centre of his theory of processual meaning. That 'our muscles are perceptive' can be taken as applying to the whole of music rather than just the 'non-syntactic' stratum to which he confines it. Indeed, Coker (1972) persuasively extends the approach by analysing the relationships between the physiological references of musical 'gestures' and their cognitive status as logical 'operators' ('musemes' in Seeger's terms). This is important since it offers a way of bringing together generative and logic-based approaches (and, more generally, all internalist music semiology), and such neuro-physiologically rooted theories as Lévi-Strauss's and Keil's. Moreover, once again it demonstrates that the undoubted importance within much popular music of organismic references does not mean that it is thereby deprived of cognitive substance.

There is a body of research into the organismic roots of musical rhythms (for a summary, see Davies 1980: 190–6). Probably the favourite theory sees bodily processes as the source (thus, for instance, tempo is said to be experienced in relation to heartbeat rate); others favour child-rearing practices (for example, maternal rocking, and walking rates while carrying). But according to Gooddy (1977: 138), the human neuro-physiological 'clock', against which periodic processes and temporal experiences in music are measured, is actually very complex, integrating very many time-forms associated with different body processes. Starting from an assumption of the intimate connections between the workings of this 'clock', motor processes, affective states and musical forms, Clynes and Walker (1982) have analysed various 'sound-pulse forms' (repeated metric patterns, differing in duration and intensity relationships) drawn from 'folk' and popular genres (waltz, rock, blues, and so on). Their graphic analyses are meant to depict the different rhythmic forms which listeners experience as inner gesture. They also display the nuances within metric types in a way that notated scores, with their simple '4/4 at ♩ = 120' and '3/4 at ♩ = 80', cannot, and conceivably could be related to the body movements involved in the associated dance forms.

This theory, like most others in this field, is concerned with very basic rhythmic phenomena: pulse, metre and accent. But, of course, actual rhythmic gestures work within this framework in manifold ways. And, however attractive the possibility of a universal rhythmic behavioural core, working at an unconscious level, such gestures are culturally mediated: socially acquired, conventionalized in form, given meaning in the context of specific cultural practices. This cultural specificity makes comparative interpretation of rhythmic styles dangerous. For instance, to talk of twentieth-century popular music of Afro-American extraction – by comparison with, say, European 'art' music, or its pre-twentieth-century bourgeois popular derivatives – as more 'instinctive', more 'rhythmic', more 'body-orientated', misses the point. Certainly there are strong correlations in this music with physical movement. What is at issue here, however, is not a body/mind antinomy, but a structure of differences concerning the amount and kind of mediation involved. In much twentieth-century popular music, the link between body processes and musical gestures is relatively direct, and heavy with what Coker (1972) terms 'performatives'; by contrast, in European 'art' music, or nineteenth-century ballads, it is heavily mediated by syntactic and semantic conventions which transform the processes into consciously organized patterns of symbols. The argument can be extended to *connotations* of the musical/gestural structures – usually falling in the area of sexuality. Pop is not 'sexier' than Beethoven, and drawing-room ballads are not more 'spiritual' than Aretha Franklin; it is simply that the patterns of sexual energy on which all these draw are mediated in different ways, more or less directly, resulting in different patterns of connotation. To insist otherwise is almost inevitably to end in racist propositions about the superior 'natural' qualities of black music.

Words and music
Almost all popular music takes the form of songs. And if the area of denotation is a problematical one as far as the music is concerned, it is certainly an important attribute of song lyrics. Unfortunately, most study of lyrics has taken the form of content analysis – which tends to oversimplify the relationship between words and 'reality', and to ignore the structural specificity of the verbal and musical

signifying systems.[28] But in any case, what interests me here is not the lyrics themselves so much as their relationship with the music.

The point that the vagueness and ambiguity of musical meanings can be focused, pinned down, made more precise, by associated lyrics has often been made. In relation to popular music, it is well put by Dave Laing. Laing's suggestion is not the crude one that lyrics *force* the music into particular meanings but 'that the words of a song give us the key to the human universe that the song inhabits, and that the musical signifieds may best be verbalised in a meta-language whose terms refer to the structure of that human universe' (Laing 1969: 99). Laing, however, goes on immediately to argue that the words' simple meanings are often transcended or modified, either when particularly strong musical conventions take precedence, or when lyric effects are transformed by the musical treatment of the words. In fact, we can probably think of the music/lyric relationship as moving between two extremes, one characterized by verbal predominance over relatively vague musical meanings, the other by the 'musicalization' of the words, often through paralinguistic techniques.

Laing himself discusses examples of the latter, in, for example, Buddy Holly's recordings, where he finds the lyrics 'transformed by accentuations given them by voice, guitars and drums' (ibid: 102). Rhythms, vocal timbre, register and articulation (for instance, Holly's hiccupping) work to modify the ostensible meaning of the words. Similarly, he finds that the hortatory use of key words and phrases in rhythm and blues dance records ('rock me baby') functions to reinforce the *rhythmic* excitement; this tendency carries on in rock 'n' roll and mainstream pop ('come on everybody'; 'let's dance'; 'shake it baby', and so on), and, as Laing points out, it derives from the use of 'jive' and 'scat' language by jazz and swing bands of the 1930s and 1940s (Cab Calloway, Louis Jordan), in which 'words' are treated as musical elements. Without going quite that far, a song like Little Richard's 'Tutti Frutti' shows how verbal denotations can be almost completely subordinated to musical effects – through rhythmic 'nonsense' language ('awopbopaloobop alopbamboom') and the organization of inconsequential verbal phrases into rhyming 'musical' parallelisms ('Rock to the east, rock to the west, She's the girl that I love best'; 'Got a girl, her name's Daisy, She almost drives me crazy').

A similar argument is mounted by Simon Frith:

> In songs, words are the signs of a voice. A song is always a performance and song words are always spoken out – vehicles for the voice . . . structures of sound that are *direct* signs of emotion and marks of character . . . Pop songs celebrate not the articulate but the inarticulate, and the evaluation of pop singers depends not on words but on sounds – on the noises around the words (Frith 1983a:35).

The significance of lyrics is governed not primarily by their obvious denotations but by their use of conventions, and these in turn are organized in terms of musical genres: the 'poetic' techniques of progressive rock, the banal colloquialisms of pop and disco, the clever rhymes of Broadway song, the emotive paralanguage of soul. Frith even suggests that black music is in part defined by a 'struggle *against* words . . . a quality of sincerity which can *only* be described in terms of sound, in terms not of what is sung but of how it is sung: the test of soul conviction is the singer's way with non-words' (ibid: 36; see also Frith 1987c: 97–9).

For the most part, the language used is everyday language – clichéd, trite, familiar – though it may be reassembled into new combinations. The point is to 'defamiliarize the familiar', to invest the banal with affective force and kinetic grace, to draw out of the concrete world of denotation some sense of those human generalities translated by musical processes. The strategy goes back at least to the 'boiled beef and carrots' of British music hall, and is still active in the treatment of street patois in rap and reggae. Much of the success of the early Beatles is built on such magical musicalization of the everyday ('with love from me to you', 'I wanna hold your hand', 'you know what I mean', 'you know that can't be bad', for example). The result is 'to make plain talk dance . . . to make ordinary language intense and vital; the words then resonate – they bring a touch of fantasy into our mundane use of them' (Frith 1983a: 378; see also Frith 1987c: 99–100).

At the same time, much of the power of these techniques derives precisely from the rootedness of the words in the concrete reality of the here-and-now; musical fantasy is focused on a precise moment. Thus, as Laing says (1969: 82–102), it is the *language* of 'high school rock' lyrics that places the songs in a particular social setting, a 'human universe' first explored by Chuck Berry and the Coasters. Similarly, the general musical qualities of British punk are given specific point by the social concerns of many lyrics, often with contemporaneous references (Laing 1985: 27–32). But the everyday is not the only category in which the denotative focus effect of lyrics can operate. The most obvious alternatives are those of *narrative* (for example, in many traditional 'folk' songs, but also in modern pseudo-folk and folk-rock repertories, such as early Bob Dylan) and of the *political message song*. In both cases, the straightforward content of the lyrics is primary, and in both, the drastic difference between the tempo of denotative language and that of melodic and harmonic rhythms means that the latter tend to retreat into the background, typically leaving simple, supporting vamps. (The situation is the same as in operatic recitative.)

A third category worth mentioning in this context is that of the *ballad*. Verbal dominance is less clear-cut here – in fact, words and music usually merge into unified emotive phrases – and language forms are highly conventionalized (moon/June rhymes, for example); but the primary significations carried by what the singer has to say are nevertheless in the foreground. To a considerable extent, the music is a vehicle for the singer's intimate, conversational address to the individual listener. As Frith points out (1983a: 36), rock music draws from this tradition as well as from the 'musical', rhythmic use of everyday language common in black music, and merges the two in varying proportions.

In practice, then, the music/lyric relationship is a complex one, rather than a question of two extremes. In part, this is because, as we have seen earlier, music and words, as signifying systems, are not simply antithetical; music has a syntagmatic, even narrative aspect, and words have a musical side. This overlap is reflected in the structure of cognitive processes and the related brain functions. Imberty (1979: 127–80), aware that melodic contours often seem to mirror the intonations of verbal phrases, proposes the term *intonemes* for certain archetypal shapes of this sort (notably ascent ($\nearrow$), descent ($\searrow$) and wave ($\sim$)). Of course, the verbal phrases, considered in their intonational aspects (that is, paralinguistically), can in turn be linked to *musical* processes; and paralinguistic studies indeed show that such aspects are meaningful (for example, 'question', 'command', 'statement'). But Imberty's point – backed up by experiments – is that listeners interpret sung melodies with reference to known verbal intonational archetypes (which may also be connected to what I have previously called melodic deep structures or gestures). Other experiments demonstrate that vocal intensity, speed of articulation and register in singing are also heard in relation to linguistic models.

Bradby and Torode find a pervasive verbal influence even within the relatively 'delyricized' musical structures of rock 'n' roll (Bradby and Torode 1984). Buddy Holly's 'Peggy Sue' reveals not only a dramatic narrative in its apparently banal lyric; a major contribution to the course of this narrative, it is argued, is made by the way the vocal performance draws on speech-rhythms, their variants and developments, and on intonational techniques deriving from speech models. It is even suggested that the solo guitar chorus plays its part in this, since its rhythms originate in, and copy, the already established rhythms of the sung lyric. Altogether, then, Bradby and Torode (1984), in an interpretation pitted against Laing's, see the rhythms of song not as 'musical', still less as 'physiological', but as 'the rhythms of *verbal images*' (ibid: 202); and their approach to musical meaning builds on Rousseau's mimetic theory, according to which 'by imitating the inflections of the voice, melody expresses pity, cries of sorrow and joy, threats and groans . . . It imitates the tones of language, and the twists produced in every idiom by certain psychic acts' (quoted in ibid: 186). It is not necessary to go this far – and indeed Bradby and Torode in the end identify the central social categories produced in the verbal discourse of 'Peggy Sue' with purely musical devices: the (male) on-beat, march-like four-four rhythm, and the (female) syncopations which try to subvert this; but the point is well made that in the music of songs linguistic and prelinguistic levels of signification are always intermingled.

This point surfaces again in Hennion's discussion of lyrics in French pop songs (Hennion 1983). He distinguishes between two categories of words: in the first, the predominant category, the words are familiar, predictable, and relate to contemporary concerns of everyday social contexts; in the second are

> certain key words . . . [which] function as pure signifiers . . . mysteriously they have an autonomy of their own within the meaning of the text, and are selected for the way they ring, for the expressive power which gives them their opacity; they have to engage the imagination of the listener, and at the same time effect a sort of disengagement from the everyday words of the text, so that the role of dream can be given full play. These unexpected metaphorical turns of phrase interrupt the unfolding of the text, giving one a shiver of pleasure, in a way very similar to the effect of the musical 'gimmick'.

The contrast is between '*word-quotes*, which enrich the context' (and have denotative power), 'and *keywords*, which serve as metaphors' (and move on more internally referenced levels of meaning) (ibid: 179).

But the same words can function in both ways, at the same time. In Sade's

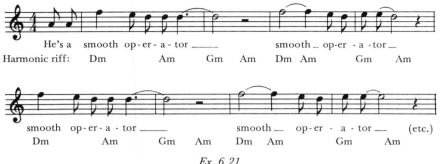

He's a smooth op-er-a-tor ____ smooth _ op-er - a -tor _

Harmonic riff: Dm   Am   Gm   Am   Dm Am   Gm   Am

smooth op-er-a - tor ____   smooth _   op-er - a - tor _   (etc.)
Dm   Am   Gm   Am   Dm Am   Gm   Am

Ex. 6.21

1985 hit 'Smooth Operator', [29] the clichéd phrase of the title is set to a melodic and harmonic riff, which is worked into a seamless musical flow, and the lyric-melodic idea takes on the 'mythic' character of a sound-gesture (see Ex. 6.21). At the same time, the quotidian quality of the words – their denotation and connotations – seems to remain important. But things are more complex than this. The words already have a 'musical' dimension, an onomatopoeic quality in their intonation, by which the 'smooth' sounds smooth and sustained, and the 'operator' has a 'mechanical' rhythm. This quality is preserved and enhanced by the melodic-rhythmic setting of the riff; it is an 'intoneme'. The extent to which, in the song as a whole, this everyday 'word-quote' is turned into a resonant, autonomous, metaphoric 'keyword' by its 'musicalization', or alternatively, the music's mythic power is brought down to earth and focused on a particular social reference, probably depends on the listener's situation and interpretation.

Such ambiguities in the music/lyric relationship may be seen as relating to a

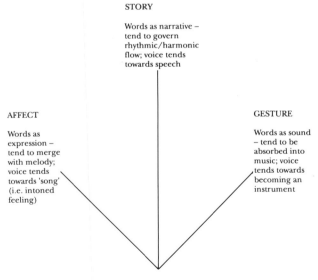

STORY

Words as narrative –
tend to govern
rhythmic/harmonic
flow; voice tends
towards speech

AFFECT

Words as
expression –
tend to merge
with melody;
voice tends
towards 'song'
(i.e. intoned
feeling)

GESTURE

Words as sound
– tend to be
absorbed into
music; voice
tends towards
becoming an
instrument

Fig. 6.13

three-pole model, in terms of which the hybrid practices of actual popular songs come into being (Figure 6.13). The links between this model and that suggested earlier (pp. 214–17) for conceptualizing the organization of difference and equivalence in musical syntax are obvious.

Secondary signification
As we have seen at several points, secondary meanings – connotations, to use traditional terminology – can arise on the basis of any of the primary signification types discussed above. There are many types of these, too. Stefani (1973: 40–1) lists the following:

Intentional values. These are recognized, intended connotations of specific structural or thematic effects: thus a cadence carries all the connotations of 'conclusion' or 'rest'; synthesizers connote 'technology' or 'modernity' or 'the future'; boogie rhythms connote 'the erotic'.
Positional implications. These are connotations arising from structural position: thus the 'bridge' in a thirty-two-bar AABA form generates the connotations of 'contrast'; a repeated 'loop' effect at the beginning of a song produces all the associations of introductory vamps while at the end of the song it carries the associations of a fade – 'unendingness' or 'continuous activity' (as against aesthetic completeness).
Ideological choices. These are particular, preferred meanings, selected from a range of possible interpretations: drug readings of psychedelic songs like 'Lucy in the Sky with Diamonds'; attributions of conservative political meanings to the styles of Country music songs.
Emotive connotations. These refer to the agreed affective implications of musical events: punk is associated with aggression; singer-songwriters with confessional intimacy; heavy soul with passionate, 'spiritual' ecstasy or striving.
Links with other semiotic systems. These are visual, kinetic, verbal, even olfactory associations: 'funky' soul; 'steamy' swamp-rock; 'highly-perfumed' Incredible String Band.
Rhetorical connotations. These are associations arising from correspondences with rhetorical forms (question, proposition, dialectic, and so on) and styles (irony, hyperbole, paradox): thus riffs generate connotations of propositions ('command', 'truth', 'authority'); call-and-response those of dialectic ('conversation', 'mutuality'); James Brown suggests hyperbole; Randy Newman irony; Public Image Ltd. paradox.
Style connotations. These are the associations summoned up by coding at the general level of style: rock 'n' roll means teds, jiving, motorbikes, violence, drainpipe trousers, and so on.
Axiological connotations. These refer to moral or political evaluations of musical pieces, styles or genres; rock 'n' roll is corrupting/liberating/lascivious/harmless and banal; Billy Bragg is a reactionary rocker/a progressive folkie and protest singer/a reformist hybridizer.

Units of secondary signification are not necessarily the same size as the associated units of primary signification. Very often they are larger. On the one hand, a single 'connotator' may be made up of several signs on the primary level; this is the case with most of the examples just given. On the other hand, whatever the size of a connotator, its *content* (what is connotated) is always, in theory, of infinite size: that is, the range of possible associations is endless; as Barthes puts it (1968: 91), 'its character is at once general, global and diffuse; it is, if you like, a fragment of ideology'. Again, some of the examples given above show the beginnings of this potentially infinite signification process.

Nattiez has suggested three methods of approach to the analysis of secondary signification: hermeneutic analysis of the text; reconstitution of the intentions of the producer(s); and experimental testing of listener responses (Nattiez 1976: 157–89). All have their problems; but in any case virtually no applications of any of these methods have taken popular music as their subject. Cooke (1959), using a combination of hermeneutics and reconstitution, made a heroic and often illuminating attempt to constitute a 'lexicon' which would account for the meanings of European 'art' music of the functional-tonal period. To the (varying) extents that nineteenth- and twentieth-century popular styles are part of that tradition, this is useful – though its success is limited by several problematical features, notably (a) a naturalistic rather than semiotic approach to acoustic material; (b) too great a reliance on the ostensible content of lyrics; (c) insufficient historical and social differentiation; and (d) a tendency to interpret procedures in isolation rather than in their musical context, where, of course, their significance varies according to the structural and functional levels on which they are considered. In a sense, Cooke's approach has been extended into the field of popular music by Philip Tagg. Tagg, however, tightens up the method by means of the techniques of 'hypothetical substitution' (see above, pp. 180–2) and 'intersubjective comparison' (a kind of experimental testing).

Tagg has applied his method in detail – rather than in a grand historical Cooke's tour – to two pieces, the *Kojak* signature tune (Tagg 1979) and the Abba hit, 'Fernando' (Tagg 1981). Having segmented the music into musemes and museme compounds (which already involves hypothetical substitution), Tagg's technique is to test his intuitive interpretations of meaning further by means of 'interobjective comparison' and 'intersubjective comparison'. The latter draws on psychological testing techniques. The former is close to Cooke's method but more selective. For any museme, Tagg assembles a large range of apparently similar usages *drawn from allied, influential, source and adjacent genres and styles*; thus for *Kojak*, comparisons are made mainly with passages from nineteenth-century concert and dramatic music, Hollywood film scores and commercial 'mood music' – the principal sources for TV theme style – but also to some extent with examples taken from jazz, rock and soul music, which were influential on much TV music of the *Kojak* period and type. Interpretations are confirmed if the meanings of the comparative material seem to be similar to those attributed to the object museme or passage (as substantiated by intersubjective testing).

This is a richly suggestive technique, easily the most fruitful method at present available for the analysis of secondary signification in popular music. There are one or two problems, however. First, the method is heavily dependent on orientations provided by accompanying extramusical aspects of the message – on 'reconstitutions' of intentions discovered in lyrics, programmatic elements (such as titles) and visual images. The lyrics of 'Fernando' and the visual sequence accompanying the *Kojak* theme, for instance, help situate the music in specific connotative worlds. It would be nonsensical to suggest that this is illegitimate:

clearly, words and images are part of the total message in these cases; nevertheless, complete correlation is purely speculative. Moreover, a great many popular songs do not possess associated visual images and have lyrics with much less specific, less concrete content than 'Fernando'. Tagg has not yet applied his analytic technique to a pop recording with relatively bland, unimportant or 'musicalized' lyrics. The less precise and the less suggestive the words, the harder it becomes to tie particular connotations to the music. The problem here also affects the comparative material, which is drawn disproportionately from the repertories of opera, song, programmatic concert music and film and mood music – all genres with extramusical aids to interpretation, which, however, may be deceptive or inapplicable.

A second problem is that Tagg appears to see TV themes (rightly, on the whole) and mainstream pop (rather more questionably) as basically still within the semiotic/aesthetic orbit of late nineteenth- and early twentieth-century European 'art' music. That repertory happened to be particularly rich in deliberately intended extramusical meanings and accompanying verbal and visual signals. Eisler has described how the semantic techniques developed in this music were taken over and mass produced by the Hollywood film industry of the 1930s and 1940s (Eisler 1948: Chapter 1). Their fixing as rationalized formulae, ubiquitous and eventually reified, testifies in favour of Tagg's view, but at the same time it seems questionable that all twentieth-century popular musics derive *solely* from this tradition, and Tagg's approach needs to be used in conjunction with concepts congruent with a critique of this approach's assumptions.

A third problem concerns one of these assumptions, namely that it is valid to interpret musemes in isolation, attributing a consistency to their effects which, in reality, varying contexts, modes of articulation and levels of listening may vitiate. While admittedly Tagg is strong on the importance of syntactic *process*, it remains true that his method is built, first and foremost, on the interpretation of segmented elements and units, and that in the assessment of how these elements and units then cohere a significant role is played by processes of aggregation. Thus the *Kojak* analysis assembles the following list of museme interpretations:

1 Bass: intense energy, action and desultory unrest, male-dominated areas of activity, unquiet, aggressiveness, atmosphere of a large North American city, the energetic and somewhat threatening excitement of its subculture.

2 Moog: general, constant bustling activity, agitated and insistent but positive, pleasant, vibrant, shimmering and luminous.

3 Brass: modern, energetic, urban American environment.

4 Woodwind: unrestful, jerky, exciting.

5 Harmony: modern, positive (perhaps cold) environment.

6 Horn: (a) call to action and attention, strong individual movement upwards and outwards, virile, energetic, heroic;
     (b) undulating, swaying, calm and confident, propelling into
     (c) fanfare of strength, breadth, boldness and confidence, something individual, martial, male and heroic.

(left margin: MELODY ACCOMPANIMENT)

Then, in the context of a reading of the texture as in a figure/ground (individual/environment) mode, these museme interpretations are summed together:

MELODY	TYPE OF RELATION	ACCOMPANIMENT		
a call to action and attention, strong	stands out against, is heard above, is	BASS	Type of relation	OTHER PARTS
individual movement up and outwards, virile, energetic and heroic, leading to undulating swaying, calm and confidence, something individual, male, martial and heroic. ↔	stronger than, is engaged in dialogue with ↔	energy, excitement, desultory unrest, male aggressive-ness, threat of sub-cultural environment in large North American city ↔	is part of, rumbles below, is heard through ↔	general, constant, bustling activity, agitated, pleasant, vibrant, luminous, modern, urban American, sometimes jerky, unresting, exciting.

This is to play down the possible semantic role of deep structures; of positional values in the syntax; of *Gestalten* and of syntactic relationships (rather than discrete terms); and the importance of historical specificity which puts in question whether *all* music tends towards combinations of 'effects' rather than synthesized wholes. True, the *Kojak* theme is rather a stylistic hotchpotch made up of strongly marked figures, harmonies and sounds; and as a result Tagg's approach works well. In a piece like 'Fernando', which is stylistically more homogeneous (though by no means totally so), the analysis seems to force more weight on to individual musemes than they want to bear. Were the approach to be applied to the average mainstream pop song, the syntax of which is even more 'synthesized', the most likely result is that the basic connotational field of *any* museme would be the same – most likely that attaching to the overall musical style. As we saw earlier (p. 182), Tagg's method is often at its most successful when dealing with *parameters*, over lengthy passages or whole pieces, rather than units; and such parameter interpretations usually refer first and foremost to style-codes, not specific affects or images.

An example may make this problem with Tagg's approach clearer. The Specials' 'Ghost Town' seems on the face of it highly appropriate for this method of analysis. There is obvious social and political content in the lyrics, relating to depression, decay and disaffection in Britain's inner cities in the early 1980s. There is an explicit contrast of vocal styles, between the semi-spoken 'rap' of the verse and the more passionate rock mode of the middle section, and these refer to differing style connotations. In the verse there are suggestions of various 'old fashioned' musical techniques: early 1960s Beat and even Tin Pan Alley har-monies; latin-tinged ballroom styles; even 'the mighty Wurlitzer'. Moreover, the diminished seventh sequence used as an instrumental intro and link has specific connotations of tension and apprehension. The stabbing rhythms and riff structure of the verse derive stylistically from ska, and more connotations enter there. In short, since the piece is so heterogeneous, there is a lot that can be said about the associations attaching to particular units and parameters.

But we have already noted the way the verse/middle contrast, and the instrumental link, work in a 'mythic' mode, on the *primary* level of signification. This involves the *structural interrelationships* of elements, not discrete elements themselves. Much the same can be said about all the components in the style collage here. Moreover, the connotational elements also function in relationship to a 'purer', more abstract level of signification. The piece is a *dance* piece, and the danceability of the song – its address to listeners as dancers rather than thinking, emoting consciousnesses – refers to kinetic elements of signification discussed earlier, as well as offering them, perhaps, as comment on or context for the more semantically translatable, secondary meanings. Similarly, while the sequence of formal sections can be interpreted connotationally, it can also be seen as an adaptation of traditional AABA ballad form which results in a satisfying (though not quite exact) arch shape, whose meaning and pleasure is 'self-reflexive' or 'introversive':

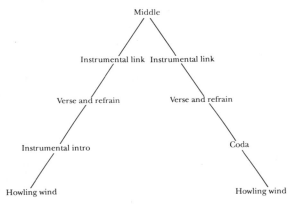

Fig. 6.14

It is precisely the tension between the, as it were, self-contained meaning of this 'circular' impulse and the 'narrative' detail constituted by sequential change – for instance, by changes in repeated material – which a semiological reading would have to account for.

Hennion argues that in most pop songs isolable 'effects' – striking figures and sounds, often functioning as the song's 'hook' – are heard against, stand out against, a much more extensive and, so to speak 'neutral' background (Hennion 1983: 172–4). This taken-for-granted, grammatically predictable framework slips by unnoticed. Now, strictly speaking, no musical device is semantically neutral; indeed it is precisely analysis of the taken-for-granted that would reveal a culture's basic assumptions. But it is true that the quantity and qualitative importance of secondary and of primary signification vary in different musical styles and types, and that in many popular song-styles the basic assumptions seem to work more on the primary than the secondary level: connotations arising from specific elements in basic syntactic frameworks are scanty, for the main function of these elements is to fulfil grammatical expectations rather than to stimulate mental associations. Adorno's argument – referring to the commercial products of the music industry – that 'As soon as music is no longer synthesised it dissolves into imagery, and that imagery accords with the accepted norms'

(Adorno 1976: 52) represents a premature closure of historical processes, and the question of the relationship in popular music between the roles of individual effects, privileging mechanisms of connotation, and of synthesized syntactic structures, privileging primary types of signification, is a general one, not limited to consideration of Philip Tagg's method of analysis.

We have seen that many secondary significations refer to social contexts. Sometimes these references are purely associative: the sound of rock 'n' roll, or Victor Sylvester, or Scott Joplin, conjures up particular social images, for historical reasons. But sometimes there seem to be more pressing links between musical structure and social structure. This, of course, is the area previously considered under the heading of *homology*. There does appear to be a widespread recognition of semantic connections between specific musical types and techniques, and specific social groups and positions. If the idea of *innate* homology is rejected, the question is how these connections work.

The most likely answer is that a *variety* of mechanisms is involved, and they are related through processes of *articulation*, which function through the operation of different structures and types of *pertinence. Behavioural connections* might be one such mechanism. The performance constructs social relationships similar to those characteristic of the society, and the connotations of the latter fall on the former. As we found in the previous chapter, much of Alan Lomax's theory of song structure is premised on this mechanism, and it can be found at work too in Keil's account of a Bobby Bland concert (Keil 1966a: 114–42). Thus a star singer backed by a restrained accompanying orchestra may suggest the spectacular but selective upward mobility available in 'mass society', and the mechanisms of hero-worship that accompany it; the antiphonal relationships of call-and-response patterns are continuous with the collective interactions of tribal and pseudo-tribal societies; the 'star unisons' and 'egalitarian' sequences of star snippets in the Band Aid and Live Aid Ethiopian hits suggest the humanitarian individualism typical of liberal bourgeois society. Some constraints on the working of this kind of mechanism were suggested in the previous chapter.

Closely related to behavioural connections are those constructed within *lyric modes of address*. The personal mode ('I love *you*') typical of ballads is commonly thought of as directed to the individual listener – alone perhaps, and certainly alone emotionally. The connotations are those of what Dave Laing has called the 'shrivelled' personal emotional life characteristic of late bourgeois society, with its retreat into sentimental fantasy (Laing 1969: 57–60). By contrast, the lyrics of rock 'n' roll address a collective ('come on everybody'). And some 'subcultural' styles have ways of trying to define specific addressees in their lyrics, as a means of delineating their social position. Again Laing (1985: 68–73) has discussed ways in which punk did this ('If the kids are united'; 'we're the people you don't wanna know').

An important way in which modes of address help to define audience position is in relation to gender. It is obvious how (reactionary) gender roles are constructed within many Rolling Stones, or heavy metal, lyrics – indeed, this applies to the whole category of what has been called 'cock rock'. The work of Bardby (1985) and Bradby and Torode (1982; 1984) has offered analyses of ways in which narrative structures in rock lyrics – the interplay of different 'voices' and the social relationships thereby represented – articulate processes of male and female socialization for adolescents. In conjunction with polyphonic behavioural aspects of performance (male singer/male vocal backing group; girl singer/girl backing group; male singer/female backing group), these structures, it is argued, offer ways of working through the processes by which teenage girls and boys acquire conventionalized though sometimes internally contradictory roles.

Of course, lyric structures do not necessarily correlate totally with musical structures. As we saw earlier, Bradby and Torode tend to elide this difference – though in the end their interpretation rests on a 'prelinguistic' reading of rhythmic patterns. Similarly, it is probably the possibility of music/lyric *dis*continuity that explains how some women can hear 'cock rock' as sexually liberating.

Musical structures, no less than lyrics, can be seen as involving an interplay of 'voices' – indeed, this takes place polyphonically as well as sequentially, as we have just seen. And, just as some words, especially pronouns, can act as 'shifters' (see p. 167 above), so musical elements can be heard as representing particular social actors, whose identity can vary according to genre conventions and social context. An instrumental or vocal solo will usually be heard as an 'I' (singular or collective), but which 'I' will depend on received connotations attaching to the genre (compare a rock 'n' roll saxophone solo with one by Lester Young); on the solo's structural position within the piece (is it highly idiosyncratic in style or not? is it taken up and repeated or varied by other 'voices' or not? is it counterpointed or harmonized by other 'voices'? is it relatively active (dominant) in the texture or relatively passive (subservient)? is it rhythmically, or harmonically, at odds, or in congruence, with its accompaniment? and so on); on the performance situation (where? when? with what function? after what, before what?); and on who is listening (compare male and female images of the social representation carried by a heavy metal guitar solo; working-class and middle-class images of the 'personality' represented in a Joe Strummer vocal).

The interplay of social 'voices' may play an important part in what Prague semiology calls the 'semantic gesture' of a piece. Indeed, in that approach musical structure as a whole is related to social function, hence to the socio-historical locations and connotations of such functions. We saw how a contrast between the open/closed principle of 'bourgeois song' and the open-ended repetitive gestures typical of many pop dance-songs could be seen from this point of view, the functions relating to private listening, on the one hand, and collective participation, on the other. A more precise example – addressing particularly the 'social' structure of musical 'voices' – would be the evolution of form in early jazz. Starting in New Orleans as open-ended collective improvisation, related to the functions of dance and parade, and reflecting the public social life of the socially mixed pre-industrial (mercantile) city, the music tended in late 1920s Chicago to turn into a string of solos, each man having his turn, the string opened and closed by a formal collective statement. This form relates to a more localized listening function (in club and bar) and more individualized social relationships, reflecting the changed circumstances of the industrial city. By the mid-1930s, much jazz displayed something closer to a star solo/big band accompaniment structure. Certainly, in the hands of the big stars – Louis Armstrong, for example – the relationship suggests the display/entertainment/

identification functions typical of the mass-disseminated forms of megalopolitan culture.

We have come very close to the area traditionally thought of in terms of homology. And it remains to reiterate that, if 'innate' homologies are suspect on epistemological grounds – for they always end in reductionism of one sort or another – it nevertheless seems likely that, at deep structural levels (historically the level of the *longue durée*, semiotically the level of *langue* and of generative gestures, ontogenetically the level of reciprocity and 'correspondence') some connections between musical and social structures are easier to make than others. And they are easier for particular social groups in particular social positions; conversely, other groups may find them hard to break and rearticulate. It would seem that the further one moves from the social towards the 'anthropological' level, the more 'natural' or innate the connections will appear.

Some examples of 'obvious' connections have already been mentioned: arch-like and centripetal melodic shapes and open/closed structures (bourgeoisie); cumulative, riff-based melodic structures (tribal societies); variative melodic structures (proletarian cultures); the narrative/lyric/epic triad and its social connotations.

Such connotations can be regarded as arising on the basis of the primary level of 'correspondence' referred to by Lévi-Strauss, Piaget and others. But the whole process is always culturally formed; it is never predetermined. All 'correspondences', and their secondary associations, however 'deep', arise through processes of socially directed learning, correlation and comparison. That is to say, all relationships are governed by criteria of *pertinence*. Objective structural possibilities are sorted into categories according to prevailing codes, values, modes of reception, and so on. The more socially specific, the less anthropologically broad, the level of processing, the finer the grid through which possibilities are sorted and the more restricted the connections that are made. Possibilities are 'rubbed against' not 'experience' (as in Willis), but against patterns of *discursive preference*, which are governed by socio-semiotic (that is, pragmatic) rules, themselves grounded in collectively operational cognitive structures. In complex societies, these structures are in part internally contradictory; hence the possibility of semiotic conflict and rearticulation. In relatively stable societies, as Geertz points out (1973: 408), such contradictions are few and mostly hidden; felt connections appear as naturally homologous structures. In dynamic societies, 'foreign' structures are forever impinging on existing situations and have to be matched against given modes and relationships. Either party in this encounter may be reinterpreted, according to new criteria of pertinence. Such reinterpretations are not a matter of 'experiential fit' but of discursive negotiation. Hence, as noted previously, their likelihood is governed by socially and historically variable 'limits of tolerance'.

The communication process – and beyond

This position carries us beyond the over-simple, internally validating systems of classical semiology. It is possible to see such internalism as a latest (final?) stage in a characteristically Western scientistic trend; or, from another perspective, as part of a parallel drive to bring all life under the principle of *exchange* (here, exchange of signified for signifier): nothing, that is to say, is allowed to be *itself* – it has to be 'understood', 'interpreted', measured and related. This leads Henri Lefèbvre to attack attempts to pin down all significations in music in terms of clear correlations between signifiers and signifieds. There is an untranslatable substratum, he argues, and it is on that level that music's function as dream, ecstasy, violence, can emerge. Drawing on a Nietzschean opposition, Lefebvre opposes to 'logogenic' semantics the moment of the 'pathogenic', which 'has its domain at this side of and beyond discourse, beyond the world of signs and of the subject; it evokes the irruption of a Dionysian space, inverse and adversary of that space of the intelligible, the specialised: [it is] the irruption of desire'. In music, he says, 'the perceptible . . . can only be musical (acoustic)' – not visual or verbal; and its meaning is what he calls 'the "sensorial"', its physical immediacy'. In music, fantasy can be realized, the distance between desire and object of desire closed. This takes place on a level 'below' that structured by the relationship between subjects and signs – a relationship which, for Lefebvre, is unavoidably implicated in projects of social control, functioning through *langue*'s appeals to 'reality' and 'reason'. Against such projects music offers a counter-space where rebellion is possible; and that is what explains music's important role in cultural contestation, subcultures and everyday imaginative life. Where, then, does music's *intelligibility* arise? Where does the structuring of logogenic and pathogenic moments come from? From the *body* (conceived as a system with cognitive and affective as well as motorial and instinctual elements). 'Musicality communicates corporeality. It renders the body into social practice . . . deploying their resources, music binds bodies together (socialises them)' (Lefebvre 1971b: 59–61).

Though there are hints here of an undesirable romanticism (music as mystery), Lefebvre's main point *can* be incorporated in a coherent model of musical communication – provided we remember the importance of a context-sensitive interpretative flexibility. Sean Cubitt suggests that

> to avoid the danger of presenting songs as referential . . . [we might] use the word 'effects' to denote . . . the signifieds or semantic effects of the song's signification. Since it is not referential, we cannot say that the song has meaning, but rather that it means, that it produces meaning (Cubitt 1984: 215).

Analytically, it is a question of the *variability* of pertinence. This applies on two dimensions: *what* is pertinent (that is, in the text); and, *to what, for whom* and *in what way* is it pertinent (the contexts, needs and place of the listening subject).

Reference has already been made to the need for flexibility in dealing with the various levels of segmentation of the expression plane. The same applies, obviously, to the semantic plane. We can conceive a spectrum running from minimal elements to whole styles and genres; any level on this spectrum is capable of producing meaning, of attaining the status of *seme*.[30] In musical 'narratives' – using the word in a broad sense – such semes can be regarded as playing the roles of what the structural analysis of verbal narrative calls *actants*, that is, structural components of plot types. The different 'voices' of musical textures no less than the different parts of formal schemes could well be approached in this way. In part, such patterns work on the primary level of signification, as we have already seen; that is, they work through purely structural interrelationships. But in part, too, they have a connotative substance – the 'semantic gestures' are filled with associations. This would account for the fact, for example, that elements which are structurally distinct (bass/vocal, verse/chorus, call/response, for instance) may substantively *agree* (the connotations of their content are similar); in these cases, one *actant* is represented by more than one *acteur*. And indeed, an interesting analytical question is the varying extents to which popular song 'plots' are built on patterns of diagetic and textural tension (and resolution), or alternatively are orientated towards relationships of unanimity. Styles and genres, too, generate connotative substance but, again, this is always interpreted in terms of structured interrelationships. Thus, in the 1930s 'hot' and 'sweet' defined each other, as did beat and rhythm and blues in the early 1960s, 'pop' and rock' in the 1970s. Punk defined itself through relationships of similarity (with previous 'hard' and 'basic' rock styles) and difference (from 'progressive' styles), and 'trad' jazz did the same in relation to commercial swing music and, later, rock 'n' roll (negatively), and New Orleans jazz (positively).

A given unit or structural relationship can produce different kinds of meaning according to the code that listeners apply. We have already seen something of the variety of codes which may operate in music. These could be grouped into categories, which, associated together in different ways and ratios, could then form analytical models appropriate to particular song-types and use situations. Such models[31] would need to take account not only of *text* but *context*. Here Jakobson's theory of the communication process is helpful (Jakobson 1960: 353ff.). He distinguishes six communication *functions*, each associated with a dimension of the process.

Dimensions

```
                     1 context
                     2 message
3 sender ---------------------------------------- 4 receiver
                     5 channel
                     6 code
```

Functions
1 *referential* (= contextual information)
2 *aesthetic* (= auto-reflection)
3 *emotive* (= self-expression)
4 *conative* (= vocative or imperative addressing of receiver)
5 *phatic* (= checking channel working)
6 *metalingual* (= checking code working)

For Jakobson, meaning resides in the total process of communication, and its nature will vary according to which function(s) predominate(s). Clearly, then – as Lefebvre suggested – 'logogenic' reference is only a part of this process. In popular songs the referential, aesthetic and emotive codes are readily recognized (and have already been discussed). The conative function operates most obviously in certain sorts of direct-address lyric (for example, 'save the last dance for me', 'come on everybody, let's rock', 'come together', 'dance while the music goes on', 'twist and shout'). It may also be associated, however, with 'imperative' rhythms, which set bodies moving in specific ways, and, in a general sense, with mechanisms of identification whereby listeners' self-image is built into the music. On this general level, it can be regarded as the function of 'interpellation', through which listening subjects are located in particular positions as addressees.

The phatic function is present in almost all popular songs, to the extent that they involve repetition – of themselves or of formulae – and quasi-ritualistic methods of establishing contact (vamps, riffs, catchphrases, and so on). The import is: 'Do you recognize this? Am I getting through? Are we on the same wave-length?' Also, channel characteristics are involved in the phatic function. We could analyse the methods through which the 'liveness' of live performance is established, the 'radio-ness' of pop radio, the 'disco-ness' of disco. On a general level, this can be regarded as the function of solidarity, cultural recognition and subcultural contact.

The metalingual function is associated with some kinds of surrounding verbal discourse: performers' introductions, DJ links, listener comments ('great, wasn't it?', 'the next song is similar to . . . ', 'anybody who doesn't recognize this, where've you been?'). On a more general level, the use of a grammar-orientated, overcoded system can act as metalingual comment: the message here is, 'This piece is not so much about itself as about the code to which it refers'.

Not only is the text governed by a variety of communication functions; it is also more than musical. Of course, meanings result from the social context of performance and reception; but the performance itself has metamusical aspects. Here it is worth noting that the analysis of bodily movement and social interaction (implicitly called for by Lefebvre) is no longer dependent on purely empirical observation or interpretative ethnographic techniques; structuralist and semiotic methods have been developed which ought to enable such analysis to be integrated with semiotic study of the musical texts (see, for example, Birdwhistell 1952; 1971; Hall 1959; 1963). Promising areas to start would be the facial expressions, body-movements and mike or instrument handling of performers, and the topography and dynamics of the performer/audience relationship. Spatial interrelationships of performers themselves are also of interest. Does the big band section standing to deliver its solo chorus represent professional guild cohesion? Compare the close spacing of rock 'n' roll and early beat groups (signifying 'gang' solidarity?) with the wide spacing of 'high-tech' pop bands (signifying individual passivity in face of technological dominance?). Or the interactive gestures of soul and rhythm and blues performers (signifying mutuality?) with the staged solo singer accompanied by hidden pit orchestra (signifying the star syndrome?). There may also be a proxemics of the musical sound itself. Even on recordings, the 'stereo picture' represents to us performer spacing and interaction. Conventions of channel balance, separation, blend and panning are probably just as significant as the conventions of distance and setting governing still and movie portraiture.

The kinesics of instrumental performance have been the subject of special study by the ethnomusicologist, John Baily (1977; 1985). Baily argues that players' movements affect musical structure in fundamental ways. The motor patterns which 'lie behind' a particular kind of music – its 'motor structure' – result from interaction between the morphology of the instrument and the player's sensorimotor capacities; and this 'motor grammar', once learned, can generate an infinite variety of specific sequences in actual performance. This means that 'through this approach we may come nearer to understanding how elements of music structure are rooted in the human body. Music can be viewed as a product of body movement transduced into sound' (Baily 1977: 330). In considering the operation and derivation of musical codes, a new factor is thus introduced – together with an extra level of *iconicity* in the semantics: music is seen as in some sense analogous to its motorial sources. Listeners, in turn, identify with the motor structure, participating in the gestural patterns, either vicariously, or even physically, through dance or through miming vocal and instrumental performance.

This is moving us close to the limits of a semiotic approach. To some degree, the correlations or correspondences here seem so direct – so close to being 'performatives', to recall Coker's term – that they have less to do with meaning than with processes in themselves, less with signs than with *actions*. 'Socialising bodies' (Lefebvre) is not to be confused with any kind of 'instinctualism' of the 'primitive herd'. Human movement and affective interaction are never culture-free; rather, as we have seen before, there are differences in kind and extent of mediation through which pre-semiotic human interaction acquires symbolic, logical and significatory superstructures. As Blacking argues (1977b: 9):

> Crucial factors in the development of cultural forms are the possibility of shared somatic states, the structures of the bodies that share them, and the rhythms of interaction that transform commonly experienced internal sensations into externally visible and transmissible forms. This process does not in theory require spoken language or even linguistic concepts [or analogous semiotic systems], though in practice language use and its cognitive consequences are an integral part of the experience of normal human beings. The shared states of different bodies can generate different sets of rules for the construction of behaviour and action by means of repeated movements in space and time that can be transmitted from one generation to another.

A similar point, from a phenomenological point of view, is made by Merleau-Ponty (1962: 184, 186):

> It is . . . quite clear that constituted speech . . . assumes that the decisive step of expression has been taken. Our view of man will remain superficial so long as we fail to go back to that origin, so long as we fail to find, beneath the chatter of words, the primordial silence, and so as long as we do not describe the action which breaks this silence . . . It is through my body that I understand other people, just as it is through my body that I perceive 'things'. The meaning of a gesture thus 'understood' is not behind it, it is intermingled with the structure of the world outlined by the gesture, and which I take up on my own account. It is arrayed all over the gesture itself . . .

The implicit desire to reach back to that pre-semiotic primordial silence is a pervasive presence in European culture; the burden of the sign is a heavy one, founded as it is on the alienation of man from nature. A pathogenic strand in popular music and dance is so widely observed as to draw extra attention to the lamentable lack of serious study of dance and its relationship to the music. Durgnat (1971: 35) writes that 'A generalised vibration invades the muscles of the body . . . the music seems to flood the listener's, or dancer's, flesh and bones . . . Even as one dances one's body becomes stacked with pulsations . . . '. Similarly, Wicke writes of rock fans that

> their . . . whole body responds to the music and not only to the rhythm but to the music as a whole – their bodies are enwrapped in the music and they transform it imaginatively into motion . . . The most important thing here are structures 'full of movement' . . . [the music] is not a sign of something beyond itself but stands for something by itself, it is the mimic presentation of movements, patterns of movement, scenes of movement . . . its semantics . . . are . . . the result of the two elements which combine here to create motion – the subject which moves and the music by which it is moved (Wicke 1985).

But in the absence of much more extensive analysis, it remains problematical whether Durgnat's conclusion:

> The music diffuses throughout one's bones and muscles, opening up the body in a compensatory fashion for the increasing irrelevance of body-experience to society . . . Rock restores, in a limited way no doubt, a primitive biological-emotional-mental unity (Durgnat 1971: 38).

represents romantic wishful thinking or a real move towards the utopian state envisioned by Blacking (1977b: 22–3):

> [if] there are forms intrinsic to music and dance that are not modelled on language[,] we may look beyond the 'languages' of dancing, for instance, to the dances of language and thought. As conscious movement is in our thinking, so thinking may come from movement, and especially shared, or conceptual, thought from communal movement. And just as the ultimate aim of dancing is to be able to move *without* thinking, to *be* danced, so the ultimate achievement in thinking is to be moved to think, to *be* thought . . . essentially it is a form of unconscious cerebration, a movement of the body. We are moved into thinking. Body and mind are one.

However far the general run of popular musical practice may be from this condition, Blacking's statement sketches a picture of the semiotic economy which all study of the music can use as a starting point.

Notes

1. A similar position is proposed in Supičic 1971.
2. See Eco (1979: 172–6); Blacking (1981); Piaget (1971: 74–96); Richman (1980). In different guises, such arguments go back to Darwin and beyond.

3. The only book-length introductions to music semiology known to me are Nattiez (1976) and Stefani (1986). There is no introduction of any sort in English. The best short account – and a very good one – is Stefani (1973). Baroni's (1983) survey of recent developments in music analysis puts music semiology in context, as does Nattiez 1989. A special issue of *Semiotica* (66: 1–3 (1987)) devoted to the semiology of music offers a useful state-of-the-art collection of conference papers.

4. An exception is Tagg (1979: 47).

5. Though acknowledging this, Nattiez (1976, pp. 45–62) is prepared to postulate for analytical purposes an objective *niveau neutre*. For an effective critique of this concept, which has been the subject of much controversy, see Ruwet (1975).

6. For influential texts, see Coons and Kraehenbuhl (1958); Youngblood (1958); Moles (1966). For a summary of the literature and a critique, see Cohen (1962). For an accessible account of the *general* theory, see Cherry (1968). For attempts to apply the approach to popular music, see Cohen (1962); Middleton (1981).

7. This concept of redundancy has a semantic orientation rather than (simply) referring to 'wastage', as in information theory. A wasted unit could have pertinence.

8. In linguistics morphemes are defined as the minimal significant units; they may coincide with words or be grammatically significant constituents of words. Phonemes are defined as the minimal distinctive units; in themselves they are meaningless but as constituents of morphemes they contribute to meaning.

9. A useful summary of the commutation principle appears in Barthes (1968: 65–9).

10. A summary of the method appears in Tagg (1982: 50–53).

11. For an explication and critique of Ruwet's method, see Nattiez (1976: 239–77).

12. Defining relations of equivalence as 'iconic' relations, Osmond-Smith refers to amount of transformation as 'iconic distance', see Osmond-Smith (1972; 1973; 1975).

13. See Boretz (1969–70); Rahn (1983); Clynes (1982); Critchley and Henson (1977); Harwood (1976); Howell *et al.* (1985); Laske (1975a; 1975b); McLaughlin (1970); Sloboda (1985). Applications of *Gestalt* theory are also relevant: see Davies (1980: 83ff.); Deutsch (1982: 99–134); Tagg (1979, *passim*).

14. In Schenker analyses, the structural pitches of the *Urlinie* are notated like this.

15. CBS Epic A6716.

16. On *Please Please Me*, Parlophone PMC 1202.

17. On circles of fifths in popular music harmony, see Winkler (1978); and cf. pp. 119–20 above.

18. For applications to tune repertories of different kinds, see Lindblom and Sundberg (1970); Baroni (1983); to ethnomusicological material, Herndon (1975); Cooper (1973); to functional-tonal musical language in general, Lehrdahl and Jackendoff (1983); Keiler (1981).

19. But for a beginning see Szabolcsi (1965); Maróthy (1974) contains a good deal of relevant pre-twentieth-century material.

20. This is also a good survey of recent literature in cognitive psychology on the subject of rhythm. On this general field, see also Fraisse (1982).

21. For a methodological outline of paralinguistic analysis, see Trager (1958). For applications to singing, see Trudgill (1983); Cogan (1984). For analogous studies of instrumental timbre, see Cogan (1984); Slawson (1985).

22. In some more recent theories (such as the later Barthes') the relationship is reversed; denotation is defined as the 'last' connotation, the 'preferred', 'imposed' or 'stereotyped' meaning through which the previously open process of meaning production is closed. But since this closure can never be absolute – the denotation can always give rise to further connotations – we should in fact think of a dialectic. Thus this does not invalidate the argument that connotation must be considered alongside denotation.

23. A not dissimilar conceptualization is Lucy Green's (1988) distinction between 'inherent meaning' and 'delineated meaning'.

24. For a study of quotation and parody in rock music, see Prato (1985). Reworking is of course one way of constructing or extending 'tune-families'; cf. pp. 136–9 above.
25. Two-Tone CHS TT17.
26. Though at rather shallower structural levels it may apply to (and differentiate) song-types within style-categories. A. Bennett (1986: 13–16) makes this argument in relation to music hall song.
27. On physical, motor, temporal and spatial symbolism, see Francès (1958: 307–36); Jiranek (1975: 28–30); Nattiez (1976: 147–57).
28. Examples of work drawing on semiotic method are contained in Laing (1969; 1985); Fiori (1987); Durant (1984). For a critique of content analysis of lyrics – and the 'realist' assumptions it is based on – see Frith (1987c: 78–85).
29. On *Diamond Life*, CBS Epic 26044.
30. On characteristic figures of various kinds (what he calls 'topos', 'tinta' and 'physiognomic sign'), see Noske (1977); on genre, see Fabbri (1982a; 1982b; 1982c); on popular music styles, see Grossberg (1984).
31. A literary example which might be used as a starting point is in Barthes (1975a).

7

'Lost in music'? Pleasure, value and ideology in popular music

The ideological field

As the previous chapter suggested, musical 'meaning' cannot be limited to translatable signification. In music we look not only for understanding but also enjoyment. Taking one style as an example, Simon Frith has concluded that after all else has been said, 'the essence of rock . . . is fun, a concept strangely neglected by sociologists' (and, we might add, by musicologists and semiologists); and fun, as he sees it, has to do with 'sensuality . . . grace . . . joy . . . energy . . . vigour . . . exhilaration' (Frith 1978: 206). By implication, two new terms enter the discussion here, most obviously *pleasure*, but – since pleasures are inextricably linked with judgements, and the euphoric exists only in comparison with its dysphoric opposite – also *value*. What does it mean to say that I like a song or a performance, and why do other people like different ones? Clearly such questions do not have disinterested answers; neither pleasure nor value can appear except through the operation of *ideology*. Their 'natural', 'innocent' and 'obvious' qualities, far from disproving this point, are precisely the mark of its truth, for their partiality and contingency have been repressed, in the interests of a false universality.

The ideological structuring of pleasure and value has both institutional and discursive supports. Even at the most general level – that of the distinction between 'popular' and 'high' practices and forms – these intermesh. As we have seen, Stefani's Model of Musical Competence reveals the existence of listening practices based on differing selections of code types, and these are associated particularly with 'high' and 'popular' competences. In given social situations, these modes of listening are attached disproportionately to particular kinds of music and audience groups, establishing both a hierarchy of value and the *kinds* of pleasure appropriate to each. As we know from the researches of Pierre Bourdieu (1968; 1980; Bourdieu and Passeron 1977)[1] and other sociologists of culture, the social organization of 'taste' in a society is a function of the overall 'force-field' through which the power relations of the society are expressed in cultural practice. Taste is 'one of the most vital stakes in the struggles fought in the field of the dominant class and the field of cultural production' (Bourdieu 1980: 225). Hence 'cultural capital' and economic capital are inextricably linked.

In the late nineteenth and early twentieth centuries, for example, British publishers' royalties on sheet music varied according to a judgement of its quality – popular songs got a lower rate than concert ballads – while classical works were subsidized by the profits on the popular product (see Peacock and Weir 1975: 3–4; Frith 1988a: 64–5, 69). English schools teaching singing from notated (that is, 'composed') music received a bigger government grant than those teaching by ear (see D. Russell 1987: 46). Similarly, the structuring of radio music channels today, the distinctions associated with the record companies' 'popular' and 'classical' divisions, the organization of advertising and image by genre and public taste, are all geared to a categorization and valuation of musical styles and audiences which are validated both ideologically and in terms of assumptions about class position and social mobility (see Barnard 1989; Green 1988: 28–31).

A considerable history lies behind such developments. The organization of cultural pleasures and values in terms of *distinction*, on the one hand, and the *consent* of those so distinguished to their apportioned pleasures, on the other, dates back – at least as it relates to the crucial restructuring of the debate about 'art' and the 'popular' which produced the recognizably modern cultural field – to that moment towards the end of the eighteenth and the beginning of the nineteenth centuries which saw the birth of modern aesthetics, of the commodification of leisure practices, and of explicit state interventions in the management of the people's cultural well-being. Thus brass bands were preferable to street ballads – especially if they played operatic transcriptions rather than popular tunes – and concert ballads or orchestral promenade concerts could be used to mark off a social divide between their audiences and that for music hall – which in any case became differentiated into various more 'respectable' or more 'vulgar' streams. The enjoyment of the highest 'art' music was reserved for those with sufficient education and free time, and the appropriate cultural competence (involving 'disinterested' contemplation).

Clearly such distinctions work (today as then) in a much more complex way than any simple high/popular (dominant/subordinate) dichotomy of musical languages and aesthetics can encompass; and they cannot be mapped easily on to any rigid ideological schema. They divide genres and styles – but also cross and interrelate them – and at times produce socially and aesthetically layered variants of a single genre (such as the waltz); they may even operate *within* genres, synthesizing divergent modes of enjoyment into new hybrids (like progressive rock) or sometimes bursting them open on the lines of their contradictions (as with punk). Certainly they play an important role in the general workings of hegemony. But as Colin Mercer points out, we inhabit an unevenly structured, *elaborated* culture. This culture has a 'density, complexity, and historical-semantic value that is so strong as to make politics possible . . . Gramsci's insight is to have recognised that subordination, fracturing, diffusion, reproducing, as much as producing, creating, forcing, guiding, are necessary aspects of elaboration' (Edward Said, quoted in Mercer 1986a: 51). The ideological work responsible for the social organization of musical taste is not the product of a simple, identifiable ideology, still less is it reducible to economic class forces; rather, it is the articulation and inflection of a multitude of lines of force, associated with different sites, audiences, media, production apparatuses and discourses, together creating the changing positions available to us on the map of pleasure.

Subjectivity and value

We do not, then, choose our musical tastes freely; nor do they reflect our 'experience' in any simple way. The involvement of subjects in particular musical pleasures has to be constructed; indeed, such construction is part and parcel of the production of subjectivity. In this process, subjects themselves – however 'decentred' – have a role to play (of recognition, assent, refusal, comparison, modification); but it is an *articulatory*, not a simplistically creative or responsive role. Subjects participate in an 'interpellative dialectic', and this takes specific forms in specific areas of cultural practice.[2]

Certainly it is clear that from the time in the late eighteenth and early nineteenth centuries when the modern musical field came into being, popular music has been centrally involved in the production and manipulation of subjectivity. From the first bourgeois domestic songs and concert ballads, the first music hall pieces, popular music has always been concerned, not so much with reflecting social reality, as with offering ways in which people could enjoy and valorize identities they yearned for or believed themselves to possess. Of course, much the same could be said of *all* music in this period. But one way of understanding the popular impulse in the field is as a tendency which foregrounds this function, while conversely the movement towards a high-art status always carries an attempt to absolutize or idealize subjectivity or otherwise 'distance' the work from the investments involved in identification.

The thrust of modernization – involving the breakdown of traditional frameworks of meaning, the growing crisis of traditional socializing institutions (family, church, school), the secularization and deritualization of life – has resulted in an increasing stress on the sphere of culture, and especially popular culture, as a primary site for the interpellation of subjects. Relatively early, as the process accelerated, an inevitable growth in intergenerational contradictions produced a 'youth question', and the identity problems of growing up became an obvious focus in the music market. The stress of most popular songs on 'story', 'character', 'feeling' and 'personality' is thus not surprising; nor is the evolution of the *star*, focus-point of identification for the listening subject. This takes place not only because of increasing division of labour, which throws the burden of performance onto specialists, but also because of certain aspects of the psychopathology of our society, which produce both individuals with the desire to act as representatives, focuses of identification, scapegoats, and so on, and mass audiences who need such individuals to offer them subject-positional opportunities for identity-confirmation, catharsis, wish-fulfilment, cannibalistic consumption or whatever. The star singer, so close and yet so impossibly far away, invitation to a life of unmatched intensity yet at the same time an institutionalized function in the ideological structure, is the most obvious transmission belt for the interpellative dialectic.[3]

The star is the focus of what we can call the *domain of identification*. But there is a partially overlapping but phenomenologically prior domain, that of *audibility*.

Colin Mercer has argued for the importance of 'conditions of legibility' in establishing the context in which popular literary and visual forms can have consensual effects.

> This does not mean just literary, visual capacities, recognition of generic forms and so on but also the institutional modes of their representation, the 'machinery' of techniques, the question of cultural, political and economic dispositions, the pre-established or formative powers of 'non-textual' categories such as entertainment, amusement, education, improvement (Mercer 1986b: 186).

Similarly, we can think of 'conditions of audibility' as governing the sites and moments of discursive consensuality in music, for

> in order to understand entertainment as a set of effective technologies concerned with the 'occupation of time' of the population . . . an 'occasion of reading' must be taken to be as real as any other social phenomenon. Occasions of viewing and listening must be construed in the same way: as invested with . . . technologies of deportment, response and inflection . . . (ibid: 184).[3]

Broadly, we can think of these technologies as organizing listening on four axes (each axis traversing economic, social, cultural and ideological structures, and moving between extremes of consensus and contradiction): (a) *the occasion* (appropriateness of environment, social function, political/moral assumptions, economic relationships, and so on); (b) the *disposition to attend* (to pay attention, to enter the space of the occasion); (c) the *recognition of codes* ('this is music'); (d) the *excitation of doxic presuppositions* ('this is appropriate music for the occasion and is doing appropriate, familiar things'). Just as the notion of an interpellative dialectic can be seen as a rewriting of the culturalist concept of 'experiential fit', so the idea of 'conditions of audibility' can be regarded as a rewriting of the social-historical and culturalist conception of *context* (reflected in, or conditioning, a text). Establishment of 'audibility' is thus a necessary precondition for the coming into operation of the signification processes discussed in the previous chapter.

The domain of audibility already implies the existence of participating subjects. But overlying and partly penetrating it is the domain of identification – or better, perhaps, of organismic involvement: for a variety of relationships between text and listening subject can be constructed here – all, however, having to do with the individual's investment and positioning in the music. Some of these relationships were discussed in Chapter 3 (pp. 93–8). We can now see, for example, that the 'three strategies' described there have definite implications for subject positioning. The auratic mode confirms identity, totality and continuity. The critical mode jerks us out of identity, fractures totality and continuity, through shock-effects and internal contradictions. The everyday mode absorbs us into a wider environment, in which the self becomes a distracted, mobile point of activity.

For the purposes of analysis, we can distinguish several factors in popular songs which bear on the construction of subjectivity. The way these are treated, and the way they are combined, will determine the mode of interpellation/listening (on this, see Frith 1987d: 140–4).

A first factor is *syntagmatic structure*: that is, the mode of time-awareness into which listeners are placed (for example, 'narrative', 'epic', or 'lyrical'). 'Narrative' structures, for example, tend towards a 'realistic' sense of temporal flow, governed by relations of tension and relaxation, disturbance and closure, and these usually work to confirm 'natural' feelings of temporal location. To quote Sean Cubitt (1984: 216), 'as diagesis, songs speak to or address us by organising a particular stretch of time into a conscious experience, and an experience of consciousness'. 'Epic' structures, by contrast, tend towards the obliteration of such experience, in a 'mythic' state of recurrence, 'emptying out' the subject. (Cf. pp. 216–17 above.)

A second way is through *emotion*: the invitation to feel. As a rule, the singer is the focus, and the twin prongs of the process work through sympathy/empathy, on the one hand, and reciprocity, on the other. Both are processes of identification, either with the position of the singer or that offered for a respondent or partner, and indeed this route usually is involved in confirming an actual, or constructing a desired, self-image for listeners.

A third factor is *character roles*, defined by social category (gender, class, and so on) and by personality type, with which listeners can identify. Again this is focused primarily on the singer; but it is also worked in the lyric structure (for example, in modes of address, or shifters: cf. pp. 167; 237–8 above), in the structure of musical 'voices', individual and collective (cf. pp. 238–9 above), and in overall musical style-connotations, both direct (via subcultural references, for instance) and intertextual (for example, the romanticized urban hustler or rebel figure in rock is linked to his appearance in Hollywood films; the warm ordinariness of a performer like Acker Bilk draws on the discourse of 'public bar conversation in the friendly English "local" '; Tommy Steele's 'cheek' refers not only to music hall antecedents but also to cockney stereotypes in film and in nineteenth-century literature).

A fourth factor is *bodily participation*: the invitation to map, trace, fill out, the patterns of movement offered by the rhythmic structure and texture (cf. pp. 226–7; 242–3). Consciously experienced representations of the body – its structure, capacities, desires, meanings – will usually be involved here, but the organismic structure thus mediated will provide input from other levels of activity too, resulting in a variety of different modes of subjectivity.

These descriptions have been written assuming a consistency of positioning within a given song; and this is generally the case in popular music. Even 'distractive' and 'epic' practices, while tending to dissolve fixed single perspective, usually maintain a given orientation within a performance: a consistent 'subject-set'. But it is possible for internal contradictions and shocks to arise. Dave Laing has discussed some of the ways in which this can happen (Laing 1985: Chapter 3, esp. 63–73, 76–81): through 'shock-effects' in lyric vocabulary, musical style or musical texture; through internal contradictions in modes of address; and through contradictions between the subject of the *énonciation* (the performance event, the principal subject of which is usually the singer) and the subject of the *énoncé* (the text: the subject here will be a protagonist in the lyric or a musical 'voice').

For most popular music, though, consistency is the key. And it becomes clear that, before there is any question of aesthetic or political value here, we are confronted by a prior level, that of *positional* values. Popular songs offer positions to subjects, who evaluate them in terms of their function as 'markers of social and individual difference' (N. Garnham, quoted in Laing 1985: 21). Of course, this is an established function for all cultural commodities. Bourgeois music genres have long had a role of identity management for their participants and audiences; behind the aesthetic of 'disinterestedness' lies the ideology of control – of self and world – which is central to the construction of the bourgeois ego. Popular music has developed an intricate variety of relationships between individuality and group norms, across the range of genres and styles. The quintessential ballad, for instance, constructs its listener as *special, unique* ('I love *you*') – but within an implicit and comforting awareness of the existence of thousands of other 'yous', suffering the same pangs, desires, frustrations. The typical rock 'n' roll song, by contrast, constructs a collective subject – but one which is only visible in a certain space: on the street, physically active, outside the realm of humdrum everyday life. The description of group positions is another way of writing the history of musical subcultures. But what is also important to remember is the role of 'mass positionality' – the positions created in Top Forty pop (and the mainstream dance band hits that went before).

The 'mass subject' is constructed serially more than simultaneously, in time as well as space – and is thus fragmentary – but, in Manfred Mann's words (quoted in Palmer 1970: 145), 'The more people buy a record, the more successful it is – not only commercially but artistically'. Far from the music's use-value being totally transformed into value in exchange – as the Adornian critique has it – there is thus a sense here in which its exchange-value functions as an aspect of its use-value. The greater its commercial success, the more the 'mass subject' is able to feel, in however reified a form, its potential power. Needless to say, such power cannot simply be read off from a calculation of quantity; and it is doubtful if 'mass positionality' exists in a pure state, rather than in dialectical interaction with other, narrower positionalities. Moreover, the politics of mass cultural practice hinge precisely on the qualitative relationships between position and response.

Positional values not only operate within the internal dynamics of groups, in a function of 'identity management'; they also work, and define themselves, through their mutual relations within the larger socio-musical field. Individual taste differences may seem the least important dimension of this, impossible to substantiate in a popular culture ruled by group norms; nevertheless, it is possible that the individual moment of reception – that is, the total matrix of positioning, in which the music finds its place within a specific organismic biography – is unique. Conflicts between subcultural positions, and between given subcultural values and those of the dominant culture, have been exhaustively discussed. At a higher level still, we can see the whole field as gripped by a dialectic between the legitimating ideology of elite art (analysed in detail by Bourdieu) and its analytically neglected antagonist, which proudly, desperately flaunts its pleasure in a part masochistic, part class-conscious, part utopian valorization of the banal, the everyday, the demotic. Intersecting and overlapping, these relations of position form an ideological cartography that feeds off but at the same time organizes the musical style-map at a given moment, the relative autonomy of the two levels making possible the dialectical movement of the relationship.

It would seem – at least at first sight – that positional values can only be assessed relative to the interests involved. There is no objective, fixed point of perspective from which they can be mapped and ranked. The same is true of the other categories of value that are found here. For example:

(a) Communicative values: does the music 'say something' and is this understandable, interesting or affecting, appropriate, relevant, adequate (to a supposed referent)? It is Jakobson's referential and emotive functions that are involved here, principally – though assessment will depend not only on what codes are deployed but also on listener competence and disposition.

(b) Ritual values: does the music perform its culturally prescribed task – for example, creating solidarity, dulling the awareness of everyday problems, constituting a special world (perhaps a liminal one, perhaps one of ecstasy, trance or 'heightened consciousness')? The phatic function is the leader here.

(c) Technical values: how skilfully is the music made, by reference to familiar codes, norms and standards? Virtuosity concerns the metalingual function more than the aesthetic one.

(d) Erotic values: does the music involve, energize, structure the body, its surfaces, muscles, gestures and desires? The conative function is closely involved, along with the referential (how is the body represented?).

(e) Political values: by which is meant explicit political content or orientation (*all* value categories being involved in less direct linkages to political interests and positions); this is a wide area,[5] but a basic distinction can be made between 'subjective' values, in which political content, references and symbols are mobilized to confirm or develop group identity and aims, and 'objective' values, in which they are put to the service of a critique of external or general positions and assumptions. 'Black power' references in soul music, and Rastafarian references in reggae, are examples of the first, and the phatic function is dominant here. Industrial disaster ballads and 1960s 'protest' songs are examples of the second and the referential and emotive functions are central.

But what is the basis for these kinds of valuation? To put it another way – and broaden the question – by what criteria can any musical values be legitimated, other than in terms of the participation of those involved? Is it just a case of 'doing your own thing'? If we regard ideology as all-pervasive rather than a removable veneer, then all guarantors of meaning, difference and position are suspect, any absolute is deceptive, any 'objectivity' at best provisional. Can we, then, justify any musical evaluation? Is any position preferable, any message more progressive than competing messages? Can we still assess music in terms of its 'adequacy' to the 'truth', and is there any point in the question whether it 'tells it like it is'? We recognize ourselves, our feelings, our bodies, our beliefs, our social positions, in popular songs; but are these simply interchangeable images in a gallery of optical illusions? If so, then perceived musical preferences cannot be treated as anything more than the result of either a trivial exercise of personal taste or the brute imperatives of power. The negotiation of hegemony turns into either a pluralistic free-for-all or a struggle between group interests based purely on conflicting motives and positions.

Conventionally, the possibility of a musical politics – as of any other politics – depends on whether it makes sense to talk about 'how things really are'; hence about how well particular musical practices measure up to this or help us to feel, understand or participate in it. In popular music, this has usually involved claims to emotional 'truth', cultural 'authority' or social 'emancipation'. But it seems less important to be able to prove the existence of objective reality than to recognize that people, in practice and in discourse, accept it, and to investigate how music offers diverse models with which to approximate or deal with it. Popular songs, no less than other cultural practices (and not just the natural sciences), produce 'orientations toward reality' – though these are linked to socially generated assumptions and conventions (coded at many levels, as we have seen). At the same time, music is – to use Wittgenstein's formulation – a 'language game' (one of many), governed by the particularities of its own rules of construction. The question, therefore, is less one of 'adequacy to' (a pre-existing reality) – this is always a circular argument and is usually dominant in periods of relative hegemonic stability[6] – than 'adequacy *as*' (a part of reality), productive of useful knowledge and effective practice. Since in complex societies there are many networks of knowledge and practice, linked to different cultural contexts, social functions, modes of agency and discursive position, there are many schemes of value, many ideological levels and types, and no single measure of 'truth' or 'progress'.

'Adequacy as' can only be assessed – or better, tested – in practice. Usefulness and effectivity relate to context – to conditions of audibility – in three particular senses. First, they are situation-dependent (thus dancing to a disco hit, listening at home to an extended album composition and drinking to a pub-band improvisation demand partly different criteria). Second, testing can only take place in relation to music which is (actually or notionally) *received*; in which, therefore, systems of pertinence and evaluation are actually applied; and to which responses are made (abstract texts have in themselves no value). Third, strategic considerations bear on value – that is, testing should take place in the light of the music's relationship to prevailing norms and power-structures in the music-political situation. Within this context, a few pragmatic tests may be suggested for trial.

(i)   *How many* positions, 'voices', identities are engaged in the musical practice in question? The more there are, the greater the possibility of comparison, hence critique.

(ii) Does the practice provoke *debate*?

(iii) Does it provoke *shock*, not necessarily of the new (it may insist on the old), but in relation to prevailing norms and self-images?

(iv) *How deep* is the potential or actual response? Here 'depth' is used not in the mystical sense of traditional aesthetics, but with reference to the engagement of structural levels, of competence levels in the codal hierarchy, and of 'organismic instances' (cognitive, affective, kinetic, and so on).

(v)   What is the music practice's *mobilizing power*? What amount and kind of activity is provoked?

(vi) To what extent does the practice engage a sense of *agency* (of the articulatory type described above)?

(vii) What is its *connective power* (with other discourses and practices)?

(viii) What order of *desire* is in play? Even if there are difficulties with evaluating and comparing different pleasures, positions, styles and structures, perhaps we can accuse some of a 'poverty of desire' (Mercer 1983) and evaluate others on this basis – rather than describing the music of Wham as 'worse', less 'authentic', more 'commercialized' and 'degraded', than that of Bruce Springsteen, some might say that it awakens fewer and shallower levels of desire. This takes us away from the sphere of an axiology and its politics into that of the internal economy of pleasure, the genesis and structure of which it is the task of psychoanalysis to explain.

It may seem that the music with the highest total score on these tests is to be attributed the highest value. In practice, context affects this judgement. Thus 'distracted listening' may appear to score relatively low on tests (ii), (iii), (iv) and possibly (vi) and (viii). But (under (iv)) a breadth of organismic involvement (even if at comparatively shallow levels of structure and coding), together with a high rating on (i) and (vii), and maybe (v) and (vi), may mean that, in the given conditions (the 'alienated' urban 'streetwalk', perhaps), this practice is the most appropriate and the best feasible.

All the tests may be seen as relating to a basic political strategy of *participation* – though participation can take many different forms, ranging from critique to appropriation, and can only be pragmatically assessed. But while such 'apprehensions of reality', such 'visions of totality', as may arise in the course of participation cannot be absolutely validated, they may actually be not devoid of substance. Pragmatically they relate to the extent to which individual values, and comparative valuations, seem to 'fit together' with others, generated within other cultural practices, to form a coherent whole. But behind this lies a deeper level responsive to processes of ontogenetic development and psychoanalytic structure. Just as a longing to penetrate beyond the 'burden of the sign' relates to a psychic memory of the pre-symbolic state when 'things' were 'themselves', so ideological 'misrecognition' – or better, partial adequacy – while inescapable, may carry an 'unconscious': the intuition of objective reality. Indeed, for Piaget (1971), these are linked, in his conception of a pre-linguistic stage, prior to the emergence of differentiation and representation, ruled instead by metaphor, equivalence and participation. Just as the symbolic order may on occasion be momentarily fractured, allowing a 'pathogenic' enjoyment of the signifier – a state which has been called *jouissance* (Barthes 1975c) – so ideologically structured valuations, as they are lived and worked against each other, may, in a shock of recognition, produce a oneness with 'things as they really are'.

We have seen that music, like myth, seems to have a privileged role in the revelation of such 'correspondences'. Of course, as the level of coding in question becomes more socially localized, more system-specific and hence semiotically more differentiated and conventionalized (as against anthropologically general), 'correspondences' become more limited, more partial, more historically particular. Still, the shock of recognition occurs. In the traditions of jazz, blues and rock music, the experience is commonplace: 'yes, that's how it is!', we say, in response to Chris McGregor, Bessie Smith, Dylan's 'Subterranean Homesick Blues', Otis Redding's 'Change Gonna Come', or whatever *you* choose. On top of whatever relatively general 'human' participation is involved, what is happening here can be expressed in terms of Frederic Jameson's notion of a 'political unconscious', the transposition of the great subjects and master narratives of history into an 'as if', 'their continuing but now *unconscious* effectivity . . . a way of "thinking about" and acting in our current situation' (Introduction to Lyotard 1984: xii). The whole structure of a 'memory of totality' can then sweep round, through its articulations in present uses, to refixings in the construction of utopian figures. We can learn from E.H. Carr that the disappearance of belief in absolute historical reference points does not thereby destroy objectivity. An objective understanding of the past – which is the present understanding its own formation – takes place in terms of a gradually evolving awareness of the future. 'Objectivity . . . does not and cannot rest on some fixed and immovable standard of judgement existing here and now, but only on a standard which is laid up in the future and is evolved as the course of history advances' (Carr 1964: 130). If it is in the present conjuncture hazardous to specify too closely what the course or even the grounds of this evolution might or should be, its 'memory structure' lies waiting, not entirely inactive, behind the presently more pervasive tactic of localized subversion and critique.

Thus, far from the impact of relativism leading to the end of politics in the sphere of cultural values, politics is all-pervasive there. But the question may be asked, what about *aesthetics*: the sphere of 'I like it' (with the focus on the 'it', for example, a tune or a chord-sequence)? Is this not an area of autonomous, interest-free values? After all positions, connections, correlations and correspondences have been accounted for, do we not find a residue of pure aesthetic quality? An elementary knowledge of the many struggles over aesthetic quality in the very home of 'aesthetics' – bourgeois music history – is enough to dispose of this argument. To this story, with its conflicts over Beethoven's 'maltreatment' of instrumental sound and texture, Wagner's harmony, Debussy's (lack of) melody, Stockhausen's 'noise', we can then add examples nearer to our subject here: ragtime's 'primitive' rhythms, the crooners' mortal blow to the art of *bel canto*, rock 'n' roll's lack of 'tune' and 'impoverished' harmony, punk's abuse of voice, instruments and eardrum, and so on. Clearly these conflicts were inextricably linked to *interests*, with moral, political and social ramifications.

I am not suggesting that the necessary sociological qualification of aesthetics – through analysis of conditions of production and consumption and through ideological critique – should be taken to reduce the aesthetic to the sociological as such. As Janet Wolff has cogently argued (Wolff 1983), to historicize the concepts and territory of 'aesthetics', and criticize its traditional universalizing claims, does not thereby destroy the specificity of 'the aesthetic' as a category of experience. Nevertheless, the aesthetic never appears in splendid isolation. The terms in which the aesthetic aspects of a popular song are felt and described will always be conditioned and mediated by other aspects. Thus a tune or a chord sequence may well have communicational, expressive, kinetic and positional values, and these will affect the form our 'liking' for it takes.

This approach to the aesthetic is derived from Prague School semiology, particularly the way Mukarovsky extends Jakobson's theory of communication functions. According to Mukarovsky (1977: xxii),

By function we understand an active relation between an object and the goal for which this object is used. The value then is the utility of this object for such a goal. The norm is the rule or set of rules which regulate the sphere of a particular kind or category of values.

For the non-aesthetic functions, the goal lies outside the object, but for the aesthetic function it is the object itself. All communicational activities – or as we might gloss this, all discursive, kinetic and perceptual interactions between ourselves and the world, human and non-human – are polyfunctional, so 'aesthetic' and 'practical' functions coexist in them all. Thus any such interaction (not just 'art') can be understood aesthetically. Whereas for the other functions value tends to be subordinated to norms, under the aesthetic function norms tend to be subordinate to value (or in other words, there is a situation of undercoding: at the extreme, the single object, experience or act offers itself as its own code; it is no longer a token but a type – it is itself).

The balance of functions varies, and the aesthetic function can be dominant, subordinate or even latent. Even the seemingly most overcoded ('banal', 'functional') popular song performance can be taken aesthetically, if predominant attention is paid to its unique features, that is, if the Op level (see p. 175 above) of coding is taken to be the pertinent one. But also, the overcoded norms themselves can be 'aestheticized', if they are regarded as a goal rather than a goal-vehicle. Criticisms of popular music for sacrificing aesthetic to commercial or functional values thus miss the point. Nevertheless, it is true that in high-culture practices a predominance of the aesthetic function is typical and the other functions blend into that, whereas in most popular culture practices the aesthetic function blends into the others. In discussing the 'genres' of 'popular melody' in similar terms – as a set of relatively autonomous but inseparable functions – Stefani refers to the aesthetic function here as precisely a 'surplus of music' (Stefani 1987a: 31): the tune's 'tunefulness' overflows its descriptive, expressive, kinetic and cultural functions. This, however, is comparatively rare. We can regard the general subservience of the aesthetic function in popular music – which explains why it is so often thought of as a non-aesthetic sphere – as an example of the 'politicization of the aesthetic' of which Benjamin spoke; at the same time, to the extent that this function is not so much subservient as *bound in* to the other functions, it is possible to see here, in a contradictory but complementary movement, a manifestation or harbinger of the aestheticization of the practical, the everyday, which brings to mind, through the action of forms however disabled and stunted, some of the characteristics of both Attali's phase of *composition* and Enzensberger's vision of a 'new ecology . . . a breaking down of environmental barriers . . . an aesthetic which is not limited to the sphere of "the artistic" ' (1976: 36–7).

The aesthetic may be defined as the hypothetically pure manifestation of our love-affair with what is really, physically, to hand (or eye or ear . . .), in our existence as social, structuring, symbol-making creatures. It is that aspect of our 'appropriation' of material reality (of the 'signifier') which, in a reversal of the semiotic norm, throws the weight of attention not on the *self*, its interests, concepts and goals, but on the object, the *other*, in all its materiality. It is, then, in the broadest sense *erotic*, and aesthetic pleasure refers to the *jouissance* resulting from the loss of self in this other. But 'practical' functions – social, emotive and cognitive interactions – have their material, even erotic roots, too, and if we acknowledge this, the basis of the intermingling of communication functions becomes clear, along with a possible route whereby the evolution of popular musical culture might help to raise this basis to a more conscious level of practice. One recalls Lefebvre's idea of music as the socializing of bodies. For Schafer (1980: 11), 'Hearing is a way of touching at a distance and the intimacy of the first sense is fused with sociability whenever people gather together to hear something special.'

Thus 'aesthetic' and 'communicational' aspects, the 'pathogenic' and 'logogenic', are inextricably mixed, and themselves mixed in with behavioural ones. But in post-Beethovenian bourgeois music the aesthetic was split off into an increasingly self-sufficient sphere, driven by sublimated energy; the tendency in popular music towards an eroticizing and 'quotidianizing' of the aesthetic may be a partial countermovement. Similarly, as Barthes points out (1977), the nineteenth-century decline of *musica practica* ('a muscular music . . . as though the body were hearing'; the possibility of 'giving oneself a place, as subject, in the scenario of the performance' (ibid: 149, 152)) is countered now only in self-made pop ('another public, another repertoire, another instrument (the young generation, vocal music, the guitar)') (ibid: 149).

There are, here, the beginnings of a basis for the formulation of a materialist approach to popular music aesthetics (see also Williams 1978; Fuller 1980). Whether or not, as has been argued, some aspects of signifying practices have their roots in certain 'relative constants' of human biological and psychological conditions, such an aesthetics could, at best, help us to find ways in which the pleasures of modern Western popular music might be located within more widespread patterns on a world-historical scale; at the very least, it might help to specify levels of relatively *longue durée* in the movement of social and cultural change to which particular enjoyments in popular musical practice correspond. It is, then, to some musical pleasures of the body that we turn.

Pleasures of the body

A widespread assumption has it that popular music has stayed especially close to 'the body' – compared to the art music of the European aristocracy and bourgeoisie – and that this intimacy has increased in the twentieth century, particularly since rock 'n' roll. Popular music, like popular culture in general, is seen as physically orientated (mentally impoverished): vulgar, spontaneous, participative, involuntary, visceral. Not surprisingly, there is less agreement over whether this is a good or a bad thing; and this divergence cannot easily be mapped on to the political spectrum: both Left and Right have their puritans and also their hedonists. There is disagreement, too, over how the connection should be conceptualized.

The most common position is the 'instinctualist' one. Here, libidinal energies are thought of as directly channelled into musical forms. Various authorities may be called upon, explicitly or implicitly, from Nietzsche through D.H. Lawrence and Reich to Marcuse; the most recent to be pressed into service are the French 'philosophers of desire', Deleuze (see Deleuze and Guattari 1984) and Lyotard (1984).

The connection between Deleuze's theory – which sees the human organism as a collection of 'desiring-machines' – and many countercultural ideas of the late 1960s is obvious; indeed, the two evolved at the same time (see Dews 1984). For many of the '68 generation, radical rock music was supposed to provide a direct route to the unconscious, a way to plug into libido. A similar vulgar Freudianism has haunted everyday popular music discourse since at least the early years of the century, colouring both the welcome given to new styles (they offered liberation from old taboos) and expressions of outrage (they released primitive instincts). Similar assumptions appear in the work of some scholars, too. Both Esman (1951) and Margolis (1954) account for the reception of early jazz by white Americans in terms of a 'return of the repressed': 'libido symbolisation' and 'regressive narcissistic gratification' (Margolis 1954: 288). Similarly, in his discussion of rock, Frith writes that

> whereas Western dance forms control body movements and sexuality itself with formal rhythms and innocuous tunes, black music expresses the body, hence sexuality, with a directly physical beat and an intense, emotional sound – the sound and beat are *felt* rather than interpreted via a set of conventions (Frith 1983a: 19).

Larry Grossberg sees rock musical practice as

> a music of bodily desire. There is an immediate material relation to the music and its movements. This relation, while true of music in general, is foregrounded in rock and roll . . . [and] . . . desire is at least conceptually independent of ideology (Grossberg 1984: 238, 239).

What is supposed to have happened is that, as someone once put it, 'the kids climbed back into their bodies' – as though these bodies, this *essence* of body, had been in store, waiting for this moment. A neglect of the *historical* body, its specific representations, culturally available shapes, desires and movements, and discursive positions, afflicts all instinctualist theories. It leads, too, to a naturalist view of musical form, in which drive-energy is directly correlated with sound-patterns, all conventions and ideology refused or treated as a superstructural veneer.

Some at least of these problems are avoided in a second common position, which draws on socialization theories. Actually, the same writers sometimes modify their instinctualism by carrying the argument in this direction. Here the relationship between music and 'the body' is seen as constructed in discourse in relation to given social roles operating in a specific historical conjuncture. Thus Esman and Margolis link the appeal of early jazz for young American whites to typical problems and processes of adolescence in that society. Because the music could easily be represented as different from the cultural norm; as a protest music; as associated with low-life, with sex and alcohol, and with a behaviourally less inhibited group (blacks); as formally less constrained (through improvisation, 'dirty' tone and so on); and as higher in kinetic symbolism than other music of the time: for these reasons it was possible for adolescents to find a position in the musical practice that they and others could define as rebellious and anti-puritan.

For obvious reasons, the socialization processes of adolescence are the usual subject of such theories. Frith and McRobbie (1978), in an influential study, focus on the construction of adolescent gender roles, which, for them, is an important part of the function of rock music. Sex-role stereotypes (where boys are seen as aggressive, dominating, group-orientated, phallocentric, and girls as passive, serious, romantic, privatist, domestic) are said to be articulated in the music in terms of two ideal types, to which all rock styles relate: 'cock rock' and 'teenybop'. Rock therefore 'operates as both a form of sexual expression and as a form of sexual control' (ibid: 5) – it reflects dominant characteristics of 'masculinity' and 'femininity', and excludes challenges to them. Heavy metal, for instance, is 'loud, rhythmically insistent, built round techniques of arousal and climax; the lyrics are assertive and arrogant' (ibid: 6). Conversely, teenybop is 'about being let down and stood up, about loneliness and frustration; . . . [it] is . . . less physical music than cock rock, drawing on older romantic conventions' (ibid: 7). Actual songs present a *range* of sexual images within this ideal-type polarity; but given the position adopted, these can only be interpreted and assessed in terms of their 'realism' and 'authenticity': do they acquiesce in dominant stereotypes or reveal contradictions relating to contradictions in society?

This, indeed, is part of the ground for Laing and Taylor's critique of Frith and McRobbie's study (Laing and Taylor 1979).[7] Without denying the relevance of 'social facts' – indeed, they stress the importance of conditions of listening as these affect interpretation – they argue that a proper attention to the relative autonomy of musical conventions would reveal the *variety* of gender-specific subject positions constructed *within* musical discourse, and of their relationships to other discourses, rather than insisting on music's representation of pre-existing social stereotypes. These positions belong to musical discourse, not (in any direct way) to generalizable social roles; thus, for example, the possible positions available to heavy metal listeners, male and female, are defined by musical, visual and theatrical structures of performances, and this gives rise to an endless stream of articulations of structures, as performers and listeners manipulate, play with, the conventions. Furthermore, genres cannot be *essentially* linked with any social category (for example, adolescents) nor with particular levels of sexual expression or repression, as these are thought to relate to any 'natural' reservoir of desire; 'what is at issue is not how much [sexuality] is revealed or expressed by a Frank Sinatra or a Thin Lizzy, but the radically different codes and conventions of representation involved in different genres' (ibid: 45–6), and it is impossible to believe that Billie Holiday is any less concerned with sexuality than is Jimi Hendrix.

Of course, what Laing and Taylor are proposing is a structuralist theory, and this in fact represents the third important position on the question of the relationship between popular music and 'the body'. A few other pieces of work have also pursued this route. Rosalind Coward (1984) has discussed the ways in which pop records are used within the divergent practices of disco and party, on the one hand, and daytime radio, on the other. The former are constructed as sites of transgression, offering opportunities for ritualized negotiations of desire, while the latter work to confirm the privatized nostalgia attending the domesticated sexual biography attributed to the 'housewife'. The work of Bradby (1985) and Bradby and Torode (1982; 1984), by contrast, focuses on musical texts, treating the interrelationships of song structures, rhythms and lyrics as constructing ways in which, positions from which, adolescent boys and girls can learn to address each other. Obviously, these positions relate to gender roles in the 'real world', but via the mediation of interdiscursive encounters, which of course open the possibility of negotiation and rearticulation of position.

In their article, Laing and Taylor draw on Barthes' notion of the 'grain of the voice'. Barthes' theory of musical pleasures has proved the most influential pointer to ways of setting these within a semiological (rather than instinctualist or sociological) account. His essay on vocal 'grain' (Barthes 1977: 179–89) links a typology of pleasure to a theory of semiosis based on a distinction between signification, on the one hand, and what he calls *signifiance*, on the other. This distinction may be considered analogous to the contrast Lefèbvre draws between 'logogenic semantics' and 'pathogenic desire', when the power of 'meaning' is broken; and it calls to mind again the haunting suspicion that behind the curtain of meaning stands the possibility of a window onto a state when 'things' might be 'themselves'. Indeed, in this sense the aesthetic mode as such could be regarded as a formalization, a systemic approximation, of the 'anarchy' of such a state: a culturally legitimated glimpse of a forbidden ecology.

For Barthes, *signifiance* arises 'when the text is read (or written) as a moving play of signifiers, without any possible references to one or some fixed signifieds' (ibid: 10). In this (erotic) process, the subject is deconstructed ('lost'), overwhelmed by the pleasures of *jouissance*. While signification covers all the processes related to communication (meaning, expression, subjectivity), *signifiance* in song concerns the 'grain' of the voice, 'where the melody really works at the language – not at what it says, but the voluptuousness of its sounds-signifiers . . . The "grain" is . . . the materiality of the body speaking its mother tongue' (ibid: 182), the physical voluptuousness of the work of tongue, larynx, muscles, teeth, the inner cavities of mouth, throat and lungs; it 'is the body in the voice as it sings, the hand as it writes, the limb as it performs' (ibid: 188).

Barthes analyses the relationship of signification and *signifiance* in terms of a contrast he draws between the singing of Dietrich Fischer-Dieskau (expressive, communicationally explicit, univocal) and that of the Swiss singer, celebrated between the wars, Charles Panzéra (the 'materiality' of his vowels, 'voices within the voice', escape from the 'tyranny of meaning'). Implicitly, here, Barthes is contrasting pleasure as *jouissance* with his conception of *plaisir*. For Barthes, *plaisir* is 'a pleasure . . . linked to cultural enjoyment and identity, to the cultural enjoyment of identity, to a homogenising movement of the ego' (ibid: 9). It is associated with the smooth movement between signifier and signified, subject and object, and acts to confirm the system of cultural conventions, the positions for subjects fixed within the system, and the pleasures felt in identity with those positions. *Plaisir* results, then, from the operation of the structures of signification through which the subject knows himself or herself; *jouissance* fractures these structures.

One obvious general point can be made: that popular music is overwhelmingly a 'voice music'. The pleasure of singing, of hearing singers, is central to it. In his discussion of popular approaches to melody, Gino Stefani even distinguishes between speech and song on this basis.

A singing voice corresponds to the principle of pleasure, as a talking voice does to the principle of reality . . . why? First, because of the conditions of production: a pitched voice requires relaxation of the muscles involved in phonation, and this implies a state of quiet, peace and *tenderness* in the person. A singing voice is therefore a love voice. Secondly, pleasure is also to be found in perception: not only because of the transmission of this state of ease through the voice, but more radically because such a type of voicing requires less effort to listen to; in fact, singing is an easier message for the brain to decode than is speaking (Stefani 1987a: 23–4).

It is easier, says Stefani – drawing on psychophonetic research – because of the higher degree of *organization* (regularity, predictability, continuity) in the singing compared to the speaking voice.

Just as the line of speech, filled with articulations by consonants, is similar to the movement of walking, so the line of vocal melody, being continuous, flowing, relaxed and free from resistance, is similar to the movement of flying. Flying and dreaming: the longing to escape, the pleasure of escape from harsh reality . . . musical melody becomes a symbol of the same profound things involved in the flying-dream (ibid: 24).

The tendency to regularity in music *as such* is by now familiar to us; periodicity, repetition and redundancy are basic to its semiology (though Stefani's bifurcation is rather too rigid: there is singing (and 'escape') in speech and there is meaning ('reality') in singing; in both, there is a constant interplay of 'grain' and 'sense'). We must return to this point later, in the context of the possible contribution of regularity to the economy of musical pleasures. What needs noting here is not only the melodic (musical) side of singing but also the *vocal* side: the *voice*, in its commonly understood significance as the profoundest mark of the human. An unsounding human body is a rupture in the sensuousness of existence. Undoubtedly this is because vocalizing is the most intimate, flexible and complex mode of articulation of the body, and also is closely connected with the breath (continuity of life; periodicity of organic processes). Significantly, technological distortion of voice-sounds (through use of a vocoder, for example) is far more disturbing than similar treatment of instrumental playing (which is regarded usually as a logical extension of manual performance). We can thus agree with Fiori (1987) that, in the context of a widespread 'dehumanization' apparent in bourgeois art, the centrality of the voice in popular music – attesting to the presence of a human body – is a mark of a certain 'humanizing' project.

Recognizing the erotic importance of the voice helps to avoid a misleading overemphasis on instrumental rhythm as the sole or predominant locus of musical sexuality; at the same time it reinforces the point that the ranking of genres and styles in terms of erotic quanta is equally misleading: what is important, rather, is the *forms* in which desires are revealed and pleasures made available.

Nevertheless, as Barthes' analysis makes clear, some performers – some performances – lend themselves more readily to *signifiant* (as against significatory) workings than others: one level is felt to predominate over the other. This may be one important way of distinguishing the effects of, say, Elvis Presley and his contemporary, Pat Boone. Presley's singing, as we saw in Chapter 1, *disrupts* language through a vivid staging of the vocal body, while Boone, marketed as a 'safe' alternative, offers unequivocal meaning in which words, melody and tone fuse into a predictable structure. (The same distinction can apply *within* a single singer's repertoire – for instance, marking the difference between Presley's 'Heartbreak Hotel' and 'Love Me Tender'.) Notice that this is not the same explanation as the usual one – that Boone 'cleaned up' Presley by exorcizing sex; there seems little doubt that Boone's fans heard him as 'sexy'. The difference lies rather in the *way* 'sex' is channelled. To an unusual degree, Presley offered an individual body, unique, untranslatable, outside the familiar cultural framework, exciting and dangerous; in Boone we hear a generalized image, the energy *bound*, tied into the conventional thoughts and sentiments provoked by the words and the intonational rhetoric – safe because explicit and unambiguous.

However, there is no clear division between the two performers – Presley's singing, for example, carries meanings as well as 'grain', and this is in fact why in some performances it could move across into a position close to that occupied by Boone. Thus, *any* singing can be analysed this way – even if, so far, the tools of analysis are largely lacking: most attempts (even Barthes') tend to relapse into descriptive accounts of subjective reactions.

It seems likely that in any singing the two semiotic modes will interact and perhaps even conflict. Laing has discussed how some of Johnny Rotten's vocals for the Sex Pistols can be interpreted differently according to whether meaning or 'grain' is felt to be dominant; and he adds that this creates problems for subcultures for it is impossible to guarantee that intended meaning and the *plaisir* of identification with it will not be subverted by a different pleasure, the *jouissance* associated with response to the 'voluptuousness of [the] . . . sound-signifiers' (Laing 1985: 55–6). Listeners can also enjoy performances with which they are ideologically out of sympathy. The fact that many Mick Jagger performances are heard as expressing misogyny, brutality and narcissism, in words and singing, and yet at the same time are enjoyed by listeners who disapprove of this message, *can* be explained in terms of a divergence between *énonciation* (Jagger as youth-hero, charismatic performer, and symbol of rebellion), and *énoncé* (Jagger as the subject of the sung lyric) (see ibid: 63–5); but a different explanation would identify two *pleasures*, one in the 'grain' of Jagger's voice (and of the musical performance in general), the other (which for some may be – perhaps in part – a *dis*pleasure) in the various layers of the message.

Similarly, the reactionary meanings often associated with the lyrics, melodic types and singing styles of many country and western songs could be understood as only one side of their semiotic work. Frith and McRobbie explain their pleasure in Tammy Wynette's 'Stand By Your Man', in spite of its submission to patriarchal ideology, with reference to the 'authenticity' of her performance: its 'country strength and confidence' (Frith and McRobbie 1978: 4). It is difficult to know how and where to locate this quality, however, except in the ideology of authenticity itself, and a far more plausible explanation is the 'grain' of Wynette's voice. When I hear Jimmie Rodgers' 'Daddy and Home', Merle Travis's 'I Am A Pilgrim' or Tennessee Ernie Ford's 'Sixteen Tons', I have to force myself to foreground the sentimentality of the first, the reactionary religious fundamentalism of the second, the gimmicks and self-pitying macho quality of the third (all of which I dislike); my attention is drawn first to three male voices, working at sound quality, movement and articulation – I *know* them, their vowels, consonants, facial resonances, falsettos and all. To some extent, what for generations of bourgeois fans of singing (especially opera-goers) was thought of as 'vocal quality' (a 'thrilling' voice, quite apart from its employment in specific musical texts) has been carried over into popular song, the admixture of 'spirituality' ('pure beauty') sloughed off to reveal the material basis of the erotic vocal body.

Nevertheless, as we have seen earlier, there is a strong tendency for vocals to act as a unifying focus within the song. The continuity and diagetic function of almost all vocal melody draw us along the linear thread of the song's syntagmatic structure, producing a 'point of perspective' from which the otherwise disparate parts of the musical texture can be placed within a coherent 'image'; even dancers, Cubitt points out (1984: 211–12), will sing along with the vocal, making it theirs, identifying with its position, message, feelings. To the extent that the voice is taken to represent a 'personality' (a unified subject, body and soul) it is more difficult for it to subvert the 'tyranny of meaning' than it is for many instrumental parts, suggesting as these do the heterogeneous functions of varied body movements (fingers, arms, feet, and so on). Despite the conflicts and possibilities of disruption, therefore, it is most common for vocal 'grain' to remain a constant but veiled underside of the syntagmatic and semantic flow. However, it is not impossible for the voice to be situated as a *constituent* of the performance rather than as a focus. In this case it acts less as a centre than as a part of the overall bodily-textural set.

If the presence of a voice is taken as a mark of the human, it is a question here of what *species* of 'humanity' is involved, a (disembodied or suprabodily) 'person' or a particular channelling of psychic-somatic processes. One of the importances of the Afro-American tradition lies in the fact that often the voice seems to be treated more as an 'instrument' (the body using its own resources to make sound) than as a soul borne on wings of song. From work-song grunts through 1930s jazz styles (Louis Armstrong singing 'like a trumpet'; Billie Holiday 'like a sax') to the short, mobile vocal phrases of funk and scratch textures (used like percussion, bass or synthesizer), we hear vocal 'personality' receding as the voice is integrated into the processes of the articulating body. Of course, at the same time, instruments in this tradition often sound like voices. But the often noted importance of 'vocalized tone' is only part of a wider development in which 'instrumental' and 'vocal' modes meet on some intermediate ground: while it is true that the instrument-as-machine (technological extension of the body) becomes a gesturing body (the 'voice' of the limb), at the same time the voice-as-a-person becomes a vocal body (the body vocalizing).

What is foregrounded here is the central role in Afro-American music of performance, for it is in performance that the ideality of vocal melody is realized through quite specific corporeal tactics, while 'logical' (that is, system-referenced) instrumental patterns are localized through equally specific, quasi-vocal articulations of the performer's body. If within bourgeois art music the pleasures of *musica practica* have generally declined, their strength within Afro-American culture has proposed for the voice in popular music a place continuously at odds with its centrality for the significatory function – a place within the erotic, sound-producing body.

Barthes himself has applied his theory to instrumental music. In a study of Schumann's collection of short, rhapsodic piano pieces, *Kreisleriana*, he again writes of two texts, one coded, the other 'distracted' (Barthes 1975b). The two are intertwined, and interpretation is a matter of extracting from beneath the stifling grip of the first the 'paragrammatic' structure articulated by the second. This is an act both of ideological critique (the signification system is a 'veil', an 'illusion', 'designed to articulate the body, not according to its own rhythm (its own dissections), but according to a known organisation which removes from the subject all possibility of delirium' (ibid: 225)) and of re-production (the listener 'executes' the body's rhythms with the performer).

Barthes' own response to the music, however, is offputtingly one-sided:

> I hear no note, no theme, no design, no grammar, no meaning, nothing that would permit me to constitute a certain intelligible structure of the work. No, what I hear is beats: I hear that which beats in the body, that which beats the body, or better: that body which beats (ibid: 217).

As this suggests, his analysis is wholly rhythmic, neglecting melodic and timbral elements which might be thought to be associated with the diverse resonances, neural tensions and kinetic interrelationships of limbs and body cavities. This is so even though Barthes recognizes not only the variety of gestural acts and corporeal-affective states with which his 'figures of the body' (or 'somathemes' as he also calls them) may be associated but even takes them so far as to include the voice. In music, he writes, the body

> speaks, it declaims, it redoubles its voice: *it speaks but says nothing*: because as soon as it is musical, speech – or its instrumental substitute – is no longer linguistic, but corporeal; it only says, and nothing else: *my body is put into a state of speech: quasi parlando* (ibid: 222).

Despite its debilitating overemphases (can the singing voice not also communicate meaning? are all significations in music no more than a mystifying 'veil'?), this is a helpful theorization of the dialectical relationship between the vocal body and the non-vocal areas of somathemic generation. Furthermore, Barthes goes on to suggest a formulation for the way this body-set gets into music. Unlike verbal language, where referents are unimportant compared to networks of signifieds, music, he argues, privileges the reference function; and its referent is the body. 'The body passes into music through no other relay than the *signifiant*. This passage – that transgression – makes of music a madness' (ibid: 225).

One may doubt if 'reference' is the best word for this process, but if we think of Barthes as talking about the area discussed earlier in terms of 'correspondences' between parallel, introversively working structures (musical and corporeal), we begin to see a way in which *signifiance* can be integrated into the basic semiotic economy of music – that economy which John Blacking's thoughts on the role of the body brought into view. Barthes is writing of an extreme; but anyone who has participated actively or vicariously in intensely 'executed' performance – who has felt the polyrhythmic interplay of hands in boogie-woogie piano, resonated with the intricacies of a bluegrass texture, played along with a B.B. King guitar solo or the bass-line in Billy Ocean's 'When the Going Gets Tough' – will recognize what he is pointing towards. At this extreme, we would indeed find 'a second semiology, that of the body in a state of music' (ibid: 228).

However, this body does not exist in any unqualified sense – only in the historical forms constructed by particular uses, representations, discourses. Barthes does not give this point enough weight, preferring vague subjective responses; and this is linked to a second point of criticism, the fact that, though he lays a theoretic stress on the interplay of signification and *signifiance*, this is insufficiently maintained in his discussion of the practices themselves. Since human beings are condemned to meaning, there is no permanent escape into *jouissance*; rather, the 'grain' of the musical body is the permanent other side of *plaisir*. To put this another way: *jouissance* is not abstract; its nature varies in relation to the positioning of the semiotically constructed subject who is 'lost'. The body – the 'real' body – cannot actually be grasped in music but only by the *hands*; in music, it is necessarily represented, positioned, analogized, (its movements) traced. There is an absence as well as a presence, and the body in a state of music is not the same as – and must coexist with – the music in a state of psychic-somatic cathexis.

There is certainly plentiful evidence that the pleasures of the musical body are inseparable from their historical construction (see Mercer 1986a: 49–50; Durant 1984: 86–98). We have only to think of the diverse erotic charges associated, in particular moments and contexts, with operatic *bel canto*, with the vocal tactics of Marie Lloyd's 'little bit of what you fancy', with the new intimacy of the crooner's voice, with Johnny Ray's histrionics or the puppy-love charm of teenybopper stars, to realize that singing mobilizes desire in many, quite specific ways. Similarly, virtually every new dance – from the sixteenth-century sarabande, through waltz, can-can, black bottom and the rest, to disco – has been associated with gestural and musical excitements given meaning by distinct, and at the time new, notions of corporeal movement, sexual expression and social relationship. We can, with Dyer (1979), reasonably think of disco (music and dance) as favouring a less phallocentric, more 'whole body' eroticism than mainstream rock; but only because the divergent social constituencies of these styles were able to locate their differing rhythmic textures within different practices and discourses of pleasure and gender.

There is thus no 'pre-historical' libidinal body, and this is why, for example, the rhythms of early jazz could be received by whites as both 'primitive' (instinctually liberating) and 'modern' (nervous, mechanical); why boogie-woogie has been associated with both low-life sexual libertinage and the industrial rape represented by railway rhythms, carrying black American bodies to factory slavery; why the rhythm of 'modern times' encapsulated in the whole cultural complex formed around ragtime, blues, jazz and Tin Pan Alley is not only that of twentieth-century, urban post-Puritan leisure but also that of the capitalist disciplines of Taylorism and its cultural spin-offs (see Ostendorf n.d.: 21).

There appears here a third point of criticism of Barthes' theory. Like other French post-structuralists who wanted to ground discourse on extralinguistic forces and dispositions, the later Barthes is open to the suspicion that 'anything goes': that along with meaning, the category of critique itself is abandoned, leaving the field to political quietism, untheorized spontaneism, or apolitical hedonism. This danger may be attributed precisely to the relative neglect of historically positioned structures of meaning. So, just as the 'anarchism' of this whole current of thought has laid itself open to infiltration by New Right 'libertarianism', so some musical forms have been narcissistically enjoyed quite in isolation from any question of their perhaps reactionary meaning. To avoid this kind of onesidedness, we need to attend not only to the pleasures of the body but also to those of the text.

Pleasures of the text

Admittedly, in his article on Schumann's *Kreisleriana* Barthes is writing about texts. Moreover, he devoted a whole book to the subject of the 'pleasure of the text' (Barthes 1975c). Nevertheless, in both cases his major project is to discover the body behind the text, not to offer or confirm a reading but to reproduce the gestural shape of its production. In a sense, then, he aims to turn the text into a performance, and so it is not surprising that most Barthesian approaches to music have concentrated on the pleasures of performance – particularly singing – rather than those of text: the transitory moment, the isolated signifier, is privileged against the syntagmatic structure. But this is an untenable distinction. On the level of semiology, musical syntaxes are not formal abstractions but, as Lefebvre reminds us, structures of relationships set up by and in physical bodies, the source of pathogenic as well as logogenic processes. Similarly, as we saw earlier, any firm distinction between 'linguistic' and 'supralinguistic' spheres cannot hold. On the level of the pleasure economy, it has become clear that we must regard signification and *signifiance* as inextricably intermingled.

Theories of musical pleasure need to keep in mind not only this intermingling but also the possibility of a *jouissance* as well as a *plaisir* of the text (of the signifying structures). We have already observed how *signifiance* may be related to the introversive tendency of musical signification as such, and hence to music's aesthetic function; and this connects it with that whole apparatus within musical semiosis which is governed by processes of 'correspondence', metaphor, and a prelinguistic iconicism. To the extent that the 'pole of equivalence' is privileged in music, we can think of musical structure itself as being located at a semiotic level prior to the development of 'rational', semantic communication. Barthes' tendency, on the other hand, is to associate *jouissance* not with structure but with fracture. In his view, the predictability of coded syntagmatic relationships, with their drive towards self-repetition, can do no more than confirm an established cultural system, and with it the identity and position of individual subjects; the effect is one of a comfortable and comforting *plaisir*, and this can only be broken by shock and dissolution. How can both these approaches be valid?

In attempting an answer to this question, a good focus would be on *repetition*. The 'tendency' of musical syntax generally towards repetition assumes a relatively high profile in most popular music; it forms, here, the essential context for assessment of value and pleasure, and at the same time is related to a variety of determinants, economic and social as well as semiological. For that very reason, however, consideration of repetition in popular music should be placed within this wider setting, which is marked by pronounced ideological conflict.

'It's monotonous'; 'it's all the same'; 'it's predictable': such 'popular common-sense' criticisms of popular music have probably filtered down from the discussions of mass culture theorists. From this point of view, repetition (within a song) can be assimilated to the same category as what Adorno termed 'standardization' (as between songs). Of course, the significance of the role played by such techniques in the operations of the music industry – their efficacy in helping to define and hold markets, to channel types of consumption, to pre-form response and to make listening easy – can hardly be denied; but as we saw earlier in this book, it is equally difficult to reduce the function of repetition simply to an analysis of the political economy of popular music production and its ideological effects. Despite Adorno's critical assault, the question of repetition refuses to go away.[8] Why *do* listeners find interest and pleasure in hearing the same thing over again, and what kind of interest and pleasure are they? To be able to answer these questions, which have troubled not only mass cultural theory but also traditional philosophical aesthetics and psychoanalysis, would tell us an enormous amount about the nature of popular music, and hence about music in general.

Common-sense criticisms of the prevalence of repetition in popular music usually derive from a specific analytical error: a particular conventionalized proportion of repetition to non-repetition is naturalized; most popular music is then said to transgress this norm. But there is no universal norm or convention here. *All* music contains repetition – but in differing amounts and of an enormous variety of types. We need to see the extent and nature of repetition in a given music as produced by and located at the point where several sets of determinations intersect: the political economy of production; the 'psychic economy' of individuals; the musico-technological media of production and reproduction (oral, written, electric); and the weight of the syntactic conventions of music-historical traditions.

Adorno saw the enjoyment of repetition as psychotic and infantile (Adorno 1973: 160ff; esp. 178–81), and this coloured his whole attitude to what he considered the pseudo-primitivism of Afro-American-derived popular music forms. Commonplace dismissals of repetitive effects in pop music as 'childish', 'primitive' or 'hysterical' clearly have the same roots. But behind the vulgar self-preservation of the virtuously civilized lies something which we can hang on to: Adorno's recognition that repetition has to do with the operation of the primary processes of the psyche. This is something we must return to. The importance of repetition in Afro-American musics hardly needs further comment by now; but before we can understand the significance of this, and of the *kind* of repetition involved, some consideration of repetition types is required.

Given the model of a syntagmatic continuum proposed earlier (pp. 214–17), it is clear that many possibilities exist for a particular music, in terms both of its location on the equivalence/difference spectrum and of its preferred route (analogue or digital). Moreover, since music is a multiple-parameter system and, almost always, a multiple-layer system (melody, bass, accompaniment, riffs, rhythm section, backing vocals, call and response, and so on), particular musical systems do not sit neatly at one particular point on the spectrum. Rather, different syntactic processes are mixed up together; and, in the mixing, they do not remain wholly themselves: they are articulated together, each mediating the other (thus, a binary switch chord-oscillation – say, a tonic-subdominant riff – can be 'worked into' a melody digitally organized as to pitch relationships (major scale, let us say), the whole being given a gradual (analogue-based) crescendo). Further, since music is a temporal system, different syntactic processes can operate simultaneously on different structural levels (thus, a digitally organized set of notes can, at the next level up, be subjected to repetition, forming a riff, and, at the next level, this whole riff-based section can be juxtaposed with different music, say, a 'middle eight', to form a binary switch).

Within a particular musical system, or individual song, the existence, role and nature of repetition is a major distinguishing tool for analysis, helping to indicate synchronically existing differences, in relation to other systems and songs, and also helping to mark out historical changes in musical styles. The significance of repetition is closely bound up with its role in the total syntactic structure, that is, first, with the nature of what is repeated, and second, with the relationship of the repetition to the other processes that are present (how dominant it is, its place in the texture, whether it is linked into the operation of another technique: thus, for example, a repeated unit can be worked into a relatively highly differentiated 'narrative' flow through the device of sequence).

The variety of ways in which repetition can be used is potentially infinite. We can, however, distinguish certain basic models. Recalling the three 'ideal' syntagmatic categories described earlier – 'narrative', 'epic' and 'lyrical' – one can consider the two types that predominate in nineteenth- and twentieth-century popular music – 'narrative-lyric' and 'epic-lyric' – as marked by contrasting modes of repetition, which I shall call *discursive* and *musematic*, respectively.

Musematic repetition is, of course, the repetition of musemes; the most immediately familiar examples – riffs – are found in Afro-American musics and in rock. Discursive repetition is the repetition of longer units, at the level of the phrase, the sentence or even the complete section. The effects of the two types are usually very different, largely because the units differ widely in the amount of information and the amount of self-contained 'sense' they contain, and in their degree of involvement with other syntactic processes. Moreover, musematic repetition is far more likely to be prolonged and unvaried, discursive repetition to be mixed in with contrasting units of various types (as in the AABA structure of the classic Tin Pan Alley ballad form). The former, therefore, tends towards a one-levelled structural effect, the latter to a hierarchically ordered discourse. Musematically recursive frameworks are often combined with a 'surface' characterized by complex, minutely inflected (that is, analogue-tending), perhaps improvised variation; while discursive processes tend to result in 'developmental' structures, most strikingly worked out in the European art tradition, in which the underlying form is often a 'one-off' while the 'surface' is in many ways relatively crude and impoverished.

The modes of repetition outlined here are often correlated with oral (or electric) and literate modes of composition, respectively. However, as we found in Chapter 3, it would be better to see them not as crudely technologically determined but as actively summoned into development and strongly mediated by the needs of distinct socio-economic configurations. The principles of musematic repetition and recursive structures are certainly suited to the methods of oral composition (because of the limits of human memory and the usefulness of a 'given', one-levelled framework); similarly, discursive repetition and hierarchically organized structures can be more easily worked out on paper. But there are plenty of examples of discursive repetition in orally created music and of musematic repetition in written pieces. Considered as social-historical categories, musematic repetition can be related to the 'collective variative' forms typical of pre-capitalist societies (in which 'individualisation comes about through a continuous approach to the typical . . . a short item . . . [reaching] full expression through countless repetitions and variations' (Maróthy 1974: 18)), while discursive repetition is strongly linked with the rise of the 'bourgeois solo song', appearing in the Middle Ages and reaching its maturity in the eighteenth and nineteenth centuries (see ibid: 17–22). It is important to stress again that these two types are historically not *entirely* mutually exclusive; indeed, they interact to form a variety of sub-types – hence the emergence of the 'narrative-lyric' and 'epic-lyric' types.

Repetition in Afro-American musics is most often musematic (riffs; call-and-response structures; short, unchanging rhythmic patterns). Even when one aspect evolves in a mildly 'developmental' way, such as the chord sequence of twelve-bar blues, there is often a substratum of riffs and other repetitive devices, and in blues the phrase structure is simple in the extreme, organized in binary parallelisms and antiphonies rather than hierarchical patterns (see Oliver 1982a; 1982b). By contrast, European popular song forms (before Afro-American influence) mostly use discursive repetition. Usually this is worked into hierarchical structures marked by a use of phrase-contrast and -development, by a stress on symmetry (open/closed and binary melodic types, with a sense of 'narrative closure'), and by 'narrative' harmonic sequences. Actual examples are likely to be 'compromises'. Nevertheless, if we look at typical songs from three historically differentiated repertories (nineteenth-century British popular song; Tin Pan Alley song; rhythm and blues, and rock music), we shall discover not only some of the important sub-types together with some interactions between them but also an overall process of change.

In music hall song, repetition is usually discursive – at the level of the phrase. It can be both immediate (Ex. 7.1), delayed (Ex. 7.2), or the two can be combined (Ex. 7.3). Quite often the repeated phrase is slightly altered for harmonic reasons (Ex. 7.4). As a rule, varied repetition, when it occurs, does not play off a relationship between recursive framework and variative detail (as is the case in a great deal of musematically organized music); rather it tends to approach either the technique of sequence (that is, it is provoked by a need to fit changing harmonies rather than by an interest in variation itself: see Ex. 7.5), or the technique of 'phrase *structure* repetition'. In the latter, the surface details change but there is a kind of 'parallelism' or 'analogical repetition' between phrases on the level of harmonic-rhythmic structure and basic melodic shape (often governed by circle-of-fifths relationships in the chord progressions) (Ex. 7.6). Maróthy has identified this type of symmetrical parallelism, or repetition by analogy, as a prime characteristic of bourgeois song as a whole (Maróthy 1974: 11–127).

Perhaps the most typical repetition technique in music hall song is that of sequence – typical because it is at the same time repetitive and non-repetitive: the unit of repetition is *worked into* a larger unit of 'narrative' flow or lyrical

Henry Clay Work, 'Come Home Father'

Ex. 7.1

Alfred Lee, 'The Man On The Flying Trapeze'

Ex. 7.2

George Le Brunn, 'Twiggy Voo'

A

Twig - gy voo, my boys, *twig - gy voo?* Well of

course it stands to rea - son that you do; All the

B   B

force and mean - ing in it you can 'tum - ble' in a min - ute, *Twig - gy*

A

voo, my boys, *twig - gy voo?*

Ex. 7.3

Charles Graham, 'Two Little Girls In Blue'

Two   lit - tle   girls   in   blue,   lad,
Harmony: G

two   lit - tle   girls   in   blue ____
(G)   C

Ex. 7.4

symmetry. The technique, clear in 'Champagne Charlie' (Ex. 7.7), had not changed some 40 years later in 'Let's All Go Down The Strand' (Ex. 7.8). Even when shorter units – approaching musemes – are repeated in music hall song, they are almost always drawn out into a longer line through sequence (Ex. 7.9). In bourgeois song in general, sequence is a way of holding on to at least some of the power of repetition while, as it were, *cutting it down* to size, and *stitching it into* other structural processes. Sequence *composes* time (rather than marking time or

Fred E. Leigh, 'Put On Your Tat-ta Little Girlie'

Ex. 7.5

Joseph Tabrar, 'Ting, Ting, That's How The Bell Goes'

Ex. 7.6

Alfred Lee, 'Champagne Charlie'

Cham - pagne Char - lie is my name,

Cham - pagne Char - lie is my name,   Good for a - ny game at

night, my boys,   good for a - ny game at night, my boys.

Ex. 7.7

Harry Castling and C. W. Murphy, 'Let's All Go Down The Strand'

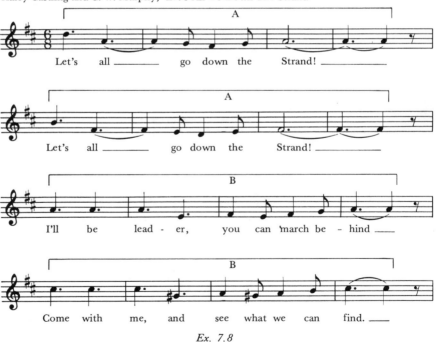

Let's   all _____   go down the   Strand! _____

Let's all _____   go down the   Strand! _____

I'll   be   lead - er,   you can 'march be - hind _____

Come with   me,   and   see what we   can   find. _____

Ex. 7.8

Henry E. Pether, 'Waiting At The Church'

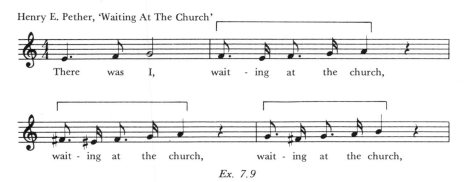

Ex. 7.9

obliterating it, as straight repetition, especially if musematic, seems to do). It makes us aware of rise-and-fall, a discursive hierarchy, and thus refers us to irreversible experiences; into the *ontology* of repetition it introduces a *teleological* directedness.

The prevalence of sequence in this kind of song confirms a general tendency there to absorb repetition into more complex macro-structures. It is a tendency which can be traced back easily to the bourgeois song styles of the eighteenth and nineteenth centuries; all the techniques mentioned above, for instance, can be found in such early nineteenth-century songs as Henry Bishop's 'Home Sweet Home' and 'The Mistletoe Bough', Joseph Knight's 'Rocked in the Cradle of the Deep' or Henry Russell's 'Woodman, Spare That Tree'. There too – as in the later music hall repertory – one notices that repetition is confined to the melodic level: at the extreme, it strikes one as an icing on the cake, the cake itself being mixed from narrative-harmonic ingredients.

The influence of Afro-American music can already be heard in some nineteenth-century popular songs, particularly in America; and with this influence came musematic repetition (see the tune of 'Zip Coon', for example).[9] When ragtime hit Tin Pan Alley, this influence became a flood. Musically, however, there was no clean break: the techniques of phrase-repetition, phrase-structure repetition and sequence remained important, and indeed Tin Pan Alley

Lewis F. Muir, 'Waiting For The Robert E. Lee'

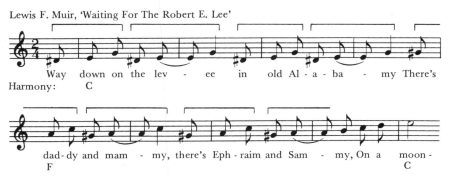

Ex. 7.10

Walter Donaldson, 'Yes Sir, That's My Baby'

Ex. 7.11

A. Harrington Gibbs, 'Runnin' Wild'

Ex. 7.12

song, from 1900 to the 1940s, can, from the point of view of repetition practice, be seen as involved in a constant struggle between the two traditions.

Classic early examples of Tin Pan Alley incorporation of musematic repetition are Irving Berlin's 'Alexander's Ragtime Band' of 1911 and Lewis Muir's 'Waiting for the Robert E. Lee', written the following year (see Ex. 7.10). By the 'jazz age', the technique was endemic (Exx. 7.11 and 7.12). As Exx. 7.10–7.12 show, musematic repetition is still generally worked in with older-established techniques: phrase-building and sequence. Often, however, the sequences are built not on 'narrative' harmonic progressions, but tonic-subdominant or tonic-dominant juxtapositions, in a way analogous to, and perhaps originating in, twelve-bar blues harmonic-structural practice; the effect is of quasi-musematic *harmonic* units, rather than a discursive flow (see Exx. 7.10 and 7.12), and the method of the overall repetition process approaches that used in later riff-based structures (for instance, Ex. 7.21, p. 281 below). In many other songs, though, more traditional sequential methods are used (see Ex. 7.13). Sometimes the musemes are coupled with longer units, also sequentially repeated (Ex. 7.14); sometimes the sequential effect is created by stretching the museme incrementally (Ex. 7.15); and sometimes this is combined with variation of the museme's melodic shape – here its impact can become rhythmic as much as melodic (Ex. 7.16).

Richard Whiting, 'Ain't We Got Fun'

Ex. 7.13

Harry Akst, 'Babyface'

Louis Silvers, 'April Showers'

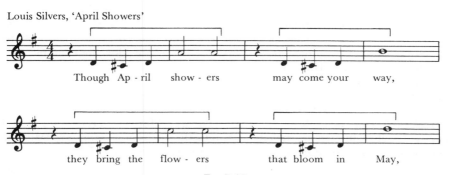

Ex. 7.15

Harry Akst, 'Am I Blue'

Ex. 7.16

Lou Handman, 'I'm Gonna Charleston Back To Charleston'

Ex. 7.17

The further we move from Tin Pan Alley towards theatre song, and from the 1920s into the 1930s (there are two relationships here, historically intertwined), the more repetition, especially musematic repetition, tends to be worked into more complex, hierarchically orientated macro-structures. In the hands of the Broadway masters, quite complex fusions can result (for an example, see Gershwin's 'A Foggy Day': Ex. 6.3, p. 184 above).

It is worth stressing, too, that at the same time as incorporating some musematic repetition, Tin Pan Alley songs retained the use of discursive techniques: indeed, the classic ballad form of the period (the thirty-two-bar AABA) relies on them for its overall structure. Moreover, repetition is still almost totally confined to melody – though the occasional song confirms the beginnings of harmonic musematic thinking noted above (Ex. 7.17).

Musematic techniques were first used as a primary structuring device – at least as far as mass-audience popular music was concerned – in the work of the

1930s swing bands (in the form of riffs). Fletcher Henderson (whose work was used and popularized by Benny Goodman) may have been a pioneer – though the Southwestern bands, notably Count Basie's, played music full of riffs, too. Black bands often made up 'head' arrangements based on simple riffs for dancing; only afterwards, if successful, were they sometimes given lyrics and worked out 'properly'. Lionel Hampton's celebrated 'Flyin' Home' can serve as a classic example of riff technique (actually *a collection* of short melodic-rhythmic riffs, heard together and successively), on its way from swing to rhythm and blues. For examples of the technique's assimilation by jump and rhythm and blues bands in the 1940s, almost any of Louis Jordan's recordings are excellent

'Do The Hucklebuck', sung by Roy Milton

Ex. 7.18

sources – or Roy Milton's 'Do the Hucklebuck', in which the principal riff (Ex. 7.18) is supplemented by a selection of supporting instrumental riffs. In all these cases, the relationship between riff-framework and variative detail (improvised solos, inflected instrumental playing) is important. From this point, riff techniques spread through almost all black popular music (see Exx. 7.19, 7.20 and 6.8, pp. 190–1 above).

As these examples suggest, the riffs can be more or less the whole piece; alternatively, they can be a framework underneath vocal and/or instrumental variative elaboration. They can be continuous, or worked into an antiphonal call-

'Searchin'', sung by the Coasters, vocal backing riff.

Ex. 7.19

James Brown (a) 'Night Train', bass riff (plus various superimposed instrumental riffs); (b) 'Out Of Sight', responsorial riff; (c) 'Papa's Got A Brand New Bag', rhythmic framework riff. All three are worked through a twelve-bar blues chord sequence.

Ex. 7.20

and-response (that is, binary) pattern. They can be unchanging in pitch, or be 'pitch-layered' (shifting in level, to use Van der Merwe's terminology (see p. 203 above) – a better one than 'sequence' in this context) against an (often twelve-bar blues) chord progression. They can be melodically memorable, or chiefly rhythmic in impact (a method leading to funk and disco styles). Their effect, to a greater or lesser extent, is always to level out the temporal flow, to challenge any 'narrative' functionality attaching to chord patterns and verse sequences, and to 'open up' the syntactic field for *rhythmic* elements (again, often short repeated patterns) to dominate (for instance, Bo Diddley's well-known 'shuffle' rhythm). The shorter and more insistently repeated the riffs, the more powerful these effects.

From rhythm and blues, these techniques permeated rock 'n' roll (see Exx. 7.21 and 7.22) and from there spread widely within rock. Again, the variety of usage is considerable. For instance, combinations of riffs can be worked into chord patterns, as often happens in, say, Rolling Stones songs (Ex. 7.23). Or the riff(s) can be virtually the whole framework, with perhaps an important role for surface variative detail (Ex. 7.24). One of the most interesting developments is the attempt by some musicians to combine musematic riff repetition with aspects of other techniques (compare the earlier Tin Pan Alley 'compromise'). In Bob Dylan's 'Masters of War', for example, a discursively constructed vocal – derived from white 'folk' traditions – with phrase repetition, sequence and phrase-structure repetition, is accompanied by a relentlessly repeated guitar riff (Ex. 7.25).

Of more general importance to a study of musematic repetition in Afro-American and rock music is the fact that it encompasses not only melody but also rhythm and harmony. Developments in rhythm are too extensive and various to be covered properly here; but it is worth noting that rhythm – treated basically as an aspect of harmonic narrativity in music hall and Tin Pan Alley song – emerges as a distinct 'layer' in jazz and rhythm and blues, notably through the use of identifiable (repeated, musematic) syntactic units by drummers: 'back beat' and eight-to-the-bar patterns among them. This usage has established both the role of rhythmic units in the formation of structural frameworks and the

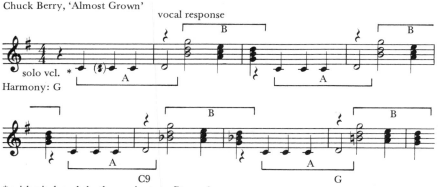

Chuck Berry, 'Almost Grown'

* with pitch and rhythm variants to fit words.

Ex. 7.21

Elvis Presley, 'All Shook Up'

Ex. 7.22

familiar relationship between such frameworks and variative (in this case rhythmic) detail. The latter is more important in jazz rock and various styles of 'progressive' rock, less so in rhythm and blues, mainstream rock, teenybopper pop and disco.

Just as melodic musematic repetition stems from Afro-American musical practice, so the harmonic equivalent – short chord sequences, usually two or three chords, treated as ostinatos – clearly has its origins in black music. The church is a likely source: the technique certainly appears early in gospel music; from there it passes into the work of secular vocal groups and early soul singers (1950s James Brown and Ray Charles, for example), and becomes a staple ingredient of black music from the 1960s on (Ex. 7.26). One route whereby it reached rock may have been through the influence of black singers and groups on the Beatles and other early 1960s British groups; at any rate, it soon became a primary rock technique. The immense significance of this is obvious, for its effect is to cut back the *differentiation* of harmonies, the 'narrativity' of harmonic syntax,

The Rolling Stones, '(This Could Be) The Last Time'

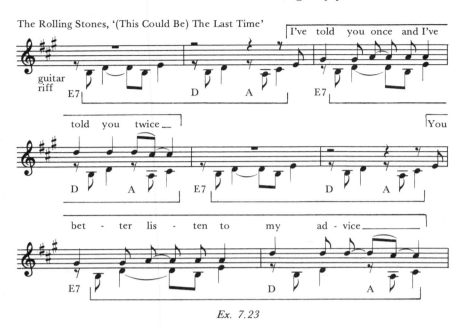

Ex. 7.23

Led Zeppelin, 'Whole Lotta Love'

Verses: quasi-improvisatory solo vocal with much variative detail and intensely vocalised effects.

Ex. 7.24

Bob Dylan, 'Masters Of War'

Ex. 7.25

to a minimum. The Who's 'My Generation', in which a continuous I-♭VII chord oscillation is supplemented by a melodic riff, illustrates one common type of application (Ex. 7.27).[10] Units combining I, IV and V chords in various sequences are also common (see Ex. 7.23; also, for example, Bob Dylan's 'Like A Rolling Stone'). Often the riff is worked into an antiphonal structure (Ex. 7.28).

Once again, some of the most interesting examples are 'compromises'; the classic source here is the work of the Beatles, a large proportion of Lennon–McCartney songs being based on the working of harmonic ostinatos into a discursive structure. Example 7.29, for example, shows the first part of 'It Won't Be Long'; this is followed by a contrasting middle eight (with no ostinatos), before being repeated. The first ostinato (C-A♭) supports phrase repetition; the second (Am-C), under antiphonal melodic riffs, is varied in order to provide a cadenced ending.

If repetition technique in popular music is marked by 'compromises' and interaction of types, we will expect its *effects* to be 'negotiable', too. But these cannot be understood except in the context of an overall theory of repetition, in music, in cultural practice more generally and in the life processes of individuals.

Returning to the problem of the meanings of repetition, we find that popular common sense not only tends to see repetition as an aspect of mass production

Otis Redding, 'Respect'

Ex. 7.26

The Who, 'My Generation'

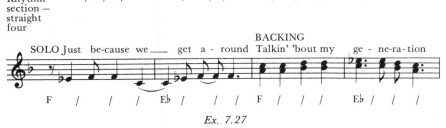

Ex. 7.27

Ex. 7.28

Ex. 7.29

and market exploitation but often also associates it with the phenomenon of being 'sent', particularly in relation to 'hypnotic' rhythmic repetitions and 'primitive' audience trance: a collective 'loss of the subject' in a state, perhaps, of *jouissance*. How can we square the two? How is it possible to square a psychology of repetition, with its biological aspects and generalizing ambition, and the historically specific Adornian notion of repetition as a function of social control? And, returning to another previously posed question, how can we square the idea of repetition as a source of trance and the Barthesian assumption that *jouissance* follows not repetition but *subversion* of the code?

Maybe the point is that, once again, it is not squaring that is needed so much as a certain relaxation of the analytical strangle-hold to allow a space in which multiple determinations can be seen to operate. The psychoanalytical interpreta- tion of repetition is itself not univocal, as we shall see; indeed, taking up Freud's metaphoric construction of the psyche as an *economy*, we may compare 'good' and 'bad' readings of repetition there with the ambiguity in the 'real' economy between repetition seen as an organic cycle (that is, in ecological processes) and repetition seen as a manifestation of 'Fordism' (mass production and the standardized series). We have already seen how the pleasures of early twentieth- century music, especially its novel rhythms, are located in a semiological dialectic, according to which they can be given both a 'modern' ('mechanical') and a 'primitive' ('corporeal') interpretation. Much the same applies to the effects of repetition. It is this, incidentally, which accounts for the fact that a writer like Deleuze, flattening the dialectic into congruence, can picture the body *as* machine: for him, human desires and the pleasures of capitalist culture are reduced to 'the common participation of the social machines *and* the organic machines in the desiring-machines' (Deleuze and Guattari 1984: 289).[11]

Repetition, then, does its work where social determinations, semiotic conventions and the 'relative constants' of the species condition intersect. Jameson (1981: 136–8), writing from an Adornian perspective, has argued that repetition in mass culture is *quite* different from repetition (generic conventions, stereotypes, and so on) in pre-capitalist forms. But popular music – which, as he himself explains, is now blurring the distinction between the individual song and the musical field as a whole, by virtue of the repetitive processes inherent in mass culture – actually provides a striking model for ways in which repetition techniques *can* overreach the needs of capitalist practice; for its reliance on repetition internally to the syntax as well as externally, as between constituents of the genre, acts to conjoin (not always harmoniously, to be sure) narrow socially functional effects and psychologically more open meanings with broad historical resonances.

Given the space opened up by this approach, what can we say about the relationship of *plaisir* and *jouissance* within the operations of repetition processes? As we saw earlier, Barthes goes to some trouble to stress that the line of division is hazy: 'the distinction will not be the source of absolute classifications' (Barthes 1975c: 4). Nevertheless, there is a tendency for Barthesian approaches to slip too easily into a dichotomy of 'message' and 'material', *plaisir* being connected with the formal relations within the signifying system, *jouissance* with the material presence of the signifier itself which breaks the code; indeed, Barthes' restriction of the deepest pleasures to instances of the deconstruction of meaning – and his resulting interest in the discontinuous, 'schizophrenic' methods of many post-modernist texts – can be regarded as continuing the traditional romantic-modernist response to the predictability and standardization taken to be characteristic of mass culture, by privileging innovation and refusal of any code (see ibid: 40–1; Jameson 1981: 135–6). But can 'message' and 'material' be demarcated quite so easily – especially in music, where the working of the signifying system is tied less to concrete external referents than to the materiality of the signifiers themselves and the correlation of that materiality with the structure of the body?

We have seen that there is some reason to consider music the primary semiotic practice. Within the process of psychological development, it can be argued (see Avron 1972: 104), its origins lie in the aural relationship of baby and mother, which, together with the tactile relationship, pre-dates the significance of visual (still more, verbal) signs (dependent as that is on an apprehension of the external world as *other*). The initial connotations of sound-structures (the origins of which may go back beyond the repetitive 'coos' of the mother even into the womb: the (equally repetitive) sound/feel of maternal breathing and heartbeat) are prior to any emergence of a subject, locating itself in opposition to external reality; for this reason the basic pleasure of music may be thought of as narcissistic – just as its quintessential structural tendency may be described as infinite repetition, or, in terms of psychological development, as the 'primal metaphor', in which everything is combined in a 'great similarity'. If these connotations and pleasures remain available in the unconscious as the subject develops, and if, as Lacan argues, the unconscious (site of *jouissance*) is not the formless jumble of vulgar pseudo-Freudianism but is structured, there is no need to limit *jouissance* in music to a level somehow beyond structure, to an assertion of materiality against form. Barthes himself offers the possibility that form – in its most extreme manifestation, 'excessive repetition' – could be a source of *jouissance* (Barthes 1975c: 41–2); but unfortunately he does not pursue the suggestion.

Rosolato (1972) has argued that the predictability of a known musical system can be ruptured not only by the presence within it of something unknown, unexpected, untranslatable (Barthes' theory) but also 'by opening it up through variation, or by carrying it to the limit' (ibid: 40). To the extent that repetition is defined, precisely, as carrying predictability to the limit, it becomes possible to link repetition not (not only?) with the *plaisir* of signification (the most obvious extrapolation from Barthes) but (but also?) with the possibility of *jouissance*. In this case, 'if the drive can be considered like the metaphoric play of music, the latter becomes the metaphoric representation of the drive substituted for the subject' (ibid: 41). A similar situation is familiar from religious practice, where 'loss of self' can be associated both with the sudden illumination of vision, conversion or miracle and with the 'oceanic' dissolution induced by mantric repetition. Interestingly enough, at least one musical movement – the countercultural rock of the 1960s – pursued both the erotic and religious pairings.

The ambiguity over the meaning of repetition – is it an aspect of the ego-function *vis-à-vis* mastering reality or is it the representant of a primary drive which may 'substitute for the subject'? – is not a purely musical problem; it informs all branches of human experience, and may be found in the work of Freud himself. The famous *fort-da* game (see Freud 1955), in which a little boy dramatizes the absence and reappearance ('gone' . . . 'there') of his mother by means of the repetitive manipulation of a wooden reel, gives rise to two possible explanations. First, it can be seen in ego-functional terms as a way of mastering reality; clearly, it is in this area – where symbol-making constantly reproduces structures of tension and de-tension – that the roots of *plaisir* are to be found (see Ricoeur 1970: 286–322). But Freud's second explanation is more radical. In a new formulation, he divides the drives into Life and Death instincts (Eros and Thanatos) and affixes repetition to the latter, which he represents as an 'expression of the inertia inherent in [all] organic life' (Freud 1955: 36). Since death represents, so to speak, a definitive 'loss of the subject' (the monadic silence of the grave), repetition, on this reading, is presumably available not only for conservative functions of control and ego unity but also moments of *jouissance*, of dissolution: revealing, as Lacan puts it (1979: 61), 'the most radical diversity constituted by repetition in itself'. (See also Heath 1981b.)

However, Eros, represented through sexuality, resists the tendency towards dissolution. Characterized in terms of 'clamour' and 'disturbance' as against the 'muteness' and 'peace' of the death instincts, this drive operates in the area where, presumably, the Barthesian *jouissance*, based as it is on disturbance and contradiction, has its roots. Are we back, then, to a simple dualism?

The answer is given in Freud's own work, for the implication is clear that Life and Death are not a mutually exclusive pair, working in a simple correlative structure (Death–repetition–ego–control–*plaisir*; Life–disruption–sexual desire–*jouissance*), but that the various terms of the psyche are *articulated together* in various ways. In the first place, the dualism appears as an overlapping of roles, since Life and Death, reproduction and extinction, define each other. In the second place, the dualism is located not on the level of concrete aims and objects but of undifferentiated *forces*, and these *cut across* the various functions of the psyche (ego-functions, sexual functions) (see Ricoeur 1970: 292–3). The energies of the two basic drives are available to be channelled in different directions. Thus, Thanatos – in the shape of repetition – can serve both ego-instincts (leading to *plaisir*), and, in the form of 'primal narcissism', sexual desire (leading to *jouissance*). Similarly, it would be surprising to find that the more physically involving forms of musematic repetition in music (boogie-woogie rhythms, for instance) have nothing to do with Eros. As Freud himself pointed out, copulative *jouissance* (the pleasure of sexual climax, one of the original meanings of the French word), though originating in the 'clamour' of erotic desire, is made possible by repetitive stimulation, and is actually felt, and often described, as a kind of *dying* (see ibid: 319). Here repetition pursues a trajectory through tension to final 'loss'. It seems likely, in fact, that *all* activities represent a complex mixture of forces, and any temptation to an either/or, *plaisir/jouissance* dichotomy must be abandoned in favour of a conception of tension, struggle, mediation – a pleasure-*field*.

Within the psychic economy, then, repetition appears to us only in complex mediated forms. Within signifying systems, too, repetition does not present itself as 'natural', nor purely as instrumental (under the function of control). Instead, we can say that its forms represent a cultural *work* – or rather they exist and are worked out at the point where socially constructed cultural codes and the structure of the subject meet. As Lacan puts it (1979: 62–3), repetition, or

> the game of the cotton-reel is the subject's answer to what the mother's absence has created on the frontier of his domain – the edge of his cradle – namely a *ditch*, around which one can only play at jumping . . . The activity as a whole symbolises . . . the repetition of the mother's departure as cause of a *Spaltung* [split] in the subject – overcome by the alternating game, *fort-da* . . . whose aim, in its alternation, is simply that of being the *fort* of a *da*, and the *da* of a *fort* . . .

Repetition, at its simplest, is the minimum step into the game of language and culture.

What this conception opens up for us is a space within which specific manifestations of repetition-practice in popular music can be located as manifestations of a complex cultural game, into which play a variety of social and psychic forces. The clarity, periodicity and importance of repetition in a particular syntax, then, can be related to the force and proximity of the death instinct, its precise effects to the nature of what is repeated and the extent to which it is mixed up with other elements (channelling repetition in particular directions). It is a question of the nature and complexity of the cultural apparatus that is constructed out of the primary energies. Thus, musematic repetition would seem *per se* to be more 'basic', discursive repetition to involve more ego functions. (Maróthy describes the form of bourgeois song as connected with the construction of the bourgeois ego, in its self-preservative little world.) At the same time, the musematic repetition of a short harmonic ostinato (in the Beatles, say) will have different effects from the musematic repetition of a physically involving, primarily rhythmic riff (in the Rolling Stones, for example), even if formally the role of this musematic repetition in the two cases is somewhat similar. The idea that 'the Stones give us energy, the Beatles take energy', a personalized form of a quite commonly felt distinction within popular music, probably refers to the ability of music with a greater reliance on musematic repetition to achieve a *resonance* with primary psychic energy flow, setting it in motion, while more discursive forms, even including repetition, demand a greater *investment* of ego-energy. Similarly, the 'constricting' effect of musematic repetition in a Bob Dylan protest song such as 'Masters of War' and its 'liberating' effect in his rhythm and blues-influenced songs ('It Takes a Lot to Laugh', for instance) is explained musically by differences in syntactic context, and psychologically by a difference in drive-channelling – into the ego instincts, on the one hand, into the sexual instincts, on the other.

Furthermore, if music's syntagmatic continuum describes a tendency towards 'extreme equivalence' – as suggested previously – the game within which repetition plays such an important role must pervade musical syntax as a whole. To the extent that all difference here can be seen in terms of transformation and analogy – that is, in terms of its 'iconic distance' from a generative monad – all syntactic moves and not just repetitive ones are involved, to a greater or lesser extent, in the interweaving of psychological effects.

The game can, of course, be disrupted, the subject 'lost'. For instance, the very force of repetition can, as it were, obliterate the significance of content; as continuous repetition approaches that point where we *know* that change is ruled out – the point of monadic unity – then the game effectively ceases. A good deal of popular music privileges this 'rhythmic obstinacy, reiteration to excess, and obliterates organisation and variety; a hypnotic abandon to this energy is also the expression of an energy' (Rosolato 1972: 43). It would be a mistake, however, to limit *jouissance* to this level, still more to separate rigidly the *plaisir* of the game from the *jouissance* of its disruption. The relationships between repetition-*jouissance* and Barthesian *jouissance* can perhaps be explained as resulting from differing proportions of Life and Death drives within the particular function: a high proportion of Eros directs the sexual instincts into desire-for-the-other (for the aural signifier, in the case of music), resulting in the pleasure of the Barthesian 'grain'; a high proportion of Thanatos channels sexuality, via repetition, towards narcissism, resulting in the pleasure of 'collective dying' – and providing the grain of truth behind the jibes about the masturbatory solipsistic nature of the pleasure of much contemporary pop music.

More generally, it seems likely that *plaisir* and *jouissance* are actually dialectically intermingled processes (thus *jouissance* is not conceivable outside a context in which *plaisir* operates, just as the unconscious, as Lacan makes clear, is not prior to the subject but comes into being as a function of the creation of subjectivity); they are continually active, in listening as in life, forever teasing and slipping. One example is Rosolato's conception of the disruption of a code (or better, the pulling aside of the curtain of predictability) 'by opening it up through variation'; the relationship between repetitive framework and variative detail, commonplace in popular music, would provide many instances. Perhaps what is needed, theoretically, is a metapleasure principle, which *organizes* the relations of its two subordinates within the pleasure-field. It might be that this could be found by looking to the notion of *suture*, developed in Lacanian psychoanalysis and subsequently in film theory; there, suture is taken to refer to an operation of *binding*, a *placing* of the subject in relation to the discourse in which it figures, but at the same time it continuously maintains the possibility that the stitching will open, revealing the gap, the *edge*, where, according to Lacan, the unconscious is to be located (see Heath 1981a).

It should by now be clear, in general terms, how the ensemble of social determinations breaks upon the pleasure-field. 'Pleasure' is a social term; similarly, people and syntaxes repeat themselves in socially determinate ways. Psychological subjects do not exist separately from social reality but take their specific forms as the result of its working of their resources. To pursue this in a more detailed way would require the application to 'repetition theory' of a *historicized* theory of psychoanalysis, taking account of the operations of specific ideological formations. Such a theory would explain, among many other things, how, in late capitalist mass culture, the 'received' role of repetition as an ego-control function was in part 'socialized' and extended into a political power, the associated *plaisir* turning masochistic, the pleasure of control sliding into that of being controlled.

There is no need, however, to see this process as monolithic, or uni-determined. It is open to struggle. Certainly the various pleasures of musical effects are not like brantub goodies, freely or randomly available; they come ideologically sorted, shaped and wrapped. But the ensemble of forces in the field is too complex and too dynamic to be regarded as a completely homogeneous totality; how can, say, a thumping rhythm and blues riff be turned *simply* into a collective rubber-stamp? The production of musical syntaxes involves active choice, conflict, redefinition; at the same time, their understanding and enjoyment take place in the theatre of self-definition, as part of the general struggle among listeners for control of meaning and pleasure.

Towards a history of the future

The idea that popular musical values and pleasures, in all their variety, can somehow be accounted for in some simple, monolithic way is thus clearly untenable. Just as listening practices in the contemporary world occupy a spectrum (one symbol of which is the antinomy of (public) ghetto-blaster and (private) walkman); just as musical politics relates to a continuum of possibilities, from the local to the tentatively global: so the pleasure-field occupies an extensive area with a complex internal structure, which, moreover, cannot be automatically mapped on to any progressive/reactionary schema of musical values.[12] *Plaisir*, for example, can refer to comfortably *doxic* cultural games, but one's comfort may produce another's discomfort; similarly, *jouissance* may on occasion represent not radical deconstruction but hedonistic abdication of interpretation. Readings of *jouissance* as wholly reactionary are also misleading, however. To see its ecstatic self-surrender now – as some have done – as a response to the inviting arms of 'the great suprapersonal system' of late capitalism itself (Jameson 1983: 13) is no less reductive than the instinctualists' vision of libidinal automata.

With the dethroning of the grand subjects of history – from God and Reason to the Proletariat, the West and even, dare one say it, the Body (life-force, sex, instinct . . .) – we are surrounded by gods that seem to have failed. This situation calls for, and is increasingly characterized by, the continuous building of *alliances*, both within individual subjects and between them. 'Valuation' and 'enjoyment' no longer have absolute references; they are phenomenological experiments, more or less intersubjectively checked, structured by and within a complex network of political strategies and working at a variety of levels in a variety of contexts. 'History', the critical reconstruction of the values and meanings of the past in the light of an evolving awareness of future needs, demands a map of the musical field sensitive to the possibility that musical action can be a model, an action model, of social change.

The shape this situation takes can be conceptualized in terms of the operation of two political axes which we may term 'localism' and 'globalism'. Within current literature, the first – focusing predominantly on the 'post-modern' culture of the metropolitan city – is at present in the ascendent (see, for example, Chambers 1985; 1986). However, to the extent that we increasingly inhabit a 'global city', the experience constituted by this culture overreaches – through the effects of the new media technologies – its ties to the metropolitan environment, penetrating and feeding back from village, desert, mountain, peasant community, suburbia and shanty town. There is here a potential not only for *fracture* – the defining characteristic of the 'local' strategy – but also for *connection*.

As the transnational corporations plunder the musical assets of the Third World, 'world music' can hardly be a neutral term. But it is not a settled, univocal one either. Struggles over the ownership, meanings and uses of these assets will have a growing importance, given wider ramifications within the 'global economy' by capital's ransacking of the *physical* assets of 'underdevelopment' as well. Thus the search for a new 'cultural ecology' is inextricably connected with responses to this threat to the physical and human environment, that is, with the search for a bio-economic ecology. It will take the redrawing of the music-historical map to a further stage, characterized by a recentring of 'world music' as a whole. This new 'holism' will be partial, provisional and concrete, fed by but also feeding its localist partner – a state

> in which the local issue is meaningful and desirable in and of itself, but is also *at one and the same time* taken as the *figure* for Utopia in general, and for the systemic revolutionary transformation of society as a whole.[13]

The musical mobilization of the 'new subject' – discontinuous but tentacular, locally rooted but a world citizen – is precisely the stage on which will now be set the struggle to redeem the democratic core of 'the popular'. The distorted premonitions of a popular utopia offered by Universal Consumerism (Enzensberger) and the 'democratic choices' of the hit parades (see Attali 1985: 106–9) provide the backcloth. Here the singular issues within which musical practices figure – in the home, at the dance, on the assembly-line, in Milton Keynes, Minneapolis, Maputo or Moscow – demand to be lived, worked out and enjoyed for themselves, but also to be articulated together and connected to the continuing attempt 'to make that construction of "the people" which unites a broad alliance of social forces in opposition to the power bloc count politically by winning for it a cultural weight and influence which prevails above others' (T. Bennett 1986b: 20).

Notes

1. On Bourdieu, see Garnham and Williams (1980).
2. The idea of subjectivity constructed through 'interpellation' comes from Althusser (1971). For modifications to Althusserian functionalism similar to the one proposed here, see, for example, Piaget (1971: 69–73, 138–40); Larmore (1981); Johnson (1979: 234).
3. On stars, see Laing (1969: 47–9).
4. Cf. Alan Durant's (1984) notion of musical 'conditions'.
5. It is surveyed, at least in relation to pop music, in Street (1986).
6. For example, the late nineteenth century or the 1930s: discussion of Victorian music hall song and of the Tin Pan Alley song of the 1930s almost always centres on the extent to which it reflects contemporary social conditions, and (from a critical point of view) on why it does not do so more adequately.
7. For a self-critique by Frith, see Frith (1988c: 163–8). See also Shepherd (1987).
8. It is still there, for example, in Jameson (1981).
9. On this moment, see Van der Merwe (1989).
10. Cf. pp. 199–200 above. Many other chord sequences mentioned in the discussion of harmonic deep structures (pp. 193–200) have been used for musematic repetition. For examples, see Burns (1987: 10–11).

11. Adorno's (1976: 52) view is preferable to this; at least he acknowledges the organic/mechanical dialectic, even if he insists that the apparent transmutation of body processes into musical rhythms is an ideological mystification.
12. On the complex politics of the pleasure-field, see Mercer (1986a).
13. Jameson (1983: 13) on what he recommends as an *allegorical* focus to cultural politics.

Appendix:
Sources of music examples

'Heartbreak Hotel' by Mae Axton, Tommy Durden and Elvis Presley, © Tree Publishing Co. Inc., 1956.
'Milkcow Blues Boogie' by Kokomo Arnold, © Leeds Music Ltd., 1934.
'All Shook Up' by Otis Blackwell and Elvis Presley, © Elvis Presley Music Inc., 1957.
'South of the Border' by Jimmy Kennedy and Michael Carr, © Peter Maurice Music Co. Ltd., 1939.
'Shake, Rattle and Roll' by Charles Calhoun, © Carlin Music Corp., 1954.
'These Foolish Things' by Eric Maschwitz and Jack Strachey, © Boosey & Co. Ltd., 1936.
'Lord Bateman', anon., transcribed by Percy Grainger, *Journal of the Folk Song Society*, 1908.
'Jumpin' Jack Flash' by Mick Jagger and Keith Richard, © Mirage Music Ltd., 1968.
'I Saw Her Standing There' by John Lennon and Paul McCartney, © Northern Songs Ltd., 1963.
'Don't Let Me Be Misunderstood' by Bennie Benjamin, Sol Marcus and Gloria Caldwell, © Bennie Benjamin Music Inc., 1964.
'When a Man Loves a Woman' by Calvin H. Lewis and Andrew Wright, © Quinvy Music Publishing Co., 1966.
'All the Things You Are' by Jerome Kern and Oscar Hammerstein II, © T.B. Harms Co., 1939.
'Caravan of Love', by Isley, Jasper and Isley, © Warner Bros., 1985.
'Memories of You' by Eubie Blake and Andy Razaf, © Shapiro, Bernstein & Co. Inc., 1930.
'Gipsy Eyes' by Jimi Hendrix, © A. Schroeder Music, 1968.
'White Riot' by Mick Jones and Joe Strummer, © Nineden Ltd./Riva Music Ltd., 1977.
'A Day in the Life' by John Lennon and Paul McCartney, © Northern Songs Ltd., 1967.
'A Foggy Day' by Ira Gershwin and George Gershwin, © Gershwin Publishing Corp., 1937.
'Hey Bo Diddley' by Ellas McDaniels, © Arc Music Corp., 1955.
'I'm Your Man' by George Michael, © Chappell & Co. Ltd., 1985.
'Twist and Shout' by Bert Russell and Phil Medley, © Robert Mellin Ltd., 1960.
'Yesterdays' by Jerome Kern and Otto Harbach, © T.B. Harms Co., 1933.
'A Hard Day's Night' by John Lennon and Paul McCartney, © Northern Songs Ltd., 1964.
'Sweet Georgia Brown' by Ben Bernie, Maceo Pinkard and Kenneth Casey, © Remick Music Corp., 1925.

'Peggy Sue' by Jerry Allison, Buddy Holly and Norman Petty, © Southern Music Publishing Co. Ltd., 1957.
'My Generation' by Peter Townshend, © Fabulous Music Ltd., 1965.
'I Feel for You' by Prince, © Island Music, 1984.
'Satisfaction' by Mick Jagger and Keith Richard, © Mirage Music Ltd., 1965.
Generative analysis of melodic phrase of the 'Kojak theme', © Philip Tagg, 1979, and Duchess Music Corp., 1973.
'Over the Rainbow' by E.Y. Harburg and Harold Arlen, © Leo Feist Inc., 1939.
'Smooth Operator', by Adu and St. John, © Angel Music Ltd., 1984.
'Yes Sir, that's My Baby' by Gus Kahn and Walter Donaldson, © Bourne Co., 1925.
'Runnin' Wild' by Joe Grey, Les Wood and A. Harrington Gibbs, © Leo Feist Inc., 1922.
'Ain't We Got Fun' by Gus Kahn, Raymond B. Egan and Richard A. Whiting, © Remick Music Corp., 1921.
'Babyface' by Benny Davis and Harry Akst, © Benny Davis Music, 1926.
'April Showers' by B.G. De Sylva and Louis Silvers, © Warner Bros., 1921.
'Am I Blue?' by Grant Clarke and Harry Akst, © M. Witmark and Sons, 1929.
'I'm Gonna Charleston Back to Charleston' by Ray Turk and Lou Handman, © Herald Square Music Co., 1925.
'The Hucklebuck' by Roy Alfred and Andy Gibson, © United Music, 1948.
'Searchin' by Jerry Leiber and Mike Stoller, © Carlin Music Corp., 1957.
'Night Train' by Oscar Washington, Lewis C. Simpkins and Jimmy Forrest, © Carlin Music, 1952.
'Out of Sight' by Brown and Wright, © Dynatone Publishing Co., 1964.
'Papa's Got a Brand New Bag' by James Brown, © Dynatone Publishing Co., 1965.
'Almost Grown' by Chuck Berry, © Arc Music Corp., 1959.
'The Last Time' by Mick Jagger and Keith Richard, © Mirage Music Ltd., 1965.
'Whole Lotta Love' by James Page, Robert Plant, John Paul Jones and John Bonham, © Superhype Publishing, 1969.
'Masters of War' by Bob Dylan, © M. Witmark & Sons, 1963.
'Respect' by Otis Redding, © Shapiro Bernstein, 1965.
'Anyway, Anyhow, Anywhere' by Peter Townshend and Roger Daltrey, © Fabulous Music Ltd., 1965.
'It Won't Be Long' by John Lennon and Paul McCartney, © Northern Songs Ltd., 1963.

Acknowledgements

Parts of Chapters 1 and 7 first appeared in (respectively) ' "Play it again, Sam": some notes on the productivity of repetition in popular music', *Popular Music*, 3, pp. 235–70, and 'Articulating musical meaning/re-constructing musical history/locating the "popular" ', *Popular Music*, 5, pp. 5–43. I am grateful to Cambridge University Press for permission to re-use this material.

Bibliography

No attempt has been made here to provide a comprehensive bibliography of popular music, which would require a book to itself. However, the following would serve as useful starting-points:

Booth, M.W. 1983. *American Popular Music: A Reference Guide* (Westport, CT and London).
Horn, D. 1977. *The Literature of American Music in Books and Folk Music Collections: A Fully Annotated Bibliography* (Metuchen, NJ and London).
Iwaschkin, R. 1986. *Popular Music: A Reference Guide* (New York and London).
Taylor, P. 1985. *Popular Music Since 1955: A Critical Guide to the Literature* (London and New York).

For updating, the journal *Popular Music* publishes an annual Booklist of recent publications.

The following is a list of works referred to in the present text.

Adamo, G. 1982. 'Ethnomusicology and mass media', paper presented to the ISME conference on 'Pop and Folk Music: Stock-Taking of New Trends' (Trento, Italy).
Adorno, T.W. 1941. 'On popular music', *Studies in Philosophy and Social Sciences*, 9, pp. 17–48.
Adorno, T.W. 1967. 'Perennial fashion: jazz' in *Prisms* (London), pp. 119–32, first published in 1955.
Adorno, T.W. 1973. *Philosophy of Modern Music* (London), first published in 1948.
Adorno, T.W. 1975. 'Culture industry reconsidered', *New German Critique*, 6, pp. 12–19, first published in 1967.
Adorno, T.W. 1976. *Introduction to the Sociology of Music* (New York), first published in 1962.
Adorno, T.W. 1978a. 'On the fetish character in music and the regression of listening' in A. Arato and E. Gebhardt (eds), *The Essential Frankfurt School Reader* (Oxford), pp. 270–99; first published in 1938.
Adorno, T.W. 1978b. 'On the social situation of music', *Telos*, 35, pp. 128–64, first published in 1932.
Adorno, T.W. and Horkheimer, M. 1972. *Dialectics of Enlightenment* (London), first published in 1947.
Aharonián, C. 1985. 'A Latin-American approach in a pioneering essay' in D. Horn (ed.), *Popular Music Perspectives*, 2 (Gothenburg, Exeter, Ottawa and Reggio Emilia), pp. 52–65.

Althusser, L. 1971. 'Ideology and ideological state apparatuses (notes towards an investigation)' in *Lenin and Other Essays* (London), pp. 127–86.

Arato, A. 1977. 'The antinomies of the neo-marxian theory of culture', *International Journal of Sociology*, 7:1, pp. 3–23.

Arato, A. and Gebhardt, E. (eds) 1978. *The Essential Frankfurt School Reader* (Oxford).

Asaf'ev, B.V. 1977. *Musical Form as a Process: Translation and Commentary* by J.R. Tull, 3 vols, Ohio State University PhD dissertation (Ann Arbor, MI).

Attali, J. 1985. *Noise*, trans. B. Massumi (Manchester).

Avron, D. 1972. 'Vers une métapsychologie de la musique', *Musique en Jeu*, 9, pp. 102–10.

Bacon, T. (ed.) 1981. *Rock Hardware* (Poole, Dorset).

Bailey, P. 1978. *Leisure and Class in Victorian England* (London).

Bailey, P. (ed.) 1986a. *Music Hall: The Business of Pleasure* (Milton Keynes).

Bailey, P. 1986b. 'A community of friends: business and good fellowship in London music hall management, *c.* 1860–1885' in P. Bailey (ed.), *Music Hall: The Business of Pleasure* (Milton Keynes), pp. 33–52.

Bailey, P. 1986c. 'Champagne Charlie: performance and ideology in the music-hall swell song' in J.S. Bratton (ed.), *Music Hall: Performance and Style* (Milton Keynes), pp. 49–69.

Baily, J. 1977. 'Movement patterns in playing the Herati *dutar*' in J. Blacking (ed.), *The Anthropology of the Body* (New York), pp. 275–330.

Baily, J. 1981. 'Cross-cultural perspectives in popular music: the case of Afghanistan', *Popular Music*, 1, pp. 105–22.

Baily, J. 1985. 'Music structure and human movement' in P. Howell, I. Cross and R. West (eds), *Music Structure and Cognition* (London), pp. 237–58.

Baraka, A. 1982. 'Black music: its roots, its popularity, its commercial prostitution', in W. Ferris and M.L. Hart (eds), *Folk Music and Modern Sound* (Jackson, MS), pp. 177–93.

Barnard, S. 1989. *On the Radio: Music Radio in Britain* (Milton Keynes).

Baroni, M. 1983. 'The concept of musical grammar', trans, S. Maguire and W. Drabkin, *Musical Analysis*, 2:2, pp. 175–208.

Barthes, R. 1968. *Elements of Semiology*, trans. A. Lavers and C. Smith (New York).

Barthes, R. 1975a. *S/Z*, trans. R. Miller (London).

Barthes, R. 1975b. 'Rasch' in *Langue, discours, société* (Paris), pp. 217–28.

Barthes, R. 1975c. *The Pleasure of the Text*, trans. R. Miller (New York).

Barthes, R. 1977. *Image-Music-Text*, trans. S. Heath (London).

Baudrillard, J. 1981. *For a Critique of the Political Economy of the Sign* (St Louis, MO).

Becker, H. 1972. 'The professional jazz musician and his audience' in R.S. Denisoff and R.A. Peterson (eds), *The Sounds of Social Change* (New York), pp. 248–60.

Béhague, G. 1973. 'Bossa and bossas: recent changes in Brazilian urban popular music', *Ethnomusicology*, 17, pp. 209–33.

Belz, C. 1967. 'Popular music and the folk tradition', *Journal of American Folklore*, 80:316, pp. 130–42.

Belz, C. 1972. *The Story of Rock*, 2nd edn (New York).

Benjamin, W. 1973a. *Charles Baudelaire: A Lyric Poet in the Era of High Capitalism* (London).

Benjamin, W. 1973b. *Illuminations*, ed. H. Arendt, trans. H. Zohn (London).

Benjamin, W. 1973c. *Understanding Brecht* (London).

Bennett, A. 1986. 'Music in the halls' in J.S. Bratton (ed.), *Music Hall: Performance and Style* (Milton Keynes), pp. 1–22.

Bennett, H.S. 1980. *On Becoming a Rock Musician* (Amherst, MA).

Bennett, T. 1986a. 'Introduction: popular culture and "the turn to Gramsci"' in T. Bennett, C. Mercer and J. Woollacott (eds), *Popular Culture and Social Relations* (Milton Keynes), pp. xi–xix.

Bennett, T. 1986b. 'The politics of the "popular" and popular culture' in T. Bennett, C. Mercer and J. Woollacott (eds), *Popular Culture and Social Relations* (Milton Keynes), pp. 6–21.

Berliner, P. 1978. *The Soul of Mbira* (Berkeley, CA).

Berman, M. 1983. *All That Is Solid Melts Into Air: The Experience of Modernity* (London).

Birdwhistell, R.L. 1952. *Introduction to Kinesics* (Louisville, KY).

Birdwhistell, R.L. 1971. *Kinesics and Context* (Harmondsworth).

Birrer, F.A.J. 1985. 'Definitions and research orientation: do we need a definition of popular music?' in D. Horn (ed.), *Popular Music Perspectives*, 2 (Gothenburg, Exeter, Ottawa and Reggio Emilia), pp. 99–105.

Björnberg, A. 1985. 'On aeolian harmony in contemporary popular music', paper presented to the Third International Conference of IASPM, Montreal.

Blacking, J. 1976. *How Musical Is Man?* (London).

Blacking, J. 1977a. 'Some problems of theory and method in the study of musical change', *Yearbook of the International Folk Music Council*, 9, pp. 1–26.

Blacking, J. 1977b. 'Towards an anthropology of the body' in J. Blacking (ed.), *The Anthropology of the Body* (New York), pp. 1–28.

Blacking, J. 1981. ' "Ethnic" perceptions in the semiotics of music' in W. Steiner (ed.), *The Sign in Music and Literature* (Austin, TX), pp. 184–94.

Blaukopf, K. (ed.) 1982. *The Phonogram in Cultural Communication* (Vienna and New York).

Bloch, E., Lukács, G., Brecht, B., Benjamin, W. and Adorno, T.W. 1977. *Aesthetics and Politics* (London).

Blum, S. 1975. 'Towards a social history of musicological technique', *Ethnomusicology*, 19:2, pp. 207–31.

Bobbitt, R. 1976. *Harmonic Technique in the Rock Idiom: the Theory and Practice of Rock Harmony* (Belmont, CA).

Boretz, B. 1969–70. 'Meta-variations: studies in the foundations of musical thought', *Perspectives of New Music*, 8, pp. 1–74; 9, pp. 49–111.

Borneman, E. 1977. 'The roots of jazz' in N. Hentoff and A.J. McCarthy (eds), *Jazz* (London), pp. 1–20.

Bourdieu, P. 1968. Outline of a sociological theory of art perception', *International Social Science Journal*, 20:4, pp. 589–612.

Bourdieu, P. 1977. *Outline of a Theory of Practice* (Cambridge).

Bourdieu, P. 1980. 'The aristocracy of culture', *Media, Culture and Society*, 2:3, pp. 225–54.

Bourdieu, P. and Passeron, J.C. 1977. *Reproduction: In Education, Society and Culture* (London).

Bradby, B. 1985. 'Do-talk and don't-talk: the division of the subject in girl-group music', paper presented to the Third International Conference of IASPM, Montreal.

Bradby, B. and Torode, B. 1982. 'Song-work. The musical inclusion, exclusion and representation of women', paper presented to British Sociological Association conference, Manchester.

Bradby, B. and Torode, B. 1984. 'Pity Peggy Sue', *Popular Music*, 4, pp. 183–205.

Bradley, D. n.d. *The Cultural Study of Music*, University of Birmingham Centre for Contemporary Cultural Studies stencilled paper SP61.

Brake, M. 1980. *The Sociology of Youth Culture and Youth Subcultures* (London).

Bratton, J.S. 1975. *The Victorian Popular Ballad* (London).

Bratton, J.S. (ed.) 1986. *Music Hall: Performance and Style* (Milton Keynes).

Bright, W. 1963. 'Language and music: areas for co-operation', *Ethnomusicology*, 7:1, pp. 26–32.

Bronson, B.H. 1969. 'Samuel Hall's family tree' in *The Ballad as Song* (Berkeley, CA), pp. 18–36.

Burke, P. 1978. *Popular Culture in Early Modern Europe* (London).

Burke, P. 1981. 'People's history or total history' in R. Samuel (ed.), *People's History and Socialist Theory* (London).

Burns, G. 1987. 'A typology of "hooks" in popular records', *Popular Music*, 6:1, pp. 1–20.

Carr, E.H. 1964. *What Is History?* (Harmondsworth).

Chambers, I. 1976. 'A strategy for living' in S. Hall and T. Jefferson (eds), *Resistance through Rituals: Youth Subcultures in Post-war Britain* (London), pp. 157–66.

Chambers, I. 1979. ' "It's more than a song to sing"; music, cultural analysis and the blues', *Anglistica, XXII*:1, pp. 9–60.

Chambers, I. 1981. 'Pop music: a teaching perspective', *Screen Education*, 39, pp. 35–46.

Chambers, I. 1982. 'Some critical tracks', *Popular Music*, 2, pp. 19–36.

Chambers, I. 1985. *Urban Rhythms: Pop Music and Popular Culture* (London).

Chambers, I. 1986. *Popular Culture: The Metropolitan Experience* (London and New York).

Chappell, W. 1859. *The Ballad Literature and Popular Music of the Olden Time* (London; reprinted New York, 1965).

Chapple, S. and Garofalo, R. 1977. *Rock 'n' Roll Is Here to Pay: the History and Politics of the Music Industry* (Chicago).

Chase, G. 1981. *America's Music, from the Pilgrims to the Present*, rev. edn (London).

Chernoff, J.M. 1979. *African Rhythm and African Sensibility: Aesthetics and Social Action in African Musical Idioms* (Chicago and London).

Cherry, C. 1968. *On Human Communication: A Review, A Survey and A Criticism* (New York).

Chester, A. 1970. 'Second thoughts on a rock aesthetic: The Band', *New Left Review*, 62, pp. 75–82.

Clarke, J. 1976. 'The skinheads and the magical recovery of community' in S. Hall and T. Jefferson (eds), *Resistance through Rituals: Youth Subcultures in Post-war Britain* (London), pp. 99–102.

Clarke, J. n.d. *The Skinheads and the Study of Youth Culture*, University of Birmingham Centre for Contemporary Cultural Studies stencilled paper, SP23.

Clarke, J., Hall, S., Jefferson, T. and Roberts, B. 1976. 'Sub-cultures, cultures and class', in S. Hall and T. Jefferson (eds), *Resistance through Rituals: Youth Subcultures in Post-war Britain* (London), pp. 9–74.

Clynes, M. 1977. *Sentics: the Touch of Emotions* (New York).

Clynes, M. (ed.) 1982. *Music, Mind and Brain* (New York).

Clynes, M. and Walker, J. 1982. 'Neurobiologic functions of rhythm, time and pulse in music' in M. Clynes (ed.), *Music, Mind and Brain* (New York), pp. 171–216.

Cogan, R. 1984. *New Images of Musical Sound* (Cambridge, MA).

Cohen, E. and Shiloah, A. 1985. 'Major trends of change in Jewish Oriental ethnic music in Israel', *Popular Music*, 5, pp. 199–223.

Cohen, J.E. 1962. 'Information theory and music', *Behavioral Science*, 7, pp. 137–63.

Cohen, N. 1970. 'Tin Pan Alley's contribution to folk music', *Western Folklore*, 29, pp. 9–20.

Cohen, N. 1981. *Long Steel Rail: the Railroad in American Folksong* (Urbana, IL).

Cohen, N. and Wells, P.F. 1982. 'Recorded ethnic music: a guide to resources' in *Ethnic Recordings in America: A Neglected Heritage* (Washington, DC), pp. 175–229.

Coker, W. 1972. *Music and Meaning* (New York).

Collins, J. 1985. *African Pop Roots: The Inside Rhythms of Africa* (London).

Cook, L. 1983. 'Popular culture and rock music', *Screen*, 24:3, pp. 44–9.

Cooke, D. 1959. *The Language of Music* (London).

Coons, E. and Kraehenbuhl, D. 1958. 'Information as measure of structure in music', *Journal of Music Theory*, 2, pp. 127–61.

Cooper, R. 1973. 'Propositions pour un modèle transformationnel de description musicale', *Musique en Jeu*, 10, pp. 70–88.

Coplan, D. 1980. 'Marabi culture: continuity and transformation in African music in Johannesburg, 1920–1940', *African Urban Studies*, 6, pp. 49–78.

Coplan, D. 1982. 'The urbanisation of African music: some theoretical observations', *Popular Music*, 2, pp. 113-29.

Cosgrove, S. 1982. 'Long after tonight is all over - Northern Soul', *Collusion*, 2, pp. 38-41.

Courlander, H. 1970. *Negro Folk Music USA* (New York).

Coward, R. 1977. 'Class, "culture", and the social formation', *Screen*, 18:1, pp. 75-105.

Coward, R. 1984. 'Our Song' in *Female Desire: Women's Sexuality Today* (St Albans), pp. 145-50.

Critchley, M. and Henson, R.A. 1977. *Music and the Brain* (London).

Crombie, D. 1982. *The Complete Synthesiser* (London).

Cubitt, S. 1984. ' "Maybelline": meaning and the listening subject', *Popular Music*, 4, pp. 207-24.

Cutler, C. 1984. 'Technology, politics and contemporary music: necessity and choice in musical forms', *Popular Music*, 4, pp. 279-300.

Cutler, C. 1985a. 'What is popular music?' in D. Horn (ed.), *Popular Music Perspectives*, 2 (Gothenburg, Exeter, Ottawa and Reggio Emilia), pp. 3-12.

Cutler, C. 1985b. *File Under Popular. Theoretical and Critical Writings on Music* (London).

Dahlhaus, C. (ed.) 1967. *Studien zur Trivialmusik des 19. Jahrhunderts* (Regensburg).

Dallas, K. 1975. 'The roots of tradition' in D. Laing, K. Dallas, R. Denselow and R. Shelton (eds) *The Electric Muse: the Story of Folk into Rock* (London), pp. 83-136.

Davies, J.B. 1980. *The Psychology of Music* (London).

Deleuze, G. and Guattari, F. 1984. *Anti-Oedipus*, trans. R. Hurley, M. Seem and H.R. Lane (London).

Denisoff, R.S. 1975. *Solid Gold: the Popular Record Industry* (New Brunswick, NJ).

Deutsch, D. (ed.) 1982. *The Psychology of Music* (New York).

Dews, P. 1984. 'Power and subjectivity in Foucault', *New Left Review*, 109, pp. 72-95.

Douglas, M. 1970. *Natural Symbols* (London).

Dundes, A. (ed.) 1965. *The Study of Folklore* (Englewood Cliffs, NJ).

Durant, A. 1984. *Conditions of Music* (London).

Durgnat, R. 1971. 'Rock, rhythm and dance', *British Journal of Aesthetics*, 11, pp. 28-47.

Dyer, R. 1979. 'In defense of disco', *Gay Left*, 8, pp. 20-3.

Eberley, P.K. 1982. *Music in the Air: America's Changing Tastes in Popular Music, 1920-1980* (New York).

Eco, U. 1979. *A Theory of Semiotics* (Bloomington, IN).

Ehrlich, C. 1985. *The Music Profession in Britain since the Eighteenth Century* (Oxford).

Eisler, H. 1948. *Composing for the Films* (New York).

Eisler, H. 1978. *A Rebel in Music: Selected Writings*, ed. M. Grabs, trans. M. Meyer (Leipzig).

Enzensberger, H.M. 1976. 'Constituents of a theory of the media' in *Raids and Reconstructions* (London), pp. 20-53.

Epstein, D. 1982. 'Myths about black folk music', in W. Ferris and M.L. Hart (eds), *Folk Music and Modern Sound* (Jackson, MS), pp. 151-60.

Erenberg, L. 1981. *Steppin' Out: New York Nightlife and the Transformation of American Culture 1890-1930* (London).

Esman, A.H. 1951. 'Jazz: a study in cultural conflict', *American Imago*, 8:2, pp. 219-26.

Evans, D. 1982a. 'Blues and modern sound: past, present and future' in W. Ferris and M.L. Hart (eds), *Folk Music and Modern Sound* (Jackson, MS), pp. 163-76.

Evans, D. 1982b. *Big Road Blues: Tradition and Creativity in the Folk Blues* (Berkeley, CA).

Ewen, D. 1964. *The Life and Death of Tin Pan Alley* (New York).

Fabbri, F. 1982a. 'A theory of musical genres: two applications' in D. Horn and P. Tagg (eds), *Popular Music Perspectives* (Gothenburg and Exeter), pp. 52-81.

Fabbri, F. 1982b. 'Musical genres and their metalanguages', paper presented to the ISME conference on 'Pop and Folk Music: Stock-Taking of New Trends' (Trento, Italy).

Fabbri, F. 1982c. 'What kind of music?' *Popular Music*, 2, pp. 131–43.

Fairley, J. 1985. 'Annotated bibliography of Latin-American popular music with particular reference to Chile and to *nueva canción*', *Popular Music*, 5, pp. 305–56.

Fairley, J. 1989. 'Analysing performance: narrative and ideology in concerts by ¡Karaxu!', *Popular Music*, 8:1, pp. 1–30.

Feld, S. 1982. *Sounds and Sentiment: Birds, Weeping, Poetics and Song in Kaluli Expression* (Philadelphia).

Ferris, W. 1978. *Blues from the Delta* (New York).

Finnegan, R. 1977. *Oral Poetry* (Cambridge).

Fiori, U. 1985. 'Popular music: theory, practice, value' in D. Horn (ed.), *Popular Music Perspectives*, 2 (Gothenburg, Exeter, Ottawa and Reggio Emilia), pp. 13–23.

Fiori, U. 1987. 'Listening to Peter Gabriel's "I Have the Touch" ', *Popular Music*, 6:1, pp. 37–43.

Fletcher, C. 1966. 'Beat and gangs on Merseyside' in T. Raison (ed.), *Youth in New Society* (London).

Forte, A. and Gilbert, S.E. 1982. *Introduction to Schenkerian Analysis* (New York).

Fowler, P. 1972. 'Skins rule' in C. Gillett (ed.), *Rock File* (London), pp. 10–24.

Fraisse, P. 1982. 'Rhythm and tempo' in D. Deutsch (ed.), *The Psychology of Music* (New York), pp. 149–80.

Francès, R. 1958. *La perception de la musique* (Paris).

Freud, S. 1955. *Beyond the Pleasure Principle* (London), standard edition of the Complete Psychological Works of Sigmund Freud, trans. J. Strachey, 18, pp. 7–64.

Frith, S. 1978. *The Sociology of Rock* (London).

Frith, S. 1981. ' "The magic that can set you free": the ideology of folk and the myth of the rock community', *Popular Music*, 1, pp. 159–68.

Frith, S. 1983a. *Sound Effects: Youth, Leisure and the Politics of Rock 'n' Roll* (London).

Frith, S. 1983b. 'The pleasures of the hearth', in *Formations of Pleasure* (London), pp. 101–23; reprinted in Frith (1988c, pp. 24–44).

Frith, S. 1986. 'Art versus technology: the strange case of popular music', *Media, Culture and Society*, 8:3, pp. 263–79.

Frith, S. 1987a. 'The industrialisation of popular music' in J. Lull (ed.), *Popular Music and Communication* (Newbury Park, CA), pp. 53–77; reprinted in different form in Frith (1988c, pp. 11–23).

Frith, S. 1987b. 'The making of the British record industry 1920-64' in J. Curran, A. Smith and P. Wingate (eds), *Impacts and Influences* (London), pp. 278–90.

Frith, S. 1987c. 'Why do songs have words?' in A.L. White (ed.), *Lost in Music: Culture, Style and the Musical Event* (London), pp. 77–106; reprinted in Frith (1988c, pp. 105–28).

Frith, S. 1987d. 'Towards an aesthetic of popular music' in R. Leppert and S. McClary (eds), *Music and Society: the Politics of Composition, Performance and Reception* (Cambridge), pp. 133–49.

Frith, S. 1988a. 'Copyright and the music business', *Popular Music*, 7:1, pp. 57–75.

Frith, S. 1988b. 'Playing with real feeling - jazz and suburbia', *New Formations*, 4, pp. 7–24; reprinted in Frith (1988c, pp. 45–63).

Frith, S. 1988c. *Music for Pleasure: Essays in the Sociology of Pop* (Cambridge).

Frith, S. and McRobbie, A. 1978. 'Rock and sexuality', *Screen Education*, 29, pp. 3–19.

Fuller, P. 1980. *Art and Psychoanalysis* (London).

Gammon, V. 1980. 'Folk song collecting in Sussex and Surrey, 1843-1914', *History Workshop Journal*, 10, pp. 61–89.

Gammon, V. 1984. ' "Not appreciated in Worthing?" Class expression and popular song texts in mid-nineteenth-century Britain', *Popular Music*, 4, pp. 5–24.

Gammon, V. 1985. 'Popular music in rural society: Sussex 1815-1914', PhD thesis, University of Sussex.

Garnham, N. and Williams, R. 1980. 'Pierre Bourdieu and the sociology of culture: an introduction', *Media, Culture and Society*, 2:3, pp. 209–23.

Gasparov, B. 1975. 'Some descriptive problems of musical semantics' in *Actes du 1er Congrès Internationale de Semiotique Musicale, Beograd* (Pesaro), pp. 183–96.

Geertz, C. 1973. *The Interpretation of Cultures: Selected Essays* (New York).

Gendron, B. 1986. 'Theodor Adorno meets the Cadillacs' in T. Modleski (ed.), *Studies in Entertainment: Critical Approaches to Mass Culture* (Bloomington, IN), pp. 18–36.

Gillett, C. 1975. *Making Tracks: the History of Atlantic Records* (London).

Gillett, C. 1983. *The Sound of the City: the Rise of Rock and Roll*, rev. edn (London).

Goldberg, I. 1961. *Tin Pan Alley: A Chronicle of American Popular Music* (New York).

Gooddy, W. 1977. 'The timing and time of musicians' in M. Critchley and R.A. Henson, *Music and the Brain* (London), pp. 131–40.

Gramsci, A. 1971. *Selections from Prison Notebooks*, ed. and trans. Q. Hoare and G. Nowell-Smith (London).

Green, A. 1965. 'Hillbilly music: source and symbol', *Journal of American Folklore*, 78: 309, pp. 204–28.

Green, A. 1972. *Only a Miner: Studies in Recorded Coal-Mining Songs* (Urbana, IL).

Green, L. 1988. *Music on Deaf Ears: Musical Meaning, Ideology and Education* (Manchester).

Gregson, K. 1983. *Corvan. A Victorian Entertainer and his Songs* (Banbury, Oxon).

Gronow, P. 1982. 'Ethnic recordings: an introduction' in *Ethnic Recordings in America: a Neglected Heritage* (Washington, DC), pp. 1–49.

Gronow, P. 1983. 'The record industry: the growth of a mass medium', *Popular Music*, 3, pp. 53–75.

Grossberg, L. 1984. 'Another boring day in paradise: rock 'n' roll and the empowerment of everyday life', *Popular Music*, 4, pp. 225–58.

Hall, E. 1959. *The Silent Language* (New York).

Hall, E. 1963. 'A system for the notation of proxemic behavior', *American Anthropologist*, 65:5, pp. 1024–6.

Hall, S. 1977. 'Culture, media and the "ideological effect" ' in J. Curran (ed.), *Mass Communication and Society* (London), pp. 315–48.

Hall, S. 1978. 'Popular culture, politics and history', in *Popular Culture Bulletin*, 3, Open University duplicated paper.

Hall, S. 1981. 'Notes on deconstructing "the popular" ' in R. Samuel (ed.), *People's History and Socialist Theory* (London), pp. 227–40.

Hall, S. and Jefferson, T. (eds) 1976. *Resistance through Rituals: Youth Subcultures in Post-war Britain* (London).

Hamm, C. 1979. *Yesterdays: Popular Song in America* (New York).

Hamm, C. 1980. Contribution to entry on 'popular music' in S. Sadie (ed.), *The New Grove Dictionary of Music and Musicians*, 20 vols (London).

Hamm, C. 1982. 'Some thoughts on the measurement of popularity in music' in D. Horn and P. Tagg (eds), *Popular Music Perspectives* (Gothenburg and Exeter), pp. 3–15.

Hampton, B. 1979–80. 'A revised analytical approach to musical processes in urban Africa', *African Urban Studies*, 6, pp. 1–16.

Hardy, P. n.d. *The British Record Industry*. IASPM Working Paper 3.

Harker, D. 1980. *One for the Money: Politics and Popular Song* (London).

Harker, D. 1981. 'The making of the Tyneside concert hall', *Popular Music*, 1, pp. 27–56.

Harker, D. 1985. *Fakesong: the Manufacture of British 'Folksong', 1700 to the Present Day* (Milton Keynes).

Harwood, D.L. 1976. 'Universals in music: a perspective from cognitive psychology', *Ethnomusicology*, 20:3, pp. 521–33.

Hatch, D.J. and Millward, S. 1987. *Promised Land: Pop Music Development from Blues to Rock* (Manchester).

Heath, S. 1981a. 'On suture' in *Questions of Cinema* (London), pp. 76–112.

Heath, S. 1981b. 'Repetition time: notes around structural/materialist film' in *Questions of Cinema* (London), pp. 165–75.

Heath, S. 1981c. 'The cinematic apparatus: technology as historical and cultural form' in *Questions of Cinema* (London), pp. 221–35.

Hebdige, D. 1976a. 'Reggae, Rastas and Rudies' in S. Hall and T. Jefferson (eds), *Resistance through Rituals: Youth Subcultures in Post-war Britain* (London), pp. 135–54.

Hebdige, D. 1976b. 'The meaning of mod' in S. Hall and T. Jefferson (eds), *Resistance through Rituals: Youth Subcultures in Post-war* Britain (London), pp. 87–96.

Hebdige, D. n.d.a. *Reggae, Rastas and Rudies: Style and the Subversion of Form*, University of Birmingham Centre for Contemporary Cultural Studies stencilled paper SP24.

Hebdige, D. n.d.b. *The Style of the Mods*, University of Birmingham Centre for Contemporary Cultural Studies stencilled paper SP20.

Hebdige, D. 1979. *Subculture: the Meaning of Style* (London).

Hebdige, D. 1981a. 'Towards a cartography of taste 1935–1962', *Block*, 4, pp. 39–56.

Hebdige, D. 1981b. 'Subculture and consumption', Open University course U203 *Popular Culture*, radio programme 5.

Held, D. 1980. *Introduction to Critical Theory* (London).

Hennion, A. 1981. *Les professionnels du disque* (Paris).

Hennion, A. 1983. 'The production of success: an anti-musicology of the pop song', *Popular Music*, 3, pp. 159–93.

Hennion, A. and Meadel, C. 1986. 'Programming music: radio as mediator', *Media, Culture and Society*, 8:3, pp. 281–303.

Hennion, A. and Vignolle, J.P. 1978. *L'économie du disque en France* (Paris).

Herd, J.A. 1984. 'Trends and taste in Japanese popular music: a case-study of the 1982 Yamaha Popular Music Festival', *Popular Music*, 4, pp. 75–96.

Herndon, M. 1975. 'Le modèle transformationnel en linguistique: ses implications pour l'étude de la musique', *Semiotica*, 15:1, pp. 71–82.

Herzog, G. 1949–50. 'Song: Folk song and the music of folk song', in M. Leach (ed.), *Funk and Wagnall's Standard Dictionary of Folklore, Mythology and Legend* (New York).

Hirsch, P. 1969. *The Structure of the Popular Music Industry* (Ann Arbor, MI).

Hirsch, P. 1971. 'Sociological approaches to the pop music phenomenon', *American Behavioural Scientist*, 14, pp. 371–88.

Hirsch, P. 1972. 'Processing fads and fashions: an organisation set analysis of cultural industry systems', *American Journal of Sociology*, 77:4, pp. 639–59.

Hitchcock, H.W. 1974. *Music in the United States: A Historical Introduction* (Englewood Cliffs, NJ).

Hoggart, R. 1958. *The Uses of Literacy* (Harmondsworth).

Hood, M. 1982. *The Ethnomusicologist*, rev. edn (New York).

Hopkins, J. 1971. *Elvis: A Biography* (New York).

Horkheimer, M. 1972. *Critical Theory*, trans. M.J. O'Connell. (New York).

Hosokawa, S. 1984. 'The Walkman effect', *Popular Music* 4, pp. 165–80.

Howell, P., Cross, I. and West, R. (eds) 1985. *Musical Structure and Cognition* (London).

Hustwitt, M. 1983. ' "Caught in a whirlpool of aching sound'': the production of dance music in Britain in the 1920s', *Popular Music*, 3, pp. 7–31.

Hustwitt, M. 1984. 'Rocker boy blues', *Screen*, 25, pp. 89–98.

Imberty, M. 1979. *Entendre la musique* (Paris).

Ivey, W. 1982. 'Commercialisation and tradition in the Nashville Sound' in W. Ferris and M.L. Hart (eds), *Folk Music and Modern Sound* (Jackson, MS), pp. 129–38.

Jakobson, R. 1960. 'Closing statement: linguistics and poetics' in T.A. Sebeok (ed.), *Style in Language* (Cambridge, MA).

Jameson, F. 1981. 'Reification and utopia', *Social Text*, 1:1, pp. 130–48.

Jameson, F. 1983. 'Pleasure: a political issue' in *Formations of Pleasure* (London), pp. 1–14.

Jameson, F. 1984. 'Postmodernism, or the cultural logic of late capitalism', *New Left Review*, 146, pp. 53–92.

Jefferson, T. 1976. 'Cultural responses of the teds' in S. Hall and T. Jefferson (eds), *Resistance through Rituals: Youth Subcultures in Post-war Britain* (London), pp. 81–6.

Jefferson, T. n.d. *The Teds – a Political Resurrection*, University of Birmingham Centre for Contemporary Cultural Studies stencilled paper SP22.

Jiranek, J. 1975. 'The development and present situation of the semiotics of music in Czechoslovakia' in *Actes du 1er Congrès Internationale de Semiotique Musicale, Beograd* (Pesaro), pp. 27–39.

Johnson, R. 1979. 'Three problematics: elements of a theory of working-class culture' in J. Clarke, C. Critcher and R. Johnson (eds), *Working-Class Culture: Studies in History and Theory* (London), pp. 201–37.

Jonas, O. 1982. *Introduction to the Theory of Heinrich Schenker* (New York).

Jones, A.M. 1959. *Studies in African Music* (London).

Jones, L. 1965. *Blues People: Negro Music in White America* (London).

Karpeles, M. 1968. 'The distinction between folk and popular music', *Journal of the International Folk Music Council*, 20, pp. 9–12.

Karpeles, M. 1980. Contribution on 'folk music' to entry on 'England' in S. Sadie (ed.), *The New Grove Dictionary of Music and Musicians*, 20 vols (London).

Kauffman, R. 1972. 'Shona urban music and the problem of acculturation', *Yearbook of the International Folk Music Council*, 4, pp. 47–56.

Kealy, E. 1979. 'From craft to art: the case of sound mixers and popular music', *Sociology of Work and Occupation*, 6:1, pp. 3–29.

Keil, C. 1966a. *Urban Blues* (Chicago).

Keil, C. 1966b. 'Motion and feeling through music', *Journal of Aesthetics and Art Criticism*, 24, pp. 337–49.

Keil, C. 1978. 'Who needs "the folk"?', *Journal of the Folklore Institute*, 15, pp. 263–5.

Keil, C. 1979a. 'Comment: the concept of "the folk" ', *Journal of the Folklore Institute*, 16, pp. 209–10.

Keil, C. 1979b. *Tiv Song* (Chicago and London).

Keil, C. 1980. Review of *Yesterdays* by C. Hamm, *Ethnomusicology*, 24: 3, pp. 576–8.

Keil, C. 1982. 'Slovenian style in Milwaukee' in W. Ferris and M.L. Hart (eds), *Folk Music and Modern Sound* (Jackson, MS), pp. 32–59.

Keil, C. 1984. 'Music mediated and live in Japan', *Ethnomusicology*, 28:1, pp. 91–6.

Keil, C. and Keil, A. 1984. 'In pursuit of polka happiness', *Musical Traditions*, 2, pp. 6–11.

Keiler, A.R. 1981. 'Two views of musical semiotics' in W. Steiner (ed.), *The Sign in Music and Literature* (Austin, TX), pp. 138–68.

Kidson, F. 1912. 'Folk song and the popular song', *The Choir*, March, pp. 149–51.

Korson, G. 1938. *Minstrels of the Mine Patch: Songs and Stories of the Anthracite Industry* (Philadelphia).

Korson, G. 1943. *Coal Dust on the Fiddle: Songs and Stories of the Bituminous Industry* (Philadelphia).

Kubik, G. 1974. *The Kachamba Brothers Band: a Study of Neo-Traditional Music in Malawi*, Zambian Papers no. 9, University of Zambia, Institute for African Studies.

Kubik, G. 1979–80. 'Daniel Kachamba's montage recordings', *African Urban Studies*, 6, pp. 89–122.

Kubik, G. 1981. 'Neo-traditional popular music in East Africa since 1945', *Popular Music*, 1, pp. 83–104.

Lacan, J. 1979. *The Four Fundamental Concepts of Psychoanalysis*, trans. A. Sheridan (Harmondsworth).

Laing, D. 1969. *The Sound of Our Time* (London).

Laing, D. 1985. *One Chord Wonders: Power and Meaning in Punk Rock* (Milton Keynes).

Laing, D., Dallas, K., Denselow, R. and Shelton, R. 1975. *The Electric Muse: the Story of Folk into Rock* (London).

Laing, D. and Taylor, J. 1979. 'Disco-pleasure-discourse: on "rock and sexuality" ', *Screen Education*, 31, pp. 43–8.

Lambert, C. 1966. *Music Ho! A Study of Music in Decline*, 3rd edn (London); first published in 1934.

Landau, J. 1972. *It's Too Late to Stop Now* (San Francisco).

Larmore, C. 1981. 'The concept of a constitutive subject', in C. McCabe (ed.), *The Talking Cure: Essays in Psycho-analysis and Language* (London), pp. 108–31.

Laske, O. 1975a. 'Towards a theory of musical cognition', *Interface*, 4, pp. 147–208.

Laske, O. 1975b. 'On psychomusicology', *International Review of the Aesthetics and Sociology of Music*, 6:2, pp. 269–81.

Lee, C.S. 1985. 'The rhythmic interpretation of simple musical sequences: towards a perceptual model' in P. Howell, I. Cross and R. West (eds), *Musical Structure and Cognition* (London), pp. 53–69.

Lee, E. 1970. *Music of the People: A Study of Popular Music in Great Britain* (London).

Lefebvre, H, 1971a. *Everyday Life in the Modern World*, trans. S. Rabinovitch (London).

Lefebvre, H. 1971b. 'Musique et sémiologie', *Musique en Jeu*, 4, pp. 52–62.

Lehrdahl, F. and Jackendoff, R. 1983. *A Generative Theory of Tonal Music* (Cambridge, MA).

Levin, T. 1984. 'The acoustic dimension: notes on cinema sound', *Screen*, 25:3, pp. 55–68.

Levine, L. 1977. *Black Culture and Black Consciousness* (New York).

Lévi-Strauss, C. 1970. *The Raw and the Cooked*, trans. J. Weightman and D. Weightman (London).

Lévi-Strauss, C. 1972. *Structural Anthropology* (Harmondsworth).

Lindblom, B. and Sundberg, J. 1970. 'Towards a generative theory of melody', *Svensk Tidskrift för Musikforskning*, 52, pp. 71–88.

Lloyd, A.L. 1944. *The Singing Englishman: An Introduction to Folk Song* (London).

Lloyd, A.L. 1967. *Folk Song in England* (London).

Lloyd, A.L. 1970. 'Towards a distinction between "popular" and "folk": a bit of history', *Club Folk*, March–April, pp. 8–11.

Lloyd, A.L. 1982. 'Electric folk music in Britain' in W. Ferris and M.L. Hart (eds), *Folk Music and Modern Sound* (Jackson, MS), pp. 14–18.

Lomax, A. 1959. 'Folk Song Style', *American Anthropologist*, 61:6, pp. 927–54.

Lomax, A. 1962. 'Song structure and social structure', *Ethnology*, 1:4, pp. 425–51.

Lomax, A. (ed.) 1964. *The Penguin Book of American Folk Songs* (Harmondsworth).

Lomax, A. 1968. *Folk Song Style and Culture* (New Brunswick, NJ).

Lord, A. 1960. *The Singer of Tales* (London).

Lyotard, J.-F. 1984. *The Postmodern Condition*, trans. G. Bennington and B. Massumi (Manchester).

Mâche, F.B. 1971. 'Méthodes linguistiques en musicologie', *Musique en Jeu*, 5, pp. 75–91.

McColl, E. 1954. *The Shuttle and the Cage* (London).

Mackay, A. 1981. *Electronic Music* (Oxford).

McLaughlin, T. 1970. *Music and Communication* (London).

McLuhan, M. 1962. *The Gutenberg Galaxy: the Making of Typographic Man* (Toronto).

McLuhan, M. 1964. *Understanding Media* (London).

McLuhan, M. 1967. *The Medium is the Massage: an Inventory of Effects* (London).

McRobbie, A. 1980. 'Settling accounts with Subcultures', *Screen Education*, 34, pp. 37–49.

McRobbie, A. and Garber, J. 1976. 'Girls and subcultures: an exploration' in S. Hall and T. Jefferson, *Resistance through Rituals: Youth Subcultures in Post-war Britain* (London), pp. 209–21.

Malone, B. 1982. 'Honky tonk: the music of the Southern working class' in W. Ferris and M.L. Hart (eds), *Folk Music and Modern Sound* (Jackson, MS), pp. 119–28.

Malone, B. 1985. *Country Music USA*, rev. edn (Austin, TX).

Mandel, E. 1975. *Late Capitalism*, trans. J. de Bres (London).

Manvel, P. 1988. *Popular Musics of the Non-Western World: An Introductory Survey* (New York).

Margolis, N.M 1954. 'A theory on the psychology of jazz', *American Imago*, 2:3, pp. 263–91.

Maróthy, J. 1974. *Music and the Bourgeois, Music and the Proletarian* (Budapest).
Maróthy, J. 1981. 'A music of your own', *Popular Music*, 1, pp. 15–25.
Martin, B. 1983. *A Sociology of Contemporary Cultural Change* (Oxford).
Martin, G. 1979. *All You Need Is Ears* (London).
Marx, K. 1973. *Grundrisse* (Harmondsworth).
Marx, K. 1975. *Early Writings* (Harmondsworth).
Mellers, W. 1964. *Music in A New Found Land* (London).
Mellers, W. 1971. 'Pop as ritual in modern culture', *Times Literary Supplement*, 19 November.
Mellers, W. 1973. *Twilight of the Gods: the Beatles in Retrospect* (London).
Mellers, W. 1984. *A Darker Shade of Pale: A Backdrop to Bob Dylan* (London).
Mellers, W. 1986. *Angels of the Night* (Oxford).
Melly, G. 1972. *Revolt into Style: the Pop Arts in Britain* (Harmondsworth).
Mercer, C. 1983. 'A poverty of desire: pleasure and popular politics' in *Formations of Pleasure* (London), pp. 84–100.
Mercer, C. 1986a. 'Complicit pleasures' in T. Bennett, C. Mercer and J. Woollacott (eds), *Popular Culture and Social Relations* (Milton Keynes), pp. 50–68.
Mercer, C. 1986b. 'That's entertainment: the resilience of popular forms' in T. Bennett, C. Mercer and J. Woollacott (eds), *Popular Culture and Social Relations* (Milton Keynes), pp. 177–95.
Merleau-Ponty, M. 1962. *Phenomenology of Perception*, trans. C. Smith (London).
Merriam, A. 1955. 'The use of music in the study of a problem of acculturation', *American Anthropologist*, 57, pp. 28–34.
Merriam, A. 1959. 'Characteristics of African Music', *Journal of the International Folk Music Council*, 2, pp. 13–19.
Merriam, A. 1962. 'The African idiom in music', *Journal of American Folklore*, 75: 296, pp. 120–30.
Merriam, A. 1964. *The Anthropology of Music* (Evanston, IL).
Middleton, R. 1972. *Pop Music and the Blues* (London).
Middleton, R. 1981. *'Reading' Popular Music*, Open University course U203 *Popular Culture*, Unit 16 (Milton Keynes).
Miller, J. 1971. *McLuhan* (London).
Moles, A. 1966. *Information Theory and Esthetic Perception* (Urbana, ILL).
Mouffe, C. 1979. *Gramsci and Marxist Theory* (London).
Mowitt, J. 1987. 'The sound of music in the era of its electronic reproducibility' in R. Leppert and S. McClary (eds), *Music and Society: the Politics of Composition, Performance and Reception* (Cambridge), pp. 173–97.
Mukarovsky, J. 1977. *Structure, Sign and Function. Selected Essays by Jan Mukarovsky* ed. J. Burbank (Cambridge, MA).
Mulhern, F. 1980. 'Notes on culture and cultural struggle', *Screen Education*, 34.
Murdock, G. and McCron, R. 1976. 'Consciousness of class and consciousness of generation' in S. Hall and T. Jefferson (eds), *Resistance through Rituals: Youth Subcultures in Post-war Britain* (London), pp. 205–6.
Nanry, C. 1972. *American Music from Storyville to Woodstock* (New Brunswick, NJ).
Narmour, E. 1980. *Beyond Schenkerism: the Need for Alternatives in Music Analysis* (Chicago).
Nattiez, J.-J. 1976. *Fondements d'une sémiologie de la musique* (Paris).
Nattiez, J.-J. 1989. 'Reflections on the development of semiology in music', trans. K. Ellis, *Music Analysis*, 8: 1–2, pp. 21–75.
Nettl, B. 1957. 'Preliminary remarks on urban folk music in Detroit', *Western Folklore*, 16, pp. 37–42.
Nettl, B, 1965. *Folk and Traditional Music of the Western Continents* (Englewood Cliffs, NJ).
Nettl, B. 1972. 'Persian popular music in 1969', *Ethnomusicology*, 16, pp. 218–39.

Nettl, B. (ed.) 1978. *Eight Urban Musical Cultures: Tradition and Change* (Urbana, IL and London).

Nketia, J.H.K. 1957. 'Modern trends in Ghana music', *African Music*, 1:4, pp. 13–17.

Nketia, J.H.K. 1979. *The Music of Africa* (London).

Noske, F. 1977. *The Signifier and the Signified. Studies in the Operas of Mozart and Verdi* (The Hague).

Oliver, P. 1970a. *The Story of the Blues* (London).

Oliver, P. 1970b. *Savannah Syncopators: African Retentions in the Blues* (London).

Oliver, P. 1982a. 'Blues and the binary principle' in P. Tagg and D. Horn (eds), *Popular Music Perspectives* (Gothenberg and Exeter), pp. 163–73.

Oliver, P. 1982b. 'Binarism, blues and black culture', *Popular Music*, 2, pp. 179–200.

Oliver, P. 1984. *Songsters and Saints* (Cambridge).

Orlov, H. 1981. 'Towards a semiotics of music' in W. Steiner (ed.), *The Sign in Music and Literature* (Austin, TX), pp. 131–7.

Osmond-Smith, D. 1972. 'The iconic process in musical communication', *Versus*, 3:2, pp. 31–42.

Osmond-Smith, D. 1973. 'Formal iconism in music', *Versus*, 5, pp. 43–53.

Osmond-Smith, D. 1975. 'Iconic relations within formal transformation' in *Actes du 1er Congrès Internationale de Semiotique Musicale, Beograd* (Pesaro), pp. 45–55.

Ostendorf, B. n.d. 'Ethnicity and popular music', IASPM Working Paper 2.

Ostendorf, B. 1982. *Black Literature in White America* (Brighton).

Paddison, M. 1982. 'The critique criticised: Adorno and popular song', *Popular Music*, 2, pp. 201–18.

Paetzoldt, W. 1977. 'Walter Benjamin's theory of the end of art', *International Journal of Sociology*, 7:1, pp. 25–75.

Palmer, R(obert) 1981. *Deep Blues* (London).

Palmer, R(obert) 1982. 'Folk, popular, jazz and classical elements in New Orleans' in W. Ferris and M.L. Hart (eds), *Folk Music and Modern Sound* (Jackson, MS), pp. 194–201.

Palmer, R(oy) 1974. *A Touch on the Times: Songs of Social Change 1770–1914* (Harmondsworth).

Palmer, T. 1970. *Born Under a Bad Sign* (London).

Paredes, A. and Stekert, E.J. (eds) 1971. *The Urban Experience and Folk Tradition* (Austin, TX).

Parry, H. 1899. 'Inaugural address to the Folk Song Society', *Journal of the Folk Song Society*, 1, pp. 2–3.

Peacock, A. and Weir, R. 1975. *The Composer in the Market Place* (London).

Perlman, A.M. and Greenblatt, D. 1981. 'Miles Davis meets Noam Chomsky: some observations on jazz improvisation and language structure' in W. Steiner (ed.), *The Sign in Music and Literature* (Austin, TX), pp. 169–83.

Peterson, R.A. (ed.) 1976. *The Production of Culture* (London).

Peterson, R.A. 1982. 'Five constraints on the production of culture', *Journal of Popular Culture*, 16:2, pp. 143–53.

Peterson, R.A. and Berger, D.G. 1971. 'Entrepreneurship in organisations: evidence from the popular music industry', *Administrative Science Quarterly*, 16, pp. 97–106.

Peterson, R.A. and Berger, D.G. 1975. 'Cycles in symbol production: the case of popular music', *American Sociological Review*, 40, pp. 158–73.

Piaget, J. 1971. *Structuralism*, trans. C. Maschler (London).

Pickering, M. 1982. *Village Song and Culture* (London).

Pickering, M. 1986. 'White skin, black masks: "nigger" minstrelsy in Victorian Britain' in J.S. Bratton (ed.), *Music Hall: Performance and Style* (Milton Keynes), pp. 70–91.

Pickering, M. and Green, T. 1987. 'Towards a cartography of the vernacular milieu' in M. Pickering and T. Green (eds), *Everyday Culture: Popular Song and the Vernacular Milieu* (Milton Keynes), pp. 1–38.

Prato, P. 1984. 'Music in the streets: the example of Washington Square Park in New York City', *Popular Music*, 4, pp. 151–63.

Prato, P. 1985. 'They all laughed: irony and parody in popular music', paper presented at the Third International Conference of IASPM, Montreal.

Pribram, K. 1982. 'Brain mechanism in music' in M. Clynes (ed.), *Music, Mind and Brain* (New York), pp. 21–35.

Rahn, J. 1983. *A Theory for All Music: Problems and Solutions in the Analysis of Non-Western Forms* (Toronto).

Raven, J. 1977. *The Urban and Industrial Songs of the Black Country and Birmingham* (Wolverhampton).

Raynor, H. 1978. *A Social History of Music* (New York).

Redfield, R. 1947. 'The folk society', *American Journal of Sociology*, 52, pp. 293–308.

Richman, B. 1980. 'Did human speech originate in coordinated vocal music?', *Semiotica*, 32, pp. 233–44.

Ricoeur, P. 1970. *Freud and Philosophy*, trans. D. Savage (London).

Riesman, D. 1950. 'Listening to popular music', *American Quarterly*, 2, pp. 359–71.

Roberts, J.S. 1973. *Black Music of Two Worlds* (London).

Roberts, J.S. 1979. *The Latin Tinge: the Impact of Latin American Music on the United States* (New York).

Rogers, E. 1964. *Tin Pan Alley* (London).

Rosselli, J. 1984. *The Opera Industry in Italy from Cimarosa to Verdi* (Cambridge).

Rosolato, G. 1972. 'Répétitions', *Musique en Jeu*, 9, pp. 33–44.

Roth, E. 1969. *The Business of Music* (London).

Russell, D. 1987. *Popular Music in England 1840–1914* (Manchester).

Russell, I. 1987. 'Parody and performance' in M. Pickering and T. Green (eds), *Everyday Culture: Popular Song and the Vernacular Milieu* (Milton Keynes).

Russell, T. 1970. *Blacks, Whites and Blues* (London).

Rutten, P. and Bouwman, H. n.d. *Popular Music in the Netherlands*, IASPM Working Paper 4.

Ruwet, N. 1967. 'Musicologie et linguistique', *Revue Internationale des Sciences Sociales*, 19, pp. 85–93.

Ruwet, N. 1975. 'Théorie et méthodes dans les études musicales: quelques remarques rétrospectives et prélimenaires', *Musique en Jeu*, 17, pp. 11–36.

Ruwet, N. 1987. 'Methods of analysis in musicology', *Music Analysis*, 6:1–2, pp. 11–36; translation of 'Méthodes d'analyse en musicologie', *Revue Belge de Musicologie*, 20 (1966), pp. 65–90.

Rycroft, D. 1961–2. 'The guitar improvisations of Mwenda Jean Bosco', *African Music*, 2:4, pp. 81–98; 3:1, pp. 86–102.

Sadie, S. (ed.) 1980. *The New Grove Dictionary of Music and Musicians*, 20 vols (London).

Sanjek, R. 1988. *American Popular Music and Its Business*, 3 vols (New York).

Saussure, F. de. 1960. *Course in General Linguistics*, trans. W. Baskin (London), first published in 1915.

Schafer, R.M. 1973. 'The music of the environment', *Cultures*, 1:1, pp. 15–52.

Schafer, R.M. 1980. *The Tuning of the World* (Philadelphia).

Schüller, D. 1982. 'Documentation of stage-amplified music: some methodological and technological problems', paper presented at the ISME conference on 'Pop and Folk Music: Stock-Taking of New Trends' (Trento, Italy).

Schuller, G. 1968. *Early Jazz* (New York).

Scott, D. 1989. *The Singing Bourgeois: Songs of The Victorian Drawing Room and Parlour* (Milton Keynes).

Seeger, C. 1949–50. 'Oral tradition in music' in M. Leach (ed.), *Funk and Wagnall's Standard Dictionary of Folklore, Mythology and Legend* (New York).

Seeger, C. 1977a. 'The folkness of the nonfolk and the nonfolkness of the folk' in *Studies in Musicology 1935–1975* (Berkeley, CA), pp. 335–43.

Seeger, C. 1977b. 'Versions and variants of "Barbara Allen" in the archive of American song to 1940' in *Studies in Musicology 1935–1975* (Berkeley, CA), pp. 273–320.

Seeger, C. 1977c. 'On the moods of a music logic' in *Studies in Musicology 1935–1975* (Berkeley, CA), pp. 64–101.

Seeger, C. 1980. Contribution to 'folk music' section of entry on 'United States of America' in S. Sadie (ed.), *The New Grove Dictionary of Music and Musicians*, 20 vols (London).

Sharp, C. 1972. *English Folk Song: Some Conclusions* (Wakefield, Yorks.), first published in 1907.

Shepherd, J. 1977. 'Media, social process and music', 'The "meaning" of music', 'The musical coding of ideologies' in J. Shepherd, P. Virden, G. Vulliamy and T. Wishart, *Whose Music? A Sociology of Musical Languages* (London and New Brunswick, NJ), pp. 7–124.

Shepherd, J. 1982. 'A theoretical model for the sociomusicological analysis of popular musics', *Popular Music*, 2, pp. 145–77.

Shepherd, J. 1985. 'Definition as mystification: a consideration of labels as a hindrance to understanding significance in music' in D. Horn (ed.), *Popular Music Perspectives*, 2 (Gothenburg, Exeter, Ottawa and Reggio Emilia), pp. 84–98.

Shepherd, J. 1987. 'Music and male hegemony' in R. Leppert and S. McClary (eds), *Music and Society: the politics of Composition, Performance and Reception* (Cambridge), pp. 151–72.

Škvorecký, J. 1980. *The Bass Saxophone*, trans. K. Polackova-Henley (London).

Slawson, W. 1985. *Sound Color* (Berkeley, CA).

Slobin, M. 1982. 'How the fiddler got on the roof' in W. Ferris and M.L. Hart (eds), *Folk Music and Modern Sound* (Jackson, MS), pp. 21–31.

Sloboda, J. 1985. *The Musical Mind: An Introduction to the Cognitive Psychology of Music* (Oxford).

Small, C. 1980. *Music-Society-Education* (London).

Small, C. 1987a. 'Performance as ritual: sketch for an enquiry into the true nature of a symphony concert' in A.L. White (ed.), *Lost in Music: Culture, Style and the Musical Event* (London), pp. 6–32.

Small, C. 1987b. *Music of the Common Tongue: Survival and Celebration in Afro-American Music* (London).

Souster, T. 1975. 'Elektronik in der Rockmusik' in E. Pütz and H.W. Schmidt (eds), *Musik International. Informationen über Jazz, Pop, aussereuropäische Musik* (Cologne), pp. 125–34.

Stedman-Jones, G. 1974. 'Working-class culture and working-class politics in London, 1870–1900: notes on the remaking of a working class', *Journal of Social History*, 7:4, pp. 460–508.

Steedman, M. 1984. 'A generative grammar for jazz chord sequences', *Music Perception*, 2:1, pp. 52–77.

Stefani, G. 1973. 'Sémiotique en musicologie', *Versus*, 5, pp. 20–42.

Stefani, G. 1984. 'An interview with Gino Stefani', by U. Fiori, IASPM Newsletter, 5, pp. 18–19.

Stefani, G. 1986. *Semiotica della musica* (Palermo).

Stefani, G. 1987a. 'Melody: a popular perspective', *Popular Music*, 6:1, pp. 21–35.

Stefani, G. 1987b. 'A theory of musical competence', *Semiotica*, 66: 1–3, pp. 7–22.

Stefani, G. n.d. 'A new theory of intervals', unpublished paper.

Stigberg, D.K. 1978. '*Jarocho, Tropical*, and "Pop": aspects of musical life in Veracruz, 1971–72' in B. Nettl (ed.), *Eight Urban Musical Cultures* (Urbana, IL and London), pp. 260–95.

Stokes, G. 1976. *Star-Making Machinery* (Indianapolis).

Stratton, J. 1983. 'Capitalism and romantic ideology in the record business', *Popular Music*, 3, pp. 143–56.

Street, J. 1986. *Rebel Rock: the Politics of Popular Music* (Oxford).

Struthers, S. 1987. 'Technology in the art of the recording' in A.L. White (ed.), *Lost in Music: Culture, Style and the Musical Event* (London), pp. 241–58.

Supičic, I. 1971. 'Expression and meaning in music', *International Review of the Aesthetics and Sociology of Music*, 2:2, pp. 194–211.

Szabolcsi, B. 1965. *A History of Melody*, trans. C. Jolly and S. Karig (Budapest).

Szemere, A. 1983. 'Some institutional aspects of pop and rock music in Hungary', *Popular Music*, 3, pp. 121–42.

Szwed, J. 1969. 'Musical adaptation among Afro-Americans', *Journal of American Folklore*, 82, pp. 112–21.

Tagg, P. 1979. *Kojak – 50 Seconds of Television Music. Towards the Analysis of Affekt in Popular Music* (Gothenberg).

Tagg, P. 1981. *Fernando the Flute – Analysis of Affekt in an Abba Number*, stencilled papers from Gothenberg University Department of Musicology, no. 8106.

Tagg, P. 1982. 'Analysing popular music: theory, method and practice', *Popular Music*, 2, pp. 37–67.

Tagg, P. 1983. Review of *Les professionnels des disques* by A. Hennion, *Popular Music*, 3, pp. 308–13.

Tagg, P. 1984. 'Understanding musical "time sense" – concepts, sketches and consequences', in *Tvärspel. Festskrift för Jan Ling*, Studies from Gothenberg University Department of Musicology, no. 9, pp. 21–43.

Tarasti, E. 1979. *Myth and Music. A Semiotic Approach to the Aesthetics of Myth in Music* (The Hague).

Tarasti, E. 1983. 'Reflections on the logic of musical discourse', *Suomen Antropologi*, 4/83, pp. 242–4.

Titon, J.T. 1977. *Early Downhome Blues: A Musical and Cultural Analysis* (Urbana, IL).

Toop, D. 1984. *The Rap Attack: African Jive to New York Hip Hop* (London).

Tracey, H. 1948. *Chopi Musicians: Their Music, Poetry and Instruments* (London).

Trager, G.L. 1958. 'Paralinguistics: a first approximation', *Studies in Linguistics*, 13, pp. 1–12.

Trudgill, P. 1983. 'Acts of conflicting identity: the sociolinguistics of British pop song pronunciation' in *On Dialect* (Oxford), pp. 141–60.

Turner, V.W. 1969. *The Ritual Process: Structure and Anti-structure* (London).

Van der Merwe, P. 1989. *Origins of the Popular Style* (Oxford).

Van Elderen, P.L. 1984. 'Music behind the dykes: Dutch rock music and its audience', *Popular Music*, 4, pp. 97–116.

Vega, C. 1966. 'Mesomusic: an essay on the music of the masses', *Ethnomusicology*, 10:1, pp. 1–17.

Vicinus, M. 1974. *The Industrial Muse* (London).

Volosinov, V.N. 1973. *Marxism and the Philosophy of Language*, trans. L. Matejka and I.R. Titunik (New York and London).

Vulliamy, G. 1976. 'Definitions of serious music' in G. Vulliamy and E. Lee (eds), *Pop Music in School* (Cambridge), pp. 33–48.

Vulliamy, G. 1977. 'Music and the mass culture debate' in J. Shepherd, P. Virden, G. Vulliamy and T. Wishart, *Whose Music? A Sociology of Musical Languages* (London and New Brunswick, NJ), pp. 179–200.

Waites, B. 1981. *The Music Hall*, Open University course U203 *Popular Culture*, Unit 5 (Milton Keynes).

Wallis, R. and Malm, K. 1984. *Big Sounds from Small Peoples* (London).

Ware, N. 1978. 'Popular music and African identity in Freetown Sierra Leone' in B. Nettl (ed.), *Eight Urban Musical Cultures* (Urbana, IL and London), pp. 296–320.

Waterman, R. 1952. 'African influence on the music of the Americas' in S. Tax (ed.), *Acculturation in the Americas* (Chicago), pp. 207–18.

Weber, W. 1975. *Music and the Middle Class* (London).

Whitcomb, I. 1973. *After the Ball* (Harmondsworth).
Whitcomb, I. 1975. *Tin Pan Alley: A Pictorial History (1919–1939)* (New York).
Wicke, P. 1982. 'Rock music: a musical aesthetic study', *Popular Music*, 2, pp. 219–43.
Wicke, P. 1985. 'Aesthetic aspects of rock music', paper presented to the Third International Conference of IASPM, Montreal.
Wilder, A. 1972. *American Popular Song: the Great Innovators 1900–1950* (New York).
Wilgus, D.K. 1971. 'Country-western music and the urban hillbilly' in A. Paredes and E.J. Stekert (eds), *The Urban Experience and Folk Tradition* (Austin, TX), pp. 137–59.
Williams, R. 1974. *Television: Technology and Cultural Form* (London).
Williams, R. 1976. *Keywords: A Vocabulary of Culture and Society* (London).
Williams, R. 1977. *Marxism and Literature* (London).
Williams, R. 1978. 'Problems of materialism', *New Left Review*, 109, pp. 3–17.
Williams, R. 1979. *Politics and Letters: Interviews with New Left Review* (London).
Williams, R. 1981. *Culture* (London).
Williams, R(ichard) 1974. *Out of His Head: the Sound of Phil Spector* (London).
Willis, P. 1978. *Profane Culture* (London).
Willis, P. n.d. *Symbolism and Practice: A Theory for the Social Meaning of Pop Music*, University of Birmingham Centre for Contemporary Cultural Studies stencilled paper SP13.
Winkler, P. 1978. 'Towards a theory of popular harmony', *In Theory Only*, 4:2.
Winkler, P., forthcoming. 'The Harmonic Language of Rock'.
Wishart, T. 1977. 'Musical writing, musical speaking' in J. Shepherd, P. Virden, G. Vulliamy and T. Wishart, *Whose Music? A Sociology of Musical Languages* (London and New Brunswick, NJ), pp. 125–53.
Wishart, T. and Virden, P. 1977. 'Some observations on the social stratification of twentieth-century music' in J. Shepherd, P. Virden, G. Vulliamy and T. Wishart, *Whose Music? A Sociology of Musical Languages* (London and New Brunswick, NJ), pp. 155–77.
Wolfe, C. 1981. ' "Gospel Boogie": white Southern gospel music in transition, 1945–55', *Popular Music*, 1, pp. 73–82.
Wolff, J. 1981. *The Social Production of Art* (London).
Wolff, J. 1983. *Aesthetics and the Sociology of Art* (London).
Youngblood, J.E. 1958. 'Style as information', *Journal of Music Theory*, 2, pp. 24–35.
Zak, V. 1982. 'Asaf'ev's theory of intonation and the analysis of popular song', *Popular Music*, 2, pp. 91–111.
Zeppenfeld, W. 1979. 'The economics and structure of the record and tape industry: the example of West Germany' in H.D. Fischer and S.R Melnik (eds), *Entertainment: A Cross-Cultural Examination* (New York), pp. 248–57.

Song index

Name index

Subject Index